MASTERING TRUSTS AND ESTATES

CAROLINA ACADEMIC PRESS MASTERING SERIES

RUSSELL WEAVER, SERIES EDITOR

For other titles, please go to caplaw.com.

Mastering Administrative Law, Second Edition
Linda D. Jellum

Mastering Adoption Law and Policy
Cynthia Hawkins DeBose

Mastering Alternative Dispute Resolution
Kelly M. Feeley, James A. Sheehan

Mastering Appellate Advocacy and Process, Second Edition
Donna C. Looper, George W. Kuney

Mastering Art Law, Second Edition
Herbert Lazerow

Mastering Bankruptcy
George W. Kuney

Mastering Civil Procedure, Fourth Edition
David Charles Hricik

Mastering Constitutional Law, Second Edition
John C. Knechtle, Christopher J. Roederer

Mastering Contract Law
Irma S. Russell, Barbara K. Bucholtz

Mastering Corporate Tax, Second Edition
Gail Levin Richmond, Reginald Mombrun, Felicia Branch

Mastering Corporations and Other Business Entities, Second Edition
Lee Harris

Mastering Criminal Law, Third Edition
Ellen S. Podgor, Cynthia E. Jones, Peter J. Henning, Neil P. Cohen, Sanjay K. Chhablani

Mastering Criminal Procedure, Volume 1: The Investigative Stage, Third Edition
Peter J. Henning, Cynthia E. Jones, Ellen S. Podgor,
Karen McDonald Henning, Sanjay K. Chhablani

Mastering Criminal Procedure, Volume 2: The Adjudicatory Stage, Third Edition
Peter J. Henning, Cynthia E. Jones, Ellen S. Podgor,
Karen McDonald Henning, Sanjay K. Chhablani

Mastering Elder Law, Third Edition
Ralph C. Brashier

Mastering Employment Discrimination Law, Second Edition
Paul M. Secunda, Jeffrey M. Hirsch, Joseph A. Seiner

Mastering Environmental Law
Joel A. Mintz, Tracy D. Hester

Mastering Evidence
Ronald W. Eades

Mastering Family Law
Janet Leach Richards

Mastering First Amendment Law
John C. Knechtle

Mastering Income Tax, Second Edition
Gail Levin Richmond, Christopher M. Pietruszkiewicz

Mastering Intellectual Property
George W. Kuney, Donna C. Looper

Mastering International Sales Law
Herbert Lazerow

Mastering Interviewing and Counseling
Kelly M. Feeley, Rebecca C. Morgan

Mastering Labor Law
Paul M. Secunda, Anne Marie Lofaso, Joseph E. Slater, Jeffrey M. Hirsch

Mastering Legal Analysis and Communication
David T. Ritchie

Mastering Legal Analysis and Drafting, Second Edition
George W. Kuney, Donna C. Looper

Mastering Legislation, Regulation, and Statutory Interpretation, Third Edition
Linda D. Jellum

Mastering Native American Law, Third Edition
Angelique Wambdi EagleWoman, Stacy L. Leeds

Mastering Negotiable Instruments (UCC Articles 3 and 4) and Other Payment Systems, Second Edition
Michael D. Floyd

Mastering Negotiation
Michael R. Fowler

Mastering Partnership Taxation
Stuart Lazar

Mastering Products Liability, Second Edition
Tim Kaye

Mastering Professional Responsibility, Second Edition
Grace M. Giesel

Mastering Property Law, Revised Printing
Darryl C. Wilson, Cynthia Hawkins DeBose

Mastering Sales
Colin P. Marks, Jeremy Kidd

Mastering Secured Transactions: UCC Article 9, Third Edition
Grace M. Giesel

Mastering Tort Law, Third Edition
Russell L. Weaver, Edward C. Martin, Andrew R. Klein,
Paul J. Zwier, II, John H. Bauman

Mastering Trademark and Unfair Competition Law, Second Edition
Lars S. Smith, Llewellyn Joseph Gibbons

Mastering Trusts and Estates, Second Edition
Gail Levin Richmond

MASTERING TRUSTS AND ESTATES

SECOND EDITION

Gail Levin Richmond

EMERITA PROFESSOR OF LAW
NOVA SOUTHEASTERN UNIVERSITY
SHEPARD BROAD COLLEGE OF LAW

CAROLINA ACADEMIC PRESS
Durham, North Carolina

LIBRARY OF CONGRESS CATALOGING-IN-PUBLICATION DATA

Names: Richmond, Gail Levin, author.
Title: Mastering trusts and estates / Gail Levin Richmond.
Description: Second edition. | Durham : Carolina Academic Press, 2025. | Series: Mastering series | Includes bibliographical references and index.
Identifiers: LCCN 2024061346 | ISBN 9781531031442 (paperback) | ISBN 9781531031459 (ebook)
Subjects: LCSH: Trusts and trustees—United States. | Estate planning—United States. | Wills—United States.
Classification: LCC KF730 .R56 2025 | DDC 346.7305/6—dc23/eng/20250107
LC record available at https://lccn.loc.gov/2024061346

Carolina Academic Press
700 Kent Street
Durham, North Carolina 27701
(919) 489-7486
www.cap-press.com

Printed in the United States of America

CONTENTS

Series Editor's Foreword xxv
Preface xxvii
About the Author xxix

Chapter 1 • Introduction to Trusts and Estates 3
Roadmap 3
A. Options for Transmitting Property 3
B. Questions to Consider 5
1. Casebook Questions 5
2. Questions Concerning Transfers 5
3. Fiduciary Questions 7
Checkpoints 7

Chapter 2 • Sources of Law 9
Roadmap 9
A. Chapter Overview 9
B. Uniform Acts and Model Acts 9
1. Acts Related to Trusts and Estates 10
2. Organization of Uniform Probate Code and Uniform Trust Code 12
a. Uniform Probate Code 12
b. Uniform Trust Code 13
3. Focus of Book 13
C. Restatements 14
D. Federal Statutes 15
E. State Statutes 16
F. Judicial Decisions 16
G. Multiple States' Involvement 17
Checkpoints 17

Chapter 3 • Terminology and Abbreviations 19
Roadmap 19
A. Chapter Overview 19
B. Terminology and Potential Areas of Confusion 20
1. Ademption by Extinction; Ademption by Satisfaction; Advancement 20
2. Augmented Estate; Elective Estate; Gross Estate; Probate Estate; Trust Estate 20
3. Beneficiary; Devisee; Heir; Legatee; Qualified Beneficiary 21
4. Capacity 22
5. Child; Descendant; Heir; Issue 22
6. Codicil; Incorporation by Reference; Separate Writing 22
7. Constructive Trust; Express Trust; In Trust for Account; Resulting Trust 23
8. Corpus; Principal; Res 23
9. Cy Pres; Interpretation; Modification; Reformation 24
10. Execution; Expression; Inducement 24
11. Fiduciary 25
12. Governing Instrument; Instrument 25
13. Grantor; Grantor Trust; Settlor 25
14. Representation 26
15. Revocation; Termination 26
16. Valid; Void; Voidable 26
C. Abbreviations 27
Checkpoints 29

Chapter 4 • Probate and Options for Avoiding It 31
Roadmap 31
A. Chapter Overview 31
B. Probate 31
C. Avoiding Probate 32
1. Pay on Death Accounts; In Trust for Accounts 33
a. Terminology 34
b. Single-Party and Multiple-Party Accounts 34
c. Relationship of Parties in Multiple-Party Accounts 35
d. Rights of Beneficiaries in Pay on Death Accounts 36
e. Liability of Beneficiaries for Claims Against the Estate 36
2. Transfer on Death Securities Accounts 36

3. Transfer on Death Real Property Deeds 37
4. Survivorship Tenancies 37
   a. Joint Tenancy with Right of Survivorship 37
   b. Tenancy by the Entirety 38
5. Life Insurance Beneficiary Designations 38
6. Annuities and Payments from Retirement Plans 39
   a. Annuities 39
   b. Retirement Plans 41
   c. Social Security Benefits 42
7. Inter Vivos Gifts 42
8. Inter Vivos Trusts 43
Checkpoints 44

Chapter 5 • Intestate Succession **45**
Roadmap 45
A. Chapter Overview 45
B. Terminology 46
C. Property Distributed by Intestate Succession 46
1. In General 46
2. Rights of Creditors 47
3. Family Protection Statutes 47
D. Intestacy Statutes 48
1. Features 48
2. Limitations 49
   a. Division of Property 49
   b. Characteristics of Eligible Heirs 49
   c. Family Dynamics 49
3. Other Relevant Statutes 50
E. Marital Relationships 50
1. Common Law Marriages 51
2. Domestic Partnerships 51
3. Spouse of Decedent's Relative 51
F. Lineal and Collateral Relationships 52
1. Lineal Relationships in General 52
2. Parent-Child Lineal Relationship 53
   a. Birth 53
   b. Adoption 54
3. Remote Lineal Relationships 54
4. Collateral Relationships 55

a. In General 55
b. Half-Blood Statutes 56
1. Relationships Covered 56
2. Statutes 56
3. Limitations 58
4. Relevance of Relationships to Decedent's Ancestor 58
G. Ordering of Heirs and Share of Surviving Spouse 59
1. UPC 59
a. Ordering Rules 59
b. Surviving Spouse 59
1. Surviving Spouse Takes 100% 60
2. Surviving Spouse Takes Less Than 100% 60
3. Surviving Spouse Takes Nothing 61
c. Descendants 61
d. Parents and Their Descendants 61
e. Siblings and Their Descendants 62
f. Grandparents and Their Descendants 62
2. State Variations 63
H. Avoiding Escheat 64
1. Survival Requirement 64
2. Fallback Rules 64
I. Taking by Representation 66
1. Representation Rules 66
2. Applying Representation Rules 67
a. Children and Their Descendants 67
b. Collateral Relatives and Their Descendants 69
c. Remote Relatives 70
J. Degrees of Relationship 70
K. Aliens 71
L. Parent-Child Relationship 71
1. Adoption 71
a. Traditional Treatment 71
b. Relationship to One Decedent Through More than One Line 73
c. Adult Adoptee 73
d. Equitable Adoption 73
2. De Facto Parentage 74
3. Assisted Reproduction 75
4. Posthumous Birth and Posthumous Conception 75
5. Nonmarital Births 76

6. Foster Children 76
M. Advancements 77
1. Application to Donee 77
2. Application to Deceased Donee 79
3. Application to Heirs in Different Priority Groups 80
N. Loans to Heirs 81
Checkpoints 81

Chapter 6 • Will Validity and Components 85
Roadmap 85
A. Chapter Overview 85
B. Testamentary Capacity 86
1. Age 86
2. Mental Capacity 86
a. Potential Challenges to Capacity 87
b. Documents Establishing Capacity 87
c. Witnesses Establishing Capacity 88
d. No-Contest Provisions 88
C. Testamentary Formalities 89
1. Written Will 89
2. Holographic Will 89
3. Signatures and the Attestation 90
4. Placement of Signatures 92
5. Number and Qualifications of Witnesses 92
6. Integration and Harmless Error 93
D. Validating an Invalid Will 94
E. Components of a Will 94
1. Format of a Will 95
2. Commonly Appearing Terms 95
a. Introductory Language 95
b. Statement of Residence 95
c. Devises and Administrative Provisions 97
d. Signature, Attestation, and Date 97
e. Self-Proof 98
3. Formalities and Admission to Probate 99
Checkpoints 99

Chapter 7 • Categorizing Devises 101
Roadmap 101
A. Chapter Overview 101
B. Language Used to Describe Devises 101

C. Precatory Language 102
D. Types of Devises 102
1. Specific 103
2. General 104
3. Demonstrative 104
4. Residuary 105
Checkpoints 106

Chapter 8 • Amending, Revoking, and Reviving a Will; Reformation and Modification 107
Roadmap 107
A. Chapter Overview 107
B. Amending a Will 108
1. Codicil 108
2. Revocable Inter Vivos Trust 108
3. Acts of Independent Significance 109
4. Incorporation by Reference 110
5. Separate Writing 110
6. Distinguishing Between Incorporation by Reference and Separate Writing 112
7. Using Incorporation by Reference to Re-Establish a Revoked Trust 112
C. Revoking a Will or Codicil 113
1. By a Writing 113
a. In General 114
b. Complete Disposition 114
c. Inconsistency 116
2. By Act 116
3. By Change of Circumstances 117
D. Reviving a Revoked Will or Codicil 118
1. By Revoking the Revocatory Document 118
2. Dependent Relative Revocation 119
E. Timing Versus Importance of Inconsistent Documents 121
F. Waivers and Succession Agreements 121
G. Reformation and Modification 123
Checkpoints 124

Chapter 9 • Family Protection Statutes 127
Roadmap 127
A. Chapter Overview 127

B. Homestead 128
1. UPC Homestead Allowance 128
2. UPC Constitutional Homestead Provision 129
3. State Provisions 130
C. Exempt Property 130
D. Family Allowance 131
E. Omitted Spouse or Child (Pretermission) 132
1. Omitted Spouse 133
a. Qualifying as Omitted 133
b. Computing and Satisfying the Spouse's Share 134
2. Omitted Child 135
a. Qualifying as Omitted 135
b. Computing and Satisfying the Child's Share 136
F. Elective Share 138
1. Computing the Augmented Estate 139
a. Decedent's Net Probate Estate 139
b. Transfers the Decedent Made to Third Parties 139
1. Property Owned or Owned in Substance 139
2. Property the Decedent Transferred During Marriage 140
3. Property the Decedent Transferred Within Two Years of Death 141
c. Transfers the Decedent Made to His Spouse 142
d. Property the Surviving Spouse Owned or Transferred to Third Parties 143
e. Exclusions, Overlaps, and Valuation 143
2. Computing the Elective Share 144
3. Funding the Elective Share 144
4. Elective Share and Other Spousal Rights 146
G. Forced Heirship 147
H. Community Property 147
I. Waiver of Spousal Rights 148
1. Overview 148
2. UPC Provisions 148
Checkpoints 150

Chapter 10 • Introduction to Trusts 153
Roadmap 153
A. Chapter Overview 153
B. Sources of Modern Trust Law 153

C. Terminology 154
D. Express Trusts 156
E. Resulting and Constructive Trusts 156
1. Resulting Trusts 156
2. Constructive Trusts 157
F. Other Usages of the Term Trust 158
Checkpoints 159

Chapter 11 • Creating an Express Trust 161
Roadmap 161
A. Chapter Overview 161
B. Settlor Capacity 162
C. Settlor Intent 163
1. Precatory Language 163
2. Power of Appointment 164
3. Custodial Arrangement 164
D. Beneficiary 165
1. Definite Beneficiary 165
2. Charitable Trusts 166
3. Certain "Honorary" Trusts 166
E. Trustee with Duties 167
F. Merger of Legal and Beneficial Interests 168
Checkpoints 169

Chapter 12 • Trust Purpose, Formalities, and Funding 171
Roadmap 171
A. Chapter Overview 171
B. Purpose 171
C. Formalities 173
1. Inter Vivos Trust 173
2. Testamentary Trust 174
3. Secret or Semi-Secret Testamentary Trust 174
D. Funding 175
1. Trust Principal 175
2. Trust *in Futuro* 176
3. Delivery 176
Checkpoints 177

Chapter 13 • Trust Distribution Provisions 179
Roadmap 179

A. Chapter Overview 179
B. Distributions by the Trustee 179
1. Mandatory Distributions of Income 180
2. Discretionary Distributions of Income 180
3. Distributions of Principal 181
C. Third-Party Powers over Trust Principal 182
Checkpoints 183

Chapter 14 • Specific Uses for Trusts 185
Roadmap 185
A. Chapter Overview 185
B. Reasons for Creating a Trust 186
1. Privacy 186
2. Control Until Death or Incapacity 187
3. Flexibility 187
4. Professional Management 188
5. Avoiding Successive Probates 188
6. Protecting Family Wealth 188
7. Avoiding Ancillary Administration 189
8. Other Uses for Trusts 189
C. Trusts for the Care of Animals 190
D. Trusts for a Noncharitable Purpose 191
E. Trusts for Spouses 192
1. Trusts Qualifying for the Marital Deduction 192
2. Trusts Used in Satisfying the Elective Share 194
F. Trusts Holding Life Insurance Policies 194
G. Charitable Trusts 197
1. Beneficiary 197
2. Purpose 197
3. Cy Pres 198
4. Split-Interest Trusts 198
Checkpoints 198

Chapter 15 • Creditor Access to Trust Assets 201
Roadmap 201
A. Chapter Overview 201
B. Creditors of the Settlor 201
1. Insolvent Settlor 201
2. Retained Power or Interest in Trust 202
3. Creditors of Settlor's Estate 202

4. Asset Protection Trusts 202
C. Creditors of a Beneficiary 203
1. Spendthrift Provisions 204
a. Requirements for Spendthrift Provision 204
b. Effect on Creditors and Beneficiaries 205
c. Creditors with Access 205
2. Discretionary Trusts; Effect of a Standard 207
3. Forfeiture Provisions 209
4. Beneficiary with General Power of Appointment 210
a. Power of Withdrawal 210
b. Lapsing Power of Withdrawal 210
D. Creditors of the Trustee 211
Checkpoints 211

Chapter 16 • Modification, Reformation, Termination, and Revocation 213
Roadmap 213
A. Chapter Overview 213
B. Uniform Act Provisions 214
1. Relevance of the Rule Against Perpetuities 214
2. Trust Termination: Revocation; Expiration; Failure of Purpose 214
3. Modification or Termination by Consent 215
4. Unanticipated Circumstances or Inability to Administer the Trust Effectively 216
5. Cy Pres 216
6. Uneconomic Trust 217
7. Reformation to Correct Mistakes 218
8. Modification of Trusts to Achieve Tax Objectives 219
9. Combination and Division of Trusts 219
10. Challenging Modification, Reformation, or Termination 220
C. Trust Decanting 220
1. Trusts for Which Decanting Is Permitted, Prohibited, or Restricted 221
2. Notice to Beneficiaries and Other Persons 222
3. Extent of the Fiduciary's Power 222
a. Expanded Distributive Discretion 223
b. Limited Distributive Discretion 223
D. Revocation and Amendment by Settlor 225

1. Capacity 225
2. Formalities 226
3. Trust with More Than One Settlor 227
Checkpoints 228

Chapter 17 • Interpreting Instruments and Rules of Construction 231
Roadmap 231
A. Chapter Overview 231
B. Ambiguities and Other Interpretation Issues 232
1. Ambiguity 232
2. Devises or Trust Interests Based on Identity 233
3. Devises or Trust Interests Based on Class Characteristics 233
4. Devises or Trust Interests Based on Activity 234
5. Devises or Trust Interests Based on Indefinite Terminology 234
6. Devises or Trust Interests Administered in a Different State 235
C. Class and Individual Gifts 235
1. Transfer to an Individual or to a Class 235
2. Qualifying for Class Membership 236
3. Share of Each Class Member 236
4. Transfers Using Both Individual and Class Terminology 237
D. Rules of Construction 238
Checkpoints 239

Chapter 18 • Rules of Construction for Wills 241
Roadmap 241
A. Chapter Overview 241
B. Property Owned at Death and After-Acquired Property 242
C. Antilapse; Deceased Devisee; Class Gifts 243
1. Common Law and Statutes 243
2. Relevant Relationships 244
3. Devises to Individuals and to Classes 245
4. Substitute Takers 246
5. Effect of Survivorship Language 247
6. Language Naming an Alternative Taker 247
7. Residuary Devise 248
D. Failure of Testamentary Provision 249
E. Increase in Securities; Accessions 250
1. Definition of Securities 250

2. UPC Provisions 251
   a. Stock Splits, Stock Dividends, and Single-Entity Reorganizations 251
   b. Securities of Another Entity 252
   c. Securities Acquired Through a Plan of Reinvestment 253
   d. Cash Dividends 253
   e. Other Situations 253
3. State Statutes 254

F. Nonademption of Specific Devises 254
1. Language Used in Devise 254
2. UPC Provisions 255
   a. UPC § 2-606(a) 255
   b. UPC § 2-606(b) 257

G. Nonexoneration 258

H. Exercise of Power of Appointment 259

I. Ademption by Satisfaction 261
1. Requirements 261
2. Application 261
3. Computing Partial Satisfaction 262
4. Comparing Ademption by Satisfaction and Ademption by Extinction 263
5. Comparing Ademption by Satisfaction and Advancement 264

Checkpoints 265

Chapter 19 • Rules of Construction for Governing Instruments 269

Roadmap 269

A. Chapter Overview 270

B. Survival Requirements 270
1. Language of the Instrument 270
2. UPC Default Provisions 271
   a. 120-Hour Survival Requirement 271
   b. Exceptions to the 120-Hour Survival Requirement 272
3. Provisions in the Governing Instrument 274
4. Deemed Failure to Survive 274
5. Alternative Taker 275

C. Choice of Law 275

D. Power of Appointment Specific Reference Requirement 276

E. Construing Class Gifts 277
1. Terms of Relationship 277

a. Relatives by Marriage 277
b. Transferor Is Not the Parent 278
2. Class-Closing Rules 279
F. Deceased Beneficiary 279
G. Survivorship with Respect to Future Interests in Trust 282
H. Class Gifts to Descendants and Similar Categories 284
I. Representation 285
J. Worthier-Title Doctrine Abolished 286
K. Future Interests in Heirs 286
L. State Statutes 286
1. Survival 287
2. Relationships 287
3. Other Differences 287
Checkpoints 288

Chapter 20 • Disqualifying Acts 291
Roadmap 291
A. Chapter Overview 291
B. Marital Dissolution 292
1. Effect on Treatment as Surviving Spouse 292
2. Effect on Devises and Other Transfers to Former Spouse or Former Spouse's Family 293
a. Revocable Instrument 293
b. Former Spouse 294
c. Family of Former Spouse 295
d. Effect of Remarriage 295
C. Killers and Abusers 295
1. UPC 295
2. State Law 296
D. Disclaimers 297
1. Terminology 297
2. Interests and Powers That Can Be Disclaimed 298
a. Fee Simple Ownership 299
b. Interests in a Survivorship Tenancy 299
c. Beneficial Interest in an Express Trust 300
d. Status as a Beneficiary 300
e. Parties to a Power of Appointment 300
f. Power as a Fiduciary 301
3. Requirements for Disclaiming 301

a. Eligibility 301
b. Formalities 302
c. Time Period for Disclaiming 302
d. Disclaimer Valid for Federal Tax Purposes 303
4. Effective Date of Disclaimer 304
5. Taker of Disclaimed Property 305
a. General Rules 305
b. Acceleration of Future Interests 307
c. Survivorship Tenancies 307
E. Undue Influence 308
F. Duress 309
G. Fraud or Mistake 310
H. Relationship to Lack of Capacity 310
I. Spoliation or Alteration 311
J. Remedies 312
Checkpoints 313

Chapter 21 • Powers of Appointment 315
Roadmap 315
A. Chapter Overview 315
B. Relevant Uniform Acts 316
C. Terminology 316
1. Parties 316
2. General and Nongeneral Powers 317
3. Powers of Invasion and Ascertainable Standards 317
4. Powers of Invasion and Powers of Withdrawal 318
5. Power to Revoke and Powers of Appointment 319
6. Exclusionary and Nonexclusionary Powers 319
7. Presently Exercisable and Testamentary Powers 320
D. Exercising the Power 320
1. Purpose 320
2. Manner of Appointee's Enjoyment 320
3. Method of Exercise 321
4. Exercise in Favor of a Deceased Appointee 321
5. Disclaimer of Power or Property Subject to Power 321
E. Elective Share 322
1. Computing the Powerholder's Elective Estate 322
2. Valuing the Spouse's Elective Share 322
F. Creditor Access 323

1. Settlor's Interest 323
2. Trust Beneficiary as Settlor 323
3. Trustee as Settlor 324

G. Miscellaneous Powers of Appointment Issues 324
1. Rule Against Perpetuities 324
2. Federal Estate and Gift Taxes 325
a. General and Nongeneral Powers 325
b. Powers of Invasion 325
c. Powers of Withdrawal 326
d. Marital Deduction 326

Checkpoints 327

Chapter 22 • Rule Against Perpetuities 329

Roadmap 329
A. Chapter Overview 329
B. Historical Context 329
C. Potential Benefits and Downsides of Avoiding Vesting 330
D. Relevant Uniform Probate Code Provisions 331
1. Statutory Rule Against Perpetuities 331
a. Application to Interests in Property 331
b. Application to Powers of Appointment 332
1. Nontestamentary General Powers Subject to a Condition Precedent 333
2. Nontestamentary Limited Powers and Testamentary Powers 334
2. Posthumous Child Exception 335
3. Nondonative Transfer Exception 335
4. Charity to Charity Exception 336
5. Other UPC Exceptions 336
6. Determining When Interest or Power Is Created 337
7. Distribution of Trust Property 338

E. State Laws 339

Checkpoints 340

Chapter 23 • Claims, Expenses, and Distributions to Beneficiaries 341

Roadmap 341
A. Chapter Overview 341
B. Expenses and Claims 342
C. Abatement of Devises 342

1. Will Clauses 342
2. Statutory Defaults 343
3. Claims Against the Estate 344

D. Tax Apportionment 345
1. Overview 345
2. Tax Apportionment Provisions 346
3. Applicable Federal Statutes 347

E. Beneficiary Requests and Private Agreements 349
1. Beneficiary Requests 349
2. Private Agreements 349

Checkpoints 350

Chapter 24 • Trustees and Other Fiduciaries 353

Roadmap 353
A. Chapter Overview 353
B. Fiduciaries Other Than Trustees 353
1. Agent Under a Power of Attorney 353
a. Creation and Termination of Power of Attorney 354
b. Agent's Authority 355
c. Agent's Duties and Liability 355
2. Conservator or Guardian 356
3. Custodian for UTMA Account 358
4. Health Care Fiduciary 359
5. Personal Representative 359
a. Powers 359
b. Duties 360
c. Liability 360

C. Trustees and Trust Directors 361
1. Powers 361
2. Duties 363
3. Liability 366
a. Liability to Trust Beneficiaries 366
1. Exculpatory Language in Instrument 367
2. Consent, Release, or Ratification 368
b. Liability to Third Parties 368
c. Liability to Settlor 368
4. Multiple Fiduciaries 368

Checkpoints 369

Chapter 25 • Income, Expense, and Investment 371
Roadmap 371
A. Chapter Overview 371
B. Relevant Documents 372
C. Overview of Accounting Principles 373
1. Accounting Period 373
2. Accounting Method 373
D. Principal and Income: Probate Estate 375
1. Overview 375
2. Uniform Act Provisions 376
E. Principal and Income: Property Held in Trust 377
1. Overview 377
2. General Uniform Act Provisions 377
3. Beginning and Ending an Income Interest 378
4. Allocation When Interest Begins and Ends 379
5. Trustee's Power to Adjust 380
6. Conversion to a Unitrust 381
7. Allocation of Receipts and Disbursements Between Income and Principal 381
F. Investing Trust Assets 382
Checkpoints 384

Chapter 26 • Federal Transfer Taxes 387
Roadmap 387
A. Chapter Overview 387
B. Gift Tax 388
1. Completed Gift 388
2. Gift Tax Exclusions 389
a. Gifts of a Present Interest 389
b. Transfers to Educational Institutions and Medical Care Providers 390
c. Gift-Splitting 390
d. Effect of Exclusions on Trusts and Estates Concepts 391
3. Gift Tax Deductions 391
a. Transfers to a Spouse 391
b. Transfers to a Charity 392
C. Estate Tax 392
1. Gross Estate 393
2. Estate Tax Deductions 395

a. Expenses, Debts, and Taxes; Losses 395
b. Transfers to a Spouse 395
c. Transfers to a Charity 396
3. Tax Base, Tentative Tax, and Exemption 396
D. Generation-Skipping Transfer Tax 396
E. Miscellaneous Tax Consequences 398
1. Tax-Inclusive and Tax-Exclusive Transfers 398
2. Income Tax Basis Rules 399
3. Trust Income Tax Rates and Creditor Access to Trust Assets 400
Checkpoints 400

Mastering Trusts and Estates Checklist 403
Table of Cases 423
Table of Statutes 425
Table of Regulations 429
Table of Restatements and Uniform Acts 431
Index 439

SERIES EDITOR'S FOREWORD

The Carolina Academic Press Mastering Series is designed to provide you with a tool that will enable you to easily and efficiently "master" the substance and content of law school courses. Throughout the series, the focus is on quality writing that makes legal concepts understandable. As a result, the series is designed to be easy to read and is not unduly cluttered with footnotes or cites to secondary sources.

In order to facilitate student mastery of topics, the Mastering Series includes a number of pedagogical features designed to improve learning and retention. At the beginning of each chapter, you will find a "Roadmap" that tells you about the chapter and provides you with a sense of the material that you will cover. "Checkpoints" at the end of each chapter encourage you to stop and review the key concepts, reiterating what you have learned. Throughout the book, key terms are explained and emphasized. Finally, a "Master Checklist" at the end of each book reinforces what you have learned and helps you identify any areas that need review or further study.

We hope that you will enjoy studying with, and learning from, the Mastering Series.

Russell L. Weaver
PROFESSOR OF LAW &
DISTINGUISHED UNIVERSITY SCHOLAR
UNIVERSITY OF LOUISVILLE,
LOUIS D. BRANDEIS SCHOOL OF LAW

PREFACE

This book is designed for students who have completed the basic course in property and are now studying trusts and estates. At one time, many law schools allotted five or six credits for the basic course and another four to six credits for the advanced course. That is no longer the case at many schools. As a result, you may not have encountered, or may have spent relatively little time on, the common-law rule against perpetuities, life estates, or powers that do not rise to the level of ownership.

Differences in coverage extend to the upper-level curriculum. Trusts and estates courses may be offered in as few as three credits or as many as six credits. They may focus on wills, trusts, and intestacy, but they may also consider inter vivos gifts, survivorship tenancies, and other ownership forms. They may limit themselves to actual transfers, or they may add fiduciary powers and duties. They may even include potential changes in the law in response to changing social norms. They may cover only doctrinal law, or they may include drafting exercises. They may focus on statutes and judicial decisions in a single state, or they may cover uniform acts, Restatements, and decisions from several jurisdictions. Some courses may include relevant federal tax consequences.

This book is structured to respond to these potential differences. It covers both lifetime and at-death transfers. It considers how possible transfer options might affect other transfers. It explains various types of ownership interests, which you can skim if your introductory property course covered those in detail. It begins with chapters focusing on terminology, relevant uniform acts, and questions that you might consider in studying trusts and estates. Its overall focus is on uniform act provisions and possible state variations. A book of this nature cannot comprehensively cover the law of every jurisdiction.

Federal transfer tax consequences are described at various points. Those descriptions use 2024 federal transfer tax numbers for gift tax exclusions and the overall transfer tax exemption. Although the slightly larger 2025 amounts now apply, there is uncertainty as to what will happen when the 2017 Tax Cuts and Jobs Act expires at the end of 2025. It is even possible, although probably unlikely, that the current 2025 amounts will change before year-end. In any event, the 2025 numbers will be obsolete by 2026.

I hope you enjoy studying trusts and estates as much as I enjoy teaching it.

Gail Levin Richmond
February 2025

ABOUT THE AUTHOR

Gail Levin Richmond is Emerita Professor of Law at Nova Southeastern University Shepard Broad College of Law. Her teaching interests include income tax, trusts and estates, and will drafting. She practiced law in Ohio and has taught on a full-time or part-time basis at several law schools. She is the author or co-author of books and articles on topics related to her teaching interests.

MASTERING
TRUSTS AND ESTATES

CHAPTER 1

Introduction to Trusts and Estates

ROADMAP

- Options for transmitting property
- Questions to consider

A. Options for Transmitting Property

A property owner has goals for transmitting her property and many options for satisfying those goals. If she wants to retain her property until she dies, she can use a will to dispose of it or she can die intestate and let the state's default disposition rules apply. She could instead transfer property into a revocable trust and retain all property rights until she dies. Or she can open a bank account in her name and include a "pay on death" designation in the account. The POD beneficiary will receive the property when she dies, but he has no rights before then. Indeed, she can withdraw her money, or select a different POD beneficiary, at any time. She is not limited to a single method for transmitting property. She can, for example, place some property in a revocable trust, open a POD bank account with other funds, and devise the rest of her property in her will.

Given the flexibility described above, you might wonder why anyone would make an irrevocable gift before dying. That question has many answers. One answer relates to privacy. A will is filed in court before it is probated and might become a public record. A property owner might not want members of the public to know how her property is being distributed. Another answer relates to cost. The process for transferring property at death, referred to as probate, is often viewed as lengthy and expensive. Transfers before death, including the revocable transfers described in the preceding paragraph, might avoid the probate process. A third answer relates to federal (and, in some jurisdictions, state) tax rules. Transfers above a certain threshold amount are currently subject to federal gift or estate tax at the rate of 40%. Gifts made during life that qualify for statutory exclusions avoid the gift tax and reduce the amount subject to estate tax. One such exclusion allows an individual to transfer up to $18,000 per year (2024 amount) to each donee. I.R.C. § 2503(b). Those transfers escape both gift and estate taxation.

> **Example 1-1.** Estelle accumulated an estate (net of debts) worth $13,750,000 and never made any large gifts to her four children and 10 grandchildren. If she had died in 2024, her taxable estate would have exceeded the 2024 exemption amount ($13,610,000) by $140,000 and would be subject to a $56,000 estate tax.
>
> **Example 1-2.** Assume Estelle followed her attorney's advice and made inter vivos gifts of $18,000 to each of her 10 grandchildren in February 2024, reducing her potential taxable estate to $13,570,000. Because that amount is below the 2024 exemption, her estate would owe no federal estate tax.

Another reason for making outright gifts before death relates to a donee's ability to handle funds. After watching how they use those gifts, the property owner can better determine which family members should receive funds outright when she dies—and which require the professional management that a trustee can provide.

This book devotes several chapters to trusts, because those entities are more flexible than outright transfers during life or at death. A trust can provide income for one or more generations, with ultimate distribution to a more remote generation or to charity. A trust can limit access by a beneficiary's creditors or provide for a beloved family pet. A trust offers professional management and investment decisions. And, assuming the trust is established before the property owner dies, its terms are not a public record unless there is litigation.

B. Questions to Consider

A trusts and estates class can appear daunting because there are so many ways to transfer property, different rules apply to different types of transfers, and transfers during life often affect how property is disposed of when the owner dies. In addition, there is a new vocabulary. Words might have different meanings depending on the type of transfer and might vary from jurisdiction to jurisdiction. Vocabulary also changes over time. Language used in a judicial decision might differ from the language in the relevant statute because the decision was rendered when the statute was worded differently or before any statute was enacted.

1. Casebook Questions

Your trusts and estates casebook includes both statutes and judicial decisions and probably includes problems based on those materials. Unless your course focuses exclusively on a single state, your casebook will include material from different jurisdictions and is likely to use the uniform acts listed in Chapter 2 as exemplars. In reading each assigned decision, ask yourself why the authors included it. Does it help interpret a current statute? Was it based on societal norms that have changed? If so, has its reasoning been overruled by statute? Does it illustrate problems caused by a lawyer who misunderstood what the client wanted or did a poor job drafting a will or trust?

2. Questions Concerning Transfers

Throughout your studies, and in using this book, you should focus on any of the questions below that are relevant. Note that the term "transfer" is used below. As you will see in later chapters, discussion often involves potential transfers rather than actual transfers. For example, a person who executes a will today might not die for several years. His will might devise property to a person who later predeceases him, or it might devise property he no longer owns when he dies. In determining how his property is distributed, you will consider Questions 7 and 17 from the list below; perhaps you will decide that other questions also apply.

1. Is the transfer one that occurred during life or one that will not occur until death?
2. Is the transfer outright or in trust?

3. Is the transfer revocable or irrevocable?
4. If the transfer is revocable, under what circumstances is it revocable?
5. Did the transferor observe any required formalities in making or revoking the transfer?
6. Did the transferor have the capacity and the intent to make or revoke the transfer?
7. Does the transferee have to meet survival or other requirements to receive the property?
8. Is the transfer to a single person or to a group?
9. Do any family protection statutes affect the transfer?
10. Did the transferor intend that a lifetime gift reduce the recipient's share of the transferor's estate?
11. Was the transfer made by an owner or by a powerholder chosen by the owner?
12. Must a potential transferee accept the property?
13. Did the potential transferee's actions prevent him from receiving property he wanted to accept?
14. When can transferees vary the terms of the transfer?
15. What rights do the transferor's creditors have?
16. What rights do the transferee's creditors have?
17. What rights do potential transferees have if the decedent no longer owns the property covered by his will?
18. What rules of construction or reformation apply to a will or trust that is ambiguous or that misstates the transferor's intent?
19. What happens if the terms of a transfer are contrary to a state's public policy?
20. Which law applies if the decedent resided in one state but owned property in a different state?
21. When can a transfer be challenged?
22. Who is eligible to challenge the transfer?
23. What evidence must the challenger present?
24. What burden of proof applies to the challenge, and who bears that burden?

3. Fiduciary Questions

In Example 1-2 above, Estelle made gifts by transferring money, possibly by writing a check to each grandchild. But who will transfer the rest of Estelle's property to her chosen beneficiaries after she dies? What if one of those beneficiaries is a minor? At various points in your course, you will consider fiduciaries who act on behalf of a property owner, both during that person's life or at his death. You will also consider fiduciaries, such as trustees, with ongoing responsibilities for managing and distributing property. The two fiduciaries you will encounter most often are those who take charge of a decedent's estate and those who manage a trust. Fiduciaries are introduced at various points in this book. When considering fiduciaries, ask yourself if the fiduciary had the power to act, had a mandatory or discretionary duty to act, to whom the fiduciary owed duties, and whether the fiduciary acted properly.

CHECKPOINTS

- Property owners have many options for transferring property to their beneficiaries.
- Their choices include waiting until death, transferring property inter vivos, or using a combination of timing methods.
- They might choose to make outright transfers or transfers in trust.
- If they wait until death to transfer property outright, they might do so by will or allow the relevant state intestacy statute to apply.
- Their choices are affected by considerations related to privacy, transfer costs, tax rules, and a donee's ability to manage funds.
- Trusts and estates law involves not only transferors and their beneficiaries but also fiduciaries who act on their behalf.

CHAPTER 2

Sources of Law

ROADMAP

- Uniform acts and model acts
- Restatements
- Federal statutes
- State statutes
- Judicial decisions
- Multiple states' involvement

A. Chapter Overview

Donative transfers, whether outright or in trust, must comply with the law of the relevant jurisdiction. This chapter describes sources of law you can consult in determining how to make a valid transfer, the grounds for challenging a transfer, and the consequences of invalidity.

B. Uniform Acts and Model Acts

The National Conference of Commissioners on Uniform State Laws (Uniform Law Commission) approves and recommends uniform acts that, if enacted by individual states, reduce differences in how states treat various topics. The ULC site states: "An act is designated as a 'Uniform' Act if there is substantial reason to anticipate enactment in a large number of jurisdictions, and uniformity of the provisions of the act among the various jurisdictions is a principal objective."

If you studied sales in Contracts or an upper-level Uniform Commercial Code course, you have already encountered a uniform act. The UCC is more widely accepted than many of the acts listed below. That should not surprise you. Parties involved in commercial transactions often live (or are incorporated) in different states; a common set of statutes facilitates business activity. Transfers of real estate, on the other hand, are local; the land does not move across state lines merely because the purchaser and seller (or donor and donee) live in different states.

A state might enact a uniform act in its entirety, enact it in part, or ignore it altogether. Even if a state initially enacts a uniform act, it might not enact amendments or might enact them long after the Uniform Law Commission recommends them. If a state statute reflects a uniform act, you can use the act's comments as interpretive aids. Those comments accompany the acts on the Uniform Law Commission website, https://uniformlaws.org. Many of the comments include useful examples in addition to explanations and citations to authority. Use the uniform act's PDF version to obtain the comments.

With one exception, the acts listed below are designated Uniform Acts. The one exception is the Model Marital Property Act. The ULC uses this designation if the act's purposes "can be substantially achieved even though it is not adopted in its entirety by every state." For these acts, "uniformity may be a desirable objective, though not a principal objective."

1. Acts Related to Trusts and Estates

The Uniform Law Commission lists several acts in a Probate, Trusts, and Estates category. It also lists some of them under other categories, primarily family law and medical & public health laws. This should not surprise you; the activities discussed in this book could have consequences that go beyond mere transfer of ownership from one person to another.

- Uniform Adult Guardianship and Protective Proceedings Jurisdiction Act
- Uniform Anatomical Gift Act
- Uniform Community Property Disposition at Death Act
- Uniform Custodial Trust Act
- Uniform Determination of Death Act

- Uniform Directed Trust Act
- Uniform Disclaimer of Property Interests Act
- Uniform Electronic Estate Planning Documents Act
- Uniform Electronic Wills Act
- Uniform Estate Tax Apportionment Act
- Uniform Fiduciary Access to Digital Assets Act, Revised
- Uniform Fiduciary Income and Principal Act
- Uniform Guardianship, Conservatorship, and Other Protective Arrangements Act
- Model Marital Property Act
- Uniform Multiple-Person Accounts Act
- Uniform Partition of Heirs Property Act
- Uniform Power of Attorney Act
- Uniform Powers of Appointment Act
- Uniform Probate Code
- Uniform Prudent Investor Act
- Uniform Prudent Management of Institutional Funds Act
- Uniform Real Property Transfer on Death Act
- Uniform Recognition of Substitute Decision-Making Documents Act
- Uniform Simultaneous Death Act
- Uniform Statutory Rule Against Perpetuities
- Uniform Testamentary Additions to Trusts Act
- Uniform TOD Security Registration Act
- Uniform Transfers to Minors Act
- Uniform Trust Code
- Uniform Trust Decanting Act
- Uniform Wills Recognition Act

Several of these acts exist both as standalone acts and as parts of the Uniform Probate Code or the Uniform Trust Code; this book notes that status when discussing the topics those acts cover. A state statutory compilation might group them within its probate or trust provisions or list them separately. Although not bearing a ULC "Probate, Trusts, and Estates" tag, the Uniform Health-Care Decisions Act, Uniform Parentage Act, and Uniform Premarital and Marital Agreements Act might also be covered in a trusts and estates course.

Other uniform acts could be relevant in the practice of law and the actual administration of estates and trusts. For example, a decedent might own a condominium that his estate's personal representative will ultimately sell or distribute to a beneficiary. In the period between the decedent's death and the property's disposition, the personal representative might need to consult a state statute based on a version of the Uniform Common Interest Ownership Act.

2. Organization of Uniform Probate Code and Uniform Trust Code

The UPC and UTC are the primary uniform acts covered in this book. Each is organized into Articles. UPC Articles are subdivided into Parts, some of which are further divided into Subparts. UPC section numbers reflect both the Article and Part number. For example, UPC § 2-302 (Omitted Children) is in UPC Article II, Part 3. UTC section numbers reflect the Article number. For example, UTC § 803 (Impartiality) is in UTC Article 8. State statute numbers might reflect the uniform act numbering system, but that is not required. The lists below should help you find UPC and UTC provisions if you lack a reference to the appropriate section number.

a. *Uniform Probate Code*

The UPC has the following Articles:

I General Provisions, Definitions and Probate Jurisdiction of Court
II Intestacy, Wills, and Donative Transfers
III Probate of Wills and Administration
IV Foreign Personal Representatives; Ancillary Administration
V Uniform Guardianship and Protective Proceedings Act (1997/1998)
5A Uniform Adult Guardianship and Protective Proceedings Jurisdiction Act (2007)
5B Uniform Power of Attorney Act (2006)
VI Nonprobate Transfers on Death
VIII Effective Date and Repealer

Former Article VII, entitled Trust Administration, was withdrawn after the UTC was widely adopted by the states. Articles 5A and 5B do not use the Roman numerals of the other Articles.

The UPC was last substantially revised in 2010; additional revisions were made in 2019. Several UPC Articles and Parts are separately named uniform acts, with approval dates that might differ from those of the overall UPC. A state that enacted the UPC when it was first recommended by the Commission might not have amended its statutes to reflect UPC amendments or inclusion of a separately named act. And, because some of the separately named acts were approved many years ago, states might have enacted quite different language in dealing with the topics covered by those acts.

b. Uniform Trust Code

The UTC has the following Articles:

1 General Provisions and Definitions

2 Judicial Proceedings

3 Representation

4 Creation, Validity, Modification, and Termination of Trust

5 Creditor's Claims; Spendthrift and Discretionary Trusts

6 Revocable Trusts

7 Office of Trustee

8 Duties and Powers of Trustee

9 Uniform Prudent Investor Act (placeholder)

10 Liability of Trustees and Rights of Persons Dealing with Trustee

11 Miscellaneous Provisions

The UTC was approved in 2000 and revised several times since, most recently in 2018. Its comments have also been updated, most recently in 2024.

3. Focus of Book

This book focuses on UPC and UTC provisions for (1) creating valid wills and trusts; (2) amending, modifying, reforming, revoking, or terminating those instruments; (3) distributing property to heirs, devisees, trust beneficiaries, and beneficiaries or surviving tenants of other nonprobate transfers; (4) rights of family members and creditors; (5) beneficiary misconduct; and (6) fiduciary powers and duties. It covers the rule against perpetuities, disclaimers, and powers of appointment; provides an overview of principal and income, investment of trust and estate assets, and federal transfer taxes; and briefly discusses other related topics.

C. Restatements

The American Law Institute (ALI) produces "scholarly work to clarify, modernize, and otherwise improve the law." Its publications include Restatements of the Law and Model Codes. The original Restatement of Trusts condensed and digested decisions from all U.S. jurisdictions. It published the consensus of those decisions as the apparent majority view. The Restatement (Second) updated those rules, taking into account later decisions. It also based the promulgated rules primarily on published decisions. Both Restatements were often cited and widely adopted by the courts. The ALI's coverage of wills began with the Restatement of Property, followed by the Restatement (Second) of Property: Donative Transfers.

The Restatement (Third) of Trusts and the Restatement (Third) of Property: Wills and Other Donative Transfers continue the process of updating the promulgated rules based on later decisions. Both have expanded the scope from "restatement" to "reform," in some cases championing rules that are based on the Uniform Trust Code or the latest revisions of the Uniform Probate Code. Some of these revised rules, while based on cogent reasoning, have little or no case law or statutory support. To the extent that a revised rule is based upon proposed statutory reform, a court might leave such reform to the legislature and reject the revised rule of the Restatement.

The Restatements include numerous comments on general rules and possible exceptions that states might have adopted. This book refers to both current and prior Restatements because they are useful for historical purposes and because some states continue to rely on earlier versions. Some citations to Restatements are made to indicate changes made by the UPC and UTC. As is true for the UPC and UTC, Restatement comments are useful interpretive tools.

D. Federal Statutes

The administration of trusts and estates is primarily a function of state law. Federal courts hear disputes in these areas only if a federal statute applies or there is a dispute between states, for example, over where a decedent is domiciled. *Marshall v. Marshall*, 547 U.S. 293 (2006), indicated that the so-called "probate exception" to federal jurisdiction is not required by either the Constitution or by federal statutes. Nevertheless, federal courts do not generally involve themselves in state law probate and trust administration matters.

Despite these limitations, federal law affects trusts and estates in numerous ways. Federal bankruptcy courts might have to determine whether property is part of a debtor's bankruptcy estate and distributable to his creditors or is instead available for distribution to his beneficiaries. The Employee Retirement Income Security Act of 1974 (ERISA) might mandate that a surviving spouse receive a share of an employee's pension rights. The Social Security Act provides benefits for surviving spouses and dependent children.

The Internal Revenue Code is most likely to affect wealthier individuals, and it does so in a variety of ways. The income tax might be an incentive for higher-income individuals to make inter vivos gifts of income-producing property to lower-income family members. The income produced by that property would then be subject to a lower rate of income tax. But if the property is significantly appreciated, the owner might decide to hold it until death. Under current law, the donee of a devise or inheritance takes a basis equal to the property's value at the decedent's death. The donee of an inter vivos gift takes the donor's lower basis for the appreciated property.

The gift tax exclusions for annual, present interest gifts of $18,000 or less to a single donee (2024 amount) and for direct payment of a donee's medical and educational expenses provide a means for ultimately reducing the donor's estate and gift tax liability. The deduction for gifts to charity and to a spouse also provide transfer tax protection. Transfers to take advantage of these protections must follow the rules provided in the federal statutes in addition to satisfying any state law transfer requirements.

If an estate tax is due when an individual dies, the personal representative confronts the question of which beneficiaries should receive less because the tax must be paid. The federal estate tax is imposed on the value of what the decedent owned. It is also imposed on the value of property he previously transferred without giving up all interests in or powers over the property. For example, if the decedent transferred Blackacre in trust but retained the right to all income it produced until his death, the value of Blackacre is in his gross estate even if the trust was irrevocable. For our purposes here, keep in mind that the Internal Revenue Code includes provisions covering which beneficiaries must contribute to the estate tax, and state statutes will also include tax apportionment provisions. Federal tax provisions are discussed at various points in this book, particularly in Chapter 26.

Finally, as discussed at relevant points in this book, a state might use federal estate and gift tax definitions in statutes governing powers of appointment, disclaimers, or spousal rights to a portion of a decedent's estate.

E. State Statutes

Relevant state statutes might be grouped together or scattered throughout the state's statutory compilation. Statutes based on uniform acts are most likely to be grouped together and often bear a short title, such as "The statutes in this [subdivision] may be referred to as the [State] Probate Code" or the "[State] Uniform Fiduciary Income and Principal Act." If you use an annotated set of statutes, you might find references to each section's history and to judicial decisions interpreting it. You will probably have to look elsewhere for actual legislative history documents.

Relevant statutes also appear in other parts of the state statutes. For example, statutes dealing with transferring real property into a trust are likely to appear with provisions dealing with property transfers rather than in the state's trust code.

F. Judicial Decisions

Judicial decisions can be important aids in interpreting statutes, but there are limits on their significance. Because you will probably read appellate decisions, you might not discover all the evidence relied on by the trial court. In addition, many appellate decisions focus on whether a grant of summary judgment was appropriate rather than on the merits of the dispute.

Don't be surprised if you cannot locate the ultimate decision in a case. If an appellate court sends the case back for trial or retrial, the parties might settle rather than continue the litigation. And, as is true in other areas of the law, don't be surprised if intermediate appellate courts within the same state appear to issue conflicting decisions. Slightly different facts, or a judge's view of them, could lead to different outcomes at trial, and appellate courts will rarely overturn the trial judge's factual determinations. If appellate courts differ on a question of law, the state's highest court might eventually resolve the issue.

G. Multiple States' Involvement

Real property generally has situs in the state in which it is located even if the property owner is domiciled elsewhere. When the reason for transferring property is the owner's death, her will (or intestate estate) is administered in the state of her domicile, and there is ancillary administration in the state in which the real property is located. The laws of her domicile will govern transfers of real property located in that state and personal property located everywhere. The laws of the state in which her real property is located govern transfers of property in that state.

Several states, primarily in the Western United States, use the community-property system of law for property owned by a married couple. Although most states do not use that system, residents of those states might own community property because they once lived in a community-property jurisdiction and own assets traceable to that earlier domicile. Likewise, residents of a community-property state might own property acquired in a state with a different property regime. This book includes only limited discussion of community property.

CHECKPOINTS

- The rules regarding trusts and estates can be found in federal and state statutes and judicial decisions.
- State laws might reflect uniform acts, particularly the Uniform Probate Code and the Uniform Trust Code, and various Restatements, but they are not required to do so.
- Uniform acts and Restatements include helpful explanatory comments.

- Although federal statutes often affect the transmission of wealth, most disputes concerning transfers from an owner to a beneficiary are based on state law and litigated in state courts.
- Residents of community-property states have different wealth transmission rules for marital property than do residents of other states.

CHAPTER 3

Terminology and Abbreviations

ROADMAP

- Terminology and potential areas of confusion
- Abbreviations

A. Chapter Overview

This chapter covers relevant trusts and estates terminology and definitions. Some terms are fixed in their meaning; the meaning of others depends on their context. State statutes might use different terms for the identical concept. Judicial decisions might use terminology that has been superseded by subsequent legislation. Documents or judicial decisions might also use initials to refer to fiduciaries or types of property ownership. The lists below cover terms you are likely to encounter, particularly those that could cause confusion, and commonly used initials. Additional terms appear, and are defined, in later chapters.

B. Terminology and Potential Areas of Confusion

The terms discussed in this chapter are not the only terms defined in this book. The terms included here either have multiple meanings in a single context or are used in different contexts. As indicated below, a term's meaning in one statute might differ from its meaning in another statute. In addition, the meaning of terms used for trusts and estates, and for other types of transfers, might differ from their everyday meaning. When dealing with a set of provisions, you should consider definitions for terms used in a provision or group of provisions. These definitions usually appear at the beginning of a relevant set of provisions or at the beginning of a single statute.

1. Ademption by Extinction; Ademption by Satisfaction; Advancement

Both ademption by extinction and ademption by satisfaction reduce or eliminate a devise. Ademption by satisfaction applies if the beneficiary has already received property from the testator and there is a writing indicating that what he received was in satisfaction of his devise. The term advancement is used when the transferor died intestate and a potential heir received property before that death. Ademption by extinction occurs when the testator no longer owns the property devised or owns less than the amount devised.

2. Augmented Estate; Elective Estate; Gross Estate; Probate Estate; Trust Estate

The term estate, without modification, is commonly used to describe property that is subject to administration when the property owner dies. Because that process is referred to as probate, the term probate estate is also appropriate. If a property owner has transferred property to a trust, it is possible that the trust assets will be referred to as the trust estate.

If a surviving spouse has rights to a percentage or other portion of a decedent's estate, the value used in computing her rights is referred to as the augmented estate or elective estate. This estate is comprised of the property in the probate estate and property over which the decedent had interests or powers when he died. It could also take into account property he transferred before death and property owned or transferred by the surviving spouse.

A property owner's probate estate, plus property over which he had interests or powers, is referred to as the gross estate for purposes of computing the federal estate tax. The federal gross estate is similar to the elective estate in that neither is limited to property passing through probate. It is not necessarily identical to it, however. Federal tax law governs which property rights and interests comprise the gross estate; individual state laws might include the same amounts, larger amounts, smaller amounts, or even different items in computing the elective estate.

As the paragraphs above indicate, the term estate has a variety of meanings. This book often uses a modifier, such as probate estate or gross estate, to help you focus on which rules apply.

3. Beneficiary; Devisee; Heir; Legatee; Qualified Beneficiary

The terms devisee and legatee refer to persons (individuals or entities) that receive property under the terms of a will. The term devisee originally referred to recipients of real property, while legatee referred to recipients of personal property. Many jurisdictions now use the term devisee for both types of property. Devisees and legatees are beneficiaries of the decedent's probate estate.

The term heir refers to individuals who receive property under the laws of intestacy. An heir is also a beneficiary of the probate estate. An individual who would be an heir if a will is declared invalid might have standing to challenge that will even if he is not a devisee.

The term beneficiary is also used in other settings. It includes persons who receive benefits from a trust, from a life insurance policy, and from pay on death and transfer on death accounts.

A beneficiary's rights depend on context. For example, a trust beneficiary may be entitled to know the trust's terms. The beneficiary of a pay on death account does not even have the right to know the account exists.

Statutes governing trusts often differentiate between persons who are beneficiaries and those who are qualified beneficiaries. Qualified beneficiaries are already, or currently are next in line to become, recipients of trust income or principal or would receive principal if the trust terminated. They generally have greater rights to notice and reporting than do other potential beneficiaries.

4. Capacity

Transfers are not effective unless the transferor and any necessary witnesses have the requisite capacity. But the capacity required varies by the role an individual plays and by the type of transfer being made. The capacity required to execute a will or create a revocable trust is usually less than the capacity required to make an outright gift or create an irrevocable trust. The capacity to witness a document is likely to be even lower.

In addition to requiring capacity when a will is executed or a trust is created, statutes require that an individual have capacity when revoking or modifying a will or trust.

5. Child; Descendant; Heir; Issue

The term descendant includes the transferor's child and anyone descended from that child. The term issue might be used interchangeably with descendant. The term heir, on the other hand, refers to those individuals who would receive property through intestate succession. In addition to children and more remote descendants, it includes spouses, ancestors, siblings, aunts and uncles, nieces and nephews, and cousins. Each state determines how close a relationship must be to qualify an individual as an heir.

6. Codicil; Incorporation by Reference; Separate Writing

A testator may revoke a will and execute a new one as many times as she wishes, assuming she has testamentary capacity and follows any required statutory formalities. Instead of executing an entirely new will, she may use other documents to amend portions of her estate plan. A codicil is the most formal of these documents; it requires the same capacity and formalities as a will. A separate writing is much less formal, requiring only the testator's signature, and can be used only to dispose of tangible personal property not specifically devised by the will or a codicil. Incorporation by reference is a method of incorporating the terms of another document into the testator's will. Although the other document can cover any type of property, only the document as it existed when the will was executed can be incorporated into the will. A separate writing, on the other hand, can be executed or amended before or after the will is executed.

7. Constructive Trust; Express Trust; In Trust for Account; Resulting Trust

An express trust is an ownership device that separates the legal title to property from its beneficial interest. The legal title holder is the trustee; the persons holding beneficial interests are the beneficiaries. A single beneficiary (or group of beneficiaries) might have rights to both income and trust principal. Alternatively, one beneficiary (or group of beneficiaries) might have rights to income, while a different beneficiary (or group) has rights to the principal. Express trusts are governed by a jurisdiction's trust code.

Constructive trusts do not require intent to create a trust. Rather, they are imposed by a court as a remedy to prevent unjust enrichment. Resulting trusts generally arise in two instances: property placed in trust has no eligible takers, in which case there is a reversion to the grantor; or one person provided funds to another person, who was supposed to hold on the first person's behalf and transfer the property to the first person at a later date. Trust codes refer to constructive and resulting trusts but, because they are judicially declared, do not govern them.

A financial institution might offer accounts with "in trust for" designations. For example, an account could be titled George in trust for (or ITF) Fred. Despite the terminology, this arrangement is not a trust. George has the legal title, the right to the account income, and the right to cancel the beneficiary designation at any time. If George dies without changing the designation, Fred will receive the account balance without its going through probate. Many states have replaced statutes authorizing ITF accounts with statutes authorizing a similar account, the pay on death (POD) account.

Trusts are used in many other contexts, which are not covered in this book. You might have encountered voting trusts in a course covering corporations. Companies whose employees have been exposed to toxic substances might establish settlement trusts to fund payments to future victims. Real estate investment trusts (REITs) are investment vehicles subject to various federal tax and securities requirements.

8. Corpus; Principal; Res

Corpus, principal, and res are all terms used to describe the trust's assets. The trustee manages those assets, distributes (or accumulates) the net income they produce, and ultimately distributes the assets themselves. She follows mandatory or discretionary powers granted in the trust instrument or by statute.

The term principal is also used in another fiduciary-related context. It can refer to an individual who is represented by an agent under a power of attorney.

9. Cy Pres; Interpretation; Modification; Reformation

If a dispositive document is ambiguous or otherwise susceptible of multiple meanings, a court might take evidence as to its meaning and might also rely on rules of construction to aid in its interpretation. If a document does not reflect the property owner's intent, a court might reform its terms to reflect that intent; reformation usually requires a higher standard of proof than interpretation, especially if the court is being asked to modify an unambiguous document. A court could modify a document, particularly a trust, for a variety of reasons. Perhaps the trust terms no longer serve the transferor's original purpose, modification is in the best interests of the beneficiaries, or the trust has become uneconomical to administer. When a charitable trust is involved, modification is referred to as cy pres.

10. Execution; Expression; Inducement

Inducement and execution are terms used in challenging why a document included or excluded particular terms or why a property owner signed the document. Generally, a document is void if its execution was a product of fraud, duress, mistake, or undue influence. Thus, a will that was executed under duress is void, as is a trust created by an individual who was led to believe he was signing a different document. A document with terms that were the product of a mistaken belief or fraudulent conduct by another person involves errors in the inducement. The document might also incorrectly express the transferor's intent. Perhaps the drafter misinterpreted what the transferor wanted, or the transferor acted under an incorrect understanding of the facts or law. Some jurisdictions allow reformation to correct mistakes of inducement or expression.

11. Fiduciary

A fiduciary is an individual or entity selected by a property owner, by a court, or by beneficiaries to carry out a particular function. The fiduciary is subject to rules provided by the property owner, by statute, or—in appropriate cases—by a court.

The fiduciary's name depends on the event giving rise to her appointment. A fiduciary administering a probate estate is usually referred to as a personal representative, an executor, or an administrator. A fiduciary administering a trust is a trustee. A fiduciary administering the property of an individual who has been declared incapacitated is a guardian, a guardian of the property, or a conservator. A fiduciary holding a power of attorney is an agent but is often referred to as an attorney in fact. A fiduciary holding property transferred to a minor is a custodian. A fiduciary with the power to make health care decisions for another is a health care surrogate.

Although different statutes govern each fiduciary relationship, there are two important common features. Fiduciaries have powers, and they also have duties. Both arise by statute or by the instrument creating the relationship.

12. Governing Instrument; Instrument

Documents that govern the disposition of property are often referred to as instruments. If more than one document applies, and their terms conflict, the governing instrument applies. If the instruments, such as a will and a trust, do not indicate which governs, a statute or judicial decision might resolve the question.

13. Grantor; Grantor Trust; Settlor

The meaning of grantor depends on its context. When it stands alone, it refers to a person who transferred property to a trust; another term used in that context is settlor. When it is used as a modifier (grantor trust), it is a federal income tax term. The income of a grantor trust is taxed to the grantor (or sometimes to the grantor's spouse or another person with power over the trust) rather than to the beneficiary or the trust itself.

14. Representation

The term representation describes how property is distributed when the originally designated beneficiary or heir predeceases the testator, intestate decedent, or other transferor. The relevant antilapse statute or intestate succession statute might provide that the deceased beneficiary's descendants take by representation. The method used for determining a descendant's share is provided in the relevant statute.

The term representation is also used to describe persons who can bind others with respect to the administration of a trust or a probate estate. For example, unless there is a conflict of interest, a parent may be able to bind a child; one sibling may be able to bind another.

15. Revocation; Termination

Revocation generally refers to an action taken by a transferor to revoke a transfer and regain his property. The right might appear in an instrument, particularly an inter vivos trust, or it might be a statutory default. While a revocation essentially terminates any interest another person might have had in the property, termination is also used to indicate the end of an entity or an interest in that entity by other means. For example, a trust established to pay income to a beneficiary for 10 years and then pay principal to his children terminates at the end of 10 years. A court might terminate a trust if it determines that the trust no longer serves its purpose and cannot be reformed in a manner that does so.

Revocation can also occur with respect to a will. A testator with capacity can revoke a will in whole or in part by following the state-required formalities. The same is true with respect to beneficiary designations on bank accounts, life insurance policies, and retirement accounts.

16. Valid; Void; Voidable

Some documents are either entirely valid or entirely void. For example, a will executed by an individual who lacks testamentary capacity is void. It does not become valid merely because the individual has testamentary capacity when he dies.

Other documents might be partially valid and partially void. A will executed by an individual who has testamentary capacity, and that was executed and witnessed with the required formalities, is valid. But one of its provisions might be void if the testator was induced to include it because of duress. A provision might also be void if it violates state law, but the rest of the document could still be valid. For example, some states treat a "no contest" clause as valid; these clauses disinherit anyone who challenges a will or trust containing such a clause. Other states impose limitations on these clauses; they might disinherit a challenger only if he acted in bad faith. Still other states treat these clauses as void under all circumstances.

A provision's status as valid or void could change over time. Statutes void a devise to a spouse if the marriage is dissolved before the testator dies. Other statutes void a devise to someone who kills the testator. In Florida, the devise of the testator's homestead is void if the testator is survived by a minor child. These provisions are tested for validity when the testator dies, not when the will is executed.

In some instances, a transfer can be voided only by particular individuals but is otherwise valid. In that case, the transfer is referred to as voidable.

C. Abbreviations

- CLT refers to a charitable lead trust. These entities are often used to reduce a settlor's income and estate taxes.
- CRT refers to a charitable remainder trust. These entities are often used to reduce a settlor's income and estate taxes.
- CSV refers to cash surrender value. A whole life insurance policy has a CSV because the premiums charged in the policy's early years are greater than the amount the insurer needs to cover the risk of the insured's death and the insurer's expenses and profit. A term insurance policy does not have a CSV; the premiums charged each year cover only the risk of death and the insurer's expenses and profit. The CSV might be a factor in determining a spouse's elective share.
- DRR refers to dependent relative revocation. Courts use DRR to reinstate a previously revoked will on the theory that its revocation was conditional on the validity of a later will that turned out to be invalid.
- GAL refers to a guardian ad litem. A court can appoint a GAL to represent a minor's interest if a potential conflict of interest prevents the parent from representing the minor during trust or estate litigation.

- ILIT refers to an irrevocable life insurance trust. These entities are often used to reduce estate taxes.
- I.R.C. refers to the Internal Revenue Code of 1986.
- ITF refers to in trust for designations, generally on bank accounts.
- JT refers to joint tenancy or joint tenants.
- JTROS or JTWROS refers to joint tenants with right of survivorship.
- LDPS refers to lineal descendants per stirpes. It can be used in an instrument to indicate a substitute beneficiary if the primary beneficiary has died.
- PC refers to per capita. It can be used on a beneficiary designation form to indicate how property interests are to be divided.
- POA refers to a power of appointment. It can also refer to a power of attorney.
- POD refers to pay on death designations, generally on bank accounts or securities accounts.
- PS refers to per stirpes. It can be used on a beneficiary designation form to indicate how property interests are to be divided.
- QTIP refers to qualified terminable interest property. A QTIP trust is used to qualify for an estate tax marital deduction.
- RAP refers to the rule against perpetuities. A state's RAP requires property rights to vest in possession within a period based on measuring lives or a state-legislated length of time.
- SUB BENE refers to a substitute beneficiary, who will take if the primary beneficiary predeceases the owner of an account with a beneficiary designation.
- TBE or TE refers to tenancies by the entirety or entireties. Only spouses can hold property in this manner and neither spouse can unilaterally sever the tenancy. The surviving spouse takes title to the property as sole owner when the other spouse dies.
- TC refers to tenancy in common or tenants in common. Tenancies in common do not include a survivorship feature. If one tenant dies, she can devise her interest to whomever she wishes.

- TOD refers to transfer on death designations, generally on securities accounts. Some states have adopted the Uniform Real Property Transfer on Death Act for real property.
- UPC refers to the Uniform Probate Code.
- U.S.C. refers to the United States Code.
- UTC refers to the Uniform Trust Code.
- UTMA refers to the Uniform Transfers to Minors Act. Its predecessor was the UGMA, the Uniform Gifts to Minors Act. These acts might allow a donor to treat a donee as a "minor" even though the donee is older than 18.

CHECKPOINTS

- Terminology used for one type of transfer might differ from that used for other types.
- Some terms, such as representation, might have multiple meanings.
- Many of the statutes covering a type of property transfer include definition sections.
- Several types of property transmission are commonly referred to by initials.

CHAPTER 4

Probate and Options for Avoiding It

ROADMAP

- Probate
- Avoiding probate

A. Chapter Overview

This chapter expands on a concept introduced in Chapter 1, selecting the time and manner of property transmission. It begins with probate as a default mechanism and then covers options that are available for avoiding probate. The discussion of probate continues in later chapters covering distributions when the decedent is intestate and distributions when she has a will.

B. Probate

Probate is a statutory process for gathering the decedent's assets, paying claims and expenses, and distributing the remaining assets to his beneficiaries. In other words, it is a process for administering the decedent's estate. Property subject to probate might also be referred to as the property under administration or property subject to administration.

The probate process is carried out by a fiduciary. A fiduciary nominated by the decedent might be referred to as an executor (or executrix, if the court uses male and female word endings). If there is no will, or if the will does not nominate a fiduciary, the person selected might be referred to as an administrator (or administratrix). If the state does not distinguish between categories of fiduciary, the fiduciary might simply be called the personal representative. A court can appoint a curator or a special personal representative to protect the estate if there is a dispute over a personal representative's ability to serve or before a successor personal representative is appointed to replace one who is no longer able to serve.

Not every asset that the decedent owned or controlled goes through probate before passing to beneficiaries. Property is subject to probate if the decedent owns it in fee simple absolute. Her interest in property she owns as a tenant in common is also subject to probate. If she has a vested remainder interest or reversion in property, that interest is also subject to probate.

Common-law states that have adopted the Uniform Community Property Disposition at Death Act might trace a decedent's property back to its origin in a community-property state. The decedent's interest in community property, but not his surviving spouse's interest, is also subject to probate. The Uniform Probate Code includes several provisions dealing with the decedent's one-half interest in community property. These provisions apply, unless a state statute provides otherwise, to residents of community-property states in addition to residents of other states who own property traced to community-property origins.

C. Avoiding Probate

A property owner can avoid probate by making inter vivos transfers, outright or in trust. She can also use beneficiary designations or survivorship tenancies. Various methods for avoiding probate are discussed below (and, for trusts, in several later chapters).

In considering these options, keep several principles in mind. First, her attempt to avoid probate could fail if the beneficiary or co-owner dies first. Unless the instrument or relevant statute names a substitute beneficiary or she creates a new survivorship tenancy, she will die owning the property and it will be in her probate estate.

Failure to avoid probate might also occur because the beneficiary disclaims the property interest. A disclaimer is a refusal to accept benefits, including an outright gift, a devise, an inheritance, or an interest by survivorship. A disclaimer might result in the property that would otherwise pass to another person being included in the decedent's probate estate.

Second, even if a property transfer avoids probate, it does not necessarily escape federal estate tax or contribution to paying that tax (or similar state taxes). In addition, its value might be used in computing the surviving spouse's elective share rights. Some nonprobate transfers, particularly to revocable trusts, may be subject to contribution to pay claims against the decedent's estate and expenses of administration.

Third, the dividing line between probate and nonprobate property is not the same as the dividing line between property passing by virtue of a will provision and property passing by other means. A testator might have a power of appointment that allows her to name the ultimate taker of property she never owned and never had the right to own. Even if she can exercise that power only in her will, the property involved is not probate property.

Example 4-1. Ted receives the income for life from a trust his grandmother established. He also has the power to distribute the trust principal among a group of charities. Ted is to select the charities by a provision in his will referring to the power. The trust includes provisions for distributing the property if Ted fails to exercise his power of appointment. The trust principal will not be included in Ted's probate estate even if he exercises the power.

Fourth, a state law might exempt property from probate and override will provisions devising it even though the decedent owned it in fee simple absolute. Such statutes are designed to protect family members. For example, Fla. Stat. § 732.4015 invalidates a devise of homestead if the testator is survived by a minor child. The homestead passes to his heirs pursuant to the homestead statute and is not part of his probate estate.

1. Pay on Death Accounts; In Trust for Accounts

UPC Article VI, entitled Nonprobate Transfers at Death, includes several sets of provisions that the Uniform Law Commission has also adopted as standalone acts. The UPC provisions on pay on death accounts (also called payable on death accounts) can also be found in the Uniform Multiple-Person Accounts Act. Discussion in this book uses the UPC section numbers.

The UPC covers accounts between a depositor and a financial institution. Checking accounts, savings accounts, certificates of deposit, and share accounts are all included. UPC §6-201(1). These accounts are not testamentary even though the beneficiary does not receive funds until all parties to the account are dead. UPC §6-214. As a result, the parties establishing the account need not follow the formalities required for executing a valid will.

a. *Terminology*

Keep three terms in mind in describing pay on death and in trust for accounts: beneficiary; party; and multiple-party.

A beneficiary is a person who is named in the account and can request the account balance *after* all the parties have died. If the account has an "In Trust for" (ITF) designation, the term beneficiary also includes any person for whom a party is named as trustee. UPC §6-201(3). The UPC treats "Totten Trusts" as pay on death accounts. *In re Totten,* 71 N.E. 748 (N.Y. 1904). They are not covered by the state's trust code.

A party is a person, other than the beneficiary, who has a present right to payment from the account. If there is more than one such person, the account is a multiple-party account. UPC §6-201(5)–(6).

b. *Single-Party and Multiple-Party Accounts*

Pay on death accounts fall into two categories. There might be a single party, who controls the funds during her life, and one or more beneficiaries, who receive the account balance when she dies. There might instead be multiple parties, who control the funds while at least one of them is alive, and one or more beneficiaries who will receive the account balance when the last party dies.

The parties owe no obligation to the beneficiaries; they can remove funds from the account at any time. If there are multiple parties, their rights to account funds are generally based on their respective contributions to the account. A party can withdraw more than his contribution without obligation to another party if there is clear and convincing evidence that the party who contributed more meant a gift to the other party (or parties). UPC §6-211. There is, in fact, no requirement that a party have actually deposited funds into the account.

The account might bear the designation P.O.D. or POD. The distinction between a single-party and a multiple-party account reflects the number of parties, *not* the number of beneficiaries.

c. Relationship of Parties in Multiple-Party Accounts

If there are multiple parties, the surviving parties continue as owners of the account when a party dies. UPC § 6-212(a). The UPC differentiates the surviving parties' rights based on their status. If a surviving party is the surviving spouse of a deceased party, she becomes the owner of his share of the account. In all other cases, the surviving parties become equal owners of the deceased party's share. State law or the deposit agreement might instead provide that all surviving parties share equally.

> **Example 4-2.** Pam and Paula each transferred $100,000 to the XYZ Bank to establish a savings account in the names of Pam and Paula POD Bob. Pam died, survived by Paula and Bob. Paula becomes the only party to the account. She can leave funds in the account, add funds to the account, remove funds from the account, or close the account. Bob receives any account balance when Paula dies unless she previously removed him as beneficiary or he predeceased her.
>
> **Example 4-3.** Jack, Joe, and Jerry each transferred $100,000 to the XYZ Bank to establish a savings account in the names of Jack, Joe, and Jerry POD Rita. Jack died, survived by Joe, Jerry, and Rita. Joe and Jerry become the only parties to the account. They can leave funds in the account, add funds to the account, remove funds from the account, or close the account. When either of them dies, the survivor has the same rights. Rita receives any account balance when all parties have died unless she was previously removed as beneficiary or she predeceased a party.
>
> **Example 4-4.** Same as Example 4-3 except that Jack and Joe were married to each other. When Jack died, Joe's share of the account balance was increased by Jack's share if the UPC provision applies. If the UPC provision does not apply, Joe and Jerry split Jack's share. In either event, Joe and Jerry continue as parties to the account. Rita's rights are as described in Example 4-3.

Although an account opened in more than one name is likely to be a true multiple-party account, it is possible that the account is instead meant to be a convenience account. The true account owner adds the name of another individual, who is supposed to use funds only to benefit the true account owner and is not meant to take the account as a surviving party. Any funds in the account when the true owner dies are part of her probate estate unless the account also had a POD designation.

UPC § 6-204 allows an account owner to include an agency designation on an account, but this designation is meant for the holder of a power of attorney. Some state forms allow a convenience party designation. Tex. Est. Code § 113.052. If the financial institution is unaware that a convenience account was intended, it might allow the other person to access account funds on his own behalf. Statutes generally protect financial institutions that act without notice of the relationship.

d. *Rights of Beneficiaries in Pay on Death Accounts*

Pay on death account balances pass outside probate if there is at least one surviving beneficiary. The beneficiaries take equal shares of the account, and they take as tenants in common. UPC § 6-212(b)(2). If the deposit agreement so provides, a deceased beneficiary's descendants might take as substitute beneficiaries in her place.

Note the difference in the ownership arrangements. Parties own in a survivorship tenancy, while beneficiaries own as tenants in common. The UPC specifically provides that a POD designation in a multiple-party account without a survivorship right for parties is ineffective. UPC § 6-212(c).

e. *Liability of Beneficiaries for Claims Against the Estate*

Although funds in a pay on death account are not part of the deceased party's probate estate, they might be subject to certain claims against the party's estate and to contribution toward statutory allowances enacted to protect certain family members. UPC § 6-102.

2. Transfer on Death Securities Accounts

Transfer on death (T.O.D. or TOD) accounts resemble POD accounts. They are authorized by the Uniform TOD Security Registration Act, which has been incorporated into the UPC; the discussion below uses UPC section numbers. The discussion is relatively brief because the governing rules are similar to those described above for POD accounts.

UPC § 6-302 allows securities to be registered with a beneficiary designation if there is a sole owner or if there are multiple owners who hold as joint tenants with right of survivorship, as tenants by the entirety, or as owners of community property in survivorship form. The designation of one or more beneficiaries is done by indicating "transfer on death," "TOD," or even "POD."

UPC §6-305. When all owners have died, any surviving beneficiaries own their interest as tenants in common. UPC §6-307. Transfers made pursuant to these provisions are not treated as testamentary. UPC §6-309.

3. Transfer on Death Real Property Deeds

The Uniform Real Property Transfer on Death Act, which has been incorporated into the UPC, authorizes the use of a transfer on death deed to transfer real property from an owner to a beneficiary. UPC §6-405. The UPC provides that the deed is revocable even if it contains a contrary provision. UPC §6-406. As is true for POD and TOD accounts, transfers pursuant to these deeds are not treated as testamentary. UPC §6-407. Nevertheless, UPC §6-408 provides that testamentary capacity is required to make or revoke the deed. Unlike a will, however, a recorded transfer on death deed cannot be revoked by act; a writing authorized by UPC §6-411 is necessary.

As of mid-September 2024, 21 states had adopted this act. They are not the only states with statutes that authorize this type of transfer. Colo. Rev. Stat. §15-15-404; Ohio Rev. Code §5302.22. States might use the term beneficiary deed rather than transfer on death deed. Another option for passing real property outside of probate, the enhanced life estate deed ("Lady Bird deed"), is available in Florida and a handful of other states.

4. Survivorship Tenancies

Survivorship tenancies avoid probate until the last surviving tenant dies. Because that tenant becomes the sole owner, the property is included in his probate estate unless he disposes of it outright or through a nonprobate device before his death.

a. *Joint Tenancy with Right of Survivorship*

At one time, the creation of a joint tenancy with right of survivorship (JTROS) required that the acquisition satisfy four unities (time; title; interest; and possession), but that is no longer necessary. Spouses who desire a survivorship tenancy can own as joint tenants with right of survivorship, or they can own as tenants by the entirety. If the co-owners are not married to each other, they can own as joint tenants with right of survivorship but not as tenants by the entirety.

Two or more persons can jointly own real estate, tangible personal property, bank accounts, securities, and other types of property. If the joint ownership includes a right of survivorship, the surviving joint owners continue the tenancy after one of them dies. Unless the tenancy is severed and converted into a tenancy in common, the last surviving tenant becomes the sole owner of the entire property.

A state's requirements for establishing the survivorship feature that distinguishes a JTROS from a tenancy in common might vary based on the type of property involved. If the state requires that a deed specify "with right of survivorship," a deed that merely says "joint tenants" does not convey a right of survivorship and is treated like a tenancy in common.

b. *Tenancy by the Entirety*

Tenancies by the entirety can have only two tenants, and those tenants must be married to each other. At common law, a tenancy by the entirety required five unities: time; title; interest; possession; and person (husband and wife then being treated as one person). The spouses had to acquire their interests at the same time and in the same instrument while they were married. Neither spouse could unilaterally end the tenancy. If they were still married when one of them died, the surviving spouse became the owner in fee simple absolute. If the spouses divorced, the tenancy was converted into a tenancy in common. Each former spouse could dispose of that spouse's one-half during life or at death.

Many state statutes have eliminated the need to strictly comply with all the unities. For example, if one spouse owns property, she can transfer it to herself and her spouse as husband and wife (or as wife and wife) and create a tenancy by the entirety. She does not have to first convey it to an intermediary and have that person convey it back to the spouses.

For some types of property, a tenancy by the entirety is presumed even if the property is not titled to the owners as spouses. Joint bank accounts between spouses fall into this category if the relevant state statute provides that as the default for such accounts.

5. Life Insurance Beneficiary Designations

A life insurance policy is a contract between the owner and an insurance company. In exchange for premiums (which might be paid in a lump sum or in installments), the insurance company promises to pay a death benefit when the insured dies. The persons who will receive that benefit are the beneficiaries of the policy. These beneficiaries generally have only an expectancy until the insured dies. Unless he has irrevocably relinquished his right to change the beneficiary, the policy owner could substitute a different beneficiary at any time before the insured dies.

The person whose life is insured might be the owner of the policy, but that is not required. If the insured person owns the policy, the death benefit will be part of his gross estate because he has incidents of ownership. I.R.C. § 2042. It will not be part of his probate estate unless the estate is the beneficiary. If the beneficiaries die before the insured, the death benefit could end up payable to the insured's probate estate if the contract with the insurance company or the governing statute does not provide for substitute beneficiaries. Even if it is not part of the probate estate, a life insurance policy might affect the computation of the surviving spouse's elective share and could be included in the insured owner's gross estate for federal estate tax purposes.

If the policy is owned by someone other than the insured, its value is included in the owner's probate estate if he dies before the insured. The policy value is not the same as the death benefit. It is the smaller amount the owner would receive if he cashed the policy in while the insured was still alive.

Policies owned by trusts escape probate when the insured dies. Irrevocable life insurance trusts are often established as a means for reducing estate taxes in addition to avoiding probate.

6. Annuities and Payments from Retirement Plans

We consider annuities and payments from retirement plans together for two reasons. First, they have many common features. Second, employees often receive plan benefits in the form of an annuity.

a. Annuities

An annuity is simply a series of periodic payments made pursuant to a contract. The person receiving the payments is the annuitant; the person making the payments is usually an insurance company or other financial institution, but it might be a charity or an individual. When the person making the payments is an individual, there is often a family relationship between the parties; these private annuities are beyond the scope of this book.

If someone will receive payments after the annuitant dies, that person is referred to as a beneficiary. If payments cease when the annuitant dies, there are no future payments to include in her probate estate. If payments continue to a beneficiary, those payments are not part of the annuitant's probate estate. They are potentially part of her gross estate for estate tax purposes and part of the elective estate used in computing the rights of her surviving spouse.

The contract between the payor and the annuitant is based on consideration. The annuitant (or someone acting on her behalf) transfers funds to the payor. These funds are often referred to as premiums. The annuity could be purchased for a lump sum (single-premium annuity), or the premiums could be paid over time. The payor might begin payments as soon as it has received the contracted-for premiums, or the parties might contract for deferring payments to a future date.

The payor promises to make payments for the annuitant's life, for the life of the annuitant and another person, or for a fixed period that does not depend on someone's life. The annuity amount is computed based on the number of years for which payments will be made, the premiums paid, and the payor's estimate of how much it can earn by investing those premiums.

> **Example 4-5.** Alberta entered into a contract with Annuity Company. In exchange for $100,000, Annuity Company will pay Alberta a fixed amount for the rest of her life. That amount will be based on her life expectancy when payments begin and on how much Annuity Company believes it can earn by investing the $100,000 she paid. If annuity payments cease at Alberta's death, there will be nothing to include in her probate estate.
>
> **Example 4-6.** If Annuity Company instead agrees to pay Alberta a fixed amount for the rest of her life and then pay her husband Bob the same amount for the rest of his life, the fixed amount will be smaller if their joint life expectancy is longer than her single life expectancy. By taking smaller payments during her life, Alberta is funding potential future payments to Bob. Those future payments are not part of Alberta's probate estate.

In pricing annuity contracts, insurance companies consider average life expectancy. Some annuitants will live longer than expected. Others will die sooner than we would expect based on their age when they began receiving payments. An annuitant who worries about dying "before her time" might purchase an annuity that guarantees a certain number of payments. Each payment will be less than it would be with an annuity that ended at her death because the guarantee increases the company's risk of paying out more than it received in premiums and its earnings from investing those premiums.

Example 4-7. If Annuity Company agrees to pay Alberta a fixed amount for the rest of her life and guarantees that it will make at least 10 annual payments, the fixed amount will be smaller than it would have been without that guarantee. If Alberta named a beneficiary for the future payments, that beneficiary will receive any payments due after Alberta's death. These future payments are not part of Alberta's probate estate.

b. Retirement Plans

The two basic types of employer-funded retirement plans are defined benefit and defined contribution. Although each can be funded completely by the employer, it is more likely that each is funded partially by the employer and partially by the employee.

A defined benefit plan pays the employee a fixed amount for life (or for the life of the employee and a beneficiary). The benefit received from a defined contribution plan is based on the amount invested in the plan and earnings on that amount. The employee could exhaust the plan balance before he dies if he withdraws too large an amount each year. A defined benefit plan is often referred to as a traditional pension plan. Although these plans were once common, many employers now offer only defined contribution plans. They thus avoid the risk of poor performance by the plan's assets or retired employees' unexpectedly long lives.

Defined contribution plans vary slightly, based on the type of employer. They are frequently referred to by the Internal Revenue Code section that governs them, I.R.C. § 401(k) or I.R.C. § 403(b).

Individual retirement accounts (IRAs) are like defined contribution accounts. An employee might fund an IRA in addition to contributing to her employer's retirement plan. Individuals with self-employment income might also contribute to self-employed retirement plans.

When a worker dies, we consider the probate, gross estate, and elective share consequences of his vested retirement account balances. His own contributions often vest from the beginning of his employment. If he has not worked long enough to vest an employer's contributions, the employer regains those funds. The discussion below applies to whatever amounts have vested when he dies.

If he dies before he has begun receiving benefits, those benefits will be paid to the beneficiary named in the plan. If he dies after he has begun receiving benefits, payment rights resemble those for annuities. They might cease at his death, continue for a fixed period, or continue for the life of a beneficiary. Those continued payments might be for the same amount he received or for a smaller amount.

IRAs differ from employer plans in one important aspect. Employer plans are governed by the Employee Retirement Income Security Act of 1974 (ERISA). That act's features include one designed to protect a surviving spouse. In the absence of a spousal waiver, the employee must elect to take a qualified joint and survivor annuity. The surviving spouse's benefit must be equal to at least 50% of the employee's benefit. 29 U.S.C. § 1055. The owner of an IRA can provide a benefit for the surviving spouse but does not have to do so.

The value of any benefit received after the employee's death is not included in his probate estate unless it is the beneficiary. The value of any survivor benefit is included in computing the gross estate and elective estate.

c. Social Security Benefits

Social Security payments are made to individuals whose earnings subject to Social Security tax qualify them for benefits. The annual benefit primarily reflects how old the worker was when she began receiving benefits and the amount of her earnings previously subject to Social Security tax. Her surviving spouse may receive payments based on his own earnings record or based on her record. Surviving dependent children may also be entitled to benefits. 42 U.S.C. § 402. Social Security survivor benefits are not included in the decedent's probate estate, gross estate, or elective estate.

7. Inter Vivos Gifts

Although transfers made before death avoid probate, they might affect how the probate estate is distributed. An inter vivos gift that counts against the donee's share of the estate results in a reduction for ademption by satisfaction (testate estate) or advancement (intestate estate). Inter vivos gifts might also affect the computation of the elective share and of any estate tax due when the donor dies. Inter vivos gifts might be used as evidence that the donee was exerting undue influence on the transferor.

The decision between inter vivos and at-death gifts often reflects potential income tax consequences. If a property owner sold an asset that appreciated in value since she acquired it, she would pay income tax on her gain. She would not pay income tax if she transferred it to a beneficiary as an inter vivos or testamentary gift; the beneficiary would not pay income tax on receiving the gift or devise. I.R.C. § 102(a). The beneficiary would have better income tax consequences, if he later sold that asset, if he received it when the donor died than if he received it as an inter vivos gift. That difference is based on the income tax "basis" rules. Because the donee has no actual cost for the property received, these rules assign him one—thus, the term basis instead of cost. The donee of an inter vivos gift generally takes the donor's basis for the asset; the donee of an at-death gift takes a basis equal to the asset's value at the donor's death (or at an alternate valuation date six months later). I.R.C. §§ 1014, 1015.

> **Example 4-8.** Mary purchased investment land 10 years ago for $100,000. It is currently worth $350,000. If Mary sold her land for $350,000, she would pay income tax on her $250,000 gain. If she gave the land to her son Dan, and Dan sold the land for $350,000, he would pay income tax on a $250,000 gain. If Mary devised the land to Dan and died when it was worth $350,000, Dan could sell the land for $350,000 and have no taxable gain.

8. Inter Vivos Trusts

An individual can transfer property to a trust before he dies. He can make the trust revocable, in which case he retains the power to regain his property. He can instead make the trust irrevocable when he creates it or at a later date before his death. He can fund the trust by inter vivos transfers, by devises in his will, by making the trust the beneficiary of a life insurance policy or a POD account, or through all of those means. He can serve as trustee, but he need not do so. He can retain the right to trust income during his life even if the trust is irrevocable.

An individual might transfer property in trust to a charity as a split-interest gift. If he retains an income interest, and the charity receives a vested remainder, the trust is a charitable remainder trust. If payments cease when the settlor dies, there are no assets to include in his probate estate. These trusts are covered in estate and gift tax, income taxation of trusts and estates, or estate planning courses. Keep in mind that a trust that escapes probate does not necessarily escape estate tax or elective share computations.

CHECKPOINTS

- Probate involves administering property the decedent owned at death.
- A property owner has many options for avoiding probate. These include outright inter vivos transfers and transfers that take effect at death.
- Probate-avoiding transfers are not necessarily treated as testamentary even though they take effect at the transferor's death. As a result, they are not subject to the formalities for a valid will.
- Transfers that avoid probate do not necessarily avoid the transferor's creditors, the elective share rights of a spouse, or federal taxes.

CHAPTER 5

Intestate Succession

ROADMAP

- Terminology
- Property distributed by intestate succession
- Intestacy statutes
- Marital relationships
- Lineal and collateral relationships
- Ordering of heirs and share of surviving spouse
- Avoiding escheat
- Taking by representation
- Degrees of relationship
- Aliens
- Parent-child relationship
- Advancements
- Loans to heirs

A. Chapter Overview

This chapter focuses on probate assets that are not governed by a will. It covers the general rules for determining eligible heirs and distributing the intestate's assets among those heirs. It also covers exceptions to those rules and the treatment of advancements and loans made by an intestate decedent.

B. Terminology

A decedent who dies without a valid will is an intestate. Even if he has a valid will, he will be partially intestate if his will does not dispose of all of his probate property. The beneficiary of an intestate's probate property is an heir.

Intestacy statutes are also referred to as statutes of descent and distribution. Do not confuse descent with descendant. Descendants are simply one category of potential heir. A surviving spouse, ancestors, siblings, and other relatives can also be heirs even though they are not the intestate decedent's descendants.

Although individuals who are likely to inherit might be referred to casually as heirs, only the intestate's death gives them that status. Until his death occurs, they have at most an expectancy.

Intestate succession statutes cover inheritance directly by one individual from another. This type of inheritance occurs between spouses, between a parent and a child, and between siblings. The statutes also cover inheritance through a potential heir who predeceased the intestate. For example, if Son predeceased Mother, but was survived by his own children, they might inherit some of Mother's property if she died intestate. They would be inheriting from Mother (their grandmother) through Son (their father). As discussed later in this chapter, an adoptee's rights to inherit through his adoptive parent might vary based on his age when the adoption occurred. His rights to inherit from or through his birth parents could vary based on the identities of the adoptive parents and other factors described later in this chapter.

When individuals inherit through another, the intestacy statutes prescribe the method of representation used to determine the share of each heir. Methods include per stirpes, per capita with representation, and per capita at each generation. In some states, the degrees of kinship are relevant in determining the distribution of property.

C. Property Distributed by Intestate Succession

1. In General

Intestate succession statutes generally apply to property that meets two tests. First, it must be subject to the probate process. Second, it must not pass pursuant to the terms of the decedent's will. Obviously, a decedent who owns probate property and does not have a valid will is intestate. But even a decedent with a valid will can be at least partially intestate. If, for example, her will lacks a residuary clause, some probate property is likely to pass by intestate succession.

If property is not subject to probate, it generally does not matter if the decedent has a valid will. That property is not governed by the terms of the will. Situations that avoid probate include survivorship tenancies and property beneficiary designations (such as life insurance proceeds and pay on death accounts). Property over which the decedent had only a power of appointment also avoids probate. But nonprobate property could ultimately be included in the decedent's probate estate if the named beneficiary predeceases him.

2. Rights of Creditors

Before distributing the probate estate, the personal representative must satisfy claims allowed by statute. UPC § 3-805 lists those claims. They include debts owed by the decedent, funeral expenses, and expenses of administering the estate. Estate or inheritance tax liabilities are usually governed by a separate tax apportionment statute. Intestate heirs receive the property that remains after the personal representative satisfies claims and makes distributions required by family protection statutes.

If claims exceed the value of probate assets, some creditors could receive less than they are owed or nothing at all. The order of priority in UPC § 3-805 or the governing state statute determines which claims are satisfied first. In some instances, recipients of nonprobate assets might be called upon to pay claims. The trustee of a revocable trust, for example, might be required to transfer trust assets to the estate's personal representative. UTC § 505(a)(3).

Creditors do not have greater or lesser rights in an intestate estate versus an estate covered by a will. The major difference relates to which beneficiaries receive less because creditors have rights. A decedent can use a will to specify which devisees will receive less if creditors must be paid. An intestate decedent forgoes that power.

3. Family Protection Statutes

State family protection statutes affect the distribution of certain types of property that would otherwise pass by intestate succession or under the terms of a will. Family members covered by these statutes are likely to receive that property in addition to their intestate share (or devise under a will). The most common family protection statutes are those governing homestead, exempt property, and family allowance. Although these statutes apply to both testate and intestate estates, they might operate differently if a will addresses those rights. A surviving spouse might also have elective share rights, which reflect both probate and nonprobate property.

> **Example 5-1.** Izzy died intestate, owning two assets, $160,000 in a checking account and an automobile worth $25,000. The automobile was not subject to a loan. Debts and other expenses to be satisfied by his estate equaled $5,000. Izzy was survived by his second wife, Wanda, and by Beth, his child from his first marriage. Under his state's intestacy laws, Wanda and Beth would share his estate equally. Although Izzy had assets of $185,000, Wanda and Beth will receive only the $180,000 remaining after paying his debts and other expenses. If the automobile is exempt property that the statute awards to a spouse, Wanda will receive it. In that case, she and Beth will split the remaining $155,000 equally. If the automobile is not exempt property, Wanda and Beth will split $180,000 equally. The personal representative can sell the automobile and give them each $90,000. The personal representative could instead transfer the automobile plus $65,000 to one of them and transfer $90,000 to the other.

D. Intestacy Statutes

If the decedent owned property covered by the intestate succession rules, the relevant state intestacy statutes guide us in dividing that property among the potential heirs. Do not assume that every relative is a potential heir. Each state determines how close a relationship must be for an individual to qualify as an heir.

1. Features

Intestate succession statutes reflect the state's beliefs about how a decedent would want her probate property distributed if it was not covered by a valid will. These statutes have several common features: (1) they list the categories of heirs (including the state through escheat if the decedent has no heirs);

(2) they order those categories; (3) they determine the share taken by each category if a higher priority category does not receive the entire intestate estate; (4) they provide representation rules for the descendants of certain deceased heirs; (5) they cover the effect of "atypical" situations, such as half-blood relationships, adoptions, and nonmarital births; and (6) they provide rules for reducing the share of an heir who has received an advancement or who owes money to the decedent.

A state might base its intestacy statutes on the UPC, or it might enact a different distribution pattern. In either case, its statutes will have the features listed above.

2. Limitations

a. *Division of Property*

Intestacy statutes do not specify how property will be divided. Thus, if a decedent with two heirs owned stocks worth $500,000 and investment land worth $500,000, the intestacy statutes do not indicate which heir should receive the stocks and which the land or whether they simply share each asset.

b. *Characteristics of Eligible Heirs*

Intestacy statutes do not consider need or ability to manage funds. An heir who is significantly wealthier than other heirs does not receive a smaller share merely because of that wealth. An heir who has declared bankruptcy multiple times is not automatically bypassed in favor of his children or other descendants who might better manage the inheritance. An heir who is a minor receives her inheritance outright or in a custodianship account rather than in a trust that continues until she is much older than the age limit provided by the state's Uniform Transfers to Minors Act.

c. *Family Dynamics*

An individual must generally be related to the intestate decedent by blood (including adoption) or marriage to inherit by intestate succession. Relatives who are likely to qualify are the decedent's surviving spouse, children and more remote descendants, parents and grandparents, brothers and sisters, aunts and uncles, nieces and nephews, and cousins.

Intestacy statutes ignore family dynamics. With limited exceptions, an heir who is estranged from the decedent receives his statutory share. In-laws and stepchildren, who might have close relationships with the decedent, receive nothing unless the state's intestacy statute includes those relationships; the same is true for registered domestic partners and de facto parents. Conversely, a relative who never met the decedent could qualify as an heir.

The UPC responds to some of these limitations. First, it allows an individual who has a valid will to use that will to disinherit an individual or group of individuals who would otherwise take by intestacy. UPC § 2-101(b). The UPC provision applies only to property that would otherwise pass by intestate succession, as would be the case if the will lacked an operative residuary devise. If UPC § 2-101(b) applies, the interest that would have passed to the disinherited heir passes as if she had disclaimed her inheritance. The comments to UPC § 2-101 indicate that it reverses the common-law rule that prevented such disinheritance and thus ignored the testator's intent.

Second, it includes stepchildren and their descendants as eligible takers under limited circumstances. UPC § 2-103(j). These individuals are included as heirs only if the decedent is not survived by a spouse, descendants, parents, descendants of parents, grandparents, or descendants of grandparents. In addition, they are included only if they are descendants of the intestate decedent's *deceased* spouse (or spouses). They are not included, even if there are no otherwise eligible takers, if their parent's marriage to the intestate ended in divorce.

State intestacy statutes might follow the UPC, make other provisions related to family dynamics, or ignore family dynamics altogether.

3. Other Relevant Statutes

Statutes other than those dealing exclusively with intestacy might also be relevant. Several of them are discussed in other chapters. Intestacy might be an unintended consequence when a devisee kills the testator, disclaims a devise, or makes an agreement to forgo a devise.

E. Marital Relationships

Because intestacy statutes begin with the rights of a surviving spouse, it is important to determine if an individual qualifies. State statutes vary in their requirements for recognizing a marital relationship. Since the Supreme Court's decision in *Obergefell v. Hodges,* 576 U.S. 644 (2015), a state cannot bar a marriage between two members of the same sex. Because that decision involved only the issue of same-sex marriage, it did not affect state domestic relations laws that do not recognize plural marriage or marriage between certain categories of relatives.

1. Common Law Marriages

If the couple failed to obtain a license, be married by an individual authorized to conduct marriages, or otherwise follow the statutory requirements, they are not considered married unless they satisfy state law requirements for common law marriage. They must have held themselves out as married and satisfy any other requirement imposed by statute or judicial interpretation. A minority of states recognize common law marriage. Statutes recognizing common law marriage might apply for all purposes—including spousal inheritance rights—or might be limited to particular purposes, such as support obligations. The National Conference of State Legislatures website (https://www.ncsl.org) includes lists, updated in March 2020, of states that allow common law marriage and states that previously allowed it.

2. Domestic Partnerships

Prior to the Supreme Court's decision in *Obergefell*, state laws varied with respect to the recognition they awarded same-sex relationships. Several jurisdictions expressly allowed marriage between individuals of the same sex or at least recognized those marriages if validly contracted elsewhere. Other states did not allow such marriages but authorized registered domestic partnerships either for same-sex couples or for both same-sex and opposite-sex couples. Still other states provided no recognition or alternate status. These differences might be reflected in the various state inheritance laws.

Now that *Obergefell* has legalized same-sex marriages in all states, it is important for you to check whether the state continues to recognize registered domestic partnerships. Such action could affect the inheritance rights of couples who chose this option instead of marriage.

3. Spouse of Decedent's Relative

Note that the only marital relationship listed in Section D is that of the decedent's surviving spouse. Spouses of the decedent's blood relatives (for example, her brother-in-law or daughter-in-law) are unlikely to qualify as her intestate heirs.

F. Lineal and Collateral Relationships

Blood relationships are either lineal or collateral. A lineal relationship is a direct relationship to an ancestor (sometimes referred to as an ascendant) or to a descendant. Any ancestor of the decedent is also an ancestor of the decedent's descendants; any descendant of the decedent is also a descendant of the decedent's ancestors. There is a direct bloodline (again, including adoptive relationships) linking these individuals.

Although all the decedent's descendants are also descendants of his ancestors, the reverse is not necessarily true. The decedent's ancestors are likely to have descendants who are not the decedent's descendants. For example, his parents could have other children; they are the decedent's brothers and sisters. Those brothers and sisters could have children, who are the decedent's nieces and nephews. The decedent's grandparents could have children other than the decedent's parents; they are the decedent's aunts and uncles. All of these relationships are collateral relationships. The potential heir is a descendant of one of the decedent's ancestors but is not the decedent's ancestor or descendant. Some states distinguish between collateral relatives based on how many ancestors they share with the decedent; other states treat such "half-blood" relationships identically to whole-blood relationships.

> **Example 5-2.** Ivan currently has a wife (Wanda), his and Wanda's child (Calvin), a brother (Brad), a mother (Myra), and a grandmother (Georgia). Calvin, Myra, and Georgia are Ivan's potential lineal heirs. Brad is his potential collateral heir. Ivan's wife Wanda is also a potential heir. She is neither a lineal nor a collateral heir because she is not related to Ivan by blood or adoption.
>
> **Example 5-3.** Calvin is a descendant of Ivan, Wanda, Myra, and Georgia. Brad is a descendant of Myra and Georgia. Brad and Calvin could not inherit from each other as lineal heirs, because neither is the other's ancestor or descendant. Each could inherit from the other as a collateral heir.

1. Lineal Relationships in General

A lineal relationship exists between an ancestor and a descendant. These relationships include parent and child, grandparent and grandchild, and so on. For purposes of intestate succession, any share of the estate not received by the surviving spouse will be received by the decedent's descendants. If the intestate decedent has no descendants, the UPC divides the estate between the decedent's surviving spouse and the decedent's parents. UPC §§ 2-102(2), 2-103(d). State intestacy statutes might ignore the decedent's parents if there is a surviving spouse even if the decedent had no descendants.

2. Parent-Child Lineal Relationship

An individual acquires descendants through her children. She is an ancestor of those children and their descendants. Inheritance rights of these individuals depend on whether a parent-child relationship has been established and, if so, on whether it continues until the intestate's death. In addition to acquiring a child by birth, a parent could acquire a child by adoption. He could acquire a stepchild by marrying one of the child's parents. If a state has adopted the Uniform Parentage Act (UPA), he could also acquire parental status after being adjudicated a "de facto parent." A parent-child relationship can also be terminated, at least for purposes of inheritance, if the relevant statute provides for such termination.

a. Birth

As a general rule, a genetic child is the child of his genetic parents. He can inherit from and through them. They and their families can inherit from and through him. The UPC eliminates a genetic parent's right to inherit from or through his child if parental rights were terminated and not restored in a judicial proceeding. UPC § 2-114(a)(1). Even if parental rights were not terminated, the parent cannot inherit based on a showing that those rights could have been terminated based on "nonsupport, abandonment, abuse, neglect, or other actions or inactions of the parent towards the child." UPC § 2-114(a)(2). This provision applies only if there is clear and convincing evidence that parental rights could have been terminated, and the child died before attaining age 18.

A parent to whom UPC § 2-114(a) applies is treated as predeceasing the child for purposes of intestate succession. UPC § 2-114(b). Note that this UPC section treats each parent separately and does not distinguish between genetic and adoptive parents. Not does it prevent the family of the ineligible parent from inheriting from or through the child.

Example 5-4. There was clear and convincing evidence that Fred abandoned his daughter Deanna when she was 12. Fred's wife Myra divorced Fred but never sought to have his parental rights terminated. Myra died when Deanna was 15; she devised her entire estate to Deanna. Deanna died intestate when she was 16, survived by Fred and by Myra's brother Bart. Fred will be treated as predeceased; Bart will inherit Deanna's property. If Deanna had lived until she was at least 18, Fred could have inherited her property.

b. Adoption

The treatment of adopted children varies from state to state. Depending on the order of death, we must ascertain whether the adopted child can inherit from members of the adoptive family, and whether they can inherit from her. We ask the same questions with respect to the adopted child's descendants. We must also ascertain whether the adopted child can inherit from members of her original family, and whether they can inherit from her. We ask the same questions with respect to her descendants.

Individuals whose inheritance rights are potentially affected by an adoption include the adopted child and her descendants; the adopting parents, their ancestors, descendants, and collateral heirs; and the genetic (birth) parents, their ancestors, descendants, and collateral heirs.

State laws vary in how they refer to the child's original parents. Some states refer to them as birth parents; others use the term natural parents. At one time, the UPC called them genetic parents.

The rights of adopted individuals and members of their original and adoptive families are discussed in Section L.

3. Remote Lineal Relationships

A state is likely to treat relationships between the intestate and his ancestors less favorably than relationships between the intestate and his descendants. This is not surprising. Most individuals who own property are already adults. Their ancestors, particularly those more remote than grandparents, are unlikely to have long life expectancies and would thus enjoy the inherited property for a relatively short period. In addition, remote ancestors might devise the property among their descendants, many of whom will be only collateral relatives of the original decedent. A descendant, on the other hand, is likely to enjoy the property for a longer period and then pass it on (though a will or intestacy) to her own descendants. Those descendants are also descendants of the original intestate.

Example 5-5. Isaac's great-grandmother Gilda had three children: Edna, Lana, and Susan. Edna is Isaac's deceased grandmother. If Gilda inherited property from Isaac, she might devise it to Isaac's great-aunts, Lana and Susan, each of whom would probably devise the property to their own children, Isaac's cousins.

Example 5-6. Ilene has four children, each of whom has children of his or her own. If Ilene's children inherited property from Ilene, they presumably would later devise it to their own children, Ilene's grandchildren. The property would remain with Ilene's lineal heirs.

State intestacy statutes are, of course, based on assumptions as to what might occur. Property owners who want to benefit a remote relative can do so by using a nonprobate transfer or by devising property to that relative in a will.

States use different cut-offs for determining which higher-generation relatives are in too remote a higher-generation relationship to the decedent. For example, UPC § 2-103(g) stops at the decedent's grandparents (and their descendants). A great-grandmother would not qualify; nor would a grandparent's brother or sister. Virginia, on the other hand, allows a great-grandparent to inherit. Va. Code § 64.2-200(A)(5)(c). A state might even look simply to kindred and not specify a cut-off point.

Example 5-7. Isabelle died intestate at age 19. She never married or had descendants, and her great-grandmother Grace is her only living relative. If the relevant intestacy statute mirrors UPC § 2-103, Isabelle's property will escheat to the state. If the statute instead mirrors the Virginia statute, Grace will inherit Isabelle's property.

Although state statutes limit inheritance by remote ancestors and their descendants, they do not necessarily limit inheritance by remote descendants. Thus, Isabelle could inherit from Grace, if Grace died intestate, even in states that would prevent Grace from inheriting from Isabelle.

4. Collateral Relationships

a. In General

A relationship by blood or adoption that is not lineal is collateral. Some collateral relationships are ranked higher than lineal relationships. For example, an intestate's brothers and sisters (collateral heirs) are ranked higher for purposes of intestate succession than his grandparents (lineal heirs). But the intestate's descendants, even remote descendants, are likely to be preferred even to such closely related collateral relatives as his siblings.

If a state cuts off ancestors it considers too remotely related to the intestate, it will do the same for those ancestors' own descendants. This rule does not apply to the intestate's own parents, who can inherit based on their status as his parents rather than as descendants of his grandparents or more remote ancestors. It does apply to collateral relatives who are descended from remote ancestors. If, for example, the decedent was survived only by his grandmother's sister, his property would escheat in a state that did not treat descendants of great-grandparents as heirs.

b. Half-Blood Statutes

1. Relationships Covered

A half-blood statute applies only to collateral heirs. It does not apply to lineal heirs because the decedent cannot have a half-blood parent, grandparent, child, or more remote descendant.

Half-blood relationships arise when an intestate decedent and his collateral heir have less than all their ancestors in common. An intestate decedent might have a half-brother or half-sister, someone with whom he has only one parent in common. Not only are the half-brother and half-sister his half-blood heirs; their children are also related to him by the half-blood. An intestate decedent's parents might have half-brothers or half-sisters; those individuals (and their descendants) are also half-blood relatives of the intestate decedent.

2. Statutes

UPC §2-107 treats half-blood and whole-blood relationships identically. Its current version refers to the number of common ancestors in the same generation. The comments indicate that references to blood are outdated in light of relationships formed by adoption, assisted reproduction, and de facto parentage. State laws might still use the half-blood/whole-blood terminology.

State law either treats half-blood and whole-blood relationships identically or it disadvantages half-blood heirs. A half-blood relationship matters only if the state intestacy statute treats the two categories differently, and the decedent has *both* whole-blood and half-blood heirs. Florida and Oklahoma exemplify different ways of disadvantaging half-blood collateral heirs.

Florida provides that half-blood collateral heirs inherit only half as much as whole-blood heirs. Fla. Stat. §732.105. If an intestate decedent is survived only by his two half-brothers, each inherits one-half of his estate. If he is survived by one whole-blood brother and one half-blood brother, the whole-blood brother receives twice as much as the half-blood brother. The former receives two-thirds of the estate; the latter receives one-third.

The computation is based on the number of half-blood heirs and the number of whole-blood heirs. It is not based on transferring two-thirds of the estate to the whole-blood heirs and one-third to the half-blood heirs. That was the result in the preceding paragraph only because there were only two heirs.

> **Example 5-8.** Irving died intestate, survived only by his five whole-blood sisters and by his two half-blood brothers. If the state has a half-blood statute like Florida's, each sister receives twice as much as each brother. Each sister receives one-sixth of the estate; each brother receives one-twelfth. The source of Irving's assets is irrelevant.

If a potential intestate heir predeceases the intestate decedent, the half-blood statute also applies to the deceased heir's descendants, who take that share by representation. Thus, if one of Irving's sisters predeceased him, but was survived by her own descendants, those descendants would share the sister's one-sixth of Irving's estate.

The treatment of half-blood heirs in Oklahoma depends on the type of property involved and the degree of relationship between the heirs and the intestate decedent. Okla. Stat. tit. 84, § 222. The Oklahoma statute provides: "Kindred of the half-blood inherit equally with those of the whole blood in the same degree, unless the inheritance come to the intestate by descent, devise or gift of some one of his ancestors, in which case all those who are not of the blood of such ancestors must be excluded from such inheritance."

> **Example 5-9.** Ilene died intestate, survived only by her five whole-blood sisters and by her two half-blood brothers. If the state has a half-blood statute like Oklahoma's, the source of Ilene's assets will determine the share each of her siblings takes.

> **Example 5-10.** Inez had a whole-blood sister, Wilma, and a half-blood brother, Hal. Wilma and Inez had the same mother and father. Hal and Inez had the same mother. If Inez dies intestate in Oklahoma, Hal and Wilma will share equally assets Inez acquired on her own or acquired from their mother. Only Wilma will inherit assets Inez received from her and Wilma's father. If Inez dies intestate in Florida, Wilma will receive twice as much of Inez's property as Hal receives; it will not matter from whom Inez received those assets. In a state that follows UPC § 2-107, Hal

and Wilma will each receive one-half of all Inez's property; it will not matter from whom Inez received those assets.

3. Limitations

A half-blood statute either reduces the half-blood relative's potential inheritance or does not affect it. It does not create an inheritance right where none would otherwise exist.

Example 5-11. Irene has only three relatives, all from her mother's side of her family: her grandmother Gillian's whole-blood sister Winifred, her grandmother Gillian's half-blood sister Henrietta, and Henrietta's son Charles. If UPC § 2-103 applied, neither Winifred, Henrietta, nor Charles could inherit from Irene. None of them is Irene's grandmother, and none of them is descended from Irene's grandmother. The fact that Winifred is Gillian's whole-blood sister and that Henrietta is her half-blood sister is irrelevant.

4. Relevance of Relationships to Decedent's Ancestor

If an intestate is survived by relatives from each parent's side of her family, two statutory provisions might apply in states with schemes like Florida's. The general intestacy statute splits the family into maternal and paternal branches, while the half-blood statute gives larger shares to whole-blood relatives.

Example 5-12. Igor is survived by only two relatives: his father's whole-blood brother and his mother's half-blood sister. If the whole-blood/half-blood distinction is more important, Igor's whole-blood uncle will receive twice as much as his half-blood aunt. If the estate is first split between his mother's and his father's sides of the family, his whole-blood uncle and his half-blood aunt will receive the same amount.

As noted above, the UPC does not make a whole-blood/half-blood distinction; each relative would receive the same amount. In Florida, which does make that distinction, the relevant statute splits the property between each parent's kindred first and applies the half-blood statute second. Fla. Stat. § 732.103(4). In the example above, Igor's half-blood maternal aunt will inherit as much as his whole-blood paternal uncle.

G. Ordering of Heirs and Share of Surviving Spouse

When an intestate dies, we do not simply count the potential heirs and divide the probate estate among them. Instead, we follow the statutory ordering of heirs. Higher-ranked potential heirs reduce or completely eliminate the share of lower-ranked potential heirs. Thus, if a decedent is survived by a spouse and a brother, the brother is unlikely to inherit at all. If she is survived by a spouse and descendants, the share—if any—of the descendants is affected by whether the decedent and the spouse had all their descendants in common or not. This section covers the ordering of heirs and the spouse's share based on UPC provisions. It concludes with examples of state variations. Various methods for computing the share of heirs who take by representation or who take as kindred or next of kin are discussed later in the chapter.

Note that if the intestate is not survived by anyone described in this section or in Section H, the state receives her property by escheat. UPC § 2-105.

1. UPC

a. Ordering Rules

UPC §§ 2-102 and 2-103 order heirs as follows: surviving spouse; descendants; parents; descendants of parents (the intestate's siblings and their descendants); grandparents and their descendants; descendants of any predeceased spouses. If there are no relatives in any of those categories, the property escheats to the state.

After we determine the order of heirs, we begin with the highest ranked eligible heir. If that heir takes 100% of the probate estate, our inquiry ends. If that heir takes less than 100%, we compute the share of the next highest ranked taker. We stop our inquiry when we have distributed 100% of the intestate estate. If there are multiple takers within a particular group, we allocate the group's share among those takers.

b. Surviving Spouse

Intestacy statutes begin with the decedent's spouse. Since the Supreme Court decision in *Obergefell v. Hodges*, the spouses' genders (same sex or opposite sex) should not matter. Nor should it matter whether the marriage was contracted in the state in which the decedent resides or elsewhere.

The surviving spouse's share might be a percentage of the probate estate or a fixed dollar amount plus a percentage of the remaining estate. The governing state law provides the formula used for determining the spouse's share. If the formula includes a fixed amount, it might include an inflation adjustment for any fixed dollar amount. We consider other potential heirs only if the surviving spouse receives less than 100% of the intestate estate.

1. Surviving Spouse Takes 100%

UPC § 2-102(1) gives the surviving spouse 100% in the following scenarios: (1) the decedent has no surviving descendants or parents; or (2) the decedent has surviving descendants but all of them are also the descendants of the surviving spouse and the surviving spouse has no descendants who are not the decedent's descendants. In many jurisdictions, the surviving spouse will receive 100% if the decedent has no surviving descendants even if the decedent is survived by parents.

> **Example 5-13.** Imogene died, survived by her husband Harry. Imogene had no surviving descendants or parents. If the relevant statute mirrors UPC § 2-102(1), Harry inherits 100% of Imogene's intestate estate. Harry would inherit 100% even if he had a descendant from another relationship because Imogene was not survived by descendants or parents.
>
> **Example 5-14.** Irma died, survived only by her husband Hank and by their grandchildren Greta and Gabe. Greta and Gabe were the children of Irma and Hank's deceased daughter Selma. Irma had no surviving parents. Hank had no descendants other than Greta and Gabe. If the relevant statute mirrors UPC § 2-102(1), Hank inherits 100% of Irma's intestate estate.

2. Surviving Spouse Takes Less Than 100%

The share of a spouse who fails to satisfy the requirements of UPC § 2-102(1) is computed using a formula. Depending on the size of the estate, she might end up receiving 100% or a lesser percentage. The three formulas in UPC § 2-102(2)–(4) define the spouse's share as a fixed dollar amount plus a percentage of the remaining estate. Each computation is made after the estate is reduced by the spouse's homestead allowance, exempt property, and family allowance.

Because each fixed amount is subject to a cost-of-living adjustment, the spouse could receive more than the amount described here if the decedent died in a state that makes those adjustments. The spouse receives $300,000 plus three-fourths of the remaining estate if the decedent is not survived by descendants but is survived by one or both parents. She receives $225,000 plus one-half of the remaining estate if all of the decedent's descendants are also her descendants but she has at least one descendant who is not his descendant. Finally, she receives $150,000 plus one-half of the remaining estate if the decedent had at least one descendant who was not her descendant.

> **Example 5-15.** Irwin died intestate, survived by his father Fred, his wife Wendy, his son Seth, and Wendy's daughter Diana. After taking Wendy's allowances and claims against the estate into account, Irwin's personal representative had $220,000 to distribute. Because Irwin had at least one descendant who was not Wendy's descendant, she receives only $150,000 plus one-half of the $70,000 balance. Wendy thus receives $185,000 of the $220,000 available for distribution. If she had adopted Seth, she would have received all $220,000 even though she had a descendant (Diana) who was not Irwin's descendant. That is because the formula amount ($225,000 plus one-half of the remaining estate) exceeds the total estate available for distribution.

3. Surviving Spouse Takes Nothing

The spouse will receive nothing if she waived her intestate share in a valid prenuptial or postnuptial agreement, disclaimed her rights after the decedent died, or committed a disqualifying act, such as murdering the decedent. Those situations are discussed in other chapters.

c. Descendants

UPC § 2-103(c) assigns the remaining estate to the intestate's descendants, if any. If the intestate had no surviving spouse, the estate goes 100% to his descendants, if any. Because descendants take their share by representation, the estate might be divided among several generations of a decedent's descendants. Representation methods are discussed in Section I.

d. Parents and Their Descendants

Parents traditionally share the entire estate if both survive the intestate, and the intestate had no surviving spouse or descendants. They share the portion not received by the surviving spouse if the intestate had no descendants and the relevant statute was based on UPC § 2-103(d).

Parents share equally if both survive the decedent. If only one parent survives, the outcome depends on whether the state allocates the entire amount to the surviving parent or follows the allocation provided in UPC § 2-103(d). That section applies if the deceased parent had one or more descendants who were not descendants of the surviving parent. UPC § 2-103(e). The UPC allocates the entire amount to the surviving parent only if the two parents had all their descendants in common or the deceased parent had no separate descendants. If the deceased parent had a descendant who was not the surviving parent's descendant, the surviving parent receives only half. The descendants of the deceased parent receive the other one-half.

> **Example 5-16.** Ilya died intestate, survived only by his father Felix, his mother Melina, and Melina's daughter Delilah. Felix was not Delilah's father and did not adopt her. Felix and Melina share Ilya's estate equally.
>
> **Example 5-17.** Same as Example 5-16 except that Felix died a day before Ilya. Melina receives all of Ilya's estate.
>
> **Example 5-18.** Same as Example 5-16 except that Melina died a day before Ilya. If UPC § 2-103(d) applies, Felix receives one-half of Ilya's estate; Delilah receives the other one-half. If a state instead uses the traditional treatment of surviving parents, Felix receives all of Ilya's estate.

e. *Siblings and Their Descendants*

If the intestate had no surviving spouse, descendants, or parents, the descendants of his parents (his brothers, sisters, nieces, and nephews) take the entire estate by representation. UPC § 2-103(f). The UPC refers to these individuals as surviving descendants of a deceased parent. A state statute might instead refer to brothers and sisters (or siblings) and descendants of deceased brothers and sisters.

f. *Grandparents and Their Descendants*

If no one survives the intestate in any of the preceding categories, the estate is distributed to the grandparents or descendants of deceased grandparents. UPC § 2-103(g). Grandparents share equally if all survive the decedent. As was true for computing the share of the intestate's parents, the UPC does not divide the estate equally between surviving grandparents if a deceased grandparent had a surviving descendant who was not a descendant of at least one surviving grandparent. UPC § 2-103(h). In determining grandparents' shares, the UPC treats grandparents who had only common descendants as a single grandparent for determining shares. A descendant of a deceased grandparent who is also the descendant of a surviving grandparent is treated as predeceased.

Example 5-19. Irma was survived by her mother's parents Minnie and Leo, her father's parents Lew and Felicia, and Felicia's son Roger. Roger was not Lew's child. Minnie, Leo, Lew, and Felicia each receive one-fourth of Irma's probate estate.

Example 5-20. Same as Example 5-19 except that Lew died a day before Irma. If UPC § 2-103(g) applies, Minnie, Leo, and Felicia each receive one-third of Irma's probate estate. If a state instead uses the traditional treatment of surviving grandparents, Minnie and Leo will share one-half of Irma's probate estate; Felicia will receive the other one-half.

Example 5-21. Same as Example 5-19 except that Felicia died a day before Irma. If UPC § 2-103(g) applies, Minnie, Leo, Lew, and Roger each receive one-fourth of Irma's probate estate. If a state instead uses the traditional treatment of surviving grandparents, Minnie and Leo will share one-half of Irma's probate estate; Lew will receive the other one-half.

As was true for parents, the UPC follows the Uniform Parentage Act by ignoring gender and providing for the possibility of an intestate having more than four grandparents.

States that focus on maternal and paternal lines are likely to divide the estate between those lines. Within each line, grandparents share equally. If one is deceased, the other grandparent receives the entire share. If both are deceased, their descendants take their share. If there are no descendants, their share is received by the other line of grandparents. If none of the intestate's grandparents survive, their descendants take by representation. UPC § 2-103(i).

Example 5-22. Inez was survived only by her mother's father and by her father's sister. Although her paternal grandparents did not survive, one of their descendants did. Inez's maternal grandfather and paternal aunt will share her estate equally.

2. State Variations

States that vary from the UPC might, as in Virginia, determine maternal and paternal kindred at the great-grandparent level. They might ignore parents if the decedent had no descendants. They might focus on maternal and paternal lines instead of treating parents and grandparents as a group. They might use a different formula to determine the surviving spouse's share of the estate. The UPC is a guide to ordering rules, but it is not a substitute for reading the relevant state statute.

H. Avoiding Escheat

1. Survival Requirement

To receive an intestate share, an heir must actually survive and must avoid any disqualifying event. Disqualifying events include killing the intestate, disclaiming the intestate share, and (for a spouse) entering into a prenuptial or postnuptial agreement waiving intestate rights. Because survival and not committing a disqualifying act apply to both testate and intestate estates, these characteristics are discussed in greater detail in other chapters.

UPC § 2-104(b) requires survival by 120 hours, and survival must be established by clear and convincing evidence. The UPC waives this requirement if necessary to avoid escheat. If the last eligible heir survives for any length of time, that individual receives the intestate's property. UPC § 2-104(c).

The UPC provision does not apply in every state. Survival by as little as one second is sufficient in jurisdictions that do not require a particular survival period. Those states do not modify the term "survival" in the specific intestacy provision or in more-general provisions applying to transfer of the decedent's property. Simultaneous death acts are likely to apply in states that require mere survival. If the court cannot determine whether the intestate or the heir died first, the intestate is treated as surviving. Simultaneous death statutes apply to both testate and intestate estates.

2. Fallback Rules

Rather than allowing property to escheat to the state because the decedent was not survived by an eligible relative, the jurisdiction's intestacy statute might provide a fallback rule. For example, it might look to the family of the intestate decedent's deceased spouse. In these situations, we pretend that the spouse did not predecease the decedent but instead died intestate immediately after the decedent did. Certain relatives of the deceased spouse take the decedent's property in that situation. If the state has a survival provision, these potential takers are subject to that requirement.

UPC § 2-103(j) allows the descendants of all the intestate's deceased spouses to take by representation. The UPC ignores a deceased spouse's other relatives, and it ignores any will a deceased spouse might have executed. The UPC uses per capita at each generation is determining each descendant's share.

> **Example 5-23.** Isaac died intestate, five months after his wife Wanda died, in a jurisdiction that follows UPC § 2-103(j). He had no surviving relatives. Wanda was his second wife; he married her two years after his first wife, Wendy, died. At the time of Isaac's death, Wendy's grandson Sidney, and Wanda's granddaughters Dora and Donna, were alive. Wendy died intestate. Wanda had a will in which she devised her property to Isaac if he survived her and, if not, to her sister Sue. Because the UPC uses per capita at each generation in dividing the estate, Sidney, Dora, and Donna each receive one-third. The fact that Wanda favored Sue in her will is irrelevant. The number of descendants in existence when Wanda or Wendy died is also irrelevant. Only descendants who survived Isaac share the estate.

Although both involve the family of a deceased spouse, Florida and California use slightly different mechanisms for avoiding escheat. The Florida statute applies if the intestate is not survived by a spouse, descendants, parents, siblings (or the descendants of deceased siblings), or grandparents (or the descendants of deceased grandparents) but did have one or more predeceased spouses. Those individuals who would be the kindred of the decedent's *last* predeceased spouse take the property. In computing the share of those heirs, we assume that the predeceased spouse died intestate immediately after the intestate decedent. Fla. Stat. § 732.103(5). Florida thus differs from the UPC in two ways. First, it gives rights only to relatives of the last predeceased spouse. Second, it allows that spouse's intestate heirs to take. It does not limit the inheritance to the predeceased spouse's descendants.

The California statute applies if the intestate is not survived by a surviving spouse, issue, parents, issue of parents, grandparents, issue of grandparents, issue of a predeceased spouse, or next of kin. Cal. Prob. Code § 6402. Its last takers before escheat are the parents of the intestate's predeceased spouse and the issue of such parents. Note that in California, the issue of the deceased spouse rank ahead of the intestate's next of kin. Cal. Prob. Code § 6402.5 provides a separate set of rules covering real property if the intestate's deceased spouse died no more than 15 years before the intestate and personal property if the spouse died no more than five years before the intestate. These rules apply to property attributable to that deceased spouse if the decedent was not survived by a spouse or issue. In those situations, the spouse's next of kin are added as takers to avoid escheat.

I. Taking by Representation

With the exception of the decedent's spouse, most relationships between the decedent and potential heirs are relationships by blood or adoption. We should not be surprised that intestacy statutes preserve the share of an heir—even if she predeceased the decedent—if she was survived by descendants of her own. In other words, the order of death is deemed less important than retaining the property within that family group. When the descendant of a deceased heir takes, she is taking by representation.

> **Example 5-24.** Ilene died, survived by her brother Bill. Bill died two weeks later, survived by his son Seth. Ilene and Bill had no other relatives and both died intestate. Seth will inherit both the property Bill owned before Ilene died and the property Bill inherited from Ilene.
>
> **Example 5-25.** Bill died two weeks before Ilene instead of two weeks after. Seth inherits the property Bill owned at death. He also inherits the property Ilene owned at death. Seth would take Bill's potential share of Ilene's estate. The intestacy statute gives the descendants of deceased heirs the share their ancestor would have taken.

Descendants take by representation; spouses do not. If, in Example 5-25, Bill was survived by both his wife Willa and his son Seth, Seth—not Willa—would inherit Ilene's property.

1. Representation Rules

Taking by representation can be complicated when more than one potential heir predeceases the intestate. What if, for example, Ilene was survived only by her brother Bill's son Seth and her sister Sally's five children? If Bill and Sally had both survived, each would take one-half of Ilene's estate. If only Sally had survived, she would have taken one-half of Ilene's estate, and Bill's son Seth would have taken the other half. To correctly divide Ilene's estate when she is survived *only* by her six nieces and nephews we follow the state's representation rules. The discussion below reviews three possible representation rules: per stirpes; per capita with representation; and per capita at each generation. The UPC follows the third rule.

The per stirpes representation system is literally based on branches of a family tree being treated equally no matter how many twigs (descendants) are in a given branch and no matter how remotely those twigs are related to the intestate. The estate is divided into as many branches as are represented by living highest-generation members or by deceased highest-generation members with living descendants. If an intestate had three children, each of whom had descendants who survived her, we divide her estate into thirds even if all three children predeceased the intestate.

Per capita with representation divides the family into branches at the highest generation of heirs with at least one living member. It then divides the estate using the per stirpes method for all other takers. Per capita with representation operates identically to per stirpes if the highest generation of potential heirs has at least one living member. It diverges from it if the first generation with a living member is not the highest generation of potential heirs. Note that both per capita systems begin at the highest generation that actually has a living member.

UPC §2-106 uses a per capita at each generation system that treats individuals in the same generation equally. This method of division begins at the highest generation with a living member. If, for example, the intestate is survived by at least one child, the division occurs at that level. If, on the other hand, the intestate is survived only by grandchildren, the division occurs at that level. Once we determine the level at which we begin dividing the decedent's estate, we determine the number of shares. We assign one share to each survivor in the first generation with survivors and one share to each deceased member of that same group who is survived by descendants.

Per capita at each generation initially resembles per capita with representation because it divides the family at the highest generation with at least one living member. It diverges from per capita with representation because it does not use representation to distribute the shares of deceased members among their own descendants. Instead, it pools the shares of deceased members and distributes the pooled shares among their combined descendants.

2. Applying Representation Rules

a. Children and Their Descendants

The examples below are based on Isabelle, who will die intestate. Isabelle had three children, Cindy, Cal, and Cody. Each of them had children, as described in the examples below. As the first three examples indicate, the three systems often give identical results. Per stirpes diverges from other systems when every member of the highest generation predeceases the intestate.

Example 5-26. Isabelle died, survived by her three children, Cindy, Cal, and Cody. The three children share Isabelle's intestate estate equally. This is the outcome under all three representation systems. A surviving higher-generation member cuts off the inheritance rights of his or her descendants.

Example 5-27. Isabelle was instead survived only by Cindy, Cal, and Cody's daughter Dorothy. The estate is still divided into three parts; Cindy, Cal, and Dorothy share the estate equally under all three representation systems. If Dorothy also predeceased Isabelle and left no survivors, Cindy and Cal would share the estate equally because Cody's line would have disappeared.

Example 5-28. Isabelle was instead survived only by Cindy, Cal, and Cody's granddaughter Gretel. The estate is still divided into three parts; Cindy, Cal, and Gretel share the estate equally under all three representation systems. The descendants can be more remote than children.

Example 5-29. Isabelle was instead survived only by Cindy, by Cal's daughters Donna, Debby, and Darla, and by Cody's daughter Dorothy. In the per stirpes system, we divide Isabelle's estate into three equal shares, one for each child who survived or who was survived by descendants. Cindy receives a one-third share; Cal's one-third share is divided equally between Donna, Debby, and Darla; Cody's one-third share goes to Dorothy. The results would be the same using per capita with representation. Because Cindy survived, we divide the estate into thirds; Cal and Cody's children each take the share their parent would have received. Using per capita at each generation, we would divide the estate differently. Because Cindy survived, the initial division is again into thirds; Cindy takes one-third. We then combine the shares attributable to Cal and Cody and divide them equally between Donna, Debby, Darla, and Dorothy. Each of them takes one-fourth of two-thirds.

Example 5-30. Isabelle was instead survived only by Cindy's sons Sam and Sid, by Cal's daughters Donna, Debby, and Darla, and by Cody's daughter Dorothy. In the per stirpes system, we divide Isabelle's estate into three equal shares, one for each child who was survived by descendants. Cindy's one-third share is divided equally between Sam and Sid; Cal's one-third share is divided equally between Donna, Debby, and Darla; Cody's one-third share goes to Dorothy. In both per capita systems, we divide the estate into six parts because the grandchildren are the highest generation surviving heirs.

b. Collateral Relatives and Their Descendants

Collateral heirs who share the decedent's property are also subject to representation rules. These rules apply if an intestate is survived only by siblings or the descendants of deceased siblings or by aunts and uncles or the descendants of deceased aunts and uncles—this includes nieces, nephews, and cousins or the descendants of deceased nieces, nephews, and cousins.

> **Example 5-31.** Isaac is survived only by his brother Bob and by his deceased brother Ben's daughter Dina. Isaac's estate is divided into two equal shares under all three systems of representation. Bob and Dina share the estate equally. The systems would give different results if Bob also predeceased Isaac, but was survived by his sons Seymour and Sylvester. If the estate was divided using the per stirpes system, Dina would still take one-half of Isaac's estate. Seymour and Sylvester would divide the other one-half. If the estate was divided using either of the per capita systems, Dina, Seymour, and Sylvester would each take one-third. The estate would initially be divided at their level.

The results differ if the state has a half-blood statute, which applies if the intestate decedent has both half-blood and whole-blood collateral heirs. Some half-blood statutes assign half as much of the estate to each half-blood sibling as to each whole-blood sibling. In other words, *each* whole-blood sibling takes twice as much as *each* half-blood sibling. Other half-blood statutes, such as the Oklahoma statute cited earlier, might prevent the half-blood relative from inheriting property attributable to his stepparent's family.

If a half-blood statute applies, we divide the estate into the share each sibling would take before applying the representation rules to descendants of deceased siblings. Because an adopted child is treated as the child of the adoptive parent, adoption can affect the application of a half-blood statute. If, for example, a stepparent had adopted her spouse's children, they would become whole-blood siblings with any child the adoptive parent has with the genetic parent. In that case, the half-blood statute would not apply.

Stepbrothers and stepsisters have no parents in common. As a result, they are not affected by the half-blood statute. Unless a state intestate succession law includes them, they do not inherit from each other.

If the state intestacy statute covers nonmarital children, it does so for all purposes. A child who is treated as his mother's child is also treated as a member of his mother's family. A child who is treated as his father's child is also treated as a member of his father's family. Nonmarital relationships might trigger the half-blood statute in states that apply those statutes.

c. Remote Relatives

A state might apply its representation rules to more remote collateral relatives, such as aunts, uncles, nieces, nephews, and cousins. If it extends intestate inheritance rights to even more remote relatives such as next of kin or kindred, it might apply representation rules to them. Alternatively, it might use a degrees-of-relationship test. In that situation, it would prefer relatives who are related more closely to the intestate over those who are less closely related.

J. Degrees of Relationship

States that rank heirs based on how closely they are related to the intestate focus on the degree of relationship. They trace the intestate and his surviving relatives to a common ancestor. At that point, they count how many degrees apart each relative is from the decedent. The closer the relative is, the more likely he is to inherit. If the relatives are from different sides of the decedent's family, we trace to the common ancestor on each side. These relationships are often illustrated in "degrees of consanguinity" charts.

> **Example 5-32.** Ingrid was survived by George, the great-grandson of her father's brother, and by Sam, the son of her paternal grandfather's sister. Assuming the relevant state law considers both George and Sam eligible heirs, we determine the degrees of relationship between each of them and Ingrid. Ingrid and George are descended from her paternal grandparents. Ingrid is two degrees below them; George is four degrees below them. Ingrid and Sam are descended from her paternal great-grandparents. Ingrid is three degrees below them; Sam is two degrees below them. If the state treated descendants of Ingrid's grandparents the way the UPC does, George would inherit even though he is more remotely related to Ingrid than Sam. If the state focused only on degrees of relationship, Sam would inherit.

K. Aliens

Aliens generally have the same inheritance rights as U.S. citizens. UPC § 2-111. If an alien dies intestate while present in the United States, the distribution of her property might be subject to the laws of her home country. That topic is beyond the scope of this book.

L. Parent-Child Relationship

Unlike the marital relationship, which generally requires adhering to state-imposed formalities, a parent-child relationship might be the result of an informal relationship as well as the product of a marriage. It might involve a child conceived through sexual intercourse or through assisted reproductive techniques. It might be established through adoption as well as through birth. It might last until the parent or child's death or be severed sooner through adoption away from the parent or through abandonment by the parent. State statutes deal with most, if not all, of these issues.

In 2019, the Uniform Law Commission revised the UPC to reflect the Uniform Parentage Act. The revised provisions include name changes (eliminating the terms half-blood and whole-blood; maternal and paternal; and genetic parent) and substantive changes (providing for the possibility that a child will have more than two parents and more than two sets of grandparents; adding de facto parentage; and providing that per capita at each generation was used for all forms of intestate inheritance). Currently only eight states have adopted the 2017 UPA; another group has adopted a version revised in 2002. Approximately half of the states have enacted neither version. No states have adopted the 2019 UPC revision. As a result, you should not be surprised if state law differs from the UPC provisions described below.

1. Adoption

a. Traditional Treatment

The traditional treatment of an adopted child looked to both the child's birth parents ("genetic parents") and adoptive parents. An adopted child was treated as the child of her adoptive parents. Her relationship to the families of those parents was the same as it would be if she were their birth child. In other words, for purposes of intestate succession, relationships created by adoption are treated the same as blood relationships. UPC § 2-118(a).

Before she was adopted, the child could inherit from her genetic parents (and members of their family), and they could inherit from her. If the adoption severed the relationship between the child and her genetic parents (and their families), she could no longer inherit from them, and they could no longer inherit from her. The general rule, that the adoption severed the child's relationship to her genetic family, was subject to exceptions. If an exception applied, the child retained the right to inherit from members of her birth family. Their right to inherit from her was governed by the state's statute.

The three typical exceptions involved adoption by a genetic parent's spouse, adoption by a genetic parent's relative, and adoption after the genetic parents died. UPC § 2-119(b) keeps these exceptions and adds an additional exception. The relationship between the genetic parent and the child is not severed despite the adoption if there is a court order or other statute so providing.

> **Example 5-33.** Harry and Wendy had one child, Carl, before Wendy died. Harry later married Marge, and she adopted Carl. Carl can inherit from Harry and Harry's family, from Wendy's family, and from Marge and her family through intestate succession. If Carl died intestate, Harry and his family could inherit from Carl; Marge and her family could also inherit from Carl.
>
> **Example 5-34.** Cory's genetic parents died in an automobile accident. His father's sister and her husband adopted him. For purposes of intestate succession, Cory is a member of three families, that of his genetic mother, that of his genetic father (which is also the family of his adoptive mother), and that of his adoptive father (his aunt's husband). If Cory's father and his father's sister were only half-siblings, Cory could also acquire additional relatives through his new mother.
>
> **Example 5-35.** Hector and Wilma had a child, Donna, while serving as medical missionaries in an underdeveloped country with an unstable government. Wilma's sister Sarah adopted Donna, who maintains contact with Hector and Wilma—when possible—by videoconferencing. Donna can inherit from or through Hector, Wilma, and Sarah.

Keep three rules in mind when determining how state law treats that individual's original family. First, it is possible that the child will retain rights to inherit from that family even if they do not retain rights to inherit from the child. Second, the state might continue the child's inheritance rights through the genetic parent only if that parent was deceased when the adoption occurred. Third, non-inheritance rights, such as grandparent visitation, are generally governed by the state's domestic relations law rather than its inheritance law; those rights are not necessarily co-extensive.

b. Relationship to One Decedent Through More than One Line

When a child is adopted by a relative, he might have more than one status vis-à-vis that relative's family. The comments to the UPC indicate this could happen if the surviving genetic parent married the deceased genetic parent's sibling, who then adopted the child. In that case, the child would be both the natural (through the deceased genetic parent) and adopted (through the adoptive parent) grandchild of the siblings' parents. This issue is not limited to adoption. The UPC provides that his inheritance rights would be based on whichever relationship resulted in the largest inheritance. UPC § 2-113.

c. Adult Adoptee

The UPC does not include a body of domestic relations or parent-child provisions. Its purpose is the transmission of an individual's property at death, not the formation of families. State law, on the other hand, generally includes both sets of provisions, usually in different parts of the state statutes.

If state law allows the adoption of an adult, presumably it would treat the adult adoptee the same as an individual who was adopted as a child. But that is not necessarily the case. In Wisconsin, for example, the relationship of an adoptee and her adopting parents is treated the same as the relationship of an individual and her birth parents. Her age when the adoption occurred is not relevant. The adoptee's relationship with the adopting parents' other relatives is ignored unless one of two conditions is satisfied. Either the adoption occurred when she was a minor, or the "adoptive parent raised the adopted person in a parent-like relationship beginning on or before the child's 15th birthday and lasting for a substantial period or until adulthood." Wis. Stat. § 854.20(a)–(b). The UPC § 2-115(1) definition does not mention age. The comments indicate that the definition includes individuals adopted as adults.

d. Equitable Adoption

Equitable adoption, sometimes referred to as virtual adoption, is a judicial doctrine that provides rights to an individual who was never formally adopted. UPC § 2-122 indicates that its parent-child provisions do not affect the doctrine of equitable adoption.

An individual is treated as equitably adopted if the individual, his parents, and the intestate decedent all met the state's performance requirements. The individual's parents perform by allowing the individual to become a member of the intestate's household. The individual performs by living in that household. The intestate performs by including the individual in her household even though she never formally adopted him. If those requirements are met, he is an heir of the intestate. Equitable adoption does not sever the parent-child relationship between him and his birth parents. Nor does it make the person with whom he resided his heir if he predeceases. The doctrine is likely to apply only if the person with whom he resided dies intestate.

> **Example 5-36.** Vincent's birth parents agreed with Alice that their son would become a member of Alice's family. Vincent moved into Alice's home and remained there until he left for college at age 18. He returned to Alice's home on college vacations. Alice died when Vincent was 20; she had never formally adopted him. Vincent is treated as Alice's child for purposes of intestate succession. If Vincent had died intestate survived by Alice, she would not be treated as his parent for purposes of inheriting from him.

2. De Facto Parentage

UPC § 2-115(3) defines a de facto parent as a person who was adjudicated to be a parent based on the person's status as a de facto parent. UPC § 2-118(b) establishes a parent-child relationship between the child and her de facto parent. UPA § 609 lists seven factors an individual can establish when he claims to be a child's de facto parent. These include being a member of the child's household for a significant period; engaging in consistent caretaking for the child; undertaking full and permanent parental responsibilities without expectation of compensation; holding the child out as his own; and establishing that this treatment is in the best interest of the child. The factors must be established by clear and convincing evidence. A stepparent or another person engaged in an intimate relationship with the child's parent might be able to establish de facto parentage.

3. Assisted Reproduction

UPC § 2-115(2) defines assisted reproduction as a method of causing pregnancy other than sexual intercourse. The comments list intrauterine or intracervical insemination, donation of gametes, donation of embryos, in-vitro fertilization and transfer of embryos, and intracytoplasmic sperm injection as examples. UPC § 2-120 provides that parentage is determined under UPA Article 7 unless the child is born to a gestational or genetic surrogate. In those cases UPC § 2-121 provides that parentage is determined under UPA Article 8.

4. Posthumous Birth and Posthumous Conception

Intestacy statutes treat a child in gestation as being alive when the intestate dies if the child is born alive and meets the relevant survival period. That period will be based on the date of the child's birth rather than on the date of the intestate's death. UPC § 2-104(b)(2).

> **Example 5-37.** Harry died, survived by Sam, the child of his first marriage, and by his second wife, Wanda. Wanda was pregnant with their daughter Delores. Delores was born two months after Harry died and lived three days. If the state had a 120-hour survival requirement, Wanda and Sam will split Harry's estate. If the state requires only a live birth, Delores and Sam will split the portion of the estate that does not go to Wanda. Because Delores will be intestate, her mother Wanda will inherit any property that Delores received from Harry's estate.

Posthumous birth statutes do not limit their coverage to a child born after her parent's death. These statutes cover any child who would have taken by intestate succession if born before the intestate dies.

> **Example 5-38.** Harry's mother Mary died intestate one week after Harry died. When she died, Sam was her only relative. Assuming Delores, who was born less than two months after Mary died, meets the relevant state survival period after her birth, she will inherit equally with Sam.

A posthumous birth can also involve a child who was not in gestation when the intestate died. UPC § 2-104(b)(3) treats a child conceived in this manner as being alive when the intestate died if two requirements are met. First, the decedent's personal representative must be notified of the intent to use genetic material in the assisted reproduction. Second, the embryo must be in utero no more than 36 months after the decedent's death or the birth must occur no more than 45 months after the decedent's death. State law will treat a child in gestation as a potential heir but might not include a posthumously conceived child.

5. Nonmarital Births

State statutes often distinguish between fathers and mothers when a child is born to parents who are not married to each other when the child is born. For purposes of the intestacy statutes, the child is a member of the mother's family. The nonmarital aspect of his birth is irrelevant because this aspect of his parentage is easily proven. The child is a member of the father's family if parentage is established under the relevant state statutes. These are likely to focus on the father's admission of paternity or an adjudication of paternity. The situation becomes more complicated if the birth involves an assisted reproduction method, such as artificial insemination or gestational surrogacy. UPC § 2-117 provides a general rule: a parent-child relationship exists between the child and his parents. The parents' marital status is irrelevant.

6. Foster Children

Most jurisdictions do not include foster children in their intestacy statutes. The foster child does not inherit from a foster parent or a foster parent's family. A foster parent and his family do not inherit from a foster child.

California has a limited exception to this rule. Cal. Prob. Code § 6454. A foster child (and the foster child's issue) can inherit from a foster parent or from members of a foster parent's family if two conditions are met. First, the relationship must have begun while the foster child was a minor and must have continued until severed by death. Second, it must be shown that the foster parent would have adopted the foster child but for a legal barrier. The second prong must be established by clear and convincing evidence. The California statute applies to inheritance by the foster child. It does not give the foster parent a right to inherit from the foster child. The same requirements also apply to inheritance by a stepchild (and the stepchild's issue).

M. Advancements

An intestate decedent might have made lifetime gifts to an individual who qualifies as an heir. In that situation, we must determine if the gift was in addition to any amounts the heir would receive by intestacy or if it was an advancement against his inheritance. An analogous concept, ademption by satisfaction, applies to inter vivos gifts to a devisee.

UPC § 2-109 applies if any of the decedent's estate would pass by intestacy. It reduces the share of the heir who received an inter vivos gift only if a writing treats the gift as an advancement against the recipient's share. A writing by the decedent must be made contemporaneously with the transfer. It must indicate that the transfer is an advancement, or it must provide that the gift is to be taken into account in distributing the donor's intestate estate. A writing by the donee acknowledging that the gift was an advancement, or that it is to be taken into account in distributing the donor's intestate estate, also suffices. The donee's writing does not have to be contemporaneous with the gift. UPC § 2-109(a).

1. Application to Donee

The advancement rules merely reduce the donee's share of the intestate estate. They do not require him to return property he received as an inter vivos transfer. And if he is not eligible to inherit, the advancement rules do not apply.

> **Example 5-39.** Ilene gave her grandson George $15,000 two years ago. She declared in a contemporaneous writing that the $15,000 was an advancement. Ilene died intestate, survived only by her daughter Dina, her son Seth, and George. If George is Seth's son, he would not have taken anything by intestate succession. Under the intestate succession rules, Dina and Seth would split Ilene's estate equally. If, on the other hand, George was the son of Ilene's deceased daughter Deborah, his share of Ilene's estate (which would otherwise have been one-third) will be reduced.

When the advancement rules apply, we must determine two amounts: the amount the donee would otherwise receive through intestate succession and the amount that should be treated as an advancement. We subtract the second amount from the first amount to determine how much, if anything, he will receive from the decedent's estate. We determine the first amount using the jurisdiction's rules of intestate succession. The second amount varies based on what the donee received and when he received it.

We value the amount the donee received as an advancement at the earlier of the date he came into possession or enjoyment of the advancement or the date on which the intestate died. UPC § 2-109(b). If the advancement was an outright inter vivos gift, the date of the gift is the earlier date. If the donee was instead made the beneficiary of another transfer, such as taking trust property after a preceding interest ended, the date of the decedent's death might be the earlier date. The value of the property on the date the personal representative distributes estate assets does not affect the amount treated as an advancement. The donee's decision to dispose of the property before the decedent's death is also irrelevant.

Once we determine the relevant value of the advancement, we add it to the actual value of the intestate estate. Then we determine the donee's share of that larger amount. He receives that amount, reduced by the value of the advancement. If the advancement exceeds his share of the larger amount, he receives nothing. This method of determining the donee's share is referred to as a hotchpot. It is a creature of judicial decisions and is referred to in the comments to UPC § 2-109.

> **Example 5-40.** Irwin gave his son Sam 100 shares of stock in XYZ Corporation, valued at $30,000, five years ago. Irwin died intestate today, survived only by his sons Sam and Sylvester, with a probate estate worth $100,000. One hundred shares of XYZ Corporation stock are worth $40,000 today. Sam sold the stock last year for $36,000. If the transfer to Sam was not an advancement, Sam and Sylvester each receive $50,000 from Irwin's estate. If the transfer was an advancement, the hotchpot is $130,000. That is the sum of the stock's value when Sam received it and the value of Irwin's probate estate. Sam and Sylvester would each be entitled to $65,000. Because Sam has already received $30,000, he receives only $35,000 of the probate estate; Sylvester receives the remaining $65,000. The value of the stock when Sam sold it or when Irwin died had no effect on the computation.
>
> **Example 5-41.** If Irwin's probate estate was only $20,000 when he died, the hotchpot is $50,000. Sam and Sylvester would each be entitled to $25,000. Because Sam has already received more than that, he receives

none of the probate estate. Sylvester receives the entire $20,000. He has no claim against Sam for the extra $5,000.

2. Application to Deceased Donee

UPC §2-109(c) provides that the advancement rules do not automatically apply if the donee fails to survive the decedent. It does not matter if the deceased donee's descendants received any of the advanced property or not. The advancement reduction applies to them only if the decedent's contemporaneous writing provides for that reduction.

Example 5-42. Isabelle made an inter vivos gift of $20,000 to her daughter Dahlia five years ago. Isabelle died intestate this year, with a probate estate of $100,000. Isabelle was survived only by two grandchildren, her deceased son Seth's daughter Darleen and her deceased daughter Dahlia's daughter Denise. If the transfer to Dahlia was an advancement, but Isabelle's contemporaneous writing did not indicate that it applied if Dahlia failed to survive, Darleen and Denise each receive $50,000. If Isabelle's contemporaneous writing indicated that the advancement would apply even if Dahlia predeceased her, we add the $20,000 to $100,000 to get a $120,000 hotchpot estate. We reduce Denise's one-half interest by the $20,000 her mother received. Darleen receives $60,000, and Denise receives $40,000.

A donee who received an advancement might actually survive the intestate but be treated as predeceasing. For example, the donee might have killed the intestate or might simply disclaim any interest in the intestate's estate. In these situations, the donee is treated as predeceasing the intestate donor. If the donor's contemporaneous writing reduced the share of the donee's descendants, the results are the same whether or not the donee predeceased the donor. But what if the declaration did not cover the donee's descendants? Do they now take a greater share than their living, but ineligible, ancestor would have taken? The comments to UPC §2-109 indicate that their share is still reduced. UPC §2-1106(b)(3)(B) provides that the disclaimed interest passes as if the disclaimant predeceased the decedent. UPC §2-803 provides that the killer is treated as disclaiming the intestate share. The comments to UPC §2-109 focus on the "interest" language in the disclaimer statute. The interest of the donee who received an advancement is less than his intestate share because of the advancement.

3. Application to Heirs in Different Priority Groups

In the examples in Subsections 1 and 2, the heirs were in the same priority groups: Sam and Sylvester were both Irwin's sons; Darleen and Denise were both Isabelle's grandchildren. When the remaining heirs are in different priority groups, the computation can be more complicated. For example, an intestate might be survived by a spouse and multiple children, at least one of whom is not the child of that spouse. In that instance, the spouse's share might be less than 100% of the probate estate, so we cannot simply say that she receives all the probate assets.

The comments to UPC § 2-109 provide examples of how the hotchpot would work in those situations. It includes examples in which the donee has received less than his intestate share and is entitled to some of the estate assets. It also includes examples in which the donee has received more than his intestate share. In the latter case, the remaining estate is divided without reference to the property received as an advancement. Because the advancement is completely ignored, the amount allocable to the other heirs is reduced and recomputed.

The first example below gives the surviving spouse a 50% share of the intestate estate. Although that is less than she would receive under UPC § 2-102, which provides a dollar amount plus a percentage of the remaining estate, it makes the computations easier to understand. The second example uses the formula in UPC § 2-102.

> **Example 5-43.** Igor made a $50,000 advancement to his son Sigmund several years ago. Igor died intestate, survived by his second wife Winifred and their daughter Doris and also by Sigmund, who was the child of Igor's first wife. Igor's probate estate was $120,000; the initial hotchpot amount was $170,000. Because Igor had descendants who were not Winifred's, his state of residence gives her only 50% of the probate estate. Winifred would be entitled to 50% of the hotchpot, or $85,000; Doris and Sigmund would each be entitled to 25%, or $42,500. Because Sigmund's advancement exceeds his share, he receives nothing from the estate and his advancement is ignored. The recomputed hotchpot of $120,000 is divided equally between Winifred and Doris; each receives $60,000.
>
> **Example 5-44.** Ivan made a $50,000 advancement to his son Seth several years ago. Ivan died intestate, survived by his second wife Wanda and their daughter Dee and also by Seth, who was the child of Ivan's first wife. Ivan's probate estate was $120,000; the initial hotchpot amount

was $170,000. Because Ivan had descendants who were not Wanda's, the UPC gives her $150,000 plus one-half of the remaining probate estate. Wanda would initially be entitled to $160,000; Dee and Seth would each be entitled to $5,000. Because Seth's advancement exceeds his share, he receives nothing from the estate and his advancement is ignored. Wanda receives the entire recomputed hotchpot of $120,000.

N. Loans to Heirs

If an heir has not repaid a debt owed the intestate, the personal representative can offset the unpaid loan against the heir's intestate share. If the heir has predeceased the intestate, the personal representative cannot offset the loan against the share of his descendants. UPC § 2-110.

The comments to UPC § 2-110 indicate that the rules applied to disclaimers under the advancement provisions also apply to loans. A debtor who survives the intestate but is treated as predeceased because he disclaimed his interest cannot prevent the debt from reducing the share his own descendants would take.

CHECKPOINTS

- An individual who owns probate property that is not disposed of through his will is referred to as an intestate. He might be totally intestate or partially intestate.
- A beneficiary who receives property by intestate succession is an heir.
- Intestacy statutes determine who qualifies as an heir. Heirs are usually related to the decedent by blood (including adoption) or marriage.
- Heirs other than the decedent's surviving spouse are either lineal or collateral. Lineal descendants are ancestors or descendants. Collateral heirs are other blood relatives, including siblings, aunts, uncles, nieces, nephews, and cousins.
- The UPC and many state statutes limit the rights of remote ancestors to inherit. Each jurisdiction determines how remote an ancestor can be before he becomes ineligible to inherit.

- Intestacy statutes rank heirs in terms of priority and establish the share that each heir takes.
- The intestate's surviving spouse is the highest-ranked heir. The surviving spouse's share is usually smaller if she and the decedent did not have all their descendants in common.
- The remaining ordering generally covers the decedent's descendants, parents, siblings and their descendants, grandparents, and descendants of grandparents.
- Some jurisdictions include stepchildren or great-grandparents.
- Some jurisdictions treat half-blood collateral heirs less generously than they treat whole-blood heirs who share both sets of ancestors with the decedent.
- Some jurisdictions determine the share of heirs by degrees of relationship.
- If the intestate decedent has no heirs, including in some states relatives of a deceased spouse, the state takes the property by escheat.
- When a deceased heir's descendants take in her place, they take by representation.
- The UPC uses the per capita at each generation method for determining representation. That method begins dividing the estate at the first generation with at least one surviving member. It pools the shares of deceased heirs in the same generation and redistributes those shares among their combined descendants.
- Some states use the per stirpes method for determining representation. That method begins dividing the estate at the highest generation, even if all members of that generation are deceased. Descendants of deceased heirs take only the share their ancestor would have taken.
- A third method, per capita with representation, has features of both of the other two methods.
- UPC provisions for adoptions, nonmarital births, de facto parentage, assisted reproduction, and posthumous conception reflect language in the Uniform Parentage Act. A state might enact some of these rules or ignore them.

- An inter vivos gift to an heir reduces the heir's share of the intestate estate only if that outcome is declared in a contemporaneous writing by the donor or an acknowledgement by the donee.
- Because the advancement was a gift, a donee who receives more than his intestate share does not have to transfer the excess back to the estate.
- If the donee predeceases the decedent, the advancement does not count against the amount his descendants receive by representation unless the donor's contemporaneous writing provides for it to count.
- If the intestate loans money to an heir, the unpaid loan reduces the heir's share of the estate. It does not reduce the share of the heir's descendants if the heir predeceases the intestate donor.

CHAPTER 6

Will Validity and Components

ROADMAP

- Testamentary capacity
- Testamentary formalities
- Validating an invalid will
- Components of a will

A. Chapter Overview

Property will not pass under the terms of an invalid will. This chapter describes two requirements for validity: testator capacity and compliance with any necessary formalities. These are determined as of the date the will is executed, but subsequent actions might validate a will that initially failed to comply.

This chapter concludes by describing items that might appear in a will. Some, such as the testator's signature, might be required. Others, such as nominating a personal representative, are elective. Their absence does not invalidate the will.

B. Testamentary Capacity

1. Age

A testator must have testamentary capacity. Testamentary capacity has two aspects. First, the testator must have attained a prescribed age when she executed her will. That age is usually the age of majority. There is no maximum age for executing a will, but challenges based on the testator's mental capacity are more likely if she is relatively elderly when she executes her will.

A jurisdiction might waive the age requirement if the testator is an emancipated minor. Statutes covering emancipation are likely to appear in the state's domestic relations code rather than in its probate code. Emancipation might be based on the testator's having been married; it might also be based on the testator's being self-supporting. The relevant statute might require that a court adjudicate the minor emancipated. Each state sets its own exceptions to the age requirement. Texas, for example, validates wills by an under-age testator who was (or had been) married or was a member of the military (or a military auxiliary) when he executed his will. Tex. Est. Code § 251.001.

A minor who has earnings, perhaps from appearing in motion pictures or endorsing products, might need court approval for the activity. That approval is not necessarily the same as emancipation. Fla. Stat. § 743.08(4)(b).

2. Mental Capacity

A typical statute requires that the testator be of "sound mind" when she executes her will. Because the testator is dead when her will is offered for probate, lawyers for disappointed family members and other potential beneficiaries cannot cross-examine her in a judicial proceeding. Even if they could, the proceeding might only establish her competency when the proceeding occurred. She might have executed her will many years earlier.

Statutes and judicial decisions begin with the presumption of competence. A testator who met the age requirement is generally presumed to have testamentary capacity. The burden of establishing lack of testamentary capacity lies with the person challenging the will. Unless the relevant statute requires proof by clear and convincing evidence, the standard of proof is preponderance of the evidence.

The person who prepared the will might be available to testify as to conversations with the testator. A preparer who predeceased the testator, or who is otherwise unable to testify, might have left detailed notes of conversations with the testator. If the testator prepared the will himself, there might be no one who can testify to his testamentary capacity when the will is offered for probate. If a beneficiary prepared the will or was involved in its preparation, disappointed family members might bring challenges based on undue influence in addition to challenges based on lack of capacity.

a. Potential Challenges to Capacity

Challenges based on lack of capacity might reflect the testator's medical history. Disappointed beneficiaries could allege that the testator suffered from dementia, atherosclerosis, paranoia, or schizophrenia. If she executed her will shortly after undergoing surgery, they might allege that she was in too much pain to comprehend the consequences of her actions or that she was under the influence of mind-altering pain medications. Challenges are also likely if the testator had a history of substance abuse. Although a testator is generally presumed to be of sound mind, that presumption can be overcome if she has previously been adjudicated to be incapacitated. *Morris v. Trust Co. of Virginia*, 2015 WL 1475487 (M.D. Ala. 2015).

The concept of insane delusion applies, albeit rarely, when a testator acts upon a belief that has no basis in fact and persists in so acting despite being presented contrary evidence. He might be sane in all other aspects but persists in this delusion. A finding that the testator suffered from an insane delusion might invalidate his will (or at least the portions affected by the delusion). *In re Robertson's Estate,* 189 P.2d 615 (Okla. 1948); *In re Estate of Hodtum,* 267 So. 2d 686 (Fla. Dist. Ct. App. 1972).

b. Documents Establishing Capacity

We generally think of a will as representing the testator's plan for distributing her property to individuals or charities that are the objects of her bounty. A testator who can list her property and her family members, and whose conversations indicate she is aware of how her will effectuates her overall plan, has testamentary capacity. Her answers to a questionnaire prepared by her attorney might be useful evidence for establishing capacity.

The will itself might establish the testator's capacity. For example, it could list her family members, list her assets in the devises she makes, and even indicate her overall purpose in making those devises. But a will that fails to include any of that information does not automatically establish a lack of testamentary capacity. If the testator wants to preserve her family members' privacy, she might execute a will that does no more than devise all of her property to an inter vivos trust.

Many wills include introductory language indicating that the testator "is of sound and disposing mind and memory." Although this language speaks to both capacity and intent, it does not establish either. It is merely boilerplate that a drafter might include in the will form he uses.

c. *Witnesses Establishing Capacity*

Even if a jurisdiction requires that a will be witnessed, the witnesses might be unable to establish testamentary capacity. They could have met the testator for the first (and only) time when she executed her will. Even if conversation occurred at that time, it might not have concerned the will. Indeed, the relevant statute might not require that the witnesses know that they are witnessing a will as opposed to some other document.

If the testator uses long-time friends as witnesses, their testimony might be useful in establishing capacity. But even this choice of witness has risks. If the testator is elderly when she executes her will (or when she dies), her witnesses might be dead or incapacitated when her will is offered for probate. The testator's doctor or other health care professional might be useful as a witness, particularly if that person knows the document is a will. Using the doctor as a witness might be particularly important if the testator takes medication that might cause confusion or otherwise affect her mental faculties.

d. *No-Contest Provisions*

A testator might use a no-contest provision (also called an *in terrorem* provision) to prevent challenges based on capacity or other grounds. These provisions generally cancel devises to anyone who challenges the validity of the will or any of its dispositions. Jurisdictions vary in their treatment of these provisions. Two UPC sections cover these provisions. Both UPC § 2-517 and UPC § 3-905 make them unenforceable if there is probable cause for contesting the will or instituting other proceedings related to the estate. The first section appears with the UPC provisions governing wills, will contracts, and custody and deposit of wills. The second section appears with distribution provisions in sections dealing with probate. Some states simply make them unenforceable. Fla. Stat. § 732.517. Other states enforce them. New York, for example, enforces these provisions, even if there is probable cause to contest the will. The statute has exceptions, such as contests to establish that the will was forged or that there was a later will revoking the contested will and contests by an "infant or incompetent." N.Y. Est. Powers & Trusts Law § 3-3.5(b).

C. Testamentary Formalities

Testamentary formalities can serve two purposes. First, they establish testamentary intent. An individual who executes a will in the presence of witnesses presumably has done so to validate its dispositions of his property. Second, they reduce the likelihood of fraud. If the testator executes the will in the presence of witnesses, those witnesses can testify that he—and not an unauthorized third-party forger—executed the document.

Although testamentary formalities vary among the jurisdictions, most jurisdictions require that the testator have a written will. They are also likely to require execution in the presence of witnesses. The discussion below expands on those requirements and on various exceptions to them.

1. Written Will

Jurisdictions that require a written will do not specify the type of writing. The will can be valid if it is typed or if it is handwritten. Even a will that involves filling in the blanks on a form will suffice. Indeed, the state itself might provide for such wills by statute. Wis. Stat. § 853.55, for example, includes a form for a Wisconsin basic will.

A noncupative, or oral, will is valid only under limited conditions in those jurisdictions that allow it. For example, New York allows a noncupative will if at least two witnesses can establish its making and contents. The testator must be a member of the armed forces in armed conflict, a person who accompanies such individuals, or a mariner at sea. The statute provides time periods after which the will loses its operative force. N.Y. Est. Powers & Trusts Law § 3-2.2. In some jurisdictions, noncupative wills are not valid even if they were valid in the jurisdiction where the testator previously resided. Fla. Stat. § 732.502(2). A will is written, rather than oral, even if the testator only dictates it so long as it is then produced in written form.

2. Holographic Will

A holographic will is written in whole or in part in the testator's handwriting. If it satisfies the jurisdiction's execution and attestation requirements, the fact that it is handwritten is irrelevant. If it does not satisfy those requirements, it will be valid only if it satisfies the jurisdiction's requirements for a valid holographic will.

Jurisdictions treat handwritten wills that are not signed by the testator or not attested by witnesses in one of three ways. Some jurisdictions never validate such wills. Fla. Stat. § 732.502. Others validate them if the will is completely in the testator's handwriting. N.Y. Est. Powers & Trusts Law § 3-2.2 (but limiting holographic wills to the situations in which it allows noncupative wills). Finally, some validate the will even if some of it is not in the testator's handwriting. UPC § 2-502(b) validates a holographic will if the signature and material portions of the will are in the testator's handwriting. It does not require a will to be witnessed if it satisfies those requirements.

Because a holographic will requires no witnesses, disappointed heirs might have an easier time arguing that the testator lacked testamentary intent. UPC § 2-502(c) allows establishing intent using extrinsic evidence and parts of the holographic will that are not handwritten. For example, the testator might use a form that already has printed "Last Will and Testament," "Devises," or other language indicating that the document is meant to be the testator's will.

3. Signatures and the Attestation

Wills generally must be signed by the testator (execution) and by witnesses to its execution (attestation). A state might require that the parties act in each other's presence. Some jurisdictions validate notarized wills even if they are unwitnessed.

Statutes or judicial decisions provide alternatives to the testator's handwritten signature. One such alternative is having someone else sign on her behalf. The testator might be unable to sign because of physical injury, or she might be illiterate. If someone other than the testator signs the will, the testator must acknowledge that the will was signed on her behalf. An illiterate testator might also use a mark to denote her signature. If the will is witnessed, the witnesses must sign their names; the jurisdiction might allow them to use a mark if they are also illiterate. Because challengers could argue that an illiterate testator did not understand the terms of the will, having witnesses who can attest to her competency might be more important than if she is literate.

The testator must execute her will in the presence of witnesses, acknowledge to witnesses that she previously signed the will and that this is her signature, or acknowledge that another person signed the will on her behalf and at her request. The witnesses can testify to the signature actually being that of the testator only in the first situation. In the other two situations, they can testify only to what she acknowledged to them.

UPC § 2-502 adopts the "conscious presence" test instead of the "line of sight" test. The conscious presence test relies on any sense that the testator or witnesses could employ. It does not require that the testator be able to see the activity in question.

The UPC does not require that the testator tell the witnesses the document is her will, although it does allow her to do so. UPC § 2-502(a)(3). Some states do require informing the witnesses that it is a will. N.Y. Est. Powers & Trusts Law § 3-2.1(a)(3). Even if she indicates that it is her will, she does not have to share its contents with them. Unless she does so, they can attest only to the will's execution. This distinction becomes important if the will is lost or destroyed. Disinterested witnesses to its contents may be necessary to establish the will for probate.

The UPC does not require the witnesses to sign in the testator's presence or to sign in each other's presence. It even allows the witnesses to sign within a "reasonable time" after witnessing the testator sign or acknowledge. The comments to UPC § 2-502 indicate that a witness's signature can meet the reasonable time requirement even if it occurs after the testator's death. New York requires witnesses to sign within a single 30-day period. N.Y. Est. Powers & Trusts Law § 3-2.1(a)(4).

The UPC dispenses altogether with the requirement of witnesses if the testator acknowledges the will before a notary public or other individual authorized to take acknowledgements. The notary need not see the contents of the will. Because the individual must be personally known to the notary or must establish identity, acknowledgement before a notary satisfies the fraud prevention function served by witnesses.

Many states reject some or all of the UPC provisions. They might adopt the more stringent line of sight presence test. They might require that the testator and witnesses all act in each other's presence. They might not provide for acknowledging the will before a notary.

In recent years, many states have allowed electronic signatures by the testator and witnesses, and the Uniform Law Commission has adopted the Uniform Electronic Wills Act (UEWA). The signing "ceremonies" are supervised by a notary public who authenticates the identities of individuals he does not personally know. The parties use audio-visual technology for this purpose. UEWA § 5. A state that allows electronic wills may impose more requirements than those in the UEWA. Indiana, for example, requires the testator or witnesses be in the same room; if they are not, the ceremony must be supervised by an attorney or a directed paralegal. Ind. Code § 29-1-21-4(b).

4. Placement of Signatures

The UPC § 2-502 signature and acknowledgement provisions do not specify where any signatures must appear. The comments to that provision indicate that a signature that appears in the body of the will is acceptable. By allowing the signature to appear anywhere, the UPC avoids the litigation over whether the signature appeared—as many states require it to—at the "end" of the will. But the UPC approach could make it easier for unauthorized alterations following the testator's signature, particularly if the witnesses' signatures appear after the testator's rather than at the end.

Courts in jurisdictions that require signatures to appear at the will's end might have to determine whether a signature complied. Litigation often involves wills prepared by the testator rather than by a lawyer. The testator might have used a fill-in-the-blank paper will form designed to be folded into thirds or halves. It might include space for the testator's name on what would become the outside after the will was folded, but it would also include space for the actual signature on the inside. If the testator signed on the outside, instead of on the inside, does that constitute a signature? This could be relevant in a state such as Florida, which requires the testator and the witnesses to sign at the end. Fla. Stat. § 732.502(1)(a). The statute does not indicate whether "end" means physical end, logical end (as in following all devises), or simply the testator's last act with respect to the will.

The New York statute treats language before the testator's signature differently from language following it but does not automatically invalidate a will because the testator's signature is not at "the end." Language following his signature, other than that related to the witnesses' attestation, is simply ignored. Language preceding his signature is given effect if it is comprehensible without resort to the post-signature language and doing so would not subvert his general disposition plan. N.Y. Est. Powers & Trusts Law § 3-2.1(a)(1)(A)–(B).

5. Number and Qualifications of Witnesses

The UPC requires at least two witnesses if the testator uses witnesses rather than acknowledging her will before a notary. UPC § 2-502(a)(3)(A). The capacity requirement for being a witness is much lower than that for executing a will. A person is qualified to witness a will if he is generally competent to serve as a witness. Even a person who might benefit from the will may serve as a witness. Use of an interested witness does not invalidate the will or the devise to that person. UPC §2-505. But a devisee's participation as a witness might make it easier for challengers to succeed in claiming undue influence.

Some jurisdictions have purging statutes that apply if a witness is also a devisee. New York, for example, has alternative treatments in this situation. N.Y. Est. Powers & Trusts Law §3-3.2. First, although its statutes normally require only two witnesses, and allow a devisee to be a witness, New York voids any devise to a witness unless there are at least two witnesses who are not devisees or appointees under the will. This requirement looks to the time the will was executed and attested. Second, even if there are at least two non-beneficiary witnesses, the beneficiary-witness's devise is void if her testimony is needed to prove the will. If her devise is voided, she might recover the intestate share she would have received if the will was not admitted to probate. That amount cannot, however, exceed the amount devised to her.

The Washington statute does not automatically void a devise to an interested witness. It raises a rebuttable presumption that the devisee-witness exerted duress, menace, fraud, or undue influence unless at least two witnesses to the will were not interested. If the interested witness is unable to rebut the presumption, she cannot receive an amount greater than what she would receive if the will was not admitted to probate. Wash. Rev. Code §11.12.160.

6. Integration and Harmless Error

The testator's will (and any later codicils or separate writings) constitutes the integrated expression of her dispositive plan—at least as it relates to her probate property. For that reason, a state might require strict compliance with the execution and attestation requirements and not give effect to post-execution changes that are not made with the requisite formalities. Because the court might not always be able to determine if, when, or how an alteration occurred, the attorney who drafts the will should take additional steps to prevent post-execution changes. These steps include instructions to the testator (such as "do not make changes to the document" and "safeguard the will"). They could also include having the testator (and even the witnesses) initial each page and using a numbering system (such as Page 1 of 8) that makes it harder for anyone to insert substitute or additional pages.

UPC §2-503 provides a harmless error exception to the testamentary formalities. The will can be probated if there is clear and convincing evidence that the testator intended the document to serve as her will. This statute also applies to validate partial or complete revocation of the testator's will, additions to her will, or partial or complete revival of a revoked will (or revoked portion of a will). The comments to this section indicate that the drafters contemplate it applying in two situations: (1) the testator failed to have two witnesses; or (2) the testator made handwritten changes to the document after it was executed.

D. Validating an Invalid Will

If a testator was an unemancipated minor when he executed his will, he has three options when he reaches the age of majority: do nothing and die intestate; execute a new will; or revive his previously invalid will. The same is true for an individual who was not of sound mind when he executed his will or who failed to obtain the required number of witnesses.

If he wants to die with a valid will rather than die intestate, reviving a previously invalid will might be the best immediate solution. For example, he might be facing a medical procedure that could result in death or incapacity, embarking on a long journey, or preparing for deployment into a combat zone. He might prefer a new will but does not have time to wait for its preparation and execution.

To revive a previously invalid will, he can simply re-execute it with the formalities required for executing a will. He could also execute a codicil that revives the will; the codicil's execution would also need to follow the necessary formalities.

E. Components of a Will

We traditionally think of a will as a document that disposes of a testator's property. But that is not always the case. If an individual uses nonprobate transfers, her will might dispose of a relatively small amount of her property.

Wills have functions other than disposing of property. A testator can use a will to nominate fiduciaries. One such fiduciary is the personal representative who will administer her probate estate. If her will establishes a testamentary trust, it can name one or more trustees to manage that trust. If she devises property outright to a minor, she can indicate the person who will receive and manage the property on the minor's behalf. She can also use a will to indicate which devises bear the burden of expenses and debt. She can even use her will to revoke a prior will and die intestate.

1. Format of a Will

With the exception of requiring a signature—and perhaps requiring it to appear at the end of the will—and requiring witnesses or notarization in states that do not allow holographic wills, statutes generally do not require a will to follow any particular format. Wills prepared by an attorney, or an online provider, generally are arranged thematically—with devises in one section and administrative provisions in another—but that is not required.

2. Commonly Appearing Terms

a. Introductory Language

Despite the lack of requirements, wills often contain certain boilerplate language. The document often begins with a heading such as "Last Will and Testament of" or "Will of." Such language arguably establishes intent, as the testator presumably read the document before signing it. The "Last" language is, of course, misleading. A testator retains the right to execute a new will at any time if she has testamentary capacity, follows any necessary formalities, and is not constrained by contract or judicial decree.

Wills also commonly begin with one or more declaration sentences. There is often language that echoes the heading language regarding "Last Will and Testament." Again, that sentence does not bind the testator. Other language might indicate that the testator is "of sound and disposing mind and memory." While this language might also support a finding of testamentary intent, it is self-serving language as to capacity. A third boilerplate provision relates to revocation. A will often states: "I revoke all wills and codicils heretofore made by me" or simply "I revoke all wills and codicils." This language might appear even if this is the testator's first will. Although it is probably part of the drafter's standard will form, it does provide evidence for denying probate to a prior will.

b. Statement of Residence

The initial language usually indicates the testator's state, and perhaps city or county, of residence. In most instances, this language determines which jurisdiction's law governs the will's validity. Even if the testator later moves, the new jurisdiction will generally allow the will to be probated. UPC § 2-506 provides validity rules based on the jurisdiction in which the will was executed. A jurisdiction that adopted this section would admit a will to probate if it satisfied the execution rules, including those covering harmless error. It also validates wills that complied with the laws of the jurisdiction in which it was executed when the testator executed it. Post-execution changes in those laws would not invalidate the will. Finally, it validates wills that complied with the law of the place where the testator is domiciled, has a place of abode, or is a national at either the time of execution or the time of her death.

States that reject the expansive rules of UPC § 2-506 generally do so based on state policies regarding formalities. Jurisdictions that do not allow unwitnessed wills may refuse to admit one to probate despite its being valid in the testator's previous domicile.

Including a statement of residence does not, of course, prevent another state from asserting that the testator was actually domiciled in the second state. These challenges are most likely to involve testators with ties to more than one state, particularly those who own residences in both, when the will was executed and at death. These disputes often involve attempts to impose state estate or inheritance taxes. To avoid such post-death disputes, the attorney preparing the will is likely to counsel the testator to concentrate indicia of domicile as much as possible in the desired state. One such indicia—the driver's license—might cause problems. An individual who fears he will not pass a vision or driving test might resist surrendering a license obtained in the prior state of domicile.

The statement of residence is not the same as a choice of law provision. That provision indicates which jurisdiction's law applies during probate. UPC § 2-703 provides choice of law provisions for wills and other documents governing property dispositions. The UPC provides for allowing the governing instrument to indicate which jurisdiction's laws should apply. It makes that choice subject to three exceptions where the chosen law might be contrary to the law of the state of domicile: computing the elective share; exempt property and allowances; and any other public policy of the state. For example, Florida invalidates devises to the drafting attorney (unless the attorney is a relative); that devise would not be validated by a will indicating that the Florida domiciliary selected the law of a different state to govern. Fla. Stat. § 732.806.

c. *Devises and Administrative Provisions*

Devises can be outright or in trust. They can be to individuals or to classes of individuals. They can be to an entity (such as a charity) or a group of entities. They can be of particular items of property, including money, or of undifferentiated assets (as in a residuary devise). They can be expressed as dollar amounts or as percentages.

Administrative provisions go beyond nominating various fiduciaries. The will can indicate whether a fiduciary must post a bond, how the fiduciary is to be compensated, and what powers the fiduciary can exercise. Because these provisions are covered by statutory defaults, their omission from the will does not prevent it from being admitted to probate.

d. *Signature, Attestation, and Date*

Although the will can simply end with the testator's signature and the signatures of witnesses, it might also include language that indicates the date and what is happening. For example, the signature might be preceded by a testimonium clause. It would include language such as "Signed this 9th day of March 2024." That language might also indicate the city and state in which the signing occurred.

The witnesses' signatures might also be preceded by an attestation clause. It includes language that establishes compliance with the relevant execution and witnessing statute. If the jurisdiction follows UPC § 2-502 and does not require the witnesses to sign in each other's presence, the statement might simply read: "Signed this 9th day of March 2024, after [Name of Testator] acknowledged his signature to me." If it instead requires the testator and witnesses to act in each other's presence, a more-detailed statement would be used. If the parties use a self-proof, it might substitute for language that might appear in an attestation clause.

Including a date serves a variety of purposes. If the testator executed more than one valid will, we need to know which one came last. The most recent will either revokes any prior wills in full or revokes them as to inconsistent provisions. The date is also relevant if the will's validity is challenged based on the testator's not being of age when she executed it or not being of sound mind.

Although the will and the self-proof discussed below are normally signed as separate instruments or parts of the same instrument, jurisdictions that follow UPC § 2-504(c) allow a signature on the self-proof to qualify as a signature on the will itself.

e. *Self-Proof*

A will is not effective for transmitting property unless it is admitted to probate. Someone must present the will to the court and ask that it be admitted to probate. The court will not admit the will to probate unless it has been appropriately executed and witnessed (or satisfies the jurisdiction's harmless error statute).

The state usually provides alternate means for accomplishing this task. One or more witnesses could testify as to the will's execution and witnessing. UPC § 3-406(3). Unfortunately, witnesses can become incapacitated, die, move to a distant location, or be unavailable for other reasons. To avoid these potential problems, a will could include a self-proof. UPC § 2-504 authorizes this method and provides a model self-proof form that will drafters can copy. State statutes use the UPC language or similar language.

A will is self-proved if the testator and witnesses appear before a notary or other official authorized to take oaths. The testator signs a statement indicating that the document is his will, which is another indicator that he had testamentary intent. The form also indicates that he is at least age 18 (or other required age) and that he is of sound mind, under no constraint or undue influence, and is acting voluntarily. Although the testator is probably certain of his age, the other statements in the self-proof are merely his opinion.

The witnesses also sign the self-proof affidavit. Their statement indicates that the testator signed the document in their presence and hearing. Because the UPC does not require that witnesses sign in each other's presence, the self-proof does not say they signed in each other's presence. A state that requires each party to be in the other's presence will use different language for this part of the self-proof. The witnesses' statement indicates that the document is a will, a requirement that does not exist when there is no self-proof, and that the testator signed willingly. The witnesses also indicate that—to the best of their knowledge—the testator meets the age and sound mind requirements and is not acting under constraint or undue influence.

UPC § 2-504(a) provides that the testator and witnesses can simultaneously execute (testator), attest (witnesses), and acknowledge before the notary or other officer. UPC § 2-504(b) authorizes completing the self-proof at a later date. Because the testator must sign the self-proof, this document cannot be used if—as allowed by UPC § 2-502—the witnesses attest the will after the testator's death.

Although a self-proof includes statements about the testator's sound mind and freedom from undue influence, it is not evidence of those characteristics. The self-proof simply provides evidence that the will was properly executed.

3. Formalities and Admission to Probate

If disappointed persons challenge a will based on improper execution, the procedure for admitting the will to probate varies based on the documents used. A self-proved will can be admitted to probate without any testimony regarding its execution. Testimony will be taken only if there is evidence of fraud or forgery regarding the acknowledgement or affidavit. UPC § 3-406(1). If the testator did not use a self-proof but had her will notarized, there is a rebuttable presumption that the will was correctly executed. UPC § 3-406(2). This option applies if the jurisdiction allows notarized, but unwitnessed, wills. If the will is neither self-proved nor notarized, the testimony of a witness can be used to establish proper execution. The witness must be present in the jurisdiction, competent, and able to testify. UPC § 3-406(3). Other evidence might be presented if there are no attesting witnesses who satisfy those requirements. An out-of-state witness could submit an affidavit. Presumably the preparing attorney—if present at the execution—could testify. If the will includes an attestation clause, UPC § 3-406(3) provides a rebuttable presumption that events stated in that clause actually occurred.

Note that the self-proof, notarization, or testimony discussed here relate solely to the execution of the will. They do not prevent challenges based on lack of capacity, fraud, mistake, duress, undue influence, or spoliation. Nor do they establish the terms of a lost will, a will destroyed by someone who was not the testator or acting at the testator's direction, or a will destroyed by the testator that might be eligible for revival based on dependent relative revocation. These issues are discussed in other chapters.

CHECKPOINTS

- A will is not valid unless the testator has testamentary capacity. She must be of age (or meet an alternate state requirement such as emancipation or marriage), and she must be of sound mind.

- Litigation over the testator's mental capacity generally focuses on whether she understood the nature of her property, the identities of the objects of her bounty, and the effect of her estate plan.
- States generally require that the testator execute the will and that at least two attesting witnesses also sign the will.
- Witnesses need not see the contents of the will and might not even know they are witnessing a will.
- The UPC requires the testator to sign the will or acknowledge a previous signature in the witnesses' presence. It does not require the witnesses to sign in each other's presence or even in the testator's presence. It allows witnesses to sign within a reasonable time after the testator executes the will.
- The UPC uses a conscious presence test for acts that must occur in the presence of the testator or a witness. This test is often easier to meet than the line of sight test that some states might use.
- The UPC validates a will (or its revocation) if there is harmless error regarding formalities for execution or revocation. The testator's intent must be proved by clear and convincing evidence.
- A minority of states allow oral wills in limited circumstances, such as a testator who will be fighting in the military.
- States that allow holographic wills might require that they be entirely in the testator's handwriting or that the material portions be handwritten. A will that is properly witnessed is not treated as holographic even if it is handwritten.
- If a testator uses a notarized self-proving affidavit, he and the witnesses indicate the steps taken in signing and witnessing the will. Self-proof forms indicate that the testator indicated that the document was his will. The witnesses do not have to see the contents of the will.
- Self-proving affidavits are a means of offering the will for probate without presenting the testimony of any witnesses to its execution.

CHAPTER 7

Categorizing Devises

ROADMAP

- Language used to describe devises
- Precatory language
- Types of devises

A. Chapter Overview

This chapter covers ways to categorize devises. Although this topic is relevant primarily to wills, you might occasionally encounter it in other situations. For example, a settlor could provide for different types of gifts when the trust terminates and beneficiaries receive the trust principal. Later chapters describe situations in which these categories are relevant to the distribution of the testator's property.

B. Language Used to Describe Devises

Although this book refers to transfers by will as devises, you might encounter other terminology. At common law, the term devise referred to a transfer of real property; bequest referred to a transfer of personal property. The recipient of a devise was a devisee; the recipient of a bequest was a legatee.

Although the UPC and many state statutes refer to the will's dispositions as devises, they do not require that the testator use that term. Do not be surprised if you encounter wills that state: "I devise," "I bequeath," "I give," or even "I give, devise, and bequeath." These examples are not exclusive. If the personal representative (or a court, if necessary) can ascertain the testator's intent to transfer property, less common language—such as "Joe is to receive"—will suffice.

C. Precatory Language

Because terminology is evidence of the testator's intent, wills that change their terminology from one clause to another can cause problems. Did the testator mean something different if one provision reads "I devise Blackacre to Joan," while another reads "I want Rob to have Whiteacre"? A will that uses each term multiple times could indicate only a desire to change language. But if the will uses "I want" only once or twice and uses more definite language many times, we should consider whether "I want" is precatory.

Precatory language expresses the testator's hopes rather than imposing an obligation on the personal representative or other person named in the precatory provision. The clearest examples of precatory language are "I hope," "It is my hope that," and perhaps even "I wish." When a provision is merely precatory, the potential beneficiary cannot enforce the devise and must rely on the goodwill of the person to whom the precatory language is addressed.

D. Types of Devises

The four types of devises are specific; demonstrative; general; and residuary. A devise's classification involves the following questions, which are covered in later chapters:

- Is the devise subject to ademption by extinction?
- Can the devise be changed by a separate writing that is less formal than a will or codicil?
- Is the devise reduced because the estate includes exempt property?
- Does the devisee take the devise subject to encumbrances?
- In what order do devises abate to pay claims, expenses of administration, elective share, and shares of an omitted (pretermitted) spouse or child?

- Does the devise include post-death earnings or interest?
- How is the devise treated for purposes of federal or state estate or inheritance taxes?

1. Specific

A specific devise is a devise of a particular item or type of item owned by the testator. It often includes the word "my" or the term "that I own." Each devise below is a specific devise:

- I devise my house to Donna.
- I devise my bracelets to Denise.
- I devise the portraits I inherited from my mother to Dean.

The devise to Denise is specific although the testator did not identify each individual bracelet. Because a will is a public document, she might not want anyone to know more about the items Denise received. In addition, she might contemplate acquiring additional bracelets after executing her will. If she listed only the bracelets she owned when she executed the will, Denise would not receive the later-acquired items.

Specific devises can involve interpretive issues. Consider the following devises by a testator who owned three sets of china when she died:

- I devise my china to Deborah.
- I devise my good china to Deborah.
- I devise my favorite china to Deborah.

The first devise arguably covers each set of china even though it doesn't say "I devise all my china to Deborah." The third devise arguably covers only one set, but the will does not indicate which one. The second devise might cover one, two, or even all three sets. Determining what is devised could involve the relative value of each set, the times each set was used, and statements the testator made when using the china.

Specific devises are usually conditional. The devisee might receive nothing unless the testator owns the property when she dies. The doctrine of ademption by extinction eliminates the devisee's rights unless the will or a statutory rule of construction provides an alternate devise.

2. General

A general devise is a devise of a sum of money or type of item that the testator might, but does not have to, own at death. In other words, a general devise is not conditioned on the testator's owning the devised property at death. A devise such as "I devise $50,000 to Doug" is a general devise. Compare it to "I devise the money in my account at the XYZ Bank to Doug." The second devise is a specific devise. Doug receives whatever funds are in that account; if the account was closed, Doug might receive nothing.

Although general devises are often used to devise money ("pecuniary devise"), a testator can make a general devise of other items. The following are arguably general devises:

- I devise $10,000 worth of Apple stock to each of my children.
- I devise a new smart phone to each of my eight grandchildren.

Neither of the devises above uses "my," "if I own it at my death," or similar language. Indeed, with respect to the second devise, it is unlikely that the testator owned the same number of smart phones as the number of her grandchildren.

3. Demonstrative

Demonstrative devises share characteristics with both specific and general devises. In common with general devises, they can be of property the testator does not own at death. But if the testator indicates property to be used first in satisfying the devise, the devise is treated as specific to the extent of that property. It is treated as general for the remainder of the devise.

> **Example 7-1.** Ted's will provides: "I devise $150,000 to Della. Take the funds from my accounts at ABC Bank before using any other assets to satisfy this devise." If Ted had $150,000 (or more) at ABC Bank, those funds will be used to satisfy the devise to Della. The devise is treated as specific for purposes of abatement and any other characteristics affected by the type of devise. If he had only $40,000 at ABC Bank, his personal representative will satisfy the remaining $110,000 from other estate assets. In that case, Della will receive a $40,000 specific devise and a $110,000 general devise.
>
> **Example 7-2.** Tillie's will provides: "I devise 100 shares of Apple stock to Dexter. Any Apple shares I own at my death shall be used to satisfy

this devise before my personal representative acquires shares from other sources." The devise to Dexter is specific to the extent, up to 100 shares, of any Apple shares Tillie owned at her death. If Tillie owned fewer than 100 shares, the remainder of the devise is general.

Although a devise is initially characterized as demonstrative, it ends up—depending on the size of the fund specified—being either totally specific, totally general, or part specific and part general.

4. Residuary

A residuary clause devises any property that was not covered by specific, demonstrative, or general devises. The testator might use language such as:

- I devise the residue of my estate to Delores.
- I devise the rest of my property to Dean.
- I devise the rest, residue, and remainder of my assets to Drew.

A testator could divide the residuary devise between devisees, either in fixed proportions or by types of property. Each of these are potential residuary devises:

- I devise the residue of my estate 60% to Delores and 40% to Drusilla.
- I devise my remaining real property to Dean and my remaining personal property to Donald.

Because the residuary devise includes only what is left after paying claims and expenses of administration and satisfying specific and general devises, it might appear the residuary devisee has no rights. That is not entirely accurate. For example, if the residue initially consists of property the residuary devisee wants, he might be able to prevent the personal representative from selling that property by transferring its cash value to the estate for payment of claims. Assuming the residue is otherwise sufficient to satisfy claims and allowances, property he desires will not be distributed to satisfy homestead rights, family allowance, or a pecuniary devise. UPC § 3-906(a)(2)(C).

Note that a will might contain only one devise: "I devise all my property to Doreen." That devise is effectively a residuary devise.

CHECKPOINTS

- In determining the testator's intent, a court distinguishes enforceable devises from precatory language. Precatory language does not create an enforceable devise.
- A will can include specific, demonstrative, general, or residuary devises.
- A specific devise is a devise of a particular asset. The devise is conditional; it could fail if the testator does not own the devised asset at death.
- A general devise is usually of a particular amount of money or easily acquired property. Because it is not conditional, the devise does not fail if the testator does not own the property at death.
- A demonstrative devise has characteristics of both specific and general devises and is ultimately treated as one or the other or partially as one and partially as the other. Although it is not conditioned on the testator owning the asset at death, it does name a fund (such as a particular bank account) from which the personal representative should satisfy the devise before looking to other estate assets.
- A residuary devisee receives probate property that was not specifically, demonstratively, or generally devised.

CHAPTER 8

Amending, Revoking, and Reviving a Will; Reformation and Modification

ROADMAP

- Amending a will
- Revoking a will or codicil
- Reviving a revoked will or codicil
- Timing versus importance of inconsistent documents
- Waivers and succession agreements
- Reformation and modification

A. Chapter Overview

If a testator executes his first will shortly before dying, we do not consider any prior will or amendments to that will. If he instead executes his first will much earlier, he might decide that its contents no longer serve his dispositive goals. If he continues to have testamentary capacity, he can amend the will or revoke it. He can also supplement it with dispositions made in other documents. This chapter considers amendments, revocation, and other means for changing dispositive provisions.

B. Amending a Will

1. Codicil

The UPC does not separately define codicil. Instead it includes codicil within its definition of will. UPC § 1-201(57). A codicil is commonly treated as a minor amendment to a will, involving changes that are not significant enough to require the preparation of a new will. The change might be dispositive, such as adding a new devise or devisee. It might instead be administrative, such as nominating a different personal representative or changing the order in which devises abate to pay debts. Because a codicil is treated as a will, the capacity and formalities requirements applied to a will also apply to a codicil.

> **Example 8-1.** Teresa's will had three provisions: "I devise my car to my sister Sue; I devise $500 to my high school English teacher, Mrs. Smith; I devise my remaining property to my brother." Two years after executing her will, Teresa executed a codicil. It provided: "I devise my car to my stepson Seth." The codicil amended Teresa's will. Seth receives the car instead of Sue.

2. Revocable Inter Vivos Trust

This book covers trusts in greater detail in later chapters. The discussion here focuses on one aspect of trusts—using a revocable inter vivos trust to amend a will. As discussed in Chapter 4, wills are only one means for disposing of property. The property owner could make outright gifts, establish a survivorship tenancy in land or other property, or use beneficiary designations for bank or securities accounts, life insurance policies, or annuities. Finally, she could transfer property to a trust. She generally retains a right to revoke or amend the trust. Instead of directly amending her will, she could devise property to a trust that she can amend until her death.

Assuming the trust was created with the requisite formalities, it can include any type of property. One set of beneficiaries might receive rights to trust income; another set might receive rights to trust principal. While she has the right of revocation, the settlor can change a beneficiary's rights or completely eliminate them.

> **Example 8-2.** Tessa created the Tessa Inter Vivos Trust and transferred property to its trustees. The trustee is to pay income to Tessa for life, then

to her children for life. When her last surviving child dies, the trustee is to pay the trust principal to Tessa's descendants. Tessa later executed a will with one devise: "I devise one-half of my property to my children and one-half to the trustee of the Tessa Inter Vivos Trust." Each time Tessa adds property to her trust, she reduces the amount her children will receive outright under the will. Each time she takes property out of her trust, she increases the amount they will receive under the will. Each time she amends the trust's distribution provisions, she changes the rights of one or more beneficiaries.

A devise to a revocable inter vivos trust is valid even though the testator can revoke or amend the trust after she executes her will. UPC § 2-511. This UPC provision is separately issued as the Uniform Testamentary Additions to Trusts Act. A state may have enacted it even if it did not enact the UPC. The devise to the trust lapses, unless the will provides otherwise, only if the trust is revoked or terminated. A partial revocation does not cause the devise to lapse.

UPC 2-§ 511 validates devises to a trust established during the testator's lifetime. It also validates devises to a trust established after his death by a devise. In the latter case, the devise is not testamentary if its terms are set forth in a written instrument that itself is executed before, after, or concurrently with the execution of the will. The term "established" is the critical term. The comments to this section indicate that this term refers to funding the trust, not to creating it.

UPC § 2-511 validates this type of devise even if made to a trust established by someone other than the testator. It provides that property devised to an inter vivos trust is administered under the terms of the trust rather than under the terms of the will.

3. Acts of Independent Significance

UPC § 2-512 allows events to affect the will's dispositions. This provision applies only if the act or event has significance beyond how it affects the testator's will. The will must refer to the event, including an event that can occur after the will is executed or even after the testator's death. UPC § 2-512 lists only one such event—the execution or revocation of another person's will. There are no comments to this UPC provision.

Example 8-3. Tom's nephew received a 20-year prison sentence two years ago. Tom wants to devise property to his nephew only if he has been released from prison before Tom dies. Tom can include a provision devising property under those circumstances. His nephew's release from prison has significance beyond its effect on Tom's will.

4. Incorporation by Reference

UPC 2-§ 510 allows a testator to incorporate another document into her will by indicating her intention to do so in the will itself. The document must exist when she executes her will, but she does not have to include the document's terms in her will. She can name the document in her will or simply describe it sufficiently to permit her personal representative to identify it. Incorporation by reference can be used to devise any type of property. Because the document must exist when she executes her will, she cannot incorporate a document that is amended after that date.

A document can be incorporated by reference even if it is not signed by the testator or by anyone else. The document does not have to be prepared by the testator.

Example 8-4. Tammy devised "Whiteacre to the individuals named in the residuary clause of my late father's will." Tammy has incorporated part of her father's will into her will.

Example 8-5. Terence devised "to my children any amounts still owed me by ABC Corporation pursuant to the February 2, 2024, contract selling my business to ABC." Terence has incorporated the contract into his will. The devise is valid even though Terence might ultimately receive all payments due before he dies. His rights would be eliminated by full payment, not by a change in the contract's language.

5. Separate Writing

As discussed earlier, a testator normally amends a will by executing a new will or by executing a codicil. Each document requires compliance with certain formalities, usually the signature of a testator and more than one witness. Rather than make the testator execute a new will or codicil to make minor changes in his devises, a state might authorize using a less formal separate writing for this purpose.

UPC § 2-513 authorizes using a separate writing to dispose of tangible personal property. The will or codicil must authorize the use of such a writing.

The writing can be made before the will is executed, or it can be prepared later. The testator can alter the list after creating it. The separate writing need not have any significance other than disposing of the testator's property. The UPC does not require that the separate writing even refer to the will.

The separate writing must identify the items and devisees with reasonable certainty, but it does not have to use specific names or list specific items. A devise of "my clothing to my children" should suffice; the testator does not have to name her children or list each item of clothing. Because the separate writing, like the will and any codicil, might be a public document, its devises need not be any more specific than those found in the more formal documents.

The testator must sign the separate writing, but no witnesses are required. Although the lack of witnesses increases the likelihood of forgery, two limitations offset the potential risk. First, as noted above, the writing can cover only tangible personal property. It cannot be used to devise real property. Nor can it be used to devise stocks, bonds, copyrights, trademarks, or other intangible property. UPC § 2-513 specifically states that it cannot devise money. Second, it usually cannot devise an item that was specifically devised in the testator's will or codicil. A testator who owns a valuable item of tangible personal property—say a painting by a famous artist—is likely to specifically devise that item in an appropriately executed and witnessed will or codicil.

A testator might be able to forgo the second protection if her will or codicil indicates that one or more devises in the will apply only if not covered by the separate writing. In this situation, the devise in the will or codicil is conditioned on the separate writing not covering the same item. Comments to UPC § 2-513 authorize this method.

Because of the limitations above, a separate writing will most likely devise items that would otherwise be part of the residue. It might also limit the items that would otherwise be sold to satisfy general devises, pay claims and expenses, and satisfy statutory family rights.

Example 8-6. Timothy's will had four provisions: "I devise my car to my sister; I devise $500 to Charity X; I devise my remaining property to my brother. I may also devise property by a separate writing." Two years after executing his will, Timothy executed a separate writing that devised his cuff links to his best friend Dean. Instead of being part of the residuary devise to Timothy's brother, the cuff links are treated as devised to Dean.

Some statutes differ from UPC § 2-513 by specifically providing for more than one writing. In those jurisdictions, each list is effective. For any inconsistencies, the most recent writing governs. For that reason, it is important that the testator be advised to date the document even if the statute does not require a date. A state might limit separate lists to items that are not used in a trade or business. Fla. Stat. § 732.515. The UPC eliminated that limitation in 1990. A statute might also differ from the UPC in its treatment of money represented by coin collections, even if the coins are also legal tender. Fla. Stat. § 731.1065.

Because the separate list items are part of the probate estate, a testator should also consider whether he wants the lapse/antilapse or ademption by extinction provisions that apply to the will provisions to also apply to items governed by the separate list.

6. Distinguishing Between Incorporation by Reference and Separate Writing

Because some documents might qualify as being incorporated by reference and as separate writings, it is easy to forget that the underlying rules are different. A document that is incorporated by reference must be in existence when the will is executed; it can cover any type of property; it does not require a signature or witnesses; it can be prepared by someone other than the testator; and it cannot be amended after the will is executed. A document that qualifies as a separate writing need not be in existence when the will is executed; it can cover only tangible personal property not specifically devised in the will; it requires the testator's signature; and it can be amended after it is initially prepared (including after the will is executed). Both documents require language in the will regarding their use. Because it is already in existence, the will must use more specificity when it incorporates a document by reference.

7. Using Incorporation by Reference to Re-Establish a Revoked Trust

Even a revoked inter vivos trust is probably represented by a document. A testator can take advantage of this fact by including a will provision that reinstates a previously revoked trust. He is incorporating the terms of the trust into his will.

This mechanism is subject to one limitation. As indicated in the discussion of incorporation by reference, its use is limited to documents in existence when the will is executed. Those documents cannot be amended at a later date. Inter vivos trusts, on the other hand, can be amended or revoked until the settlor dies or relinquishes those rights. A testator who wants to use incorporation by reference to reinstate a revoked trust can reinstate only the trust provisions that existed when he executed his will.

> **Example 8-7.** Sam established the Sam Inter Vivos Trust on March 1, Year 1. He executed his will on May 1, Year 2. His will devised the residue of his estate to the Sam Inter Vivos Trust. Sam amended the trust on August 1, Year 6. He died in Year 8. The personal representative of his estate will distribute the residue to the Sam Inter Vivos Trust, as amended in Year 6.
>
> **Example 8-8.** Sam instead revoked the trust in Year 7. The personal representative of his estate will distribute the residue to Sam's intestate heirs. The will did not incorporate the trust's terms by reference.
>
> **Example 8-9.** Assume that Sam's will provided "If the Sam Inter Vivos Trust dated March 1, Year 1, has been revoked before my death, I devise the residue of my estate to the trustees named in that trust instrument to administer the trust according to its terms on the date of this will." If Sam revoked the trust in Year 7, the personal representative will distribute the residue to the reestablished Sam Inter Vivos Trust, as it read on May 1, Year 2, not as it read after the amendment in Year 6.

C. Revoking a Will or Codicil

1. By a Writing

A testator can use a writing to revoke a will completely, revoke a codicil completely, or revoke only part of a will or codicil. Because the UPC treats a will as including a codicil to that will, it does not separately deal with revocations of codicils. Instead, they are covered by the general language of UPC § 2-507(a)(1), which provides for the revocation of a will or any part thereof by a writing. That writing can revoke the original document expressly or by inconsistency.

a. *In General*

UPC § 2-507 addresses two types of later writing: a writing that replaces the will and a writing that supplements it. The language of the new writing is our starting point. If it expressly revokes the old will, we presume that the new will replaces the old will. Even if it does not expressly revoke the prior document, UPC § 2-507(b) provides that it replaces the old will by inconsistency if that was the testator's intent.

The UPC relies on presumptions to determine testator intent. If the new document makes a full disposition of the testator's probate estate, we presume it was meant to replace the original document. A challenger who argues that the new will only supplements the old will must rebut the presumption by clear and convincing evidence. UPC § 2-507(c). If the new document does not make a full disposition of the testator's probate estate, we presume it was meant to supplement the original document. A challenger who argues that the new will replaces the old will must rebut the presumption by clear and convincing evidence. UPC § 2-507(d). In either case, a state might provide for a preponderance of the evidence standard.

Both wills are probated if the new will only supplements the old will. Because each is subject to the same testamentary formality requirements, the later document governs those inconsistencies. It is the most recent evidence of the testator's intent.

b. *Complete Disposition*

The distinction between replacement and supplementation is based on whether the new document made a complete disposition of the testator's property. The comments to UPC § 2-507 indicate that a document that does not make a complete disposition is more like a codicil to the old will than a replacement will.

That term is potentially misleading. It does not require the will to list every item the testator owned. The new will makes a complete disposition if its provisions cover all his probate property; the easiest method for doing this is to include a residuary devise.

> **Example 8-10.** Tom's first will had two provisions: "I devise $100 to Ed; I devise my car to Ella." Tom's second will also had two provisions: "I devise my stocks and bonds to Mike; I devise my stamp collection to Myra." Tom owned additional property at the time he executed these wills. Neither will made a complete disposition of Tom's probate estate; neither had a residuary clause covering items he did not list. Unless a challenger

overcomes the presumption by clear and convincing evidence, we will probate both wills. Because Tom had no residuary clause, his intestate heirs will receive any property not covered by these four clauses.

Example 8-11. Terry's first will had two provisions: "I devise my stocks and bonds to Gene; I devise the residue of my estate to Gloria." Terry's second will also had two provisions: "I devise $500 to Jeff; I devise my television to Joann." The first will made a complete disposition of Terry's probate estate; the second will did not. Unless a challenger overcomes the presumption by clear and convincing evidence, we will probate both wills. The second will merely supplements the earlier will.

Only an interested person—someone who would be affected by the outcome—can challenge the probate of a will. In Example 8-10, the dispute is between Tom's intestate heirs and Ed-Ella. If the court had found that the second will replaced the first will instead of supplementing it, his intestate heirs would receive the property devised to Ed and Ella. In Example 8-11, the dispute appears to be only between Gloria and Jeff-Joann. But that is not really the case. If the second will supplements the first will, Gloria would indeed receive less because Jeff-Joann would receive $500 and the television. But if the second will replaced the first will, neither Gloria nor Gene would receive anything. Terry's intestate heirs would receive the property that did not go to Jeff-Joann. Because the second will did not make a complete disposition of Terry's property, the potential intestate heirs could overcome the presumption only by clear and convincing evidence that Terry intended to revoke the first will.

Example 8-12. Tillie's first will had two provisions: "I devise $1,000 to Harry; I devise my book collection to Hilda." Tillie's second will also had two provisions: "I devise my car to Larry; I devise the residue of my estate to Lisa." The first will did not make a complete disposition of Tillie's probate estate; the second will did.

Example 8-13. Ted's first will had two provisions: "I devise $600 to Ned; I devise the residue of my estate to Nora. Ted's second will also had two provisions: "I devise my boat to Roger; I devise the residue of my estate to Rita." Each will made a complete disposition of Ted's probate estate.

In Examples 8-12 and 8-13, the second will makes a complete disposition of the testator's estate. In each case, we start with the presumption that the first will is revoked. Only Nora, in Example 8-13, will definitely receive nothing. If Ted's second will replaces his first will, her devise is revoked. Even if his second will only supplements his first will, her devise is revoked by the later inconsistent devise to Rita. To receive their devises, Harry and Hilda (Example 8-12) and Ned (Example 8-13) must establish by clear and convincing evidence that the second wills were meant only as supplements to the first even though they included residuary clauses.

c. *Inconsistency*

Assuming that the later document only supplements the first, we probate both. If there are no inconsistencies, the devisees of each will receive their devises. The comments to UPC § 2-507 indicate that some inconsistencies might require the court to ascertain the testator's intent. These inconsistencies are likely to involve general devises to the same person. The court must determine if the second devise replaces the first devise or is in addition to it.

> **Example 8-14.** Tyrone's first will had two provisions: "I devise $100 to Charles; I devise my car to Carol." Tyrone's second will also had two provisions: "I devise $50 to Charles; I devise my car to Chris." The devises of the cars are inconsistent. Chris receives the car under both the replacement and supplementation interpretations. If the second will replaced the first, Charles receives only $50. If the second will supplements the first, the court will try to determine whether Tyrone intended for Charles to receive $50 or $150.

2. By Act

UPC § 2-507(a)(2) applies to revocation by act. It allows a testator to revoke a will—or a part of a will—by performing a revocatory act. Alternatively, the testator can direct another person to perform the revocatory act on his behalf; that person must act in the testator's conscious presence. The testator must have the intent and purpose of revoking the document.

The UPC lists several revocatory acts: burning; tearing; canceling; obliterating; or destroying. It provides that a burning, tearing, or cancellation does not have to touch any of the document's words. The comments note that, with respect to cancellation, the UPC language is inconsistent with most of the case law. The comments also note that performing a revocatory act upon the testator's signature is generally deemed to be a revocation of the entire document.

Example 8-15. Immediately after he decided to revoke his will, Thomas ran it through his shredder. Thomas revoked his will by act. If he had shredded only a later-executed codicil, only that codicil would be considered revoked.

State law regarding revocation by act might differ from UPC § 2-507(a)(2). A state might not treat an act that does not touch any words as a revocatory act. Even if the act touches words, the state might apply an all or nothing test. For example, some statutes allow revocation of an entire document but not of a portion of the document if the revocation is by act. Fla. Stat. § 732.506; 755 Ill. Comp. Stat. Act 5 § 4-7. Finally, if the testator asks another person to destroy the will, a state that uses the line of sight test for will attestation is likely to also use it for revocation by act.

Because probate does not commence until after the testator dies, she will not be there to testify and there may have been no witnesses to the revocatory act. It could be impossible to prove that the act was performed by the testator (as opposed to a disappointed potential beneficiary) and that her intention was revocation (as opposed to an accidental act). In those situations, courts apply presumptions that might not be necessary for written revocations. We generally presume that the testator acted and had the requisite intent and purpose if we can establish certain facts. The testator must have had possession of the will. No one with an adverse interest can have had access to the will. No external event, such as a flood or forest fire, might have caused the destruction. The testator must have had the requisite capacity to form the intent to destroy.

3. By Change of Circumstances

The testator's family status might change after he executed his will. In addition to marrying or divorcing, he might have children by birth or adoption. One or more of his devisees might die before he does.

At one time, marriage revoked a woman's will, but that is no longer the case. Although a change in status might change the effect of certain devises, it does not revoke the will. UPC § 2-508. Events that invalidate devises and rights acquired by a spouse or child omitted from the will are discussed in other chapters.

D. Reviving a Revoked Will or Codicil

1. By Revoking the Revocatory Document

UPC § 2-509 covers reviving (or not reviving) a revoked will. It addresses three situations. The first two apply when the later revocation was by revocatory act. The third applies when the later revocation was done by a writing.

If a later will completely revoked an earlier will, the earlier will is not reinstated merely because the testator uses a revocatory act to revoke the later will. The earlier will is reinstated only if the testator revives it. UPC § 2-509(a) does not require that the testator follow the testamentary formalities when reviving the earlier will. Proponents of the earlier will can establish that it was revived based on the circumstances of the later revocation or based on the testator's declarations that he intended to have the original will be effective. Those declarations can be made at the time he revoked the subsequent will or later.

If the later will only partially revoked an earlier will, the revoked earlier will provisions are revived if the testator uses a revocatory act to revoke the later will. The earlier provisions will not be revived if the court determines that the testator did not intend revival. It bases its decision on the circumstances of the later revocation or the testator's declarations. UPC § 2-509(b). The UPC differentiates this situation from the first situation based on the difference between the revoking documents. The complete revocation is treated as a substitute will, while the partial revocation in the second situation is more in the nature of a codicil. The comments indicate that the testator is more likely to realize that a complete revocation vitiates the original will.

If the later will that revoked an earlier will is revoked by an even later will, the revoked original will (or revoked portion thereof) is not reinstated until it is revived. Revival can be determined based on the language of the latest will. UPC § 2-509(c). Because the testator used a writing—the "final" will—it is not unreasonable to expect that will to indicate his intentions regarding the original will.

> **Example 8-16.** Tom's original will devised $100,000 to Debby, $100,000 to Boris, and the residue to Rita. A year later, Tom executed a new will in which he devised all his property to Robert. Two years later, Tom tore up the second will. In the absence of facts indicating that Tom intended to revive the first will, he will die intestate.
>
> **Example 8-17.** Instead of an entirely new will, Tom executed a codicil eliminating the devise to Boris. Two years later, Tom tore up the codicil.

In the absence of facts indicating that Tom did not intend to revive the devise to Boris, that devise is reinstated.

Example 8-18. Instead of tearing up his second will in Example 8-16, Tom executed a third will revoking the second will. The third will did not mention the original will. If the third will itself made devises, the original will probably stays revoked. If the third will simply revoked the second will but made no devises, the court might treat it as reinstating the original will on the theory that executing a will is incompatible with a desire to die intestate.

States that have not adopted a statute resembling UPC § 2-509 may require more formality to reinstate a previously revoked will or codicil. They may follow the UPC in making it easier to infer that revocation of a codicil reinstates the earlier devise but that revocation of a revoking will does not. States that require more formality are likely to require that the revoked will be re-executed or that the testator execute a new will or a codicil reviving the revoked provisions.

2. Dependent Relative Revocation

An individual who executes a will—even an invalid will—has decided to avoid intestacy. If it is her first will, and it is valid, she has probably succeeded. If it is not valid, she has failed. But what if it is not her first will? She might have previously executed a will and later revoked it. If her new will is valid, it governs her probate property. But if her new will is not valid, we must decide whether she dies intestate or whether the terms of the revoked will govern. This decision revolves around the judge-made doctrine of dependent relative revocation (DRR).

DRR is based on the premise that the decedent would rather have her property pass under the terms of her revoked will than by intestacy. The probate court reinstates the revoked will by holding that it was only conditionally revoked rather than unconditionally revoked. The relevant condition is her new will being valid. The court will not invoke the doctrine if it cannot determine that the revocation was conditional. Nor will it invoke the doctrine unless it can determine that she would prefer the terms of the revoked will to intestacy.

The doctrine is most likely to be asserted if the testator validly revoked the prior will by act and executed an invalid later will. It is less likely to be asserted if she revoked her earlier will by a writing. Because the writing must be executed with the required testamentary formalities, there will be witnesses who can testify that the revocation occurred. When a testator revokes a will by act, she often does so without witnesses.

The validity of each event is significant. If she invalidly revoked the prior will—either by act or by a writing—it is still valid, and there is no need to assert DRR. The same is generally true if she validly revoked the prior will and executed a valid new will. In that case, the valid new will applies.

Because the testator is deceased, the court must base its decision on ascertainable events, relevant testimony, and the documents themselves. With regard to events, it is important to determine if the original will was actually revoked. If the executed will cannot be found at all, or has been burned or mutilated, the court initially presumes the testator destroyed the will with the intention of revoking it. But that presumption can be rebutted by showing individuals with an adverse interest had access to the will. If the court decides that the testator did not destroy the will with the intention of revoking it, there is no need for DRR. The will is still valid.

If the testator destroyed the will in the presence of witnesses, the court must determine if the testator intended to destroy the will, had the requisite capacity, and was revoking the will because she was replacing it by a new will. It will hear witness testimony as to what the testator said and whether the testator understood the consequences of her actions. The court will probably give more credence to testimony by disinterested witnesses than to heirs who would gain from intestacy.

The length of time between the two actions is also relevant. If the testator destroyed the old will shortly before executing the new will, the court is more likely to determine the destruction was conditioned on the new will's validity. If a year or more passed between the two actions, the court is more likely to determine the destruction was unconditional. There is no bright-line test regarding timing. For example, it might treat the situation of a testator who was hit by a car and spent two years in a coma a day after destroying her old will quite differently from that of a testator who destroyed her old will and didn't even consult her attorney about a new one for five months.

A comparison of the valid old will and the invalid new will might be the deciding factor. If the two wills were generally similar, the court is likely to decide that the testator preferred the old will to intestacy. If the two wills were quite different, the court will probably decide that she would prefer intestacy. Even the degree of similarity is subject to judicial interpretation. In one case, for example, the two wills had different primary devisees, but they had one feature in common. Neither devised property to the individuals who would take if the decedent died intestate. *Wehrheim v. Golden Pond Assisted Living Facility*, 905 So. 2d 1002 (Fla. Dist. Ct. App. 2005).

E. Timing Versus Importance of Inconsistent Documents

When two documents conflict, the later in time usually governs. But, as indicated earlier in this section, that is not always the case. There are situations in which the more important document governs. That is usually the document whose execution requires more formalities or that represents a fuller expression of the testator's plan. Thus, an earlier will prevails over the language of a later separate writing unless the will provides otherwise. A separate writing requires only a signature, while a will generally requires both a signature and witnesses (or acknowledgement to a notary in states that recognize this option).

The same rules might apply when a document that amended or revoked an earlier document is itself revoked. A will might be considered more important than a codicil because it generally addresses the testator's entire estate rather than a few provisions. If the testator revokes the underlying will, he revokes any later codicil amending it. If he instead revokes only the codicil, he does not necessarily revoke the original will. Revoking the codicil might even result in reviving the earlier, revoked will provision.

F. Waivers and Succession Agreements

Spouses might enter into agreements before or during marriage in which they waive one or more of their statutory rights. Agreements made during marriage often occur during a separation or pending divorce or annulment, and are included in a property settlement agreement, but that is not required. If the waiver is effective, the spouse is treated as renouncing any will provision benefiting her. This rule does not apply to will provisions executed after the waiver is made. It also does not apply if the waiver or property settlement provides otherwise. UPC § 2-213. Because a waiver is treated as a renunciation, the property will pass as if the spouse had predeceased the testator. Waivers are discussed in more detail in the next chapter.

Waivers involve only spouses or prospective spouses, and they cover only marital rights. Spouses might want to make an agreement based on succession by their children or other beneficiaries. For example, each spouse might be willing to devise property to the other spouse on the condition that the surviving spouse then devise it to their children. Individuals who are not married to each other might also want to memorialize certain goals in a succession agreement. One individual might agree to render services to another in exchange for receiving a devise when the service recipient dies. Not surprisingly, each party wants the agreement to be binding on the other party because neither can predict the order in which they will die.

UPC § 2-514 governs succession agreements. It covers three types of contracts: (1) to make a will or a devise; (2) not to revoke a will or devise; or (3) to die intestate. Because these contracts all limit an individual's normal right to freely dispose of her property, you should not be surprised that the UPC imposes conditions on their enforcement. Each of these methods requires a writing to establish the contract.

The first method is to include material portions of the contract in a will. The second method is to make an express reference in a will to the contract, which can then be proven by extrinsic evidence. The third method is to have a writing signed by the decedent that evidences the contract. Because a will might be lost or destroyed, the party seeking to enforce the contract might prefer that the contract be memorialized in both the will and a writing separate from the will.

UPC § 2-514 also negates a presumption that some states might use in interpreting a joint will or mutual wills. The UPC provides that the execution of either of these does not alone establish a contract not to revoke either party's will.

> **Example 8-19.** Harry and Wendy executed a single will, which was properly witnessed. Under its terms, whichever of them survives receives the other's property. When the survivor dies, their descendants will receive all their property. Unless the jurisdiction treats this joint will as contractual, the surviving spouse is free to revoke the will by executing a new will. It might be impossible for the survivor to revoke the original will by act if it is in the possession of the court that oversaw probate when the first spouse died.
>
> **Example 8-20.** Hal and Wanda executed reciprocal provisions in their wills. Hal devised all his property to Wanda; if she failed to survive, to

their descendants. Wanda devised all her property to Hal; if he failed to survive, to their descendants. Unless the jurisdiction treats mutual wills as contractual, the second spouse to die can revoke his or her original will by executing a new will or by simply destroying the old will.

A state must also determine whether contracts between spouses prevent a subsequent spouse from asserting rights to the property involved. Even if Hal did not change his will after Wanda died, the state might allow his new spouse to claim an elective share or rights as an omitted (pretermitted) spouse. If the mutual wills did not create a contract, the new spouse has such rights. Even if the new will did create a contract, state policy protecting spouses might trump the contract provisions. Situations such as this might be avoided if Hal and Wanda place their property in trust or if Hal obtains a valid waiver from his new spouse.

The UPC is concerned with establishing a contract exists. It does not cover any state law contract requirements, such as consideration or fairness. It does not address whether one party can revoke before the other party dies or what notice requirements are necessary if revocation is possible. If one party breaches the contract, the third-party beneficiaries might be able to have a constructive trust imposed on the recipient of the property following a breach.

G. Reformation and Modification

UPC § 2-805 allows the court to reform a will if there is clear and convincing evidence that the challenged terms were based on a mistake of fact or law. The proponent must establish the testator's intent by clear and convincing evidence. The will can be reformed even if it is unambiguous.

These provisions apply whether the challenged terms were caused by a mistake of expression or a mistake of inducement. The former involves erroneous language—omitting language the testator wanted included, including language she did not want, or misstating her intent. This type of error could result from a drafting error. Mistakes of inducement involve language that is accurate, but the will contains an error attributable to the testator's misunderstanding of the law or of the operative facts. She might have erroneously believed, for example, that she could not exclude one or more of her children from a devise to children.

The comments to UTC § 415, on which UPC § 2-805 is based, indicate that the standard of clear and convincing evidence is used because of the risks involved in relying on extrinsic evidence as to what the testator's intent really was. Reformation involves changing language as opposed to interpreting existing language, which is involved in resolving ambiguities.

UPC § 2-806 provides for modification of a will if its terms do not comport with the testator's tax objectives. Unlike reformation based on mistake, modification based on the testator's probable tax objectives does not include a clear and convincing evidence standard. This makes sense in view of what is likely at stake. If a will is reformed for nontax reasons, some devisees are likely to receive more at the expense of others, who will receive less. When it is modified to reflect the testator's tax objectives, the outcome is likely to be that the devisees receive more (and the taxing authorities receive less). Modification might not be effective, however, against the claims of the relevant taxing authorities.

CHECKPOINTS

- A testator can amend a will formally by executing a new will or a codicil. Each requires the same formalities as a will.
- A testator can indirectly amend a will by making an inter vivos transfer to a trust, incorporating another document into the will, or devising property in a separate writing.
- A separate writing is valid only if the will indicates that one is possible. It generally can be used only for limited types of property.
- A testator can revoke a will or codicil by a writing or by performing a revocatory act (burning, tearing, canceling, obliterating, or destroying).
- A will that makes a full disposition of the testator's property is treated as revoking the original will even if words of revocation are not used.
- A will that does not make a full disposition of the testator's property generally revokes only the inconsistent portions of the earlier will.
- A testator can reinstate a revoked will by reviving it. If the original will was only partially revoked by the later will, he might be able to reinstate the earlier will by revoking the later one.

- Dependent relative revocation revives an earlier will if the later will was invalid and the court determines the valid revocation of the earlier will was conditioned on the validity of the later will.
- A change in marital status does not revoke a will but might affect the validity of some of its provisions.
- Although a later document generally governs if it is inconsistent with an earlier document, less-formal documents such as separate writings do not supersede earlier, inconsistent will provisions.
- Individuals can make succession agreements that cover rights to make a will or a devise, not to revoke a will or devise, or to die intestate.
- Statutes generally require a writing to make such contracts enforceable.
- The mere execution of joint or mutual wills is not sufficient to establish the existence of a contract.
- A will can be reformed if there is clear and convincing evidence that one or more terms were based on a mistake of fact and law. The testator's intent would also have to be established by clear and convincing evidence.

CHAPTER 9

Family Protection Statutes

ROADMAP

- Homestead
- Exempt property
- Family allowance
- Omitted spouse or child (pretermission)
- Elective share
- Forced heirship
- Community property
- Waiver of spousal rights

A. Chapter Overview

The intestacy statutes discussed earlier divide an intestate's estate among her surviving family members. Those statutes favor her surviving spouse, descendants, and parents over other relatives. If the decedent's probate property passed under the terms of her will, the intestacy statutes do not apply. The same is true for property she owns as a joint tenant with right of survivorship and for most property that passes under a beneficiary designation, such as life insurance proceeds.

This chapter addresses several benefits available to the decedent's relatives. Some apply to both testate and intestate estates. Some apply only to probate property. Some apply only in the absence of a contrary will provision. Some affect particular items of property, while others cover a particular share of the estate. They vary in terms of which family members can claim the benefit and whether the benefit augments or substitutes for a gift, devise, or other provision for that family member.

These provisions benefit surviving family members. A state that adopts the UPC definition of survivorship requires survivorship by at least 120 hours. Other states might require only actual survivorship.

B. Homestead

1. UPC Homestead Allowance

UPC § 2-402 provides a homestead allowance. The allowance amount was set at $22,500 in 2008. States that have enacted UPC § 1-109 or a similar provision increase the amount to reflect increases in the cost of living.

Assuming no waiver or disclaimer, the surviving spouse is entitled to the homestead allowance. If there is no surviving spouse, the allowance is divided equally among the decedent's surviving minor children and dependent children. Adult, nondependent children do not receive an allowance even if the decedent had no surviving spouse, minor child, or dependent child and even if the adult, nondependent children were members of the decedent's household. The comments note that the set amount, which is relatively small, minimizes the consequences of providing for one group of children and not for another group.

The homestead allowance is superior to all claims against the estate; it cannot be reduced by those claims and is paid ahead of them. The spouse or eligible children receive it in addition to intestate share if any property passes by intestacy. They receive it in addition to any devise for them in the decedent's will unless the will provides otherwise. The spouse receives it in addition to his elective share.

UPC § 2-405(a) allows the surviving spouse (or qualifying children) to satisfy the homestead allowance from estate assets; he is not required to select money. He cannot select specifically devised property unless the estate is not otherwise large enough to satisfy the homestead allowance rights.

The homestead allowance is payable even if the decedent did not own a home. Although the allowance thus provides funds to continue rental, mortgage, or other household maintenance expenses, it is not premised on the surviving spouse or children actually needing those funds.

Example 9-1. Irene died intestate, survived by her husband Hal and three minor children. She and Hal lived in a rented home. At her death, Irene's only asset other than household furniture and clothing was a bank account that held $500,000 she had won in a lottery. Hal is entitled to a homestead allowance. The portion of the $500,000 remaining after subtracting that allowance will be used to pay claims against her estate and then divided between Hal and the children in the proportions specified in the intestacy statute.

Example 9-2. Tillie's will devised $100,000 to her husband Hiram, and devised the remainder of her property to their children and grandchildren. It did not mention any specific item of property. Hiram is entitled to the homestead allowance. He is also entitled to $100,000, assuming that much remains after the personal representative satisfies claims against Tillie's estate.

Example 9-3. Tillie's will instead provided for reducing Hiram's devise by the homestead allowance. Hiram will receive the homestead allowance. He will receive less than $100,000 of his devise because the $100,000 will be reduced by his homestead allowance.

Although Hiram received only $100,000 in Example 9-3, the fact that part of it was homestead allowance is significant. Because homestead allowance is exempt from the claims of creditors, Hiram will receive that amount even if claims eliminate the rest of his devise.

2. UPC Constitutional Homestead Provision

The UPC includes an optional section for use in states that give the surviving spouse or child a constitutional right to the homestead or to an interest in the homestead. UPC § 2-402A provides for subtracting the value of the constitutional right from the homestead allowance provided by UPC § 2-402.

Example 9-4. Irwin died intestate, survived by his wife Wilma and his daughter Deanna, who was the child of his late wife Laura. Under the state constitution, Wilma received a life estate in the homestead; the remainder would go to Irwin's descendants. Wilma's homestead allowance is reduced, and might even be eliminated, by the value of her life estate. That value will reflect both the value of the homestead and Wilma's life expectancy.

3. State Provisions

Read the state statute and constitution carefully. A state might provide homestead rights only if the decedent actually owned a home. It might give the surviving spouse only a life estate, but it might also allow her to elect a tenancy in common or other ownership interest in the property. The state might allow the decedent to offset any devise to the spouse by the value of homestead rights, or it might prevent any such offset. The Florida homestead provisions are particularly strict: a decedent who is survived by a minor child cannot make a valid devise of homestead to anyone. Fla. Stat. § 732.4015. Despite the minor child's existence preventing a devise, that child's rights to homestead are no greater than that of the decedent's adult children.

C. Exempt Property

Exempt property statutes have several common characteristics. First, they cover specific types of property. Second, they protect specific family members. Third, they do not eliminate security interests in the otherwise-exempt property. Fourth, they do not apply if the property is specifically devised.

UPC § 2-403 provides for exempt property in two ways. It sets a limit on the value of property treated as exempt, and it lists the types of eligible property. The value limit was set at $15,000 in 2008. States that have enacted UPC § 1-109 or a similar provision increase the amount to reflect increases in the cost of living. The UPC amount is based on the value of the property in excess of security interests. Thus, an automobile worth $18,000, but subject to a $4,000 loan, counts as only $14,000 of the UPC dollar limit.

The UPC treats five items as exempt property: household furniture; automobiles; furnishings; appliances; and personal effects. A state statute might differ from the UPC by including additional items or different dollar limits. A state statute might ignore dollar limits and provide limits based on other factors, such as limiting the number of automobiles. It might subject only some items to dollar limits or other limits.

The UPC provides for using other estate assets to satisfy a deficiency in exempt property. For example, if the decedent owned none of the assets listed in UPC § 2-403, the spouse (or qualified children) could select other assets equal in value to the statutory limit.

Assuming no waiver or disclaimer, the decedent's surviving spouse is entitled to the exempt property. If there is no surviving spouse, exempt property inures to the benefit of the decedent's surviving children. The children do not have to be minors or dependent on the decedent for support.

If otherwise qualifying property has been specifically devised, the spouse or children cannot claim it as exempt if their rights can be satisfied with other estate assets. UPC § 2-405(a). State statutes might follow this rule or might completely disallow claiming property specifically devised to another devisee.

> **Example 9-5.** The state in which Tasha lives follows UPC § 2-403. Tasha devised $100,000 to her husband Homer. She devised her stocks and bonds to her daughter Darlene. She devised the residue of her estate to her son Sam. If the residue includes exempt property, Homer can claim that property in addition to the $100,000. If Tasha had instead devised her car to her sister, Homer could not claim it as exempt property unless other assets were insufficient to satisfy his exempt property rights.

Exempt property rights are superior to all claims against the estate other than security interests in the exempt property. These rights cannot be reduced by those other claims and are paid ahead of them. The spouse or eligible children receive exempt property in addition to intestate share if any property passes by intestacy. They receive exempt property in addition to any devise to them unless the will provides otherwise. The spouse receives it in addition to his elective share. If the estate is not large enough to fully satisfy homestead allowance, family allowance, and exempt property rights, the personal representative is to satisfy homestead allowance and family allowance first. UPC § 2-403.

D. Family Allowance

UPC § 2-404 authorizes paying a reasonable allowance to maintain qualifying family members during the estate's administration. It imposes a one-year cut-off period if the estate is not sufficient to pay other claims. The allowance covers the surviving spouse, minor children if the decedent was obligated to support them, and children he was actually supporting. Some states also include support for other relatives the decedent was actually supporting.

The family allowance is exempt from claims against the estate. The homestead allowance is superior to the family allowance; exempt property rights are not. The family allowance is paid in addition to intestate share if any property passes by intestacy. It is in addition to any devise to eligible recipients in the decedent's will unless the will provides otherwise. The spouse receives it in addition to his elective share and other allowances.

UPC § 2-405(a) limits the family allowance to a maximum amount, which can be reduced based on the other resources available. The statutory maximum, which can be paid in a lump sum or in monthly installments, is $27,000. That amount is subject to the UPC § 1-109 inflation adjustments. A state might provide for a different maximum amount or a different time limit for payments. Although UPC § 2-405(a) limits using specifically devised property to satisfy homestead allowance and exempt property rights, it does not do so for family allowance.

E. Omitted Spouse or Child (Pretermission)

An individual might change her marital status from unmarried to married or from married to unmarried before she dies. She might also give birth or adopt a child. Unless a waiver applies, the distribution of her intestate estate is affected by the change in her marital status. It might also be affected by the birth or adoption of a child. But what about the distribution of her property if she has a valid will?

The UPC and individual state laws address the treatment of a spouse or a child who is omitted from the testator's will with statutes covering pretermitted spouses and children. The UPC refers to them as omitted spouses and children or as spouses and children who are unprovided for in wills. UPC § 2-301 applies to the surviving spouse only if the will is executed before the marriage. UPC § 2-302 generally applies only to a child who is born or adopted after the will is executed. The spouse can waive her rights in advance or can disclaim them after the decedent's death.

1. Omitted Spouse

a. Qualifying as Omitted

UPC § 2-301 applies if the testator executed his will before marrying his surviving spouse. It applies whether or not his will includes a devise to that individual. If a state adopts this section as written, its courts might still consider whether a devise made before marriage was made in contemplation of marriage—which would rule out pretermission—or not. States that require that the will omit a devise to the spouse must consider why any premarital devise occurred.

> **Example 9-6.** Tammy, an only child, lived next door to Linda, Mary, and Ned when they were children. After Tammy's parents died, she executed a will devising $15,000 each to Linda, Mary, and Ned and the residue to a charity. Tammy married Ned 15 years after that; she later died without revising or revoking her will. Ned would be entitled to his intestate share of Tammy's estate under UPC § 2-301. The $15,000 devise would not matter. Because her will did not omit him, courts in states that required omission would have to decide if the $15,000 devise was in contemplation of marriage. Because she also devised $15,000 to Linda and Mary, and the marriage occurred 15 years later, the court would probably decide that the devise to Ned was not in contemplation of marriage and that he was an omitted spouse.

The surviving spouse does not have omitted spouse rights if it appears that the testator executed her will in contemplation of their marriage. That determination can be made from language in the will or from other evidence. As noted above, a spouse is not precluded from being considered omitted merely because he received a devise in the will. Omitted spouse rights are precluded if the will expresses the testator's intention that the will should apply as written despite any subsequent marriage. Finally, the decedent can provide for the surviving spouse by another type of transfer. Her statements in providing for the spouse by a trust, by a beneficiary designation, or in some other manner are evidence that preclude omitted spouse status. Even if she made no statements regarding the other transfers, UPC § 2-301(a)(3) provides for inferring her intent based on other factors, including the relative size of the nontestamentary transfer.

b. Computing and Satisfying the Spouse's Share

An omitted spouse is entitled to receive an amount based on what would have been her intestate share if the decedent had died intestate. If the decedent is not survived by descendants (or parents in some states), her intestate share could be the entire probate estate.

UPC §2-301(a) describes the amount to which the spouse is entitled by referring to any child of the decedent who is not the surviving spouse's child. That reference has three prongs: the child must have been born before the testator executed his will; the child must not be the surviving spouse's child; and the testator must have devised property to that child. In that situation, the value devised to the child is subtracted from the estate before computing the omitted spouse's share.

> **Example 9-7.** When Harry executed his will five years ago, he was unmarried. He devised his entire estate to his sister Selma. Harry married Wendy last year. He died a month ago, survived only by Wendy and Selma. He had not executed a new will or revoked his old will. Wendy is entitled to all of Harry's probate estate. That is what she would have received if Harry had died intestate.
>
> **Example 9-8.** When Bert executed his will five years ago, he was married to Freda, but they were separated and they later divorced. Bert and Freda had a child, Cora. Bert executed his will after Cora was born but before meeting his second wife Lisa. That will divided his estate equally between Cora and Bert's sister Angie. When Bert died, he was survived by his second wife Lisa, his sister Angie, and his daughter Cora. Lisa is entitled to a portion of Bert's probate estate but not to all of it. Because Bert had a descendant who was not Lisa's, her intestate share would be only a portion of his probate estate. Lisa's share will be a portion of the property that otherwise would go to Angie.
>
> **Example 9-9.** Same as Example 9-8 except that Bert's will devised \$100,000 to Cora and the residue to Angie. The amount on which Lisa's share is computed is reduced by the \$100,000 devised to Cora. Cora met all three requirements for reducing Lisa's omitted spouse share. Angie's devise will be reduced by Lisa's omitted spouse share.

UPC §2-301(a) makes the same reduction if the devise was to the child's descendants or if property would have passed to the child or her descendants under the state's antilapse statute.

Example 9-10. Ted adopted Celina 10 years ago. Five years ago, he devised his entire estate to his mother Minnie. Last year, Ted married Wanda. Minnie died six months ago. Ted died last week without revising or revoking his will. Minnie predeceased Ted, but—because she is a descendant of Ted's grandparent—the devise to her is preserved in her descendant Celina by virtue of the antilapse statute. Although Wanda is an omitted spouse, her share is $0. All of Ted's probate property passes to Celina. She was adopted before he executed his will, and she is not Wanda's child.

To fund the spouse's share, we reduce the share of one or more devisees. If the surviving spouse received a devise in the will, that amount is treated as in full or partial satisfaction of his rights. He does not receive the devise and his omitted spouse share even if the devise was not in contemplation of marriage. The normal rules of abatement then apply, but with one exception. Devises to children or their descendants that are ignored in computing the spouse's share do not abate to satisfy it. UPC §2-301(b). As is true for actual intestacy, the omitted spouse's rights are based on the amount of the probate estate available for distribution after satisfying claims against the estate and other rights that take priority over distributions to intestate heirs or devisees.

Some states treat an omitted spouse more favorably. Those states give the omitted spouse his full intestate share even if that reduces the share of a child born before the marriage occurred.

Example 9-11. Jim adopted Alice 10 years ago. Five years ago, he devised his entire estate to her. Last year, Jim married Betsy. Jim died last week without revising or revoking his will. If the UPC provisions for omitted spouses do not govern, Betsy is likely to receive 50% of Jim's probate estate. That would likely be her intestate share because Jim had a descendant (Alice) who was not Betsy's descendant.

2. Omitted Child

a. *Qualifying as Omitted*

UPC §2-302 applies to a child who was born or adopted after the testator executed his will, and who was omitted from that will. Even if the child meets these conditions, she will not receive an omitted child share if it appears from the will that the omission was intentional or provision was made for her outside the will. As with the omitted spouse, the effect of any provision outside the will can be based on the testator's statements or on factors such as the size of the nontestamentary transfer. UPC § 2-302(b).

UPC § 2-302 uses born or adopted language in its comments. As a result, it can be interpreted as not covering a child who was born before the will was executed but whose existence was unknown to the testator.

A child is not omitted from the will, even if her name does not appear, if the will makes a class gift to children. If the will both describes a class and names the members in existence when the will was executed, the probate court will have to determine if the language created a true class gift.

UPC § 2-302(c) gives one other child omitted child rights. If the testator omitted a child from his will because he mistakenly thought the child was dead, that child shares in the estate in the manner of an omitted child. States that do not provide for a child in this situation might allow reformation of the will to cure the testator's mistake if there is clear and convincing evidence that he would have otherwise included the child.

b. *Computing and Satisfying the Child's Share*

The UPC computes the omitted child's share based on two factors: whether the testator had at least one living child when he executed his will; and what the testator devised to the omitted child's parent or to the testator's other children. UPC § 2-302(a).

If the testator did not have a living child when he executed his will, each omitted child might receive an amount equal to her intestate share. The child does not receive this amount if the testator devised the entire estate (or substantially all of it) to her other parent. The other parent must survive the testator and be entitled to take the devise. If the child receives an omitted child share, the rules of abatement in UPC § 3-902 determine which devises abate to fund it. UPC § 2-302(d).

> **Example 9-12.** Horton devised $100 to his church and the remainder of his estate to his wife Winona. When he executed his will, he had no children. Horton and Winona's child Callie was born a year before Horton died. There is no evidence that he purposely omitted her from his will. Although Callie was omitted from the will, Horton devised substantially all his estate to Winona. If Horton and Winona had divorced before his death, Callie would be entitled to an amount equal to her intestate share.
>
> **Example 9-13.** Horton instead devised one-half of his estate to his mother and the other one-half to Winona. Callie would be entitled to an amount equal to her intestate share whether or not Horton and Winona

were married when he died. Horton did not devise substantially all his estate to Winona.

If the testator had one or more living children when he executed his will, but he devised nothing to any of them, the omitted child receives nothing. In other words, she will not be in a better position than those other children. If the testator did make a devise to at least one such child, an omitted child receives a fraction of the devises made to those other children. The fraction's denominator includes all children to whom devises were made and all omitted children. It does not include children born or adopted before the will was executed but omitted from the will. If some children were devised more than others, the reduction in those shares is ratable rather than equal. To the extent possible, the court is to preserve the character of the testator's testamentary plan, including whether the gifts to the children are outright or in trust and are present or future interests.

Example 9-14. Tamara executed her will shortly after she adopted her fourth child. She devised $100,000 to her son Seth, $75,000 to her son Seymour, $75,000 to her daughter Dianne, nothing to her daughter Doris, and the residue to her brother Brad. A few years later, Tamara adopted two more daughters, Daphne and Delia. Tamara died without ever revising or revoking her will. Daphne and Delia are omitted children. They share the $250,000 devised to Seth, Seymour, and Dianne. Although Tamara had six children, we count only the three who received devises and the two omitted children. Daphne and Delia each receive one-fifth of the $250,000—$50,000 each. We reduce the devises to the other children by two-fifths to satisfy the Daphne and Delia's shares: Seth's by $40,000, Seymour's by $30,000, and Dianne's by $30,000. The amount devised to Brad is not reduced to satisfy their shares.

Some states depart from the UPC by simply giving the child the amount he would receive had the decedent died intestate. In states that give the surviving spouse a 100% intestate share if the spouses had all their descendants in common, the omitted child would receive nothing even though his siblings were provided for in the will.

Example 9-15. Same as Example 9-14, but Tamara lived in a state that gives the child his intestate share. Daphne and Delia would each receive one-sixth (because there were six children) of Tamara's probate estate. That amount would likely be taken first from Brad's residuary share, through abatement, instead of from the devises to Seth, Seymour, and Dianne.

F. Elective Share

The elective share derives from such common-law spousal protections as dower. It is designed to assure that a surviving spouse receives a specified value based on a percentage of the deceased spouse's property or of the couple's combined property. By extending spousal rights to nonprobate property, elective share statutes make it difficult for a decedent to disinherit his spouse through nonprobate transfers to others. The UPC refers to the amount used to compute the spouse's elective share as the augmented estate. UPC § 2-202(a). Some jurisdictions might call it the elective estate. Likewise, a jurisdiction might use the term forced share rather than elective share.

The UPC computation has two important features. First, the length of the marriage affects the surviving spouse's rights. A surviving spouse from a short-lived marriage may be entitled to as little as 1.5% of the augmented estate. The spouse's percentage reaches 50% for marriages that have lasted at least 15 years. UPC § 2-203(b)(Alternative A). If the spouse's rights are less than a specified amount, she receives a supplemental elective-share amount. UPC § 2-202(b). Second, the UPC takes into account the decedent's probate property, certain property interests he transferred (or is treating as having transferred) to others, certain property interests he transferred (or is treating as having transferred) to the surviving spouse, and the surviving spouse's property and transfers to others. It does not simply compute the elective share as a percentage of the decedent's probate estate or combined probate and nonprobate property.

The spouse is entitled to the elective share in addition to homestead allowance, exempt property, and family allowance rights. UPC § 2-202(c). She cannot claim both a full elective share amount and her intestate share rights, omitted spouse rights, or rights to devised property. The elective share computation takes those potential rights into account.

State versions might differ from the UPC by applying a single percentage rather than a sliding percentage. They might compute the surviving spouse's rights only with respect to the value of the decedent's probate property. They might ignore property owned by the surviving spouse. They might take into account whether the decedent had children. They might apply different cut-off dates in determining which transfers are brought back into the computations. They might provide for a different order of contribution toward the spouse's elective share. Georgia provides a year's support but no elective share. Ga. Code Ann. § 53-3-1.

In working through an elective share statute, focus on what powers, interests, and transfers are included in the computation, how those powers, interests, and transfers are valued, and how the spouse's elective share is funded.

1. Computing the Augmented Estate

a. Decedent's Net Probate Estate

The starting point for computing the spouse's elective share is the net probate estate. The personal representative determines the value of the probate assets and then subtracts the items listed in UPC § 2-204: funeral and administrative expenses; homestead allowance; exempt property; family allowance; and enforceable claims. That computation reflects two value judgments. First, claims and expenses have priority over donative transfers and allowances. Second, the spouse's rights to certain allowances and exempt property take priority over other donative transfers and are in addition to her rights to elective share, intestate share, or share of an omitted spouse.

b. Transfers the Decedent Made to Third Parties

If the decedent never made any nonprobate transfers, directly or indirectly, his net probate estate might be the only value attributable to him used in computing the spouse's elective share. If he did make such transfers, we continue with transfers he made to third parties. The three major categories of such transfers are covered by UPC § 2-205.

1. Property Owned or Owned in Substance

If the decedent, immediately before death, had ownership rights with respect to four types of property, his augmented estate includes some or all of the value of those items. UPC § 2-205(1). For property included in this category, it does not matter if he acquired the property by gift or with his own funds. The decedent had the ability to own the property in this category before his death. If he had acted on that ability, the property would have been included in his probate estate. By not acting, he is indirectly transferring it.

First, the augmented estate includes the value of any property over which he had a presently exercisable general power of appointment. Property is included in this computation if it passed to someone other than his estate or his surviving spouse. It does not matter if the property passed because he exercised the power or because he released it or allowed it to lapse.

If the decedent owned property as a joint tenant with right of survivorship, and the property passed to someone other than his spouse, the value of his fractional share is included in the augmented estate. The value of any account he owned with a pay on death, transfer on death, or co-ownership with right of survivorship registration is also included if it passed to someone other than his estate or his spouse. If the decedent was the sole owner of a POD or TOD account, the full value is included. If he was a co-owner of a multiple-party account, only the value of his ownership interest is included. That interest is not based on the number of co-owners; it is instead based on how much he could have withdrawn without being liable to his co-owners. Finally, the augmented estate includes the proceeds of a life insurance policy payable to someone other than his estate or his surviving spouse if he either owned the policy or had a presently exercisable general power of appointment.

Example 9-16. Paul had a power to appoint one-third of a trust's principal to any of his mother's descendants, including himself. He could exercise this power at any time. Paul did not exercise the power, and his sister received the trust principal as taker in default. One-third of the value of the trust principal is included in the augmented estate.

Example 9-17. Barbara placed $100,000 in a bank account, which she registered as Barbara and Sue POD Carol. Sue is Barbara's sister; Carol is Sue's daughter. Because Barbara provided the entire $100,000, the full account balance—not merely one-half—is included in the augmented estate.

2. Property the Decedent Transferred During Marriage

UPC § 2-205(2) applies to two types of transfers the decedent made while he was married to the surviving spouse. It includes the value of property that he irrevocably transferred, retaining the right to possession or enjoyment of the property's income at least until his death, after which the property passed to someone other than his estate or his surviving spouse. If he retained the right to possession or income from only a portion of the property, only the value of that portion is included.

The augmented estate also includes property the decedent transferred but over which he created a power to appoint the property or the income it produced to (or for the benefit of) himself, his estate, his creditors, or the creditors of his estate. This provision applies if he could exercise his power alone, he could exercise it in conjunction with another person, or a nonadverse third party could exercise it. Property is not included under this provision if it passes to his estate or to his surviving spouse.

Example 9-18. Several years ago, Sylvia transferred property to a trust that pays income to her daughter Dora for 15 years and then pays trust principal to Dora. The trust terms gave Sylvia the power, exercisable at any time, to retake 40% of the original trust principal. Although Sylvia did not exercise this power, 40% of the value of the trust principal is included in the augmented estate.

Example 9-19. If Sylvia could appoint the property only to her creditors, the augmented estate still includes 40% of the value of the trust principal. The power need not be exercisable in favor of all four categories listed in UPC § 2-205(2)(B).

Example 9-20. Same as Example 9-18 except that Sylvia's brother Brad had the power to appoint to Sylvia. Sylvia had no power to appoint. Brad is a nonadverse party because exercising the power does not reduce his interest in the trust; Brad had no interest in the trust. As a result, 40% of the value of the trust principal is included in the augmented estate. Dora is an adverse party; exercising the power would reduce her share of the trust. If Dora had the power to appoint to Sylvia, the augmented estate would not include any of the trust's value.

3. Property the Decedent Transferred Within Two Years of Death

UPC § 2-205(3) applies to three types of transfers that occurred while the decedent was married to the surviving spouse. It applies only to transfers made during the two years ending with his death. The two-year period is an arbitrary look-back period. A three-year look-back period applies for computing the federal estate tax. I.R.C. § 2035. Some states apply a look-back period shorter than the UPC period.

The first inclusion involves property that would have been covered under UPC § 2-205(1) or (2) (other than life insurance proceeds) if the decedent's right or power had not terminated in the two-year period before his death. The value is based on the value of the property when the right or power terminated, not at the date of the decedent's death. This provision does not apply if the property passed to the decedent, his estate, or his spouse (either before or at his death).

The second inclusion covers life insurance proceeds that would have been included under UPC § 2-205(1)(D) if the decedent had not transferred the policy before death. The third inclusion covers any transfer not included under another category and made to someone other than the surviving spouse. UPC § 2-205(3)(C) thus applies to outright transfers of property over which the decedent retained no rights or powers. This provision exempts transfers below a stated amount, or—if the state prefers—the amount treated as an excluded present interest gift for federal gift tax purposes. The UPC does not exempt transfers for medical care or education that qualify for the gift tax exclusion; state statutes might also exempt those transfers.

Example 9-21. Geraldine transferred $30,000 to her grandson 18 months before she died. The gift tax exclusion was then $18,000. Only $12,000 is included in Geraldine's augmented estate if her state of residence uses the gift tax exclusion amount rather than a fixed statutory amount.

Although UPC § 2-205(3)(C) applies only to amounts exceeding the gift tax exclusion (or fixed statutory amount), it does not preclude including a transfer under another provision. The comments indicate, for example, that the creation of a survivorship tenancy within two years of death could be covered under both UPC § 2-205(1)(B) and UPC § 2-205(3)(C).

Example 9-22. Five months before his death, Frank created a joint tenancy with right of survivorship with his daughter Dina. Frank provided all the consideration. One-half of the value of the property is included in Frank's augmented estate because it represents his fractional interest immediately before his death. The amount he paid for the other one-half—minus the exemption—is also included because it was transferred within two years of his death. Note that Frank's fractional interest is valued at his death; the transfer to Dina is valued as of the time it was made. If Frank had made this transfer four years before his death, only the value of his fractional share would be included in the augmented estate.

c. *Transfers the Decedent Made to His Spouse*

UPC § 2-206 provides that the augmented estate also includes all nonprobate property passing at his death to his surviving spouse. It lists three categories, but—because those items are listed following the word "including"—the list is not necessarily exclusive. The first item is his fractional share of joint tenancy with right of survivorship property to the extent that interest passed to the surviving spouse. The second item is his ownership interest in accounts to the extent that interest passed to the surviving spouse as co-owner. The final item includes any property that would have been included under UPC § 2-205(1) or (2) if it had passed to (or for the benefit) of someone other than the spouse, surviving spouse, decedent, decedent's estate, decedent's creditors, or creditors of the decedent's estate.

d. *Property the Surviving Spouse Owned or Transferred to Third Parties*

UPC § 2-207 includes the value of property or property interests the surviving spouse owned at the decedent's death. To prevent double counting, items covered by UPC § 2-204 or UPC § 2-206 are not also included here. Items included under UPC § 2-207 include the spouse's fractional interest in joint tenancy with right of survivorship property, her interest in co-ownership accounts with right of survivorship, and property that passed to her by reason of her spouse's death. The latter category does not include homestead allowance, exempt property, or family allowance. The spouse is entitled to those rights in addition to her elective share rights. Social Security benefits are also expressly excluded.

The comments to UPC § 2-207 indicate that the spouse's ownership includes beneficial interests in addition to outright ownership. It even includes property interests created by third parties for her benefit.

UPC § 2-207 also takes into account transfers that the surviving spouse previously made to third parties. It includes the types of nonprobate transfers that would have been part of the augmented estate if the decedent had made them.

Any enforceable claims against the spouse offset the amount included under this provision. In valuing items included under UPC § 2-207, we use the value at the decedent's death for most items. If the spouse transferred a life insurance policy, we ignore the decedent's death in valuing it.

e. *Exclusions, Overlaps, and Valuation*

The augmented estate concept treats the marriage as a partnership, with each spouse's share in "partnership" assets reflecting the length of the marriage.

UPC § 2-208 adds two exclusion rules. First, we ignore nonprobate transfers made for full and adequate consideration. The consideration received in exchange for the property substitutes for the original property. Counting both the property transferred and the property received would double count the value involved. Second, we ignore transfers made to third parties by either spouse if the other spouse joined in the transfer or consented to it. A writing is required as evidence of joinder or consent. The joinder or consent is in effect treated as a waiver of the spouse's right to include that property in valuing his or her elective share rights. The comments indicate that a mere spousal consent to split-gift treatment for gift tax purposes does not qualify as a written joinder or consent.

UPC § 2-208 also provides valuation rules. It reduces the value of property transferred by the decedent or spouse by enforceable claims against the property. That reduction treats nonprobate transfers in a manner comparable to the provisions in UPC § 2-204 and UPC § 2-207(c); those provisions cover the decedent's *net* probate estate and the reduction for enforceable claims against the surviving spouse. It also provides for using the commuted value for interests such as pension rights.

Property is to be valued only once. If more than one section applies to the same property interest, the section that gives the highest value governs. UPC § 2-208(c).

2. Computing the Elective Share

After we compute the total value of property included in the augmented estate, we divide the amount in half to reflect the partnership aspect of marriage. We then multiply the spouse's half by the UPC § 2-203 percentage that reflects the length of the marriage. If that amount does not reach the UPC minimum elective share amount, we increase it by the supplemental elective share amount. UPC § 2-202(b).

3. Funding the Elective Share

The next step is to determine if the spouse's elective share has been satisfied. If it has, no further action is necessary. She does not have to return "excess" property if she received more than her elective share. If it has not been satisfied, we reduce property interests that would otherwise go to third parties. UPC § 2-209 specifies the sources used to fund her elective share. It also indicates that the additional amount she receives is treated as a general pecuniary devise; this is relevant for purposes of her right to receive interest during estate administration pursuant to UPC § 3-904. The discussion below ignores the supplemental elective share; computations for that amount differ slightly from the computations below.

The first two sources for funding the elective share also determine if the spouse has received the amount to which she is entitled. One such source is the amount included in the decedent's probate estate that passed to the surviving spouse. We include amounts that passed under a will and amounts that passed to her by intestate succession. We also include the value of nonprobate transfers to the surviving spouse covered by UPC § 2-206. The other such source is the value of the spouse's property and transfers to third parties. We count only the spouse's "marital share" of this second source. In other words, we count only the percentage based on the length of the marriage.

Example 9-23. When Horace died this year, he and Wilma had been married 10 years. That entitled her to 60% of half of the augmented estate. Horace had a net probate estate of $1 million (ignoring property used to satisfy homestead allowance, exempt property, and family allowance). Neither Horace nor Wilma had ever made any nonprobate transfers to third parties or had any other powers or interests over property; Wilma owned no property net of claims. If Horace devised at least $300,000 to Wilma, or she inherited at least $300,000 through intestate succession, her elective share rights are fully satisfied.

Example 9-24. Instead of Horace having a $1 million probate estate, Horace and Wilma each owned property worth $500,000 net of claims. Even if Wilma receives no property by devise or intestate succession when Horace dies, her elective share rights are satisfied. Multiplying the $500,000 she owns by 60% equals $300,000. That is the amount she is entitled to, as it equals 30% of the $1 million total augmented estate.

Example 9-25. Wanda and Henry were married 10 years when she died. Wanda's net probate estate was $400,000. At her death, Wanda and her brother owned Blackacre (worth $300,000) as joint tenants with right of survivorship; each had contributed equally to its purchase. Henry owned property worth $200,000. A year before Wanda died, Henry transferred cash to his son by his first marriage; the transfer equaled $100,000 more than the federal gift tax exclusion. The augmented estate is $850,000. That amount equals the value of Wanda's probate estate ($400,000), plus one-half of Wanda's interest in the joint tenancy ($150,000), plus Henry's property ($200,000), plus the amount Henry transferred to his son in excess of the exclusion ($100,000). Because the marriage lasted 10 years, Henry is entitled to 60% of half of the augmented estate, or $255,000. Sixty percent of the marital property portion of the $300,000 Henry owned or transferred equals $180,000. If Henry receives at least $75,000 from Wanda's probate estate, his elective share rights are satisfied.

If the surviving spouse's rights have not been satisfied based on property received from the decedent and property the surviving spouse owned or transferred, we reduce the property rights of other beneficiaries. UPC § 2-209 provides for satisfying the spouse's rights with property in the decedent's probate estate and property that passed to third persons under UPC § 2-205(1), (2), and (3)(B). This provision includes transfers made with retained rights and interests and transfers within two years of death with respect to a life insurance policy. Outright transfers or relinquishment of rights or powers within two years of death are not otherwise included. Probate assets and nonprobate transfers abate pro rata to satisfy the spouse's rights.

If a deficiency remains after taking into account property that passed to the spouse and the first group of nonprobate transfers, UPC § 2-209(d) then looks to any remaining nonprobate transfers made by the decedent. Contributions from these sources are also made on a pro rata basis.

4. Elective Share and Other Spousal Rights

As indicated above, the surviving spouse is entitled to elective share in addition to homestead allowance, exempt property, and family allowance. He is not allowed elective share in addition to omitted spouse share, intestate share, or devises from the decedent. Because the elective share is satisfied in whole or part by amounts passing to the surviving spouse from the decedent's probate estate in addition to certain nonprobate transfers to him, amounts received through these other rights are used in funding the elective share.

A spouse is entitled to an intestate share if the decedent dies intestate; he is entitled to his omitted spouse share amount if he qualifies as an omitted spouse. He need not elect either right. The elective share, on the other hand, is unavailable unless the spouse elects it within the time period established by statute. Although UPC § 2-405 allows the spouse to select estate assets that will fund the homestead allowance or that satisfy his exempt property rights, it does not require that the spouse elect to take these rights.

G. Forced Heirship

Louisiana has adopted a modified version of the civil law rules for forced heirship. La. Civ. Code art. 1493 defines eligible individuals as descendants of the first degree who are age 23 or younger when the decedent dies and descendants of the first degree, no matter what their age, who are permanently incapable of self-care or of administering their estates when the decedent dies. A descendant of the first degree is the decedent's child. Forced heirship also applies by representation, if the child predeceases, to any of the deceased child's children. Forced heirship by representation requires either that the descendant of the first degree have died before attaining age 24 or that the individual who would take by representation was permanently incapable of self-care or of administering his estate. A bill was introduced in the Louisiana legislature in 2024; if enacted, it would reduce the forced heir cut-off age from 23 to 18.

The amount of the forced share takes into account the number of eligible forced heirs, the amount of transfers the decedent made during life and on account of death, and the intestate share to which the heir would be entitled. La. Civ. Code art. 1495. One exception applies to forced heirship. The child can be disinherited for just cause. La. Civ. Code art. 1494.

Note that forced heirship differs from omitted child rights. It applies whether the child was born before or after the will was executed.

H. Community Property

The community-property regime in effect in Arizona, California, Idaho, Louisiana, Nevada, New Mexico, Texas, Washington, and Wisconsin treats property acquired during marriage as owned equally by each spouse. Only one-half of the couple's property thus goes through probate when one of them dies. That spouse can devise his share of community property to the other spouse but is not required to do so. Alaska has a community-property regime that requires opt-in by the spouses. A few states allow spouses to transfer property to a community property trust.

Each community-property state enacts its own rules for the treatment of property acquired when the spouses resided in a common-law property state, property acquired as a gift, and the distribution of community property if the marriage is dissolved. If a couple moves to a state that has enacted the Uniform Community Property Disposition at Death Act, assets traced to community property are presumed to retain their community-property status. Only one-half of such assets are probated in the estate of the first spouse to die.

Several UPC provisions include alternate language for adoption in community-property states.

I. Waiver of Spousal Rights

1. Overview

Spouses might waive their rights to each other's property, or to some of that property, as part of a prenuptial agreement (sometimes referred to as an antenuptial agreement). They might also do so as part of a postnuptial agreement, whether or not that agreement is in contemplation of separation or divorce. An agreement might cover waivers made by both spouses or made by only one of them.

Spouses often enter into prenuptial or postnuptial agreements to preserve property for children and other descendants from a prior relationship. They might also do so for estate planning reasons—to avoid successive rounds of probate if both spouses are elderly or in poor health or to limit estate tax if a surviving spouse is independently wealthy.

If the agreement is valid, the spouse is treated as predeceased and does not take any of the property rights she waived. In judging the validity of these agreements, you should focus on the following factors: the formalities required to make the agreement valid; the disclosure required to make the agreement valid; any state law fairness requirements; and the rights covered by the agreement.

2. UPC Provisions

UPC §2-213 governs waivers by one or both spouses of rights attributable to the marital relationship. It focuses on the timing of a waiver, the property interests that a spouse can waive, the procedure for making a waiver, and the information the waiving spouse must receive.

The waiver can occur before the marriage takes place (prenuptial or antenuptial agreement). It can occur during the marriage (postnuptial agreement). UPC §2-213(a) provides that the waiver can cover elective share, homestead allowance, exempt property, or family allowance. It can cover all of those rights or some of them. The waiver can cover a right in full, or the spouse can make a partial waiver. For example, a spouse could waive one-half of the amount she would otherwise receive as exempt property.

A waiver must be in writing and signed by the spouse who is waiving rights. UPC § 2-213(b). The UPC does not require that the spouse receive any consideration for making the waiver, but it does not prevent the other spouse from providing consideration.

UPC § 2-213(c) sets conditions for enforcing the waiver, which it applies to both prenuptial and postnuptial waivers. Some jurisdictions apply stricter conditions to postnuptial waivers, often reflecting a partnership theory of marriage. They might require little or no disclosure for a valid prenuptial agreement. Keep in mind that a waiver that satisfies statutory requirements regarding rights at death does not necessarily satisfy the requirements for rights during divorce.

A waiver is not enforceable if the spouse did not make it voluntarily. A surviving spouse who can establish that he signed under duress can avoid having the waiver enforced. It is also unenforceable unless the surviving spouse had access to independent legal advice, received an explanation in plain language (in the absence of independent legal advice), or received adequate financial disclosure. UPC § 2-213(c)–(e). A waiver is not enforceable if it was unconscionable when it was executed or if it would result in significant hardship for the surviving spouse because of a material change in his circumstances after the agreement was signed. UPC § 2-213(f). The question of unconscionability is treated as a question of law, to be decided by the court overseeing the probate. UPC § 2-213(g).

UPC § 2-213(h) makes an agreement that waives "all rights" or comparable language effective to waive not only the rights described earlier in this section but also benefits that the spouse would receive by intestate succession or as a devise in a will executed before the waiver was made. This section applies not only to typical prenuptial and postnuptial agreements but also to property settlement agreements entered into in anticipation of or following a separation or divorce. The UPC treats waivers as renunciations of rights; it does not use the term disclaimer or the term treated as predeceased.

The failure of either spouse to execute a waiver does not mean that the spouse must accept these potential benefits. The surviving spouse can also waive rights after the decedent dies by disclaiming those rights or—in the case of elective share—not filing an election.

CHECKPOINTS

- The UPC gives the surviving spouse the right to a homestead allowance, exempt property, and a family allowance. Although the UPC limits the dollar value of these rights, individual states might address homestead and exempt property with reference to the property itself.
- If the decedent does not have a spouse, or if the spouse has waived his rights, his children might take those rights in his place. The UPC limits homestead allowance to minor and dependent children and limits family allowance to minor children the decedent was obligated to support and children he was actually supporting. It allows all children to share in exempt property. Individual states might give these rights to a wider or narrower group of the decedent's relatives.
- A spouse or child who is not mentioned in the decedent's will might be entitled to a share of the decedent's estate. Neither has omitted spouse or child rights if the omission was intentional or if the decedent provided for the spouse or child by other transfers.
- A spouse might be considered omitted even though mentioned in the will if the will was executed before the marriage. A child can be treated as omitted if born or adopted after the will was executed or if the decedent omitted the child based on an erroneous belief the child was dead. State laws might not cover children the testator erroneously believed were dead.
- The surviving spouse's rights as an omitted spouse are based on what he would take if the decedent died intestate. The omitted child's rights are generally based on sharing amounts received by the decedent's other children, if any. If the decedent had no children when he executed his will, the omitted child's rights are based on the child's intestate share.
- A surviving spouse has elective share rights, which entitle him to a percentage of the value of the deceased spouse's probate estate.
- The UPC and many states also extend the surviving spouse's rights to a percentage of the value of the decedent's nonprobate property, including property transferred outright within a certain period before death.

- The elective share computation might also include the spouse's property. This inclusion might prevent the spouse from taking an elective share if he owns significant property, received nonprobate transfers from the decedent, or gave away property before the decedent died.
- The UPC bases the elective share percentage on the length of the marriage. Some states simply apply a flat percentage to the value of the property comprising their version of the augmented (elective) estate.
- Other recipients (or potential recipients) of a decedent's property have their probate or nonprobate receipts reduced if funds are needed to satisfy rights to homestead allowance, exempt property, family allowance, omitted spouse or child shares, or elective share.
- The statutes granting those rights will determine which devises and other transfers are reduced to satisfy those rights. The statutes might allow the decedent to specify the order in which devises and other transfers abate to satisfy those rights.
- Only Louisiana requires that children under age 24 and children incapable of self-care receive a portion of the decedent's estate.
- States with a community-property form of ownership treat each spouse as owning one-half of the community property. Only the decedent's one-half is probated. If a married couple moves from a community-property state to another state, the property they own when they move is likely to retain its status as community property.
- The UPC provides a mechanism for waiving various spousal rights. An enforceable waiver must be in writing and generally requires fair and reasonable disclosure of the other spouse or potential spouse's property and financial obligations. A state might require less (or even no) disclosure for a prenuptial waiver.

CHAPTER 10

Introduction to Trusts

ROADMAP

- Sources of modern trust law
- Terminology
- Express trusts
- Resulting and constructive trusts
- Other usages of the term trust

A. Chapter Overview

This chapter briefly describes sources of trust law and trust terminology. It differentiates private express trusts and charitable trusts from resulting trusts and constructive trusts.

B. Sources of Modern Trust Law

Although there are federal tax provisions dealing with trusts, there is no federal trust law governing how a trust is created or funded. Trust law is entirely a matter of state law and once was almost entirely a matter of case law. Trust law today is the product of uniform acts, Restatements, statutes, and judicial decisions.

The Uniform Trust Code codifies, and in several significant ways reforms, the law of trusts. It was initially promulgated in 2000 and was most recently amended in 2018; its comments were most recently amended in 2024. The UTC has been adopted in more than two-thirds of the states, either entirely or with modifications. Although this book cites to Restatements when discussing trusts, its primary focus is the UTC.

The UTC and state statutes based on it include several provisions referring to the common law. In those situations, the statutes operate to provide rights, responsibilities, or remedies in addition to those provided by the common law. As a result, judicial decisions issued before a state enacted its trust code or other statutes governing trusts may have continued relevance.

Judicial decisions interpreting a statutory provision are also important. They indicate how a particular jurisdiction interprets the statutory language. If the legislature disagrees with a judicial interpretation, it can revise the relevant statute.

C. Terminology

A trust is a fiduciary relationship whereby one or more persons or an entity holds property subject to an equitable obligation to use the property for the benefit of another person or persons. Although the trust mechanism is based on three distinct roles—settlor, trustee, and beneficiary—there is no requirement that three distinct persons be involved. A settlor can be a trustee or a beneficiary. A trustee can be a beneficiary. A beneficiary can be a trustee.

The trust instrument is the document that sets forth the trustee's powers and duties and names (often only by category) the beneficiaries. Contrary state statutes sometimes override provisions in the trust instrument. In other instances, provisions in the trust instrument govern instead of statutory default rules.

The person who originally owned the property and created the fiduciary relationship is referred to as the settlor, trustor, donor, or grantor. That person created the trust by transfer, by declaration of trust, or by exercise of a power of appointment. UTC § 401. This book refers to the person who created the trust as the settlor for several reasons: the term "grantor trust" has meaning in the context of federal income tax; the term donor is also used to identify a person who creates a power of appointment or who makes an outright inter vivos gift; and trustor is not a commonly used term.

The trustee is the person or persons, including an entity, holding legal title to the property subject to the equitable obligation in favor of another. The beneficiary is the person or persons for whose benefit the trustee holds the trust property. At one time, that person was referred to as the *cestui que trust.*

A beneficiary's interest might be vested or contingent. It might be present or future. Subject to any rule against perpetuities limits on vesting periods, there might be several generations of successor beneficiaries. Some successor beneficiaries will die before their interests ever become possessory; others might not be born until decades after the trust's creation. They might be ascertainable as a class but not as individuals. Still other persons are considered beneficiaries because they hold a power of appointment over trust property in a nonfiduciary capacity. UTC § 103(3).

Statutes or trust instruments often limit the trustee's duties regarding notice to beneficiaries and beneficiaries' standing to enforce a trust to "qualified beneficiaries." Those beneficiaries are either distributees or permissible distributees of income or principal; would be distributees or permissible distributees if the prior interest terminated without terminating the trust; or would be a distributee or permissible distributee if the trust terminated on the date their status is determined. UTC § 103(13). A beneficiary who is not initially a qualified beneficiary might become one based on the passage of time, the occurrence of an event, or the termination of a predecessor interest.

> **Example 10-1.** George created a trust with the following interests: income to his children for life; income to his grandchildren for life; income to his great-grandchildren for life; principal at the death of the last surviving income beneficiary to the county library. On the day George created the trust, his children, his grandchildren, and the county library are qualified beneficiaries. His great-grandchildren will become qualified beneficiaries when his last child dies (or, if sooner, when his last grandchild dies).

The property that the trustee holds for the benefit of the beneficiaries is referred to as the trust res, principal, or corpus. This book generally refers to it as the trust principal.

D. Express Trusts

An express trust is created by the expressed intention of the settlor. It is a private express trust if it is for the benefit of a particular person or persons. It is a charitable express trust if it is for a charitable purpose that provides broad public benefit. Trusts for animals, and certain other trusts that have no definite beneficiaries to enforce their terms, were once referred to as honorary trusts. The UTC and many state codes now include several of these trusts in provisions governing private express trusts.

An express trust created during the settlor's life is an inter vivos trust. An express trust created by his will is a testamentary trust. An inter vivos trust can be revocable. If the settlor does not retain the power to revoke, or later relinquishes that power, the trust is irrevocable. A trust's status as revocable or irrevocable affects trustee duties, creditor access, and other topics discussed elsewhere in this book.

Express trusts must have a purpose. Some purposes have become shorthand designations for the trust. These include elective share trusts, which can be used to fund a surviving spouse's elective share, and marital deduction and bypass trusts, which are used to reduce federal transfer tax liability. Spendthrift trusts and asset protection trusts are designed to prevent or limit access by a beneficiary's creditors. The features of these trusts are not mutually exclusive; a settlor might, for example, create an elective share trust with a spendthrift provision. Despite the varying names, these trusts are all private express trusts and must be created according to the state's rules for such trusts.

E. Resulting and Constructive Trusts

The comments to UTC § 102 indicate that the UTC does not apply to resulting or constructive trusts because neither is an express trust. They are nevertheless relevant to any discussion of trusts and estates.

1. Resulting Trusts

If an express trust fails for any reason other than illegality, or it becomes impossible to carry out its provisions, a resulting trust arises by implication in favor of the settlor, or, if she is dead, in favor of her estate. For example, she might transfer property to a trustee to pay the income to a beneficiary for life and then distribute the principal to a different beneficiary. If the second beneficiary predeceases the income beneficiary, and neither the trust instrument nor a statutory default rule provides for a successor taker, the settlor (or her estate) becomes the beneficiary of a resulting trust. A resulting trust thus resembles a reversionary interest. Although the trust principal technically "results" back to the settlor or his estate, the term "results" is awkward. This book instead refers to the property reverting to the settlor or his estate.

A purchase money resulting trust arises when one person provides the purchase price for property, and the seller conveys the property to a second person. In that situation, a rebuttable presumption arises that the second person is to hold the property in trust for the person who provided the purchase money. The trust is not based upon proof of an agreement. If it were, it would be an express trust. Restatement (Third) of Trusts § 9.

Relief is granted if the second person cannot overcome the presumption by adequate proof. The second person might raise an overriding presumption, used when the parties are related, that the purchaser intended to make a gift to him. That overriding presumption might itself be rebutted by adequate proof that no gift was intended. In that case, the original presumption would remain in place.

The second person can also rebut the presumption by providing proof that the first person paid the purchase price as a loan to him. In that case, the first person is a creditor and not the beneficiary of a resulting trust. The second person might also rebut the presumption by offering proof that he was to hold in an express trust for a third person, rather than for the person who provided the funds, even if the express trust is not enforceable because of the Statute of Frauds.

Even if the second person cannot rebut the presumption, a resulting trust might not arise if the transfer was made to accomplish an unlawful purpose. The court must determine whether the policy against unjust enrichment of the transferee is outweighed by the policy against giving relief to the person who entered into the illegal transaction.

2. Constructive Trusts

An express trust arises out of the settlor's manifested intent, and a resulting trust arises out of his inferred intent. In contrast, a constructive trust is not based on intent. Rather, it is a remedy imposed by a court to prevent unjust enrichment. The court might impose a constructive trust when a transferee-trustee induces the transfer by fraud or breach of a confidential relationship and then refuses to carry out the trust in reliance on the Statute of Frauds. Restatement (Third) of Trusts § 24. It might impose one to prevent unjust enrichment of a person who exerted undue influence over a property owner, which resulted in diminishing the assets that would otherwise have gone to different beneficiaries. It might impose one to prevent unjust enrichment of an individual who destroyed a will that benefited other individuals or that devised him less than he would have received in intestacy.

> **Example 10-2.** Tanya devised her probate estate to her sisters Sue and Sally and intentionally omitted her son Simeon. Simeon found her will and destroyed it. If Tanya died intestate, Simeon would receive her estate and be rewarded for his wrongdoing. If Sue and Sally can establish that Simeon destroyed the will, and the distribution that Tanya provided, the court might impose a constructive trust on Simeon.

Note that Sue and Sally might be unable to prove Simeon's actions or the terms of Tanya's will. A lost or destroyed will can be offered for probate if proponents can satisfy the statutory provisions for establishing its terms. In that case, there is no need for a constructive trust.

F. Other Usages of the Term Trust

The term trust is applied in other contexts. These include "in trust for" bank accounts, which have largely been supplanted by pay on death accounts; voting trusts used to maintain control of a corporation; real estate investment trusts used as investment vehicles; blind trusts used to hold assets of government officials who need to avoid conflicts of interest; and Massachusetts business trusts used to operate a business. Courses focusing on antitrust laws cover use of concentrated business power to reduce competition. With the exception of "in trust for" bank accounts, this book does not cover these other usages.

CHECKPOINTS

- Trust law is derived from the common law, much of which appears in the Restatements.
- More than two-thirds of the states have enacted the Uniform Trust Code.
- Trusts separate legal and beneficial ownership of property.
- The trustee has legal title and acts on behalf of the trust beneficiaries. The settlor of the trust might be a trustee, a beneficiary, both, or neither.
- Trusts can be created by transfer of property to a trustee, by a settlor's declaration of herself as trustee, or by exercise of a power of appointment.
- Qualified beneficiaries generally have more rights than other beneficiaries. A beneficiary who is not initially a qualified beneficiary might become one when a predecessor interest terminates or other event occurs.
- Private express trusts generally have one or more ascertainable beneficiaries. Charitable trusts are designed to provide a public benefit.
- Constructive and resulting trusts are not governed by the Uniform Trust Code. A resulting trust is imposed based on the transferor's inferred intent. A constructive trust is imposed as a remedy to prevent unjust enrichment.

CHAPTER 11

Creating an Express Trust

ROADMAP

- Settlor capacity
- Settlor intent
- Beneficiary
- Trustee with duties
- Merger of legal and beneficial interests

A. Chapter Overview

UTC § 402 adopts, with only slight modification, the traditional requirements for creating an express trust. The settlor must have capacity to create a trust; he must indicate an intention to create a trust; the trust must satisfy the requirements for a beneficiary; the trustee must have duties; and, if there is only one trustee and one beneficiary, they cannot be the same person.

In addition to those requirements, we must consider requirements regarding formalities, purpose, and funding. They are covered in the next chapter. You should read the two chapters together if that is how your trusts and estates course is structured.

B. Settlor Capacity

Although UTC § 402(a)(1) requires a settlor to have capacity, it does not specify what constitutes capacity. The comments to UTC § 402 indicate that the capacity varies based on whether the trust is testamentary or inter vivos and whether, for an inter vivos trust, it is revocable or irrevocable.

If the settlor creates the trust by language in his will, he has created a testamentary trust. That trust is valid only if the will itself is valid. The testator-settlor must have testamentary capacity when he executes the will. It does not matter if he has testamentary capacity when he dies.

A settlor who creates an irrevocable inter vivos trust relinquishes all control over his property during his lifetime. He retains no power to retake it. Because he is making a gift to the ultimate recipients, he must have the capacity to transfer property free of trust. That is a higher standard than testamentary capacity. This standard also applies if he relinquishes his right to revoke a previously revocable trust.

A settlor can retain an interest in an irrevocable trust. For example, he might irrevocably transfer property in trust but retain the income interest for life. Or he might have a contingent reversion that arises if the ultimate takers are unwilling or unable to receive the property when the trust terminates. Because these interests are not powers to revoke, they do not change the relevant capacity standard.

A settlor who creates a revocable inter vivos trust must have testamentary capacity. UTC § 601. Because the trust is revocable, he might amend the trust and change the beneficiaries or their share of trust property. He might eventually relinquish the power of revocation. We determine whether he has testamentary capacity when he creates the trust. His capacity when he amends, revokes, or relinquishes his right to revoke will be judged when he takes those actions.

C. Settlor Intent

The settlor must intend either by her agreement with the trustee at the time of transfer, or by declaration if she is to be the trustee, to create the fiduciary relationship that the law recognizes as a trust. In other words, she must intend that the trustee, whether herself or another person, hold the property in a fiduciary capacity with an equitable obligation to use the property for the benefit of another.

The settlor need not use any particular words such as "trust" or "trustee" in either the agreement or the declaration and, in fact, need not even know that what she intends is, under the law, a trust. Conversely, if the intent is that the "trustee" is to hold the property free from any fiduciary responsibility, then the fact that the agreement uses the terms "trust" and "trustee" does not create what the law recognizes as a trust. *Ponzelino v. Ponzelino*, 26 N.W.2d 330 (Iowa 1947); *Lewis G. Allen Family Tr. v. Gov't of the United States*, 558 F. Supp. 152 (D. Kan. 1982). This situation is analogous to an "in trust for" bank account used as a probate avoidance device.

Problems arise when the settlor does not use "trust language." A court may have to decide if the instrument created an express trust or was merely precatory. If a power of appointment is involved, the court must determine who takes the property. Finally, the court may have to distinguish between a trust and a purely custodial transfer.

1. Precatory Language

Very often the language used, particularly in the case of testamentary transfers, will be ambiguous. For example, a will might provide: "I leave to my nephew, Neal, all my stocks and bonds. I hope this will be a help in the education of his children."

Such language might be deemed mandatory, thus creating a trust with Neal as trustee for the benefit of his children and their education. Or the words might interpreted as creating an outright gift to Neal. The additional words would be merely a precatory suggestion as to how Neal might use the money, but they would impose no accompanying fiduciary responsibility. The testator's failure to use trust terminology is not determinative.

Unfortunately, there is no rule of law or of construction that determines the issue. Each case is decided based upon its facts and circumstances. The resolution is made even more difficult if the court refuses to admit extrinsic evidence regarding intent.

2. Power of Appointment

The creation of a power of appointment can also cause interpretive problems. For example, a will might provide: "I leave Blackacre to my brother Brad for life. At his death Blackacre shall go to whichever of my nieces or nephews he shall select. His decision in this regard shall be final."

What if Brad dies without leaving a will or any other evidence of a chosen taker? It must be determined if the testator intended to create a trust for Brad and the testator's nieces and nephews or intended only to give Brad a life estate and a power of appointment over the remainder. If Brad received a power of appointment, Blackacre goes to the beneficiary that would take under an unexercised power of appointment. That taker in default could even be the testator's estate. But that is not the only possibility. In some jurisdictions the failure to exercise a nongeneral power in favor of a limited class results in the entire class being treated as the taker in default. N.C. Gen. Stat. §31D-3-311(2).

3. Custodial Arrangement

Not every possessory relationship is that of a trustee. For example, one person might transfer property to another to hold in safekeeping for a third person. The transfer might involve no fiduciary duties other than preserving the property while in the holder's possession and delivering it at some future time. The holder might have no duty to inquire into the wisdom of retaining the property or the advisability of investing or reinvesting.

> **Example 11-1.** Tillie devised "my collection of bronze statues to my nephew, Norris. My brother Bill is to hold them until Norris reaches 21."

If this provision creates a trust, and Bill sees a decline in the value of the bronzes, he might be under a duty to sell them and invest the proceeds. If it is merely a custodial arrangement, Bill's only responsibility is to protect the bronzes and deliver them when Norris reaches 21. Again, it is a question of intent.

D. Beneficiary

An express trust must have a definite beneficiary. The UTC provides exceptions if the trust is a charitable trust, meets the UTC requirements for a trust for an animal, or meets its requirements for a trust for a noncharitable purpose.

1. Definite Beneficiary

The common law requires that a noncharitable trust have at least one identifiable beneficiary. This reflects the fact that the trustee must have enforceable fiduciary duties and must be able to determine the appropriate recipient of distributions. Because a beneficiary might be the only person who has standing to enforce the trust, a court must be able to determine the beneficiary's identity. UTC § 402(a)(3) reflects the common-law rule. It requires that the trust have a definite beneficiary or qualify for one of its exceptions.

The definite beneficiary requirement does not require the settlor to name one or more specific individuals. UTC § 402(b) treats a beneficiary as definite if he can be ascertained now or in the future. This provision is made subject to any applicable rule against perpetuities. For example, a remainder interest to the settlor's descendants, to take effect within the relevant rule against perpetuities period, is sufficiently definite.

UTC § 402(c) provides another option. It allows giving the trustee the power to select a beneficiary from an indefinite class. That power fails unless it is exercised within a reasonable time. In that case, the property will be received by those persons who would have taken it if the trustee had not been given the power to select.

What is important is that a court can determine that any person claiming to have standing to enforce the trust, or any person to whom the trustee would make distributions, is the intended beneficiary. For example, a trust with benefits to be distributed "among such of my children as the trustee may in its sole discretion determine" is a sufficient description even though the trustee might elect to make no distribution at all to some of the settlor's children. The court can determine the breadth of the intended class to grant standing and can determine whether the trustee has acted within the limits of its authority and fulfilled its fiduciary duty. On the other hand, a trust with benefits to be distributed only "to or among such of my friends as my trustee may in its sole discretion determine" is generally held to be too vague. Because "friends" is a subjective term, the court would have no objective way to determine who was or was not within the intended class of beneficiaries. In that event, the trust would fail, and its property would revert to the settlor or the settlor's estate. The trustee would not be allowed to carry out the trust.

> **Example 11-2.** Tom created a testamentary a trust with the following provisions: "My trustee is to distribute up to one-quarter of the trust's net income to those individuals who assisted me in attaining a college education and pay the remaining trust income to my children. When my last surviving child dies, my trustee is to distribute the entire trust principal to the state library." If the trustee does not exercise his power to distribute income to the individuals who assisted Tom in attaining a college education, Tom's children will receive the entire trust income. The trust will not fail even if the trustee cannot ascertain the identity of those individuals because the trust itself provides for an alternative distribution.

2. Charitable Trusts

Charitable trusts are for the benefit of the public and thus need not have identifiable beneficiaries. The state's attorney general has historically had exclusive standing to enforce charitable trusts. Additional persons, including the settlor, might have standing by statute. Charitable trusts are discussed in Chapter 14.

3. Certain "Honorary" Trusts

The Restatement (Third) of Trusts § 47 identified two types of transfers in trust that failed to have identifiable beneficiaries. If the transfer was for indefinite or general purposes, the transferee had the power, but not the duty, to use the property for those purposes. The trustee held the property not used for those purposes for the distribution to the reversionary beneficiaries. If the transfer was for a specific noncharitable purpose, the transferee held the property as trustee, generally for a limited period (normally not to exceed 21 years). Any property not used for the designated purpose was to be held for distribution to the reversionary beneficiaries. In addition, if the amount transferred exceeded amounts reasonably needed for the trust's purpose, the trustee held the excess for distribution to the reversionary beneficiaries.

Under this traditional rule, "honorary" trusts were allowed primarily for three purposes: care of specific animals; maintenance of cemetery plots; and masses for the dead. In such cases, the persons who would receive the property if the transfer failed have raised challenges based on the absence of identified beneficiaries and violation of the rule against perpetuities. Nevertheless, many jurisdictions allowed such trusts as "honorary." The named trustee was allowed, but could not be required, to carry out the terms of the trust. If the trustee chose not to do so, a resulting trust arose in favor of the settlor or the beneficiaries of his estate.

UTC § 402(a)(3)(B) & (C) provides exceptions to the definite beneficiary requirement for two types of "honorary" trusts: trusts for animals and trusts for a noncharitable purpose. Each has its own set of requirements related to beneficiaries, purpose, or both. Each is described in Chapter 14.

E. Trustee with Duties

UTC § 402(a)(4) requires that the trustee have duties to perform. This provision does not require that the trust instrument name the trustee. A court can name a trustee if the instrument fails to do so, as might occur if the settlor initially named herself as trustee and then died or otherwise became unwilling or unable to serve.

Although UTC § 402(a)(4) makes duties critical, it does not list any duties the trustee must have. Other UTC provisions provide for trustee duties, and the trust instrument might also list trustee duties.

The comments indicate that a trustee who has only passive duties—for example, the duty not to interfere with the beneficiary's enjoyment of the property—could suffice unless the particular state's version of the Statute of Uses resulted in the trust's being terminable. If a state has adopted UTC § 402, the duties requirement is the least likely of its requirements to cause litigation.

F. Merger of Legal and Beneficial Interests

Trusts grew out of a property owner's desire to have property managed during his absence or to avoid the English rules preventing him from devising his real property at death. Because trusts separated legal and equitable ownership between the trustee and beneficiaries, a trust did not automatically terminate when the settlor or a beneficiary died. But if that trust had only one trustee and one beneficiary, and they were the same person, the legal and equitable interests merged. That merger would terminate the trust, and the beneficiary would then own the property outright. The UTC does not change this rule.

UTC § 402(a)(5) requires that the same person not be the trust's sole trustee and sole beneficiary. This requirement is not a problem, even if the sole trustee is also the sole beneficiary during her life, if there are other beneficiaries who will take after her death. The interests of those other beneficiaries can be vested or contingent.

> **Example 11-3.** Sylvia transferred property in trust. The trustee was to pay income to her son Steve for life and then distribute the trust principal to Steve's descendants. If Steve had no descendants, the trust principal would be distributed to several named charities. Steve can be the sole trustee of this trust. He is not the sole beneficiary because his descendants and the charities are alternate beneficiaries (other than his estate) after his death. If the trust principal was instead to be distributed to Steve's estate when he died, he could not be the sole trustee. The merger doctrine would apply, and the trust would not be valid.

A trust can be void from its inception if it provides for only one beneficiary and only one trustee, and they are the same person. The merger doctrine might also apply later, in which case the previously valid trust terminates. *In re Wells*, 259 B.R. 776 (Bankr. M.D. Fla. 2001).

> **Example 11-4.** Susan devised property in trust. Her daughter Dora was named sole trustee. The trustee was to pay income to Dora and her brother Barton for life and then distribute the trust principal to Dora's probate estate. When Barton died three years later, the legal and equitable interests merged in Dora.

CHECKPOINTS

- A trust is valid only if the settlor had capacity to create it. A settlor who creates a testamentary trust or a revocable inter vivos trust must have testamentary capacity. Creating an irrevocable inter vivos trust requires the capacity to make an outright gift.
- The settlor must have the intent to create a trust. An ambiguous will provision might be interpreted as precatory rather than as a transfer in trust.
- Private express trusts, with certain statutory exceptions, must have at least one definite beneficiary.
- A trust must have a trustee with duties. A court can appoint a trustee if the trust instrument fails to do so, and both the trust instrument and relevant statutes can provide duties.
- If a trust has only one beneficiary and one trustee, and they are the same person, the legal and equitable interests merge and the trust fails.

CHAPTER 12

Trust Purpose, Formalities, and Funding

ROADMAP

- Purpose
- Formalities
- Funding

A. Chapter Overview

This chapter continues the discussion of requirements for a valid trust. As discussed in the previous chapter, a trust is not valid unless the settlor satisfies the requirements of UTC § 402 or its relevant state counterpart. But even if he has the requisite capacity and intent, names a definite beneficiary, provides duties for a trustee to perform, and avoids merger, the settlor might not have created a valid trust. The trust must have an appropriate purpose, the settlor must comply with the formalities for creating the trust, and he must fund the trust.

B. Purpose

UTC § 404 provides that a trust may be created for any purpose that is lawful, not contrary to public policy, and possible to achieve. A trust created to promote wasteful or useless activities would likely fail.

The comments to UTC § 404 list purposes that should fail to satisfy its lawfulness requirement. These include situations in which the trustee would commit a criminal or tortious act in performing the trust purpose, establishing the trust for the purpose of defrauding creditors, and having illegal consideration for the formation of the trust. Its list of purposes that are contrary to public policy covers purposes that tend to encourage criminal or tortious activity, that interfere with freedom to marry or that encourage divorce, that limit religious freedom, or that are frivolous or capricious. If the trust has more than one purpose, only some of which are problematic, the comments indicate that only those provisions might be invalid.

> **Example 12-1.** Susan created a trust to benefit her children. The trustee is to distribute trust income in the amount needed to provide for her children's health, education, and support. The trustee is also to distribute trust income to cover the damages owed by any child who commits a tort. Providing for health, education, and support are valid purposes. Paying damages for tortious conduct might not be a valid purpose. A court could strike the final purpose but not invalidate the entire trust.

Some public policy limitations applied to trusts are not applied to outright devises. Marital status and religion are two areas of potential difference. Consider the following potential provisions:

- Will: I devise $100,000 to Lucy if she is not married when I die.
- Trust: I devise trust income to Larry so long as he does not marry.

Because the testator need not reveal the terms of his will, Lucy's actions with respect to marriage are not influenced by the will provision. In addition, the will does not prevent her from marrying after the testator dies, so it does not constrain her future actions. The trust provision benefiting Larry, on the other hand, constrains his future actions.

The comments to UTC § 404 might not apply in every situation. For example, a court might order one spouse to create a trust that pays income for the support of his ex-spouse until she dies or remarries. The creation of this trust is not subject to the UTC limitations regarding a valid purpose. Likewise, spouses might enter into a valid prenuptial or postnuptial agreement providing for limitations based on remarriage. The comments to UTC § 401, which lists the three methods of creating a trust (transfer, declaration, and exercise of a power of appointment), indicate that these methods are not exclusive and that a trust might be created by a different statute or by a court order. The statute or court order might also determine the trust's purpose.

UTC § 404 also requires that the trust and its terms must be for the benefit of the beneficiaries. The comments refer to UTC § 412(b), which is a trust modification provision, as a specific example related to this requirement. A court can modify trust provisions that are impracticable, are wasteful, or that impair the trust's administration.

C. Formalities

The formalities requirements in this section have some overlap with the capacity requirement in UTC § 402, and the funding requirements discussed later in this chapter. Keep in mind that a trust must meet each requirement. Also remember that the formalities requirements for trusts are not necessarily the same as the requirements for wills. For example, a jurisdiction that does not recognize oral wills might recognize oral trusts. A jurisdiction that requires wills to be witnessed might not apply this requirement to trust instruments. Even if state law is more lenient regarding the formalities for creating a trust, a drafting attorney is likely to adhere to testamentary formalities.

1. Inter Vivos Trust

UTC § 407 provides that a trust does not have to be in writing unless the jurisdiction has a statute that requires a writing. It requires proving both the creation and terms of an oral trust by clear and convincing evidence. A mere preponderance of the evidence will not suffice. Because a state's Statute of Frauds might require a writing (and perhaps other formalities) for a conveyance of real estate, an oral trust has limited utility even if its terms can be proved. The UTC formalities requirements do not mention witnesses.

UTC § 407 differs from its UPC counterpart relating to wills. As a rule, a will must be in writing and might require witnesses. UPC § 2-502. Although the UPC does not provide for oral wills, some states do allow oral wills that satisfy conditions expressed in their probate codes. N.Y. Est. Powers & Trusts Law § 3-2.2.

2. Testamentary Trust

If the intended trust will be created by a transfer to the trustee effective at the settlor's death, the trust is testamentary and can be created only by an instrument that satisfies the relevant statute concerning the execution of a valid will. The requirement that the instrument satisfy that statute exists not because a trust is intended but rather because a *testamentary trust* is intended. As noted in the previous chapter, a court might have to interpret the will to determine if a particular devise created a trust or was merely precatory.

With one exception, the testamentary instrument must contain all the requisite terms of the trust. The one exception is that the trust will not fail for want of an identified trustee. A court can appoint a trustee if the instrument does not name one. However, the trust property and the beneficiary or beneficiaries must be established or readily determinable from the terms of the will. The statute is unlikely to allow them to be proven by extrinsic evidence.

If a will manifests the testator's intent to create a trust but fails to identify a definite beneficiary, the trust fails and the property reverts to the estate. Unless the will provides otherwise, the residuary takers receive the property. If there is no residuary clause, or there are no surviving residuary takers, the property passes by intestate succession.

3. Secret or Semi-Secret Testamentary Trust

Secret and semi-secret trusts are not additional types of trusts. These terms describe private express trusts that do not indicate the trust purpose or the actual existence of the trust. If, for example, the testator's will provides that "I devise Blackacre to Ted, who is to hold the property in trust as we agreed," the trust is semi-secret. The trust will likely be invalid, even though the will clearly indicates the devise is being made in trust. A state's version of the Statute of Wills might require that all of the terms of the will be in writing and that the will be signed. In most cases, it must also be witnessed. The will itself was properly executed, but some of its terms are missing. The terms of the trust were "dictated" so to speak in a manner that does not satisfy the Statute of Wills. In this situation, the intended beneficiary cannot enforce the trust, and the trustee cannot carry out its terms voluntarily. The court could order Ted to hold Blackacre in a resulting trust for the benefit of those who take the testator's estate. It could instead order the property transferred to them.

A different result follows if the will had simply made a devise to Ted, and the will's language contained no evidence that he was to hold as trustee. If it is proven that Ted had agreed to hold in trust for a beneficiary, the trust is deemed secret. The Restatement (First) of Trusts § 55 provides for imposing a constructive trust on the devisee if the devise was made in reliance on his agreement to hold the property in trust. This provision is not limited to devises. It also imposes a constructive trust on an heir who agreed to hold the property in trust if the original owner died intestate in reliance on the heir's agreement to hold the property in trust.

This dichotomy between secret trusts, with the intended beneficiary obtaining the property by way of constructive trust, and semi-secret trusts, with the property reverting to the estate is longstanding. *Olliffe v. Wells*, 130 Mass. 221 (1881); *Pickelner v. Adler*, 229 S.W.3d 516 (Tex. App. 2007). Scholars criticize the disparity in result but disagree over how to eliminate it. Some suggest imposing a resulting trust in favor of the estate in either case. Comments to the Restatement (Third) of Trusts § 18 take the view that a constructive trust in favor of the intended beneficiary should be the remedy for either a secret or semi-secret trust.

D. Funding

1. Trust Principal

Even if the settlor executes a trust instrument with all the required formalities, property is not a trust asset unless he complies with any formalities required for transferring it to the trust. Placing property into a trust is an implied aspect of the UTC § 401 methods of creating a trust: transferring title to property to a trustee; declaring herself trustee of property; or exercising a power of appointment over property.

The settlor might transfer title to the trust property to another as trustee. UTC § 401(1). To be effective, an inter vivos transfer must satisfy the state property law requirements for transfers. Transfers of realty require a written deed duly executed and delivered. Transfers of personal property usually require either actual or constructive delivery of the property to the trustee. If his will creates a testamentary trust, the trust must be created by a validly executed will. The personal representative will be responsible for transferring the testator's probate property to the trustee.

The settlor might instead declare herself as trustee of designated property. UTC § 401(2). In this situation, no delivery is necessary. An individual who holds a power of appointment over property might be able to exercise the power to transfer the property to a trustee. UTC § 401(3). Failure to exercise a power of appointment, power of invasion, or power of withdrawal might result in the powerholder being treated as a settlor of an existing trust.

The trust principal can consist of any property or interest in property that is transferable. It might be tangible or intangible, real or personal. It might consist of future interests or even contingent interests. What matters is that the interest is presently owned and transferable by the settlor when the trust is created.

Even an expectancy can satisfy the requirement that a trust have property. For example, a trust that is the beneficiary of a life insurance policy has a principal even though the policy owner retains the right to revoke that beneficiary designation. UPC § 2-511(a). A state might have statutes in addition to those in its probate or trust code that broadly define property in this context.

2. Trust *in Futuro*

A settlor might manifest the intent to create a trust, either by transfer or by declaration, of property that does not yet exist (for example corporate stock that has not yet been issued) or of property that currently exists but that he does not yet own (for example corporate stock that has been issued but that he has not yet acquired). That manifestation is *in futuro;* no trust is created at the time of such manifested intent. A trust will exist when the identified property comes into existence and the settlor acquires it if either of two conditions is met. Either the original manifestation of intent was a promise supported by consideration, or the settlor acts in a way that demonstrates his continued intent to create the trust (even though his acts at that later time might be insufficient without the prior manifestation of intent). Restatement (First) of Trusts § 26; Restatement (Third) of Trusts § 13, comment a.

3. Delivery

The common law requires either delivery or symbolic delivery to the donee to complete a gift of tangible property. If the settlor makes a gift in trust, however, there is no requirement of delivery to the donee-beneficiary. The property must be delivered, if at all, to the trustee rather than to the beneficiary. If the trust is created by transfer, legal title must be vested in the trustee. In the case of tangible property that does not require a title document, delivery or symbolic delivery must be made to transfer title.

If the trust is created by declaration, the settlor-trustee already possesses the property, so no delivery is required. There have been cases where a donor clearly intended to make a gift to a donee, failed to accomplish the needed step of delivery, and the donee sought to have the transaction treated as a declaration of trust by a settlor-trustee. If the donee succeeded, the absence of delivery would not be fatal to his receiving the property. Because treating intended gifts that would fail for want of delivery as trusts by declaration would completely negate the delivery requirement, courts usually reject such claims.

CHECKPOINTS

- A trust must have a purpose that is not unlawful, contrary to public policy, or impossible to achieve.
- The formalities necessary to create a trust might be identical to those required for a valid will, but trusts might require fewer formalities.
- Trusts involving real estate usually require a writing to create the trust in addition to any writing necessary to validly transfer the real estate into trust.
- If a will purports to create a trust, but omits required trust terms, it is a semi-secret trust. Its terms will not be enforced, despite the evidence that the testator intended a trust, because that would violate the requirement that a will's terms be in writing.
- If the will does not include trust language, but the testator intended a trust, it is a secret trust. Its terms might be enforced as a constructive trust if the testator acted in reliance on the purported trustee's promise to carry out the trust.
- A promise to create a trust in the future might not be enforceable.
- If the settlor creates a trust by transfer, he must observe any formalities—deed, delivery, etc.—necessary to validate the transfer. Otherwise, the property meant for the trust might remain in his probate estate and be received by his devisees or intestate heirs.

CHAPTER 13

Trust Distribution Provisions

ROADMAP

- Distributions by the trustee
- Third-party powers over trust principal

A. Chapter Overview

Trust income and principal can be allocated between groups of beneficiaries and among members of a single group. Because trusts are so flexible, the settlor can mandate distributions of income or principal or leave them to the trustee's discretion. She can also give a third person the power to invade trust principal for himself, for trust beneficiaries, or for another person. This chapter outlines several distribution options.

B. Distributions by the Trustee

The Uniform Fiduciary Income and Principal Act (or other relevant state law) describes methods for determining whether a trust receipt is allocable to income or principal. This chapter's discussion assumes that the trustee has already made that determination. The concern here is what the trustee can do with trust income and principal.

The trustee's powers or duties can change based on the passage of time or some other event. A duty might initially be mandatory and later become discretionary or vice versa. The trustee might have a mandatory duty to distribute income but discretion with regard to principal or vice versa.

The trust instrument might indicate the extent of the trustee's power to distribute income or principal. It might state whether the trustee is to favor certain beneficiaries or classes of beneficiaries. In the absence of any indication, the trustee exercises its authority based on its duty of impartiality. UTC § 803.

1. Mandatory Distributions of Income

The trust instrument might require the trustee to distribute the trust's entire net income. Although income distributions are mandatory, the trustee still must determine when and how to distribute the income.

The trust instrument might, for example, require monthly, quarterly, or annual distributions. Because beneficiaries are taxed on mandatory distributions even if they did not receive them by the end of the year, distributions less frequent than annually are unlikely. I.R.C. § 652(a).

If the trust instrument requires the trustee to distribute income "to" the beneficiary, the trustee will pay the income to the named beneficiary. If it instead requires income distributions "to or on behalf of" or "to or for" the beneficiary, the trustee may also pay a beneficiary's obligations directly. If a beneficiary is under a legal disability, the trustee can satisfy the "to" requirement by distributing income to an appropriate recipient on the beneficiary's behalf. The trustee can also do so if it believes the beneficiary is incapacitated even if there has been no determination of legal disability. UTC § 816(21) lists permissible recipients. These include conservators, guardians, UTMA custodians, and adult relatives.

Trusts designed to qualify for an estate tax marital deduction or to satisfy the elective share may have to provide for mandatory income distributions to a surviving spouse. Statutes governing the estate tax and elective share also indicate how frequently the spouse must receive income and might include provisions related to unproductive property.

2. Discretionary Distributions of Income

The trustee might have discretion over whether to distribute income. It might also have discretion over how much, if any, income a particular beneficiary should receive. Its discretion might be limited by a purpose included in the trust instrument. Finally, it might have discretion to add undistributed income to principal or to hold undistributed income for later distribution to income beneficiaries.

> **Example 13-1.** Sally created a trust to benefit her descendants. The trustee has the power, in its discretion, to distribute trust income quarterly to her grandchildren until the youngest grandchild attains age 21; distributions are to be equal in amount. The trustee is to add any undistributed income to principal. When the youngest grandchild attains age 21, the trustee is to distribute all trust income to Sally's grandchildren equally for 10 years. The trustee initially has a discretionary power to distribute. It will later be subject to a mandatory distribution requirement.

> **Example 13-2.** Sam created a trust to benefit his descendants. The trustee has the power, in its discretion, to distribute trust income quarterly for his grandchildren's education until the youngest grandchild attains age 25. The trustee can consider each grandchild's other income and assets. The trustee is to add any undistributed income to principal. When the youngest grandchild attains age 25, the trustee is to distribute all trust income to Sam's grandchildren equally for 10 years. The trustee initially has a discretionary power to distribute, but one that is limited by a specific purpose. It will later be subject to a mandatory distribution requirement.

The trust in Example 13-2 indicates the settlor's purpose, which limits the trustee's discretion. Purpose has significance for topics discussed elsewhere in this book, including the requirement that a trust have a valid purpose. Courts take the settlor's purpose into account in deciding whether to modify the trust's terms.

3. Distributions of Principal

Unless the relevant jurisdiction has no rule against perpetuities, the trustee must eventually distribute trust principal to the beneficiaries. It might also have the power or duty to invade principal and distribute it before the trust terminates. As with income, the trustee's powers with respect to principal might be totally discretionary, discretionary but limited by a purpose for which distributions can be made, or totally mandatory.

Some purposes for invading principal involve ascertainable standards; others do not. Powers subject to ascertainable standards are less likely to have adverse federal transfer tax consequences if the trustee has the power to invade for the trustee's benefit. Powers to invade for health, education, support, or maintenance are powers subject to an ascertainable standard; a court can, if necessary, determine whether the trustee is acting in accord with the power. Powers to invade for happiness, while arguably limited in nature, are not considered subject to an ascertainable standard. UTC § 103(2); Treas. Reg. § 20.2041-1(c)(2).

A trustee's power to distribute principal might include transferring principal to another trust rather than distributing it outright. This power might be subject to the jurisdiction's statutes dealing with trust decanting.

As was true for income distributions, a trustee's power to distribute principal might reflect the trust's need to comply with other statutes. Provisions designed to comply with marital deduction and elective share statutes are common. Other situations include trusts designed to supplement public assistance benefits or to obtain a charitable contribution deduction.

C. Third-Party Powers over Trust Principal

A trust's provisions might grant someone other than the trustee power over trust principal. For example, a beneficiary might have a power to invade trust principal. He might be granted this power only over amounts transferred to the trust and only for a limited time after the transfer occurs. This limited power is often referred to as a withdrawal power. A settlor usually gives this power for gift and estate tax reasons. A beneficiary might instead have this power for a longer period, including until his death. A power that unlimited might have adverse estate tax consequences for the beneficiary's estate. It might also subject a portion of the trust property to the claims of her creditors. Those consequences are discussed in other chapters.

Instead of a power to withdraw contributions or a power to invade trust principal, an individual might receive a power of appointment over trust principal. That power might be exercisable during the powerholder's life or not until his death. A settlor is likely to give someone a power of appointment over trust principal for one of two reasons. First, the power might be necessary to satisfy marital deduction or elective share requirements. Second, the trust termination date might be many years in the future. Rather than having trust principal distributed equally, or according to the state's intestacy distribution provisions, the settlor might want to give someone other than the trustee the power to allocate trust principal among potential beneficiaries.

CHECKPOINTS

- A trust instrument might include mandatory provisions governing the distribution of trust income or principal.
- A trustee might instead have discretion over the timing of, and reasons for, making distributions of trust income or principal.
- A trustee's powers over distributions might be subject to purposes included in the trust instrument.
- A beneficiary or third party might have a power to withdraw contributions or invade principal.
- Powers to withdraw or invade have consequences beyond the administration of the trust. These consequences include creditor access to trust assets, computing a surviving spouse's elective share, and computing the powerholder's federal transfer taxes.

CHAPTER 14

Specific Uses for Trusts

ROADMAP

- Reasons for creating a trust
- Trusts for the care of animals
- Trusts for a noncharitable purpose
- Trusts for spouses
- Trusts holding life insurance policies
- Charitable trusts

A. Chapter Overview

This chapter describes many of the reasons for creating a trust. It then focuses on several particular uses: care of animals; noncharitable purpose; satisfying requirements for a marital deduction or elective share without giving the surviving spouse outright ownership; holding a life insurance policy; and benefiting charity. Using a trust to limit creditor access is discussed in the next chapter.

B. Reasons for Creating a Trust

Trusts are only one method for transmitting property. As discussed earlier in the book, an individual could instead make an outright transfer while she is alive or at her death. In the former situation, the donee receives an outright gift; in the latter, he receives an outright devise or intestate share. Alternatively, she could transfer property into a tenancy between herself and another individual or between individuals other than herself. If she creates a tenancy in common, she makes an outright gift to the other person(s) but does not give up her rights to any portion of the tenancy she retained. If she creates a joint tenancy with right of survivorship or a tenancy by the entirety, she also gives the other tenant(s) the possibility of taking her interest if she predeceases. Finally, she can transfer property at her death by making one or more persons the beneficiary of a life insurance policy, an annuity, a bank account, or a securities account. In some jurisdictions, she can even create a transfer on death deed in real estate.

Given those other options, why might she decide to transfer her property in trust? The answer depends on a variety of factors, including when she is making the transfer, what her goals are for herself and her beneficiaries, and her family situation (and that of her beneficiaries). Not surprisingly, given the options available for creating and funding a trust, some trusts are more appropriate than others for meeting her goals.

1. Privacy

Intestate succession provides more privacy than a will because the property owner does not execute a document that lists any property or names any recipients. But intestacy statutes might not meet her goals for distributing her property. A will devising particular items to named devisees gives her more control, but—if the will is a public record—might give the public too much information about her devisees' potential wealth.

Although survivorship tenancies and beneficiary designations might solve the privacy problem, they can backfire if the other tenant or beneficiary predeceases her. If that happens, her property ends up being transferred by will or intestacy. For that reason, she might create a trust while she is alive even though she funds it primarily at her death.

If she creates the trust while she is alive, its terms are not included in her will. She can retain her property until death, if that is her wish, and then devise it to her trust. She can make a specific, general, or residuary devise to the trust. To preserve as much privacy as possible she would use a residuary devise for this purpose. Her will would contain a "pourover" provision devising property to the trust. She could even use the doctrine of incorporation by reference to re-establish a trust she revoked before her death.

The public is not the only group without access to the trust terms. Family members might also lack access. The trustee is required to provide information only to beneficiaries, and sometimes only to qualified beneficiaries. UTC § 813.

2. Control Until Death or Incapacity

An inter vivos trust is presumed to be revocable. UTC § 602(a). The settlor can, of course, provide that the trust is irrevocable when she creates it. She can also relinquish her power of revocation later, so long as she has capacity to modify the trust. If she becomes incapacitated, the trustee will manage the trust according to the provisions in the trust instrument.

The power to revoke is not limited to all-or-nothing revocation. A settlor who has the power to completely revoke the trust also has the power to revoke it in part or modify its terms. Because the terms include the provisions for distributing income and trust principal, she can change not only the beneficiaries' identities but also their time and manner of enjoying trust assets. She can make herself a trust beneficiary if she did not do so when she created the trust. She can regain trust assets, free of the trust, for her own use. The trustee must accede to her wishes, if the trust is revocable, because its duty is to her rather than to other beneficiaries. UTC § 603(b).

3. Flexibility

The recipient of a devise or inter vivos gift can deal with the property however he wishes. He can retain it, sell, or give it away. If he transfers it, he can select one or more family members, other individuals, or charities as the recipient. He can use any income produced by the property as he sees fit.

A settlor who creates a trust can limit her beneficiaries' powers over the trust property. She can, for example, give the trustee the discretion to distribute income to current beneficiaries or retain it for future distribution. She can set the percentage of income each beneficiary receives on a yearly basis. She can list the purposes for which the trustee can distribute income or principal to a beneficiary. She can create a power of appointment that allows the powerholder to select the recipients of trust principal from among a class she defines.

4. Professional Management

The settlor can serve as trustee until her death or incapacity, but she might instead select an individual or institution to serve. She might also indicate a preference for any successor trustee. If the trust's holdings are extensive, or involve assets whose management requires particular expertise, she can select a trustee with the necessary skills to carry out those tasks. If a beneficiary is a minor, or is relatively unsophisticated about financial matters, the settlor might prefer professional management even for an uncomplicated asset mix.

5. Avoiding Successive Probates

The settlor might expect a spouse or domestic partner who is elderly or in poor health to die relatively soon after she does. Rather than have the property go through probate at her own death, and then again at the survivor's death, she might place it in trust and give that person the income for life. The trust could then terminate, and younger beneficiaries would receive the principal. Alternatively, the trust instrument could provide for successor income beneficiaries. Subject to limits imposed by the rule against perpetuities, the trust could avoid probate when successor income beneficiaries died.

Avoiding successive probates has benefits beyond probate costs. Assets that remain in the trust need not be retitled. In addition, the ultimate recipients would be those who met criteria she set rather than being the devisees or intestate heirs of her surviving spouse or partner.

6. Protecting Family Wealth

Potential claims against the beneficiary are relevant. Property that an individual owns outright might be subject to claims that would not arise if he were merely a trust beneficiary. Some of those claims might be made by creditors; others might be made by new spouses who did not waive their rights in a valid prenuptial or postnuptial agreement.

7. Avoiding Ancillary Administration

Real property has a situs in the jurisdiction in which it is located. The property owner might have previously lived in that jurisdiction. She might have never lived in that jurisdiction. When she dies, her estate will be subject to probate in her state of residence. Her personal property—and her real property located in that state—will be probated there. Her real property located elsewhere will be probated in the other state. To avoid ancillary administration in one or more other states, she might consolidate her real estate holdings in an entity that will not be subject to ancillary administration. A family limited partnership is one such entity; a trust is another. Because the trustee has legal title to the real estate, she owns no real property in those other states and avoids the need for separate probates.

To obtain this benefit, she must fund the trust before she dies. A testamentary trust does not avoid probate because she owns the property at death. The trust mechanism is probably better suited to her needs than a transfer on death deed for real estate even though that method might avoid probate. First, she might not want the beneficiary to obtain outright ownership. Second, she might own real estate located in jurisdictions that have not enacted the Uniform Real Property Transfer on Death Act or comparable legislation.

8. Other Uses for Trusts

An outright gift might disqualify a family member for public assistance for which he is otherwise eligible or might become eligible. Specialized trusts, which are beyond the scope of this book, can be used to supplement rather than supplant public assistance.

A homeowner can use a "qualified personal residence trust" to transfer a remainder interest in her home while retaining possession of the home for a fixed term. Treas. Reg. § 25.2702-5. When the term ends, she must either vacate the home or begin paying rent to the holder of the remainder interest. These trusts, which are designed to minimize federal transfer taxes, are also beyond the scope of this book.

C. Trusts for the Care of Animals

UTC § 408 authorizes trusts for the care of animals. It departs from the common law by providing that such trusts are not only allowable, but enforceable. The trust's terms can be enforced by anyone named in the instrument creating the trust. If no one is named, the court can appoint someone to enforce its terms.

The settlor might use a separate trust for each animal or might use a single trust for all her animals. The UTC allows either method but limits the trust to animals alive during the settlor's lifetime. The settlor can use an inter vivos or a testamentary trust.

The trust property can be used only for the trust purpose. The court can determine if the value of trust property exceeds the amount required for the animal's care and can even make this determination before the animal's death. Unless the trust provides otherwise, any property not required for the intended use reverts to the settlor or to her estate. The trust terminates upon the death of the last surviving animal designated for caretaking. At that time, any unexpended funds revert to the settlor or her estate unless the governing instrument provides for a different recipient.

UTC § 408 provides its own trust termination language: the death of the last surviving animal. Neither the common-law rule against perpetuities nor any statutory variation applies. Even if a state does not impose a time limit, animal life span can present problems. Some animals, including tortoises, can live for more than 100 years. Because they could outlive the original trustee or caretaker, the trust instrument might list characteristics the court should consider in appointing a successor trustee or caregiver.

The UTC does not specify how detailed the provisions for the animal's welfare can or must be. Organizations such as the American Society for the Prevention of Cruelty to Animals include sample provisions in brochures and on their websites. The ASPCA website (aspca.org) lists the states that allow animal trusts and those that allow noncharitable purpose trusts.

The UTC does not indicate how to treat animals in gestation. And, although these trusts are commonly referred to as "pet trusts," it calls them animal trusts and does not indicate whether any animals are excluded. Many state statutes mirror the UTC language, but others address those questions. Colorado addresses both. Its statute provides for "domestic or pet animals" and specifically includes offspring in gestation. Colo. Rev. Stat. § 15-11-901(2).

The Uniform Trust Decanting Act § 23 includes provisions for decanting an animal trust. Decanting might be necessary because changes in the health of the animal or its caregiver or the caregiver's employment location might necessitate moving the trust and its administration to another jurisdiction.

D. Trusts for a Noncharitable Purpose

UTC § 409 contains two provisions, one of which is a variation on common law principles for honorary trusts, and the other of which is a significant departure from the common law. This section authorizes a trust for a noncharitable purpose without a definite or definitely ascertainable beneficiary. It also authorizes a trust for a noncharitable but otherwise valid purpose to be selected by the trustee. In the first instance, the settlor indicates the purpose but not the beneficiaries. In the second instance, the settlor allows the trustee to select the purpose. Trusts authorized by UTC § 409 can be enforced for no more than 21 years. The UTC brackets this time limitation; states are free to enact different time periods for enforcement.

UTC § 409 does not apply to transfers covered by UTC § 408 or by any other statute. The trust's terms can be enforced by anyone named in the trust instrument. If no one is named, the terms can be enforced by anyone the court appoints. The trust property can be used only for the trust purpose, and the court can determine if the value of trust property exceeds that required for the purpose. Unless the trust provides otherwise, any property not required for the intended use reverts to the settlor or his estate.

The commentary to UTC § 409 indicates that its purpose is to allow trusts without definite beneficiaries for general but noncharitable purposes as well as trusts for specific noncharitable purposes. The first type, for general noncharitable purposes, would allow trusts for such things as benevolence to unidentified friends. It would also allow trusts for any other noncharitable purpose selected by the trustee so long as it does not violate any law or public policy. The second type, for specific noncharitable purposes would allow, for example, a trust calling for annual distributions of income to school children for noncharitable purposes.

Because either type is enforceable only for 21 years or other state-enacted term, the commentary recognizes that this could pose a problem for purposes such as the care of cemetery plots. The reference to "other statute" in UTC § 409 contemplates that legislatures might enact other statutes for such purposes. Nebraska's statute is typical. It validates gifts to perpetual care funds despite indefiniteness of beneficiaries and the possibility that the fund will extend beyond any perpetuities period. Neb. Rev. Stat. § 12-512.

E. Trusts for Spouses

An individual might transfer property to his spouse in trust, rather than outright, using provisions like those in trusts established for other beneficiaries. But there are potential differences. One relates to the federal estate tax; the other, to the spouse's elective share. A trust used to secure a marital deduction, and thus reduce or eliminate estate tax when the first spouse dies, must give the surviving spouse certain rights. The size of a trust required to satisfy elective share rights will be affected by the rights the spouse receives.

1. Trusts Qualifying for the Marital Deduction

The federal estate and gift taxes are discussed in greater detail later in this book. This chapter focuses on one aspect of those taxes. An individual—whether by inter vivos or testamentary transfer—can deduct qualifying transfers to a spouse (or surviving spouse) and thus reduce the amount of transfers that would otherwise be subject to federal gift or estate tax. Because the current rate of tax on transfers above a lifetime exemption is 40%, the marital deduction provides immediate benefits for individuals whose wealth exceeds the exemption.

The marital deduction is designed to delay, not eliminate, the estate tax ultimately due. In theory, the surviving spouse will either own the property received when she dies or give it away during her life—thus making it subject to gift or estate tax when she exceeds her lifetime exemption. There is, of course, no guarantee that the surviving spouse will be subject to either tax. She might incur extraordinary medical expenses that reduce her wealth below the exemption amount. She might reduce her wealth by making annual exclusion gifts to family members and friends. And, because the exemption amount is subject to an inflation adjustment, her exemption amount might exceed her lifetime and at-death transfers.

Because the marital deduction is premised on the surviving spouse being subject to transfer taxes, the transferor spouse can take this deduction only if the transfer satisfies the statutory requirements. To use transfer tax language, no deduction is allowed if the recipient spouse receives a terminable interest and the property will ultimately pass to someone other than the recipient spouse or her estate after a lapse of time or the happening of an event or contingency. I.R.C. §§ 2056(b)(1), 2523(b). For example, a trust in which the surviving spouse receives only a life estate, followed by a remainder to descendants, will not qualify. Because the spouse will not own the trust assets when she dies, they would not be included in her gross estate. If the first spouse were allowed to take a marital deduction, neither spouse would be subject to transfer tax on those assets.

Because the Internal Revenue Code includes exceptions, the first spouse can use a trust and obtain a marital deduction if the donee spouse receives the rights required by those exceptions. In addition to the possibilities discussed below, the first spouse can make a qualifying transfer using a qualified charitable remainder trust. No one other than the spouse (income) and a charity (remainder) may have an interest in the trust. I.R.C. §§ 2056(b)(8), 2523(g).

One possibility involves giving the trustee discretion over income distributions. It can distribute income to the spouse or on her behalf, or it can retain the income in the trust. In that situation, the donee spouse must receive rights to the trust principal. It must be paid to her or to her estate; it will potentially be subject to transfer tax when she makes gifts or dies.

Another possibility involves giving the donee spouse rights with respect to both trust income and trust principal. She must be entitled for life to *all* the income from the trust or from the portion of the trust qualifying for the marital deduction. The income must be payable at least annually. In addition, she must have the power to appoint the property to herself, to her estate, or to either herself or her estate. Because that power is a general power of appointment, the property subject to the power is included in her gross estate even if she fails to exercise it. The power qualifies even if she is also allowed to appoint to other persons. If the trustee has a power of invasion, it can exercise that power only in favor of the spouse during her lifetime. I.R.C. §§ 2056(b)(5), 2523(e).

A transfer might also qualify if the donee spouse receives rights with respect to trust income and the transferor spouse (for inter vivos transfers) or his personal representative (for testamentary transfers) irrevocably elects to treat the property transferred as qualified terminable interest property (QTIP). The donee spouse must be entitled for life to *all* the income from the trust or from the portion of the trust qualifying for the marital deduction. The income must be payable at least annually. Any power of invasion can be used only for the spouse's benefit during her lifetime. I.R.C. §§ 2056(b)(7), 2523(f). If a QTIP election is made, the trust principal is included in the spouse's gross estate when she dies even though she never received it or had any right to receive it. I.R.C. § 2044. Unless the resulting estate tax is apportioned to the first spouse's beneficiaries, the survivor's beneficiaries will bear the burden of the tax without necessarily receiving any of the assets giving rise to the tax.

2. Trusts Used in Satisfying the Elective Share

UPC § 2-202 indicates the percentage (sometimes augmented by a minimal value) that the surviving spouse is entitled to receive if he takes an elective share. That provision does not mandate that he receive any particular type of property interest. The UPC uses the commuted value of the spouse's interest for property he receives in other than outright ownership. Comments to UPC § 2-206. Some states use formulas that use specific percentages of the trust value rather than commuted value. For example, Florida includes 50% of the trust's value if the spouse receives the unqualified right to all trust income, 80% if he also receives a qualifying power of invasion, and 100% if he receives both a qualifying power of appointment and a qualifying power of invasion. It uses the transfer tax value (but not more than 50% of the trust value) if he does not receive at least the unqualified right to all trust income. Fla. Stat. § 732.2095(2)(d), (f).

F. Trusts Holding Life Insurance Policies

Individuals use life insurance for many reasons. One such reason is as an income substitute; the policy proceeds replace salary or professional fees the decedent would have received if he had lived. Another reason is to provide liquidity. For example, the insured might own a controlling interest in a business, which he plans to devise only to the children who participate in that business. If that interest is his estate's primary asset, life insurance policy proceeds can be used to pay claims, expenses, and taxes and to fund devises to other family members.

An insured must decide whether to own the policy himself, transfer it to a family member, or transfer it into a trust. He must also select one or more beneficiaries for the policy. If he uses a trust as beneficiary or owner, he must decide between a revocable and an irrevocable trust. Family dynamics, creditor access, and federal transfer tax consequences are relevant to these decisions.

If he makes his probate estate the beneficiary, the death benefit is included in his gross estate. I.R.C. § 2042(1). Even if he selects a different beneficiary, the death benefit is included in his gross estate if he has incidents of ownership with respect to the policy when he dies. I.R.C. § 2042(2). The death benefit is also included if he released those incidents within three years of his death. I.R.C. § 2035(a). Incidents of ownership include the right to name the beneficiary or to borrow against the policy's cash surrender value.

If the insured names an individual as beneficiary, there is a risk that the beneficiary will not be willing to contribute to estate expenses even if the estate is illiquid. This can be problematic if the estate beneficiaries and the policy beneficiaries do not get along. If the insured instead names a trust, with a trustee who is not one of the beneficiaries, he can avoid that problem. The trust instrument can allow the trustee to loan money to the estate as needed. If the trust instrument mandates such payments, the estate tax will apply. Mandated payments are the equivalent of making the insured's estate the policy beneficiary.

Example 14-1. Ted currently owns business property worth $20 million. He wants his daughter Dora to receive that property. He wants his son Seth to receive cash equal to the value of Dora's devise. If Ted purchased a $20 million term life insurance policy and made Seth the beneficiary, Seth would receive $20 million when Ted died. Because Ted retained ownership of the policy, his gross estate would equal $40 million. After deducting expenses and the applicable exemption, the estate tax might exceed $10 million.

Example 14-2. If Ted transferred the policy to Seth—and lived at least three years following the transfer—his gross estate would be only $20 million and the estate tax would be much lower. Because none of that tax would be apportioned to Seth, the personal representative would pay the tax from property otherwise going to Dora. Dora would thus receive a smaller inheritance than Seth.

Example 14-3. Ted could instead transfer the policy to the trustee of an irrevocable life insurance trust. He could make the policy subject to its share of estate taxes if he died within three years of making the transfer. He could also give the trustee the power to loan money to the probate estate if needed to pay claims and expenses. The instrument could provide that Seth received trust principal after the probate process ended. He could even make Dora a trust beneficiary to the extent needed to equalize her inheritance and Seth's.

Before transferring property to a trust, the insured must ascertain if the trustee has an insurable interest—that is, will it be affected financially by the insured's death. If the trustee does not have an insurable interest, the insurer will be excused from paying the death benefit when the insured settlor dies. UTC § 113 provides rules for determining if the trustee has an insurable interest in the life of the insured. The trustee has such an interest if the policy insures the settlor or someone in whom the settlor had an insurable interest and the proceeds are primarily to benefit trust beneficiaries with designated connections to the insured. The comments note that several states had already addressed this issue in statutes predating the UTC.

Irrevocable life insurance trusts (ILITs) raise other issues. Annual insurance premiums must be paid to keep the policy in force. The settlor can initially transfer additional property into the trust for that purpose, allowing the trustee to use the property or the income it produces for that purpose. Alternatively, the settlor can continue to pay the premiums himself, either directly or by transferring funds to the trust each year. If the premium is relatively large—as might be the case if the death benefit is substantial—that payment could be a taxable gift.

Another issue that arises relates to the policy itself. If the trust owns publicly traded stock, the trustee can determine a market value daily. If it owns rental property, the trustee can ascertain income and disbursements (or can engage a property manager to do so). But an insurance policy doesn't produce income, and there is always a risk that the insurance company's net income and reserves might be insufficient to cover the death benefit when the insured dies. The trustee might not have the expertise to monitor the strength of an insurer. A state statute, like that in Florida, may relieve the trustee of this obligation. Fla. Stat. § 736.0902.

G. Charitable Trusts

An individual can benefit one or more charities by making outright inter vivos gifts or by making outright testamentary devises. He might instead transfer property—either inter vivos or at death—in trust. He might believe that his name will be remembered longer, or he might want a mechanism for regaining his property (or for his family to regain it) if the beneficiary does not fulfill the trust's purpose. He might simply want to select the persons who will administer the assets he is allocating to charity. The discussion in this section assumes that all trust beneficiaries are charities.

1. Beneficiary

A charitable trust is an express trust, but it is not a *private* express trust. Its validity depends on its satisfying the requirements for express trusts, with one exception. It does not need to have a definite beneficiary. UTC § 402(a)(3)(A). Whether or not the trust has a definite beneficiary, its terms can be enforced by the settlor while he is alive. UTC § 405(c). If there is a definite beneficiary, that charity can also enforce the trust's terms as would be the case with a private express trust. Finally, the state's attorney general can enforce the trust.

UTC § 405(b) allows the court with supervisory powers over the trust to select a beneficiary if the trust instrument does not do so and does not delegate that power to the trustee. The court is to select one or more beneficiaries that are consistent with the settlor's intention if that can be ascertained. For example, if the settlor established a trust to provide for orphans, the court could name an orphanage as a beneficiary.

2. Purpose

A charitable trust can have a very specific purpose—for example, funding scholarships at the state's university. It can also have a more general charitable purpose. UTC § 405(a) lists the following as charitable purposes: the relief of poverty; the advancement of education or religion; the promotion of health, governmental or municipal purposes; or other purposes that are beneficial to the community. State statutes might include other purposes, such as the advancement of science or the arts.

The settlor need not indicate a particular charitable purpose. UTC § 405(b) allows the court to select a purpose if the trust instrument does not do so and does not delegate that power to the trustee. The court is to select a purpose that is consistent with the settlor's intention if that can be ascertained.

3. Cy Pres

Because a charitable trust is not subject to the rule against perpetuities, events that occur long after its creation could prevent the trust from being effectively administered. Alternatively, the settlor's purpose might have been accomplished or become impossible to accomplish. UTC § 413 gives a court the power to modify or terminate a charitable trust when its purpose becomes unlawful, impracticable, impossible to achieve, or wasteful. Cy pres is discussed in Chapter 16.

4. Split-Interest Trusts

A trust can benefit both charity and noncharitable beneficiaries. A transferor can establish a trust that pays income to charity for a set period, followed by a remainder interest in a noncharitable beneficiary. He could instead establish a trust that pays income for a set period to a noncharitable beneficiary, followed by a remainder interest in a charity. Charitable lead and charitable remainder trusts are designed to reduce transfer taxes.

CHECKPOINTS

- Inter vivos trusts offer benefits that wills do not. These include privacy, professional management, and avoiding delays caused by probate.
- A settlor might use a trust to avoid ancillary administration or the potential claims a surviving spouse's new spouse or children might make if he receives outright ownership of her property.
- Trusts for spouses are often structured to satisfy a spouse's elective share rights or reduce estate taxes.
- Although most private express trusts require definite beneficiaries that can enforce the trust, the UTC includes provisions validating trusts for animals and for noncharitable purposes.

- Irrevocable life insurance trusts can be particularly useful in funding estate expenses—through loans—without increasing the insured settlor's estate taxes.
- Charitable trusts do not have to have definite beneficiaries or a specific purpose (other than one that is charitable), but they are subject to the other requirements for creating a valid express trust.

CHAPTER 15

Creditor Access to Trust Assets

ROADMAP

- Creditors of the settlor
- Creditors of a beneficiary
- Creditors of the trustee

A. Chapter Overview

This chapter describes the rights of persons with claims against a settlor, a beneficiary, or a trustee. Claims against a settlor include those that arise during his life and those that remain unpaid at his death or that arise because of his death. As the discussion in this chapter indicates, trust language barring creditor access might be ineffective against certain types of creditors.

B. Creditors of the Settlor

1. Insolvent Settlor

If the settlor, either by declaration or by transfer, creates a trust when he is insolvent, his existing creditors can usually reach the trust assets. The transfer is treated as one in defraud of creditors. The result would be the same if he becomes insolvent as a result of the transfer. In the absence of such a fraudulent transfer or declaration, the settlor's existing or future creditors can reach the trust assets only if he retained a power or interest.

2. Retained Power or Interest in Trust

The UTC, unlike the common law, presumes that a settlor retains the power to revoke an inter vivos trust. UTC § 602. The traditional common-law rules would not allow his creditors to reach the trust assets or to force him to exercise any power to revoke that he retained when he created the trust. Restatement (Second) of Trusts § 330 comment o. Many jurisdictions have either accepted the revisions provided in Restatement (Third) of Trusts § 25 comment e or have adopted UTC § 505(a)(1). Both allow the settlor's creditors to reach the assets of a revocable trust during the settlor's life.

If the settlor retains any interest in the income or principal of an irrevocable trust, then to that extent, his creditors can usually reach trust assets. This rule applies even if the trust is a spendthrift trust, discretionary trust, or support trust. The general rule is that his creditors can reach the trust's assets to the extent of the maximum amount that the trustee could pay to him or apply for his benefit under any circumstances. Restatement (Third) of Trusts § 58(2); UTC § 505(a)(2).

> **Example 15-1.** Harley transferred $100,000 to ABC as trustee of the Harley Family Trust. ABC can distribute up to 60% of the trust's annual income to Harley. ABC is to distribute any income not distributed to Harley to his children. Harley's creditors can reach up to 60% of the trust's annual income even if ABC decides to distribute a lesser amount to him.

3. Creditors of Settlor's Estate

The personal representative of the settlor's probate estate might be entitled to use assets of his revocable trust to pay claims against his estate. UTC § 505(a)(3). The trust might also be liable for its share of any federal estate tax assessed at the settlor's death. The will or trust might include language indicating how liability is to be apportioned between the two entities.

4. Asset Protection Trusts

In 1989, the Cook Islands amended its international trust act to provide that a spendthrift provision protecting the retained interest of the settlor of a trust created under the act would be valid and enforced. Several offshore jurisdictions followed suit over the next few years. By the end of the twentieth century, variations of the asset protection trust were available in numerous Caribbean and European jurisdictions. These statutes provided the settlor with protection from creditors by recognizing spendthrift restraints, by providing that foreign judgments could not be enforced in the local courts, and by making it difficult—if not impossible—to obtain domestic judgments against nonresident trust beneficiaries.

It was not uncommon for such statutes, and trust agreements drawn under such statutes, to contain a "beneficiary under duress" provision. Those provisions allowed the trustee to disregard any instruction or direction to revoke or withdraw if the trustee determined that the beneficiary was "under duress." U.S. citizen debtors who relied on such trusts to protect assets from creditors and pled impossibility when ordered to repatriate the assets by U.S. courts, particularly U.S. bankruptcy courts, were often held in contempt and even jailed for failure to comply with the court's order. *FTC v. Affordable Media, LLC*, 179 F.3d 1228 (9th Cir. 1999). Nonetheless, offshore asset protection trusts continue to be a viable method of sheltering assets from potential creditors. However, the comfortable protections of the U.S. legal system are not available and, with offshore accounts, there is always some risk of regime change in the offshore jurisdiction.

In 1997, Alaska became the first U.S. jurisdiction to authorize similar protection for interests retained by the settlor in self-settled trusts. Several other states have followed suit. Nearly all of the domestic asset protection statutes provide protection if the settlor is a discretionary distributee.

In addition to protection against the claims of creditors generally, most of the statutes include protection against claims for tort, alimony or equitable distribution, and even child support. These provisions are in direct conflict with the U.S. and English common law, as reflected in Restatement (Third) of Trusts § 58(2) comment e, Restatement (Second) of Trusts § 156, and UTC § 505(a)(2).

C. Creditors of a Beneficiary

By definition a trust involves a fiduciary who holds property for the benefit of a beneficiary. Because his interest in the trust is a property interest, the beneficiary has the rights normally associated with that type of interest. Unless somehow restricted by the terms of the trust or otherwise, his interest is freely transferrable, and, like any other property interest owned by a debtor, is subject to the claims of his creditors. This section describes methods a settlor might use to limit a beneficiary's interest and thus prevent the beneficiary's creditors from reaching that interest.

1. Spendthrift Provisions

a. Requirements for Spendthrift Provision

Spendthrift provisions are designed to prevent alienation of a beneficiary's interest in the trust. A settlor includes spendthrift provisions in a trust instrument for one of two purposes: to prevent creditors of a beneficiary from accessing trust assets or to prevent a beneficiary from assigning or otherwise voluntarily alienating her interest in the trust. These provisions are routinely inserted in trust instruments; because they are likely to be boilerplate, they do not necessarily indicate that the settlor had any concerns about the beneficiary. Although the spendthrift language is a provision in a trust that probably has additional purposes, trusts with these provisions are often referred to as spendthrift trusts.

UTC § 502(a) provides creditor protection only if the spendthrift provision restrains *both* voluntary and involuntary transfer of a beneficiary's interest. Most states include that requirement, as does the Restatement. Restatement (Third) of Trusts § 58(1).

> **Example 15-2.** Sam created a trust for the benefit of his daughter Dora and Dora's descendants. The trust instrument stated: "No beneficiary of this trust may voluntarily assign or otherwise alienate his or her interest in this trust." That provision does not satisfy UTC § 502(a) because it restrains only voluntary transfers. The result would be the same if the trust instrument instead read: "No creditor shall have access to the interest of any beneficiary of this trust." That provision would restrain only involuntary transfers.

The provisions below are typical of the language a settlor might use to satisfy the UTC requirements:

- No beneficiary shall have the power to voluntarily assign or otherwise alienate her interest, nor shall any creditor have access to the interest of any beneficiary.
- No beneficiary hereunder may assign, sell, hypothecate, anticipate, or alienate his or her interest in either income or principal of this trust

and no creditor of any beneficiary shall be allowed to attach or subject such interest to any lien or claim.

The UTC also provides "short-hand" language. Language providing that a beneficiary's interest is held subject to a spendthrift trust is sufficient to restrain voluntary and involuntary alienation. UTC § 502(b). The settlor need not use that exact language; words of "similar import" are sufficient.

b. *Effect on Creditors and Beneficiaries*

The UTC treats a beneficiary and his creditors somewhat differently. UTC § 502(c). If the trust contains a valid spendthrift provision, the beneficiary cannot transfer an interest in the trust in violation of that provision. A creditor or assignee of the beneficiary cannot normally reach the beneficiary's interest until the beneficiary actually receives it. But a creditor or assignee might have greater access, despite the spendthrift provision, if another statutory provision provides for greater access.

The majority of U.S. jurisdictions recognize spendthrift restraints either by statute or by judicial decision based on common-law principles. The general rule is that there is no limit on the value of the interest covered by these restraints. A small number of states limit such protection either to a dollar amount of income or to the amount needed for support; any amount exceeding the limit is unprotected.

If the trust contains a valid spendthrift provision, the trustee has no liability to a beneficiary's creditor or assignee if he ignores any attempted attachment of the beneficiary's interest. A trustee that honors a voluntary assignment by a beneficiary who is *sui juris* has violated the terms of the trust but is not liable to the beneficiary. The beneficiary is, in equity, estopped from complaining of conduct that he himself authorized.

The spendthrift restraint might apply only to income interests or only to principal interests. It is usually intended to apply to both. If the spendthrift restraint is valid in a jurisdiction, it is usually valid as to either or both interests.

c. *Creditors with Access*

Both the common law and modern statutes recognize the right of select creditors to reach the spendthrift interest. UTC § 503 lists three exceptions; a spendthrift provision is unenforceable against any creditor covered by one of these exceptions. The first exception covers the beneficiary's child, spouse, or former spouse who has a judgment or court order against the beneficiary for support or maintenance. UTC § 503(b)(1). The rationale is that the trust beneficiary, whose expenses might be covered by trust distributions on his behalf, should not live well at the expense of those for whom he has a support obligation. A child is covered even if the support order was entered in another state. UTC § 503(a). A few states, by case law or statute, have limited the exception to the support of children and do not cover spouses or former spouses. N.C. Gen. Stat. § 36C-5-503.

The second exception covers a judgment creditor who provided services for the protection of the beneficiary's interest in the trust. UTC § 503(b)(2). Note that the exception applies only to a limited group of creditors. The creditor must have a judgment against the beneficiary, and the services must have been to protect the beneficiary's interest in the trust. Other types of services are not covered by this exception even if the creditor has a judgment for payment.

The third exception covers a claim of the jurisdiction in which the trust is situated or of the United States to the extent a statute of the jurisdiction or federal law so provides. UTC § 503(b)(3). The UTC adopts a slightly different rule with regard to state or federal claims against the beneficiary of a spendthrift trust. It has long been recognized that federal tax law trumps any state law, statutory or otherwise, for federal tax liens. Presumably the same is true of any other federal claims. With regard to state claims, the precedents have differentiated between state claims for unpaid taxes and other claims, such as Medicaid reimbursement. The UTC is drafted in such a way as to leave the decision regarding such issues to each state.

If a creditor is covered by UTC § 503(b), he may obtain a court order that attaches present or future distributions to the beneficiary or for the beneficiary's benefit. UTC § 503(c). This provision gives the court discretion to limit relief to that which is appropriate under the circumstances. Some jurisdictions have modified the scope of this provision. For example, Florida allows attachment of present and future distributions only as a last resort for claims by spouses, former spouses, children, and certain judgment creditors. It does not apply the "last resort" language to attachment by the state or federal government. Fla. Stat. § 736.0503(3).

Although the UTC contains no such provision, the Restatement (Third) of Trusts § 59 allows creditors who have provided necessary services or support to reach the beneficiary's interest in a spendthrift trust. The absence of such a provision in the UTC is consistent with its rejection of their right to reach the beneficiary's interest in a discretionary trust with a support standard imposed (which is the UTC's equivalent of a traditional support trust).

2. Discretionary Trusts; Effect of a Standard

A trust instrument might provide that the amount to be distributed on behalf of a beneficiary can be determined only by reference to his need for health, education, support, and maintenance. In that case, the trustee can make payments only in that amount and for that purpose. As a result, the trustee might make no payment to any of the beneficiary's assignees or creditors even if the instrument does not contain a spendthrift provision. The only exception would be a creditor whose claim was for an outlay necessary for the beneficiary's support.

The beneficiary of a support trust might compel the trustee to make distributions necessary for his support. The beneficiary generally has this right even if the instrument gives the trustee "discretion" or "sole discretion" to determine the amount necessary for such support. This rule will not apply if a court determines that the language used creates a discretionary trust instead of a support trust. The discussion below of discretionary trusts illustrates the problems with ambiguous language in jurisdictions that have not adopted UTC § 504.

The trust instrument might give the trustee discretion to determine what amounts, if any, of income or principal are to be distributed to any beneficiary. In that event, a beneficiary has no interest until the trustee exercises discretion in her favor. It is generally held that an assignment by the beneficiary or an attachment by her creditor gives neither the assignee nor the creditor any greater right than the beneficiary herself has. Because the beneficiary has no right to demand any distribution, neither an assignee nor a creditor could obtain such a right.

The trustee cannot be compelled by an assignee or creditor to exercise his discretion to make a distribution. However, if after receiving notice of an assignment or service of process by a creditor, the trustee does exercise his discretion in favor of the beneficiary, he must honor the assignment or attachment. If he fails to do so and pays the money to the beneficiary instead of the assignee or creditor, the trustee is personally liable unless the interest of the beneficiary was also protected by a valid spendthrift restraint. Restatement (Third) of Trusts § 60.

In order for the trust to be a discretionary trust for purposes of creditor access, the trustee must have discretion *whether* to make a distribution to the beneficiary; discretion that merely covers *when* to distribute is not sufficient. Often, the trust language will be ambiguous. In that situation, a court must determine whether the language used creates a truly discretionary interest that is protected from creditors or instead creates a support trust. The distinction is important, because creditors who have provided necessities for the beneficiary's support can reach the beneficiary's interest in a support trust.

The following is an example of ambiguous language. "The trustee shall distribute such sums of income and, if income is insufficient, principal, as the trustee shall in its sole discretion determine to be necessary for the comfortable maintenance and support of the beneficiary."

Cases are widely divided on this issue, and including any sort of standard regarding the discretion of the trustee should be avoided if the settlor desires a true discretionary trust protected from assignment or attachment. The UTC resolves this issue by eliminating any distinction in the rights of the creditors. UTC § 504 applies to discretionary trusts. It prevents most creditors from accessing the beneficiary's interest even if the trust does not contain a spendthrift provision. It applies even if the trustee's discretion is expressed based on a standard of distribution. It also applies even if the trustee abuses its discretion. UTC § 504(b).

> **Example 15-3.** Serena established a trust with the following provision: "The trustee is authorized to distribute income to my brother Brad in its sole discretion." Because this is a discretionary trust, most creditors cannot access it.
>
> **Example 15-4.** Serena instead used the following provision: "The trustee is authorized to distribute income for my brother Brad's support in its sole discretion." Because this is a discretionary trust, most creditors cannot access it even though the trustee's discretion is based on a standard of distribution.

If the trustee does not comply with a standard of distribution or abuses its discretion, UTC § 504(c) gives the beneficiary's child, spouse, and former spouse limited rights. A court might order a distribution to satisfy a judgment or court order against the beneficiary for the support or maintenance of these individuals. The payment is limited to an amount that would be equitable under the circumstances. In addition, it cannot exceed the amount that the trustee would have distributed to the beneficiary (or for his benefit) if the trustee had acted correctly. In other words, UTC § 504(c) does not necessarily give the child, spouse, or former spouse unlimited access to trust assets. If the trustee fails to comply with the standard or abuses its discretion, the beneficiary can also maintain an action against the trustee. UTC § 504(d).

If the trust is a traditional discretionary trust, the trustee's discretion is not subject to any standard of review other than clear abuse. UTC § 504 does not increase or decrease the rights of the beneficiary's creditors. If the trust instrument contains a standard relating to the beneficiary's support and maintenance, his creditors do not have the same rights that they would have in a common-law jurisdiction despite commentary to the UTC that provides otherwise. If there is a court order requiring the beneficiary to provide support, a creditor who has supplied support for a child, spouse, or former spouse may reach the trust in satisfaction of its claim. A creditor who has supplied necessary support to the beneficiary does not have that right.

Because a beneficiary can serve as trustee, he may have the power to make distributions to himself. A trustee who has discretion to make distributions to himself (or on his behalf) has a power of appointment over trust assets. UTC § 504(e) limits creditor access to the trustee-beneficiary's interest if the trustee's power to benefit himself is limited by an ascertainable standard. In that case, the creditor's rights are no greater than they would be if the beneficiary was not acting as a trustee.

UTC § 504(e) is intended to limit the effect of Restatement (Third) of Trusts § 60. The Restatement provision would allow the creditors of a beneficiary who is also a trustee to reach his interest in the trust. The UTC commentary explains that this provision treats creditor claims similarly to the federal transfer tax treatment of these powers. A common estate planning device gives a trustee-beneficiary a power of distribution on his own behalf, but subject to an ascertainable standard. The trust instrument would typically use the Internal Revenue Code language: "health, education, support, or maintenance." I.R.C. § 2041(b)(1)(A). Such a standard prevents the power from being deemed a general power of appointment. The property subject to the power avoids inclusion in the trustee-beneficiary's gross estate for purposes of the federal estate tax. UTC § 504(e) would likewise protect the interest from the claims of creditors.

3. Forfeiture Provisions

A forfeiture provision provides that the beneficiary's interest shall cease upon any attempted assignment of the interest or upon any attempted attachment of the interest by the beneficiary's creditors. This type of provision does not protect the beneficiary's interest but does protect the trust assets from his creditors. The trust instrument might provide that the trust will continue for any remaining beneficiaries. It might instead provide for returning the trust principal to the settlor. If the trust is what is commonly called a "protective trust," the instrument will provide that the trustee will hold the assets in either a discretionary or support trust but will make no distributions to the forfeiting beneficiary that would be subjected to the claims of the creditors or assignees.

4. Beneficiary with General Power of Appointment

a. Power of Withdrawal

In addition to an income interest, the beneficiary might have a power to withdraw trust principal. That makes her the donee of a power of appointment. If this power is not limited by an ascertainable standard, most commonly relating to "health, education, support, or maintenance," it is a general power of appointment. I.R.C. § 2041(b)(1)(A). As such, the value of the property subject to the power is included in the beneficiary's gross estate for federal estate tax purposes. It might also be subject to the claims of her creditors.

At common law, the donee of a general power of appointment had no interest in the property subject to the power unless she exercised the power. If she did not exercise the power, her creditors could not reach the property. If the power of withdrawal is presently exercisable, she can reach the property by simply appointing it to herself. Recognizing this ability, the modern movement is to subject such property to the claims of her creditors. UTC § 505(b)(2) is consistent with this view. It provides that the holder of a presently exercisable power of withdrawal is treated as the settlor of a revocable trust for the property subject to the power and is subject to the same creditor access as she would be if she was the settlor.

A beneficiary might hold a testamentary general power, which allows her to appoint to her estate or the creditors of her estate by will only, rather than a presently exercisable power, which she could use to benefit herself during her life. The decisions are mixed and the UTC is silent regarding creditor access when the beneficiary's power is testamentary.

b. Lapsing Power of Withdrawal

A beneficiary might receive a power of withdrawal that is not subject to an ascertainable standard but that is limited in time. The settlor uses that type of power to reduce the value of transfers to a trust that are treated as taxable gifts. It is a creature of federal tax law that has consequences for the rights of the beneficiary's creditors.

Unless properly drafted, this type of withdrawal power results in the beneficiary being treated as a settlor. In that case, creditors may have rights against trust property they would not otherwise have had. Creditor rights would exist while the beneficiary was able to exercise the power and could exist even after the power lapsed. UTC § 505(b).

D. Creditors of the Trustee

As a general rule, the trust is not liable to the trustee's creditors even if the trustee is insolvent or bankrupt. UTC § 507. Creditors of a trustee who is neither a settlor nor a beneficiary can access trust assets only in limited situations. If the trustee deals with those creditors as if the trust assets were his own, and the creditors had no reason to know that the trustee had title in a fiduciary capacity, they might have rights to that property under state law.

CHECKPOINTS

- The settlor's creditors can generally access trust assets while the trust is revocable.
- If the trust is irrevocable, the settlor's creditors are generally limited to accessing his retained interest, if any.
- Some jurisdictions let settlors avoid creditor access by establishing asset protection trusts.
- A settlor can limit access by a beneficiary's creditors by including a spendthrift provision in the trust or by making distributions subject to the trustee's discretion. A jurisdiction might also limit creditor access if the trust is a support trust.
- To be effective, a spendthrift provision must bar voluntary *and* involuntary transfer or alienation of the beneficiary's interest in the trust.
- Certain of the beneficiary's creditors, particularly spouses, ex-spouses, and children with court orders for support, may be able to gain access despite a spendthrift provision.

- If a beneficiary has a power of withdrawal, he could be treated as a settlor unless the power is limited by an ascertainable standard.
- Creditors of a trustee are generally unable to access trust assets to satisfy his personal obligations.

CHAPTER 16

Modification, Reformation, Termination, and Revocation

ROADMAP

- Uniform act provisions
- Trust decanting
- Revocation and amendment by settlor

A. Chapter Overview

This chapter focuses on changing the provisions of a trust. Most of this chapter covers modification, reformation, and termination of trust provisions or of the trusts themselves. Because an inter vivos trust is likely to be revocable until the settlor dies, it includes possible modifications by the settlor.

This chapter complements discussion elsewhere regarding changes caused by other events. These include the settlor's divorce from a beneficiary or death at the hands of a beneficiary, or by disclaimer, exercise of a power of appointment, or agreement between beneficiaries.

B. Uniform Act Provisions

1. Relevance of the Rule Against Perpetuities

The UPC provides for a 90-year wait-and-see rule against perpetuities period. UPC § 2-901. Some states allow much longer delayed vesting or have eliminated vesting requirements. Although the perpetuities provisions are included in the UPC, delayed vesting is really a trusts problem. The longer a trust exists, the more likely that some of its terms will not serve the settlor's original purpose or will not be in the beneficiaries' best interests. Legislatures have responded by enacting statutes allowing modification or termination of trusts. These statutes also provide for reformation of trusts.

These statutes vary in their coverage. Some require judicial approval. Others allow the trustee to make changes after giving notice. Some allow the trustee and qualified beneficiaries to agree to changes, involving a court only if there is disagreement. Some apply only if the trust provides for them; others apply only if the trust is silent. The period for which the trust will operate is relevant in some jurisdictions—changes could be easier to obtain if trust interests do not vest within a stated perpetuities period.

2. Trust Termination: Revocation; Expiration; Failure of Purpose

UTC § 410(a) provides that a trust terminates to the extent it is revoked. Although a complete revocation terminates the trust's existence, a devise to a revoked trust could be saved if the settlor's will incorporates by reference the trust's terms as they read when the will was executed. UPC § 2-510. The UTC also terminates a trust to the extent it expires according to its terms. For example, a trust that has been divided into subtrusts might terminate as to the subtrust for one group of beneficiaries while other subtrusts continue. This situation could arise if the settlor provided for dividing the trust into subtrusts for each of his children and terminating a child's subtrust when she attained a certain age.

The UTC also terminates a trust if it has no remaining purpose to be served or if its purpose has become unlawful, contrary to public policy, or impossible to achieve. This language in UTC § 410(a) tracks language in UTC § 404 stating the requirements for a trust's purpose.

3. Modification or Termination by Consent

UTC § 411 involves several scenarios, some of which allow modification or termination by consent, and some of which require court approval. It includes alternative language, so it is likely that versions will vary from state to state. The section has two constants: the trust must be both irrevocable and non-charitable. Those requirements make sense. If the trust was revocable, the settlor could unilaterally modify or terminate it. If the trust was charitable, the power to modify or terminate by consent could prevent the settlor from qualifying for a charitable contribution deduction.

The first alternative in UTC § 411(a) allows modification or termination if the settlor and all beneficiaries consent. In that case, modification or termination occurs even if that action is inconsistent with a material purpose of the trust. The second alternative is similar; it provides for a court to order modification or termination after it finds that the settlor and all beneficiaries consent to that action. An agent can consent on behalf of the settlor if his power of attorney expressly gives the agent that power. The settlor's conservator (or guardian if no conservator has been appointed) can exercise the power with court approval. There is no requirement that the trustee's consent be obtained.

UTC § 411(b) provides for modification or termination if a court finds that all beneficiaries consent. It does not require the settlor or trustee to consent. The court can terminate the trust if it determines continuing the trust is not necessary to achieve any material purpose. It can modify the trust if the modification is not inconsistent with a material purpose. An optional provision, UTC § 411(c), provides that a spendthrift provision is not presumed to constitute a material purpose and thus would not prevent termination or modification. If a state does not enact that subsection or similar language, its courts might accord more significance to spendthrift provisions when deciding whether to allow modification or termination.

If the trust is terminated under this section, its property is distributed according to terms agreed on by the beneficiaries. UTC § 411(d). Even if there is not unanimous agreement, the court may still modify or terminate the trust. It can do so if it finds that § 411 would have been applicable if all beneficiaries had consented and that the interest of any non-consenting beneficiary will be adequately protected. UTC § 411(e).

Example 16-1. Five years ago, Fred created an irrevocable inter vivos trust with ABC Bank as trustee. ABC was to distribute income to Fred for life and then distribute the trust principal to his children. Fred recently suffered financial reverses. He and all his children (all of whom were adults) agreed to terminate the trust and distribute its assets to him. ABC must terminate the trust and distribute its assets to Fred.

4. Unanticipated Circumstances or Inability to Administer the Trust Effectively

UTC § 412 differentiates between the trust's administrative provisions and its dispositive provisions. In each situation, whatever action is taken must be authorized by the court. If the trust is to be terminated, the trustee is to distribute trust assets in a manner that is consistent with the trust's purpose. UTC § 412(c).

UTC § 412(a) applies to both administrative and dispositive terms. The court can modify those terms—or terminate the trust—if that will further the trust's purposes. Before taking this action, the court must determine that this action is appropriate because of circumstances that the settlor did not anticipate. If the court modifies the trust, it must do so to the extent practicable in a manner that is consistent with the settlor's probable intent. The comments indicate that one such unanticipated circumstance might involve a beneficiary's economic condition or health. The comments also indicate that the court can modify the trust even if the circumstances existed when the trust was created, assuming the settlor was not aware of them. In that case, the trust provisions might have been based on a mistake of fact. The comments indicate that modification under this section complements reformation based on mistake of fact or law under UTC § 415.

UTC § 412(b) applies to administrative terms. The court can modify those if it determines that continuing the trust without modification would be impracticable or wasteful or would impair the trust's administration.

5. Cy Pres

A trust with only charitable beneficiaries is not subject to the rule against perpetuities. Events that occur during its potentially indefinite existence could make its original purpose impossible to achieve or unnecessary. For example, the settlor might create a trust to fund research into curing or preventing a particular disease. If scientists discover a cure or means of prevention, the trust funds may no longer be necessary for that purpose. Or a trust might be established to fund the maintenance of a new county hospital. If the county government decides not to build a new hospital, the trust's purpose becomes impossible to achieve. The doctrine of cy pres ("as close as possible") may apply in these situations.

UTC § 413(a) governs when the purpose for a charitable trust becomes unlawful, impracticable, impossible to achieve, or wasteful. It allows the court to continue the trust with a new beneficiary or purpose, modify it in some other way, or terminate it and distribute its property to a different charitable beneficiary. The goal is to adhere as closely as possible to the settlor's intent in creating the trust. Because reversion to the settlor is rarely allowed, the UTC effectively infers a general charitable intent when the settlor's purpose becomes unlawful, impracticable, impossible to achieve, or wasteful. Not every state statute infers a general charitable intent.

Reversion to the settlor or other noncharitable beneficiary is an exception rather than the rule. UTC § 413(b) allows a reversion to the settlor only if the instrument provides for such distribution and the settlor is still living. It allows distribution to a different noncharitable beneficiary only if the instrument provides for such distribution and the trust has been in existence less than 21 years. State statutes might not include either distribution provision.

6. Uneconomic Trust

UTC § 414(a) reinforces a statement in UTC § 404: a trust and its terms must be for the benefit of the beneficiaries. If trust expenses regularly exceed trust income, the trustee might find it impossible to provide for the beneficiaries without invading—and perhaps ultimately eliminating—trust principal. Rather than focus on the income produced, however, this provision focuses on the amount of trust principal, which is likely to be a good indicator of potential trust income. If the trustee determines that the value of the trust is not sufficient to justify the cost of administration, it can terminate the trust. The UTC includes $50,000 as a cut-off point; the trustee has a power to terminate only if the trust value is below that amount. The amount is bracketed so that states that wish to do so can substitute a different cut-off point.

Before terminating the trust, the trustee must give notice to the qualified beneficiaries. Unless one of them brings a proceeding to disapprove the termination, the trust avoids being further depleted by the costs of obtaining court approval to terminate.

A trust can be uneconomic even if its principal is at least $50,000. That is likely to be true if there are many income beneficiaries, the trust instrument requires outlays for expensive items (such as tuition), or the costs of administration limit the amount that can be distributed to beneficiaries. UTC § 414(b) authorizes a court to modify or terminate a trust if it determines that the value of the trust is not sufficient to justify the cost of administration. Instead of terminating the trust, the court can appoint a different trustee as a cost-saving measure. Either the trustee or any beneficiary can bring an action under this provision.

If the trust is terminated under UTC § 414, the trustee is to distribute the trust property in a manner consistent with the trust purposes. UTC § 414(c). It is possible, of course, that the trust instrument indicates how the principal is to be distributed in the event of an early termination.

This section does not apply if the trust involves an easement for conservation or preservation. UTC § 414(d). The comments indicate that the easement is likely to have more importance to the settlor and might have involved a charitable trust.

7. Reformation to Correct Mistakes

UTC § 415 allows the court to reform a trust if there is clear and convincing evidence that the challenged terms were based on a mistake of fact or law. The proponent must establish the settlor's intent by clear and convincing evidence. The document can be reformed even if it is unambiguous.

These provisions apply whether the challenged terms were caused by a mistake of expression or a mistake of inducement. The former involves erroneous language—omitting language the settlor wanted included, including language she did not want, or misstating her intent. This type of error could result from a drafting error. Mistakes of inducement involve language that is accurate, but the instrument contains an error attributable to the settlor's misunderstanding of the law or of the operative facts. She might have erroneously believed, for example, that she could not exclude one or more of her children from a trust for children.

The comments to UTC § 415 indicate that the standard of clear and convincing evidence is used because of the risks involved in relying on extrinsic evidence as to what the settlor's intent really was. Reformation involves changing language as opposed to interpreting existing language, which is involved in resolving ambiguities. The comments to UPC § 2-805 indicate it is based on UTC § 415.

8. Modification of Trusts to Achieve Tax Objectives

UTC § 416 provides for modification of a trust if its terms do not comport with the settlor's tax objectives (or probable objectives if the settlor is dead). Unlike reformation based on mistake, modification based on the settlor's probable tax objectives does not include a clear and convincing evidence standard. This makes sense in view of what is likely at stake. If a trust is reformed for nontax reasons, some beneficiaries are likely to receive more at the expense of others, who will receive less. When it is modified to reflect the settlor's tax objectives, the outcome is likely to be that the beneficiaries receive more (and the taxing authorities receive less). Modification might not be effective, however, against the claims of the relevant taxing authorities.

9. Combination and Division of Trusts

The administration of trusts must consider the beneficiaries' interests. Those interests might be satisfied (or more effectively satisfied) if multiple trusts are combined into a single trust or a single trust is divided into separate trusts. Combining separate trusts benefiting the same beneficiary or group of beneficiaries could reduce administrative costs. Separating a trust might allow the trustee to pursue one investment strategy for a beneficiary with a current need for income and a different strategy for a beneficiary who would prefer that the trustee focus on growing the trust principal that his descendants will ultimately receive.

UTC § 417 allows a trustee to take either action if it first notifies the qualified beneficiaries. The trustee cannot combine or separate trusts if the action would impair the rights of any beneficiary or adversely affect achieving the trust purposes. Although the trustee does not need court approval or beneficiary consent, the comments indicate that it might decide that obtaining approval would be appropriate. Because the trustee must give advance notice, a beneficiary can commence an action to prevent combination or separation.

10. Challenging Modification, Reformation, or Termination

UTC § 410 indicates who can bring an action to approve or disapprove an action brought pursuant to the provisions governing modification, termination, and reformation. UTC § 410(b) provides that a trustee or a beneficiary can commence a proceeding to approve or disapprove a proposed modification or termination described in UTC § 411 through UTC § 417. It adds optional language allowing the settlor to commence a proceeding to approve or disapprove a proposed modification or termination covered by UTC § 411. Finally, it allows the settlor of a charitable trust to maintain a cy pres proceeding under UTC § 413.

UTC § 410(b) does not require that all beneficiaries join in an action, that a beneficiary and a trustee act together, or that a beneficiary be a "qualified beneficiary." Some of the provisions described above do impose one or more of these requirements. The settlor often has no part to play in proceedings regarding irrevocable trusts even if he is still alive. And spendthrift provisions might not be sufficient to prevent a court from modifying or terminating a trust.

C. Trust Decanting

In 2015, the Uniform Law Commission approved the Uniform Trust Decanting Act (UTDA). Some states that adopted the UTC had already included decanting provisions in their trust codes. They might choose to maintain their originally adopted statutes or amend them to conform to the UTDA. Eighteen states have enacted the UTDA.

The UTDA allows an authorized fiduciary to distribute assets from one trust to another. It is a mechanism for amending an irrevocable trust without obtaining judicial approval under the UTC provisions described above. The act provides two options: distributing trust principal from the first trust to a second trust; or amending the terms of the first trust, after which it is treated as if it was a second trust. The comments to the UTDA indicate that the latter option eliminates the need to retitle trust assets.

Decanting might be appropriate, for example, if statutes regarding trust administration in effect when the trust was created are different from statutes currently in effect. It might also be appropriate if administrative or investment powers do not reflect changes in the law or in the general economic climate.

The discussion below generally uses the term authorized fiduciary rather than trustee. The decanting power authorized by the UTDA can be exercised only by an authorized fiduciary. A trustee might be an authorized fiduciary, but in a trust with multiple trustees, it is possible that only one of them qualifies as an authorized fiduciary. It is also possible that someone other than a trustee will be an authorized fiduciary. A person is an authorized fiduciary if that person either has the discretion to distribute the principal of the first trust to one or more of the beneficiaries or has the discretion to direct the trustee to make such a distribution. The discretion can cover the entire trust principal or a portion thereof. UTDA § 2(3)(A).

1. Trusts for Which Decanting Is Permitted, Prohibited, or Restricted

UTDA § 3 provides general eligibility rules. The decanting power is available for private express trusts. It is not available for trusts that are solely charitable. The trust generally must be irrevocable. Any right of revocation retained by a settlor must be subject to the approval of the trustee or of a party with an adverse interest.

UTDA § 3 does not prevent a settlor from limiting or prohibiting a decanting power in the trust instrument. Nor does it prevent her from including distribution provisions in the trust instrument, from creating a power of appointment that allows appointment to another trust, or from including provisions related to trust modification. It does not affect authority of a trustee, powerholder, or third party to make distributions, appointments, or modifications pursuant to the trust instrument, another statute, common law, court order, or nonjudicial settlement agreement.

UTDA § 15 prevents the fiduciary from exercising a decanting power to the extent the trust instrument expressly prohibits exercise or makes any exercise subject to restrictions in the trust instrument. Trust provisions that prohibit amendment or revocation of the trust are not prohibitions against decanting. Spendthrift provisions are not prohibitions against decanting.

If the trust instrument limited the decanting power but did not completely forbid it, the second trust must include the same restrictions that the first trust did. Because UTDA § 2(10) defines "decanting power" as a power exercisable under the UTDA, a prohibition or restriction on decanting must refer to the UTDA or to the state's law authorizing decanting.

2. Notice to Beneficiaries and Other Persons

The authorized fiduciary does not need beneficiary or settlor permission to decant, but it must notify certain persons 60 days in advance of exercising the power. The fiduciary must notify each living settlor of the first trust, each qualified beneficiary of that trust, each holder of a presently exercisable power of appointment over that trust, any person who has the right to replace the authorized fiduciary, every other fiduciary of that trust, and every fiduciary of the second trust. If there is a charitable interest, the fiduciary must notify the state attorney general or other designated state official. UTDA § 7.

The notice must include copies of both trust instruments, state the date on which the fiduciary intends to exercise the power, and indicate the manner of exercise. The fiduciary may act before the notice period expires if all persons entitled to notice provide written waivers allowing it to do so.

UTDA § 8 allows the fiduciary to give notice to a person who is authorized to represent and bind another person rather than giving actual notice to that other person. This rule mirrors representation rules in the UTC. UTDA § 8 precludes a settlor from representing or binding a beneficiary for purposes of decanting.

UTDA § 9 provides for court involvement if such involvement is requested by the authorized fiduciary, by a beneficiary, by a person entitled to notice under UTDA § 7, or by any person with standing to enforce a charity's interest. Although only qualified beneficiaries are entitled to notice, any beneficiary can request court involvement.

3. Extent of the Fiduciary's Power

The fiduciary's decanting power reflects the type of discretionary power it has over principal of the first trust. Either the fiduciary has expanded distributive discretion or limited distributive discretion. If the fiduciary's distributive discretion is not limited by an ascertainable standard or by a reasonably definite standard, it has expanded distributive discretion. UTDA § 2(11). If such limits apply, it has limited distributive discretion.

a. Expanded Distributive Discretion

A fiduciary with expanded distributive discretion may decant the principal of the first trust to a second trust. UTDA § 11(b). The fiduciary's powers are subject to limits in UTDA § 14 included to protect charitable interests.

The fiduciary has more leeway regarding powers than beneficial interests in the second trust. UTDA § 11(d) allows the fiduciary to retain or omit a power of appointment from the first trust. It cannot, however, omit a presently exercisable general power of appointment. The fiduciary can also create or modify a power of appointment held by a current beneficiary of the first trust if the fiduciary has expanded distributive discretion to distribute principal to that beneficiary. It can also do so with respect to a powerholder who is a successor beneficiary or presumptive remainder beneficiary, but the power will be exercisable only after the powerholder becomes a current beneficiary. The powers in UTDA § 11(d) are subject to the provisions of UTDA § 11(c)(3).

> **Example 16-2.** Georgia's testamentary trust provided that her children would receive income for life, with remainder to her grandchildren alive when the last child died. Georgia gave her sister Susan the authority to distribute trust principal to Georgia's children before the trust terminated. She placed no limits on Susan's power. Susan can transfer the trust property to a new trust and give Georgia's son Tony the power to distribute principal to his children before the trust terminates. Tony is a current beneficiary and Susan has expanded distributive discretion to distribute principal to him.

The fiduciary's discretion with respect to beneficiaries is limited by UTDA § 11(c). It generally prevents the fiduciary from adding new current beneficiaries or new presumptive remainder beneficiaries or successor beneficiaries. It also prevents reducing or eliminating any vested interest. It does not prevent the fiduciary from eliminating or reducing a nonvested interest. The limits in UTDA § 11(c) are subject to the provisions of UTDA § 13. That section imposes additional rules if a beneficiary of the first trust has a disability that might qualify him for government benefits.

b. Limited Distributive Discretion

If the fiduciary's distributive discretion over the principal of the first trust is limited by an ascertainable standard or by a reasonably definite standard, the fiduciary has limited distributive discretion. The term ascertainable standard reflects Internal Revenue Code definitions as to when a power of appointment is general or nongeneral for purposes of federal transfer taxes. A standard is ascertainable if the distributions are for the beneficiary's "health, education, support, or maintenance." UTDA § 2(2).

The term reasonably definite standard is also defined with reference to the Internal Revenue Code. A standard is reasonably definite if it is a clearly measurable standard under which the powerholder can be held accountable under I.R.C. § 674(b)(5)(A) and its regulations. UTDA § 2(21). Although the regulations largely mirror power of appointment language, they do add additional items. For example, a power to distribute corpus to meet an emergency is reasonably definite. Treas. Reg. § 1.674(b)-1(b)(5)(i). I.R.C. § 674 is an income tax provision related to grantor trusts and the appropriate person to be taxed on trust income.

UTDA § 12 covers the decanting power when the fiduciary has limited distributive discretion. The beneficiaries of the first trust must receive beneficial interests in the second trust that are substantially similar to their interests in the first trust. This requirement is met by considering their interests in the aggregate rather than individually. The comments indicate that splitting a trust into separate trusts, one for each of the settlor's children, could satisfy this requirement. Even though each child's rights would now be limited to a fixed portion of the original trust, no child would risk receiving less than that fixed portion.

UTDA § 12 indicates that a power to make distributions on the beneficiary's behalf is treated as substantially similar to a power to make distributions to the beneficiary. The comments indicate that this provision is important if a beneficiary is under a disability. The comments also indicate that UTDA § 12 would allow the second trust to have different administrative positions. As was true for trusts with expanded distributive discretion, the fiduciary's powers are limited by UTDA § 14 to protect charitable interests.

D. Revocation and Amendment by Settlor

Inter vivos trusts are revocable unless the trust terms expressly provide otherwise. UTC § 602(a). This UTC provision reverses the common law presumption applied in the absence of language making the trust revocable. Comments to the Restatement (Third) of Trusts § 63 indicate that the settlor's failure to include the power to revoke or to retain a beneficial interest in the trust raises a rebuttable presumption of irrevocability.

Before assuming that a particular trust is revocable, you should read the relevant state statute and note its effective date. Even if it makes trusts revocable, it is likely to follow the UTC by applying the change to trusts created after the statute's effective date.

Although UTC § 602(a) gives the settlor the power to revoke or amend, it does not require her to exercise that power. Even if she initially had the power, she might later relinquish it, often to prevent the value of the trust principal from being subject to estate tax when she dies. I.R.C. § 2038.

Until the settlor relinquishes the revocation power, she may direct the trustee to transfer trust assets back to her. She may do so even if she is not otherwise a beneficiary of the trust. Although this power resembles the power to invade, we usually refer to it as a power to revoke. This power has consequences related to creditor access to trust assets, valuing a surviving spouse's elective share, and the settlor's estate tax. If exercised in a manner that revokes the trust, it may also result in voiding any devises to the trust in the settlor's will. If she revokes the trust, the trustee will transfer the trust property according to her instructions. UTC § 602(d).

If the settlor exercises her power to simply amend the trust, she may change its administrative or dispositive provisions. She may substitute beneficiaries or change beneficial interests from vested to contingent.

Revocation or amendment by the settlor is valid only if she has the requisite capacity and complies with any formalities imposed by statute or by the trust instrument. Additional rules apply if the trust had more than one settlor.

1. Capacity

The settlor of a revocable trust must have the same capacity to amend or revoke the trust as was required to create it in the first place. She must have the same capacity as the jurisdiction requires for the execution of a valid will:

testamentary capacity. She must also have this capacity to add property to the trust or to give directions to the trustee. UTC § 601.

A settlor might be represented by an agent under a power of attorney. After she has been judged incapacitated, the agency relationship may continue if the power was durable. UTC § 602(e) allows the agent to exercise the power of revocation, amendment, or distribution on the settlor's behalf, but only if the trust instrument or the power of attorney expressly gives the agent that power.

An incapacitated settlor might also be represented by a conservator or guardian. UTC § 602(f) allows the conservator or guardian to exercise those powers only with court approval.

2. Formalities

UTC § 602(c)(1) requires that the settlor (or her fiduciary) exercise the power by substantially complying with any formalities required by the trust instrument. If the instrument is silent, the settlor may even exercise her power by a later will or codicil. If she uses this method, she must either expressly refer to the trust or she must specifically devise property that was part of the trust. This method is also available, even if the trust provides a method of revocation or amendment, if the trust does not expressly provide for its method being exclusive. UTC § 602(c)(2)(A). The settlor may also amend or revoke, assuming the trust instrument does not provide the exclusive method, by any other method that manifests clear and convincing evidence of her intent. UTC § 602(c)(2)(B).

> **Example 16-3.** Sheila executed her will five years ago. It included a devise of Blackacre to her daughter Denise. Three years ago, Sheila created an inter vivos trust for the benefit of her son Sam and his descendants. The trust instrument did not specify a method for amending or revoking the trust. Sheila transferred Blackacre and other property to the trustee. Sheila died this year without amending either the will or the trust. Blackacre remains in the trust. Although the will devised Blackacre, it was executed before Blackacre was transferred to the trust.
>
> **Example 16-4.** Sheila executed a codicil to her will six months before she died. In the codicil, she devised Blackacre to her brother Brad. Because the trust instrument did not expressly preclude using a will or codicil to revoke or amend its terms, Brad will receive Blackacre. The codicil was executed after Blackacre was transferred to the trust. Blackacre remains

in the trust until Sheila dies, because neither the will nor the codicil is effective until then.

3. Trust with More Than One Settlor

When a trust has more than one settlor, the trust instrument might include express limits on the power to revoke or amend. Five such possibilities for a two-settlor trust are (1) requiring that both settlors agree to any amendment or revocation while both are alive and allowing no amendment or revocation by the surviving settlor; (2) requiring that both settlors agree to any amendment or revocation while both are alive but allowing the surviving settlor to amend or revoke the entire trust; (3) allowing each settlor to revoke with respect to his or her property while both are alive but allowing no amendment or revocation by the surviving settlor; (4) allowing each settlor to revoke with respect to his or her property at any time; or (5) allowing each settlor to revoke with respect to his or her property while both are alive and allowing the surviving settlor to amend or revoke the entire trust. If the trust instrument does not provide rules governing amendment or revocation, we use the default rules in the relevant statute.

UTC § 602(b) distinguishes between community property and other property when a trust has more than one settlor. Either settlor can revoke a trust to the extent it contains community property, but amendment requires joint action. Both community-property states and other states might use the UTC § 602(b) language or similar language. For other types of property, either settlor can revoke or amend, but only to the extent of that settlor's contributions to the trust. Spouses residing in community-property states might have acquired separately owned property; spouses residing in other states might have acquired community property when they lived in such states. Both sets of rules could apply in those situations.

Whenever a settlor amends or revokes the trust, or portion thereof, the trustee must inform any other settlors. The comments to UTC § 602 explain the importance of such notice. First, the other settlors can take action to protect their (or their successors') interest in the trust. Second, if the settlor has breached an agreement not to amend or revoke, they can sue for breach of contract. Third, if the trustee fails to give them notice, so that they can protect their rights, the trustee may be liable to them for breach of fiduciary duties.

CHECKPOINTS

- The UTC includes provisions related to modifying, terminating, or reforming a trust.
- The UTC and UTDA include provisions regarding the receipt of notice, persons eligible to make a decision regarding modification, termination, reformation, or decanting, and situations in which court intervention is required or allowed.
- An irrevocable noncharitable trust can be modified or terminated without court approval if the settlor and all beneficiaries agree. It can be modified or terminated with court approval without the settlor's agreement if all beneficiaries consent. The court can terminate the trust if it determines continuing the trust is not necessary to achieve any material purpose. It can modify the trust if the modification is not inconsistent with a material purpose.
- A court can modify administrative or dispositive terms, or even terminate the trust, if that will further the trust's purposes. Before taking this action, the court must determine that this action is appropriate because of circumstances that the settlor did not anticipate. A court can modify administrative terms if it determines that continuing the trust without modification would be impracticable or wasteful or would impair the trust's administration.
- A court can modify or terminate a charitable trust if its purpose has become unlawful, impracticable, impossible to achieve, or wasteful. When the court applies the doctrine of cy pres, it attempts to follow the settlor's purpose as closely as possible.
- A trustee can terminate a trust if it determines that the value of the trust is not sufficient to justify the cost of administration. The trustee's power to do so without consent or court approval is limited to trusts with a value below $50,000 (or other amount provided by statute or the trust instrument). The trustee must notify the qualified beneficiaries before exercising this power. A court can modify or terminate a trust if it determines that the value of the trust (even if $50,000 or more) is not sufficient to justify the cost of administration.

- A court can reform a trust if there is clear and convincing evidence that the challenged terms were based on a mistake of fact or law. The mistake could have been made by the settlor or the person drafting the instrument. The proponent must establish the settlor's intent by clear and convincing evidence. The document can be reformed even if it is unambiguous.
- A court can authorize modification of a trust if its terms do not comport with the settlor's tax objectives (or probable objectives if the settlor is dead).
- A trustee can combine separate trusts into a single trust or split a single trust into separate trusts after giving notice to the qualified beneficiaries. The trustee cannot combine or separate if the action would impair the rights of any beneficiary or adversely affect achieving the trust purpose.
- An authorized fiduciary might have the power to decant trust assets from one trust to another or to amend the initial trust to make it into a new trust.
- The power to decant exists only if the fiduciary has discretionary powers over trust principal. The fiduciary has broader decanting powers if the power is not limited by an ascertainable standard or a reasonably definite standard.
- An authorized fiduciary cannot exercise its power to decant in a manner that eliminates or reduces vested interests even if it has expanded distributive discretion.
- An authorized fiduciary with limited distributive discretion must provide beneficiaries of the first trust with substantially similar rights in the second trust. Their rights are considered in the aggregate rather than on a per-beneficiary basis.
- The settlor can prohibit or restrict a fiduciary's power to decant by appropriate language in the trust instrument.
- The settlor of an inter vivos trust generally has the power to revoke or amend the trust or withdraw trust principal.
- Powers to withdraw, invade, or revoke have consequences beyond the administration of the trust. These consequences include creditor access to trust assets, computing a surviving spouse's elective share, and computing the powerholder's estate or gift taxes.

- The trust instrument or relevant state law requires that the settlor have the requisite capacity and comply with any requisite formalities to create, amend, revoke, or add property to a revocable inter vivos trust. An agent, conservator, or guardian acting on the settlor's behalf must have the requisite authority to take these actions.
- If a trust has more than one settlor, each settlor's rights to amend or revoke may be limited to his or her own contributions unless the trust instrument provides otherwise.

CHAPTER 17

Interpreting Instruments and Rules of Construction

ROADMAP

- Ambiguities and other interpretation issues
- Class and individual gifts
- Rules of construction

A. Chapter Overview

This chapter covers rules that guide a fiduciary in carrying out the transferor's intent. The governing instrument might provide all the instructions a fiduciary (or a court) needs to carry out the testator or settlor's dispositive scheme. Extrinsic evidence might be necessary, if allowed in the jurisdiction, to resolve interpretive questions, including those related to ambiguities or errors in descriptions.

The jurisdiction might have enacted default rules of construction to guide fiduciaries in distributing the transferor's property. As was true for intestacy statutes, these rules represent the state's view of how the average transferor would act if she had considered the issue.

B. Ambiguities and Other Interpretation Issues

1. Ambiguity

Ambiguities can be latent or patent. If an ambiguity is latent, it is not apparent from the language of the instrument. When the fiduciary begins administering the estate or trust, he finds the ambiguity. A patent ambiguity is apparent from the language of the instrument. In either case, the potential transfer might fail if the fiduciary or the court cannot ascertain the transferor's intent.

Courts generally allow extrinsic evidence to explain what the transferor meant, but some jurisdictions are less willing to do so for patent ambiguities. They might instead use canons of construction to determine what was meant. They might resolve the ambiguity in favor of the last relevant clause in the will or trust. That last clause would be considered the testator's or settlor's final statement about the item in question. While that method might suffice if the document was not prepared by an attorney, it might be inappropriate when an attorney was involved. The document's order might simply reflect the attorney's ordering preference.

Another canon of construction is that of *ejusdem generis.* A reference to an "other" or a less specific item following a list of specific items is treated as having the same characteristics as the earlier items. Yet another interpretive device is to assign everyday meanings to words that are not legal terms. If a will devises "my clothing and other personal property," a court might decide that the testator meant personally used property. It would not include her stocks and bonds—although they are personal, as opposed to real, property—if it decided that the testator did not mean to include investment assets in a devise of personal property. *Romaniello v. Romaniello*, 760 So. 2d 1083 (Fla. Dist. Ct. App. 2000).

> **Example 17-1.** Tara devised "my furniture, appliances, and other household goods" to Gillian and the residue to Gordon. A court might interpret "other household goods" to include Tara's dishes and silverware but not her clothing or jewelry.

2. Devises or Trust Interests Based on Identity

When a will or trust designates a beneficiary by name, and only one potential beneficiary has that name, the fiduciary can easily determine the beneficiary. The task is less clear if more than one person has that name or if the instrument refers to a recipient by a nickname shared by others.

Example 17-2. Tom devised "my shares of XYZ Corporation stock to my nephew John." When Tom executed his will, he had one nephew named John. When he died, he had two nephews named John. This devise involves an interpretive question. It is likely that Tom meant for this devise to go to the nephew who was alive when he executed his will.

Example 17-3. Same as Example 17-2 except that Tom had only one nephew named John when he died, and it was a different nephew. The nephew who was alive when Tom executed his will predeceased him. In this situation, a court might have to determine whether the personal representative should distribute the shares to the second nephew named John, to the descendants (through antilapse) of the deceased nephew named John, partially to the surviving nephew and partially to the descendants of the deceased nephew, or to Tom's residuary devisees.

Example 17-4. Same as Example 17-2 except Tom had two nephews named John when he executed his will, and both survived him. Unlike Example 17-3, this devise involves an ambiguity or misidentification. If Tom's will listed his relatives, including both nephews, the ambiguity is patent. If it did not include such a list (or did not list nephews), the ambiguity is latent. The situation would be the same if, when he executed his will, Tom's nephews were named Jonathan and Jonathon, and both went by the nickname John.

3. Devises or Trust Interests Based on Class Characteristics

A testator or settlor might want to treat all relatives in the same category equally, including those born or adopted after she executed the instrument. In that case, she might make a class gift. But even a class gift can require interpretation if based on gender or on other characteristics that might change before a beneficiary's interest vests. The examples below concern the trust's income. Because principal will be distributed to "descendants," gender is not an issue.

> **Example 17-5.** Sam created an irrevocable trust that provides income to his daughters for life. When the trust terminates, the trustee is to pay the trust principal to Sam's descendants. When Sam created the trust, he and his late wife had four daughters. He later had a son whose mother never married Sam.

> **Example 17-6.** Seth created an irrevocable trust that provides income to his daughters for life. When the trust terminates, the trustee is to pay the trust principal to Seth's descendants. When Seth created the trust, he and his late wife had four daughters. One of his daughters later had gender reassignment surgery and is now male.

4. Devises or Trust Interests Based on Activity

A testator or settlor who wishes to reward certain behavior might condition a gift on complying with the desired behavior or increase a gift based on the degree of compliance. Assuming the proposed condition does not violate state public policy (as could be the case with a trust that conditions a beneficiary's right to income on getting divorced), it might involve issues of interpretation.

> **Example 17-7.** Talia devised "$10,000 to each of my grandchildren. The grandchild who has earned the largest number of college degrees is to receive an additional $10,000." Talia's granddaughter Greta went to a four-year college and earned a B.A. degree. Talia's granddaughter Gillian went to a community college and earned an A.A. degree; she then continued her education at a four-year college and earned a B.A. degree. Talia's will did not define college degree.

5. Devises or Trust Interests Based on Indefinite Terminology

A testator or settlor might use the term "any" to mean "every" or "all." She might instead use it to mean "any one of a group." The interpretive issue is likely to arise because she often purchased replacement property and did not want to risk ademption of a specific devise. Rather than devise a particular car, boat, or home, for example, she might devise "any [car] [boat] [home] I own at my death." If she owned more than one of the item devised, the court must determine whether the devisee received each such item or only one of them, perhaps the most recently acquired.

6. Devises or Trust Interests Administered in a Different State

An instrument drafted when the testator or settlor resided in one jurisdiction might ultimately be administered in another jurisdiction. Interpretive issues could arise if the second jurisdiction uses different definitions for a term or still follows a common-law rule repealed in the first jurisdiction (or vice versa). The instrument might fail to indicate which jurisdiction's definitions and statutes are to apply.

C. Class and Individual Gifts

1. Transfer to an Individual or to a Class

The transferor might create a benefit by will, trust, or other instrument for a specific individual. A devise to "my sister Rachel" is an example. The transferor might instead benefit a group of beneficiaries who have common characteristics. A settlor might create an inter vivos trust, reserving the income to herself for life, and directing the remainder interest to "my sisters" or to "the members of my poker club." The remainder appears to be created in a class.

A class is a group that shares one or more common characteristics and that could possibly expand or contract. For example, the settlor could have more sisters after creating her trust, or some of her sisters could predecease her (or be treated as predeceased). If her parents are both dead when she creates her trust, the class will either stay the same or contract by the time she has died. Its inability to expand does not prevent the remainder interest from being a class gift.

Although class gifts are often of money, they could be of other personal property or even of real property. Class members will take as tenants in common unless the instrument specifies a different form of ownership.

2. Qualifying for Class Membership

Determining whether an individual is part of a class involves two questions. First, does the individual have the characteristics required for membership in the class? Second, does the individual qualify before the class closes? The former question can generally be answered rather easily for individuals related to the transferor by blood or adoption, including his children, siblings, parents, and similar relationships.

Certain relationships might involve a class for one set of relatives but not for another set. For example, a transfer to "my children" by a parent who abandoned a child and never married the other parent might nevertheless include the abandoned child. But the abandoned child's grandmother might not even know of the child's existence. Should we infer that a transfer to "my grandchildren" includes that child? Rules of construction in the next two chapters cover class membership in various family situations.

Transfers to younger generations raise questions of when to close the class. A testator might devise property to her grandchildren, or she might create a trust and give her grandchildren a remainder interest after the oldest reaches age 30. In each instance, additional grandchildren could be born after her death or after her oldest grandchild reaches age 30. Not surprisingly, class-closing rules apply in those situations. These are discussed in Chapter 19.

3. Share of Each Class Member

When a transfer is made to a class, each eligible class member receives the same percentage of the property. If a class member is ineligible to take, and has no eligible descendants to take in his place, the remaining class members receive the share of the deceased class member. If multiple class members are ineligible, but each has eligible descendants, the share of those descendants depends on the instrument's distribution system (or the state law system used when the instrument is silent). In these situations, it is important to determine whether the relevant antilapse statute applies and the representation system used in the instrument or statutory default.

> **Example 17-8.** Tom devised "$100,000 to my brothers and sisters." This is a general devise to a class. If Tom was survived by two brothers and three sisters, each receives $20,000. If one of Tom's sisters did not survive him, and had no descendants who could share the devise in her place, Tom's four surviving siblings each receive $25,000.

Example 17-9. Assume Tom's brothers also predeceased him. Brother 1 was survived by two children; Brother 2 was survived by three children. If the will (or state law) provided for per stirpes distribution, Brother 1's children would each receive one-half of $25,000; Brother 2's children would each receive one-third of $25,000. If the will (or state law) provided for per capita at each generation distribution, those five children would each receive one-fifth of $50,000. In either case, Tom's two surviving sisters would each receive $25,000.

Do not confuse a class gift with a gift to unspecified individuals who share common characteristics. If a transferor uses the terms "each" or "every," he is likely making a gift to individuals who share certain characteristics, but he is probably not making a class gift. For example, if Tom had instead devised $20,000 to "each of my brothers and sisters," he probably has not made a class gift. Instead of devising a fixed amount, to be shared by a group, he has devised a particular amount to each individual who has the characteristics he specified.

4. Transfers Using Both Individual and Class Terminology

If an instrument uses both individual and class gift language, we must interpret whether the transferor meant to include unnamed individuals who share the class characteristics. Either she meant a class that could contract but not expand—a class that included only the named individuals—or she meant to include future class members despite naming the current class members.

Example 17-10. Tess devised "$100,000 to be shared by my sisters, Sue and Sally, and by any sisters born or adopted after I execute this will." Although Tess named the sisters she had when she executed the will, she used language to indicate that the class could expand to include any additional sisters.

Example 17-11. Thaddeus created a trust with principal "to be shared by my brothers, Bob and Bill." The trust did not indicate whether future brothers would share in the gift. If another brother is born or adopted after Thaddeus created his trust, we must determine if that brother is included.

In the second example, it might be important to know if Thaddeus had any brothers other than Bob and Bill when he created his trust. If he did, a court might infer that he meant to include only Bob and Bill because he did not mention an existing brother. The distinction between individual and class gifts might be particularly important in determining if a child who is born or adopted after the testator executes his will qualifies as his omitted child.

The UPC does not provide rules to distinguish between gifts to a class and gifts to an individual. A comment to UPC § 2-603 refers to the Restatement (Third) of Property: Wills and Other Donative Transfers §§ 13.1 & 13.2. The Restatement treats the inclusion of names along with a category as creating a rebuttable presumption against class gift status.

D. Rules of Construction

The UPC has two categories of construction provisions: those that apply only to wills and those that apply to both wills and other governing instruments. The UTC has a single, optional provision: the rules that apply in the jurisdiction to the interpretation and disposition of property by will also apply to the interpretation of trusts and the disposition off trust property. UTC § 112. As the introduction to the UPC provisions indicates, these provisions create a rebuttable presumption. They are rebutted by a showing of contrary intent. But, if there is no evidence of contrary intent, these rules become mandatory. UPC § 2-601. They are rules of construction rather than rules of constructional preference. The comments to this section indicate that the current version of the UPC does not require that the evidence of contrary intention be found only in the will. State law might provide otherwise.

The discussion in the next two chapters focuses on UPC provisions. It is possible that one or more of a state's provisions differ from the UPC version. It is also possible that one or more provisions in the state's trust code differ from the corresponding provision in its probate code.

CHECKPOINTS

- A document might contain an ambiguity or an incorrect description.
- Ambiguities are latent if they are not apparent until it is time to act on the document.
- Ambiguities are patent if they are apparent from the text of the document.
- The court may have authority to take extrinsic evidence to determine what the ambiguous term meant.
- In the case of a patent ambiguity, some jurisdictions might rely solely on the language of the document to ascertain intent.
- If beneficiaries are identified only by name, the transfer is to the named individuals.
- If beneficiaries are identified only by a group characteristic, the transfer is to a class.
- If an instrument identifies the recipients by both name and group characteristic, the court must determine the transferor's intent. A gift to individuals is presumed in the absence of evidence of contrary intent.
- A class can expand or contract between the time the transfer document is executed and the time for distribution arrives. A class that can only contract is possible.
- When the time for distribution arrives, class members share the property equally unless the instrument provides otherwise. Descendants of deceased class members take the share of their deceased ancestors using the representation method provided by the instrument or by a state law default rule.
- Courts may rely on canons of construction, such as giving terms their everyday meaning. Judges might treat these as constructional preferences rather than as absolute rules.
- Courts also rely on rules of construction, which apply if they cannot determine the drafter's intent from the document or by other means.

CHAPTER 18

Rules of Construction for Wills

ROADMAP

- Property owned at death and after-acquired property
- Antilapse; deceased devisee; class gifts
- Failure of testamentary provision
- Increase in securities; accessions
- Nonademption of specific devises
- Nonexoneration
- Exercise of power of appointment
- Ademption by satisfaction

A. Chapter Overview

The rules of construction discussed in this chapter are not mandatory rules. Because they do not implement the state's public policy, they apply only if the court determines that the testator did not have a contrary intent. UPC § 2-601. But, as the language indicates, these provisions control unless the court finds that the testator had a contrary intent. They are not merely constructional preferences that a court can reject in favor of a different construction.

This chapter focuses on rules that apply only to wills. The next chapter covers provisions that apply to wills and to other instruments.

B. Property Owned at Death and After-Acquired Property

A will might provide for all property the testator owned at death. It might also provide for property acquired after she died. UPC § 2-602. A testator can use a residuary clause for one of three purposes: (1) to dispose of all property she owned when she executed her will and did not dispose of through specific, demonstrative, or general devises; (2) to dispose of all property she owned when she died and did not dispose of through specific, demonstrative, or general devises; or (3) to dispose of all property she owned when she died—and any property she acquired after her death—and did not dispose of through specific, demonstrative, or general devises. UPC § 2-602 adopts the third interpretation.

The third interpretation differs from the second in what might be considered an unusual situation. A testator devised property "to Devisee or Devisee's estate," the devisee predeceased the testator, and the devisee's will had a residuary clause. If the testator had instead devised property "to Devisee," the devise would be to a predeceased devisee. In that case, the ultimate recipient would be the devisee's descendants (if the antilapse statute applied), an alternate taker mentioned in the testator's will, the testator's residuary devisee, or the testator's intestate heirs. We would decide among the options based on the language of the testator's will and any relevant rules of construction.

> **Example 18-1.** Tom devised "Blackacre to my sister Dora or her estate, and the residue of my estate to Charity X." Dora survived Tom and received Blackacre. Dora's will, written before Tom's death, devised $10,000 to her daughter and the residue of her estate to her son. If Dora owned Blackacre when she died, her son will receive it as her residuary devisee.
>
> **Example 18-2.** The result is the same if Dora predeceased Tom, and there is no evidence that she did not intend her residuary clause to include after-acquired property.
>
> **Example 18-3.** If Dora's residuary clause instead provided that her son would receive "the remaining property I own when I die," her son would not receive Blackacre. Because it would not pass under the residuary clause, Dora's intestate heirs will receive it.
>
> **Example 18-4.** Tom instead devised "Blackacre to my sister Dora." Blackacre will not be distributed as part of Dora's estate if Dora predeceased Tom. Unless Tom's will indicated a contrary intent, Dora's descendants

(presumably her son and daughter) would receive Blackacre by virtue of the antilapse statute discussed below. If antilapse did not apply, Tom's residuary devisee, Charity X, would receive Blackacre.

A state that rejects the UPC rule would limit Dora's residuary devise in Example 18-2 to property she owned when she died. It would include after-acquired property only if her will specifically provided for including such property.

C. Antilapse; Deceased Devisee; Class Gifts

If a testator devises property to a named individual or to a class, the individual or class members normally receive the property. But what if a named devisee or a class member fails to meet survival conditions imposed by the will or by statute? The outcome depends on several factors: (1) whether the testator provided for an alternative taker; (2) the relationship of the devisee to the testator; (3) whether the devise was to an individual or to a class; and (4) whether the devise was a residuary devise or a pre-residuary devise.

1. Common Law and Statutes

At common law, property did not pass from a decedent to a deceased beneficiary. A devise to an individual who was dead when the testator executed his will was void; a devise to an individual who was alive when the will was executed but who failed to survive failed. Those rules have been replaced by statutes in jurisdictions adopting the UPC or their own provisions for lapse and antilapse.

As discussed in Chapter 5, the descendants of a deceased heir may take by representation under the relevant intestacy statutes. These apply if the decedent and his deceased heir bore a relationship covered by those statutes. Antilapse statutes provide similar outcomes for property passing by will. These statutes reflect a belief that the testator would prefer that her property go to a deceased devisee's descendants instead of to the residuary taker or by intestacy. They generally preserve the devise only if the testator and the deceased devisee bear a relationship defined in the statute.

The statutory assumption makes sense. A devisee who met the survival conditions would receive the devise and could devise it to his descendants (or to any other devisee of his choice). If he died intestate, his heirs would receive the property.

The UPC includes a comprehensive set of antilapse provisions. They cover the relationships that trigger antilapse, devises to a class and to an individual, and exercise of a power of appointment. These provisions do not use the term "surviving" in its literal sense. UPC § 2-702, which requires survival by at least 120 hours, still applies.

UPC § 2-603(b) applies when the devisee fails to survive the testator. It applies to devises of the testator's probate property. It also applies to property that would pass because the testator exercised a power of appointment in his will. The UPC does not distinguish between (1) devisees who were dead when the testator executed her will, (2) devisees who were alive when she executed her will but who failed to survive her, and (3) devisees who failed to survive to a distribution date. A state antilapse statute might cover all of these situations or only some of them.

2. Relevant Relationships

UPC § 2-603(b) is based on relationships. It applies if the devisee is the testator's grandparent, a descendant of the testator's grandparent, or the testator's stepchild. Although the UPC includes devises to stepchildren, it does not include devises to their descendants. If none of these relationships exist, the devise lapses. If a state statute differs from the UPC, it is likely to do so by omitting stepchildren from its coverage.

If a power of appointment is involved, the antilapse statute applies if the object of the power bears one of those relationships to the donor of the power. The object's relationship to the powerholder does not matter.

Antilapse can apply even if the testator and devisee are not related. But the testator must provide for its application in that situation. The testator could include a statement in his will that the descendants of the deceased devisee take in his place. He could alternatively include a statement that defines the devisee as a relative covered by the antilapse statute.

Because testator intent controls, a testator could also limit the application of an antilapse statute. He might, for example, indicate that substitute devisees taking under antilapse could be no more than two generations lower than the actual devisee.

3. Devises to Individuals and to Classes

UPC §2-603(b) provides different rules for devises to individuals and devises to a class. If the devise is not a class gift, the devisee's descendants take the property devised to their deceased ancestor. UPC §2-603(b)(1). It does not matter if the devisee executed a will. Nor does it matter that the devisee's descendants would not take all of his property by intestacy.

> **Example 18-5.** Teresa devised $100,000 to her brother Bill. Her will did not indicate an intent to prevent antilapse. Bill died a day before Teresa, survived by his wife Winnie and their sons Seth and Sam. Bill devised all his property 60% to Winnie and 40% to Seth. Bill's will and the relevant intestate succession rules do not matter. Bill's descendants Seth and Sam will each receive one-half of the $100,000 that Teresa devised to Bill.

If the devise is a class gift, UPC §2-603(b)(2) applies similar rules to each class member. The descendants of a deceased devisee take the share of the property that their deceased ancestor would have taken. When a class gift is involved, we divide the gift by the number of class members who survived plus the number of deceased class members who are survived by descendants. If a class member has no surviving descendants, the remaining class members (and descendants of deceased class members) share the amount he would have received.

> **Example 18-6.** Ted devised $60,000 to "my nephews." Ted had four nephews, Nathan, Neal, Nick, and Norris. Nathan and Neal survived Ted's death. Nick and Norris did not. Nick was survived by his granddaughter Gilda; Norris had no surviving descendants. The $60,000 is divided into thirds. Nathan, Neal, and Gilda each receive $20,000. The fact that Gilda is not Nick's child is irrelevant. The antilapse statute applies because she is Nick's surviving descendant. Nathan, Neal, and Gilda would each have received only $15,000 if Norris had survived. Because he did not, they share his portion of the class gift. The fact that Gilda is female should also be irrelevant—if Nick had survived, he could have devised his share of Ted's property to Gilda.

UPC §2-603(b)(2) provides that a devise is not a class gift for purposes of this section if it uses terms such as issue, descendants, heirs of the body, heirs, next of kin, relatives, or family. The comments indicate that antilapse statutes are not necessary in this situation, as the normal representation rules would apply to substitute a deceased family member's descendants. A gift to beneficiaries in a single generation, such as siblings, children, or grandchildren, is the type of class gift covered by the antilapse statute.

It is possible that some class members will be relatives covered by the antilapse statute and others will not be. For example, the testator might devise a sum of money to be divided among the vice presidents of his closely held company. The group of vice presidents might include both relatives and nonrelatives. Based solely on the language of the antilapse statute, it is possible that antilapse will apply only to deceased class members who were related to the testator.

4. Substitute Takers

If the antilapse statute applies, it creates a substitute gift to the deceased devisee's descendants. Because they take by representation, the jurisdiction's representation rules are important. Representation rules are generally found in the state's intestate succession statutes.

> **Example 18-7.** Trey devised $90,000 to "my sisters." Neither of Trey's sisters survived him. His sister Sally was survived by her two children, Alvin and Alina. His sister Selma was survived by her three children, Ed, Ethel, and Egbert. If the state uses per stirpes representation, each family will receive one-half of the devise because each sister was survived by descendants. Alvin and Alina will each receive $22,500; Ed, Ethel, and Egbert will each receive $15,000. If the state instead uses the UPC § 2-106 per capita at each generation rules for representation, we would allocate shares based on the number of takers in the highest generation with representatives. In that case, Alvin, Alina, Ed, Ethel, and Egbert would each receive $18,000.

As noted above, UPC § 2-603 applies both to devises and to exercises of a power of appointment. Its default rule with respect to powers of appointment provides a substitute gift to the descendants of a deceased appointee even if those descendants are not themselves objects of the power. The donor of the power can prevent this outcome by expressly prohibiting substitution of the appointee's descendants. UPC § 2-603(b)(5).

> **Example 18-8.** Gerald created a power of appointment in his inter vivos trust. It gave his daughter Daphne the power to appoint the principal of that trust. Daphne could exercise the power in her will in favor of any of

Gerald's descendants other than herself. In her will, Daphne exercised the power in favor of her daughter Denise. Denise predeceased Daphne but was survived by three children. Those children will take the property subject to the power.

Example 18-9. Gerald instead gave Daphne the power to appoint the principal among his grandchildren. In this case, Denise's children—Gerald's great-grandchildren—would not have been objects of the power. Unless the language Gerald used to create the power (or the relevant state law) expressly excluded substituting an appointee's descendants, Denise's children will take the property Daphne appointed to Denise.

5. Effect of Survivorship Language

The UPC antilapse rules do not apply if the testator expresses a different intention. UPC § 2-603(b)(3) provides that words of survivorship alone are not a sufficient indication of the testator's intent to prevent antilapse. It requires additional evidence of that intent. A state might differ from the UPC and treat words of survivorship as a sufficient indication of the testator's intent to prevent antilapse.

Comments to the UPC provide reasons for requiring additional evidence of the testator's intent. Many attorneys routinely use "if he survives me" or similar language in their will forms. If the attorney and client never discussed this language, there is no reason to assume the client meant to require survivorship. If they did discuss the language, the attorney can testify to the client's intent to require survivorship.

Example 18-10. Tillie devised $100,000 to "my daughter Delia, if she survives me." Despite the survivorship language in Tillie's will, the UPC might provide a substitute devise in favor of Delia's descendants if Delia failed to survive Tillie. It is less likely that Delia's descendants would take if the devise had instead read "to my daughter Delia, but only if she survives me."

6. Language Naming an Alternative Taker

The UPC does not apply antilapse if the testator provided for an alternative devisee in the event the primary devisee failed to survive. The alternative devisee can be a class or an expressly designated individual devisee. In either case, at least one alternative devisee must be entitled to take under the will.

Otherwise, the devise to the alternative devisee does not prevent antilapse from applying to the original devise. UPC § 2-603(b)(4). A state might differ from the UPC by treating the devise as failed if the alternative devisee was not eligible to receive the property (and was not survived by descendants).

UPC § 2-603(c) governs when there is more than one group of substitute takers. The first-named devisee is the primary devisee; the second-named devisee is the alternative devisee. If both of them fail to survive, the descendants of the primary devisee have precedence over the descendants of the alternative devisee. An exception applies if the alternative devisee is a descendant of the primary devisee. In that situation, the descendants of the alternative devisee have precedence over the other descendants of the primary devisee. This outcome reflects what appears to be the testator's decision to favor one of the primary devisee's descendants over his other descendants.

> **Example 18-11.** Ted devised $100,000 to "my brother Burt, if he survives me; otherwise, to my sister Sue." Burt is the primary devisee; Sue is the alternative devisee. If Ted is survived by Burt, Burt's daughter Dana, Sue, and Sue's son Serge, Burt receives the $100,000. If Ted is survived only by Sue, Serge, and Dana, Sue receives the $100,000. The substitute devise that Burt's daughter Dana would take by antilapse is superseded by the alternative devise to Sue. If Ted is survived only by Dana and Serge, Dana takes the $100,000." Because Sue died before Ted, she could not take under the will. Because Burt is the primary devisee, the alternative gift to Sue does not supersede the operation of antilapse in favor of Burt's daughter as the substitute taker.
>
> **Example 18-12.** Tessa devised property to her brother Ben, but if Ben did not survive, to Ben's daughter Danielle. Ben and Danielle died before Tessa. Tessa was survived by Ben's daughters Debra and Denise and by Danielle's son Seth. Although Ben was the primary devisee, the alternative devisee (Danielle) was Ben's descendant. Because Tessa is treated as preferring Danielle to her siblings, her descendant Seth takes as the substitute devisee.

7. Residuary Devise

We expect a will to include a residuary devise. Otherwise, the testator risks having property pass by intestacy if a nonresiduary devisee dies and antilapse does not apply. The comments explaining UPC § 2-603(b)(4) indicate that a residuary devise does not necessarily constitute an alternative devise to an expressly designated taker. A residuary devise that specifically includes lapsed and failed devises might constitute an alternative devise to an expressly designated taker.

D. Failure of Testamentary Provision

A devise might fail because the devisee died (or is treated as dying) before the date on which the devise vests. The testator might have provided for an alternative taker, or the antilapse statute might preserve the devise for the devisee's descendants. If neither of those possibilities applies, the devise fails. The property passes under a different provision in the will or by intestacy.

If a specific, demonstrative, or general devise fails, the property covered by the failed devise becomes part of the residue. UPC § 2-604(a). A pre-residuary devise is most likely to fail if the devisee is not related to the testator, the devise is not to a class, and the will did not provide for an alternative devisee.

> **Example 18-13.** Tina devised "$10,000 to my best friend Fred, $15,000 to my high school English teacher Mrs. Jones, and the residue of my estate to my sister Serena." Fred died three weeks before Tina. The residue received by Serena will be increased by the $10,000 that Fred would have received if he had survived.

When a residuary devisee fails to survive or is otherwise ineligible to take, UPC § 2-604(b) supplies slightly different rules. Not surprisingly, given that the testator has executed a will—thus indicating his desire not to die intestate—this section tries to prevent intestacy from occurring.

If the residue is devised to more than one individual, the other residuary devisees share the devise that would otherwise fail. This rule applies even though the residuary devise is not a devise to a class. Each survivor takes his proportionate share of the otherwise failed devise. The residue goes by intestacy only if there is no residuary taker.

> **Example 18-14.** Tamara devised: "$5,000 to my high school library fund and the residue of my estate to my friends Felix, Felicia, and Flora." Felix died five months before Tamara. Felicia and Flora will share the entire residue equally.

Example 18-15. Same as Example 18-14 except that the residuary devise was to be distributed 25% to Felix, 60% to Felicia, and 15% to Flora. Instead of dividing Felix's share equally between Felicia and Flora, we divide it in proportion to their share of the residue. Felicia will thus receive 80% of the total residue and Flora will receive the other 20%.

Example 18-16. Tillie devised "$5,000 to my high school library fund and the residue of my estate to my first cousins Flossie, Finn, and Fanny." Flossie died five months before Tillie. Because Flossie was a descendant of Tillie's grandparents, her descendants (if any) will take her one-third of the residue. Otherwise, Finn and Fanny will share the entire residue equally.

E. Increase in Securities; Accessions

Securities differ from most other assets for several reasons. First, unlike real property, securities in publicly traded companies are likely to be fungible. One share of ABC stock has the same value and rights as any other share of ABC stock of the same class. Second, the testator is likely to acquire additional securities in the same company, or dispose of only part of those securities, between the time he executes his will and the time he dies. Third, the company issuing those securities might merge with another company, split its stock, or take other corporate action that changes the nature or amount of the testator's holdings.

UPC § 2-605 covers securities and accessions. State statutes might include both ademption (or nonademption) and accessions in the relevant section title. Although this discussion primarily focuses on shares of stock issued by a publicly traded corporation, the term "securities" is much broader.

1. Definition of Securities

Each jurisdiction defines what is covered by the term "securities" for purposes of statutes governing donative or other transfers. Although definitions might not distinguish between publicly traded and closely held entities, that distinction is important. Because changes in ownership can affect the controlling owner's succession plans, the will or other governing instrument will likely treat securities in closely held entities differently from how it treats securities in publicly traded entities.

2. UPC Provisions

UPC § 2-605(a) applies to both specific and general devises of securities. It applies when the testator owned the securities devised when he executed his will. It covers the treatment of additional securities he acquired before his death. As discussed below, state provisions might differ from the UPC rules.

a. *Stock Splits, Stock Dividends, and Single-Entity Reorganizations*

UPC § 2-605(a)(1) covers securities of the same organization acquired by reason of action initiated by the organization or any successor, related, or acquiring organization, excluding any securities acquired by exercise of purchase options. Purchase options might be granted to employees, customers, lenders, or other persons. They differ from rights held by shareholders in their capacity as shareholders.

Stock splits and stock dividends are two commonly used entity-initiated actions. A stock split is based on the number of shares, not on the number of shareholders. The corporation issues additional shares based on a multiple of its existing shares. If for example, it makes a 3 for 1 split, each shareholder will own three times as many shares after the split as he owned before the split. The split might have been consummated solely to bring the price per share down. Because each pre-split share is treated identically, there is no percentage change in any shareholder's voting rights or rights to corporate distributions. The total post-split shares are the alter ego of the total pre-split shares in terms of the shareholder's rights.

The term stock dividend is a misnomer. A true dividend is a distribution of cash or other property from the corporation to its shareholders. A stock dividend is simply a distribution of more shares of the corporation's own stock. It is possible that no cash or other property will leave the corporation. As is true for stock splits, the additional shares are based on the number of pre-dividend shares, not on the number of shareholders. But, unlike a stock split, a stock dividend is not a simple multiple of the number of shares owned. Instead, it is based on a fraction or percentage of shares owned. For example, if the corporation declares a 10% stock dividend, each shareholder receives 1 share for every 10 shares owned. A shareholder who owns only 9 shares before the stock dividend is likely to receive cash instead of receiving a fractional share. Thus, some shareholders will receive only stock, others will receive stock and cash, and still others will receive only cash.

Example 18-17. When he executed his will, Thomas owned 100 shares of XYZ Corporation common stock. He devised 60 shares of XYZ Corporation common stock to his daughter Dora. He devised the residue of his estate to his sister Sharon. Two years later, XYZ split its stock 4 for 1. Dora will receive 240 of the 400 shares that Thomas owned at death; Sharon will receive the other 160 shares.

Example 18-18. One year after splitting its stock, XYZ Corporation declared a 5% stock dividend. As a result, Thomas owned 420 shares when he died. Dora will receive 252 of those shares; Sharon will receive the other 168 shares.

UPC § 2-605 distinguishes stock dividends from reinvestment plans and from cash dividends. Each of those is discussed later in this section. The Internal Revenue Code distinguishes among types of stock dividends. A distribution of common stock to holders of common stock, none of whom has a choice to instead receive cash or other property, is not taxable to any of those shareholders. I.R.C. § 305(a). But a distribution of stock to holders of preferred stock might be taxable even if the shareholders have no choice. I.R.C. § 305(b)(4). These and other exceptions are discussed in courses dealing with corporate tax or business entity tax.

UPC § 2-605(a)(1) refers to action initiated by the entity. Instead of splitting its stock or issuing a stock dividend, an entity might reorganize by issuing a different class of stock or even bonds to its shareholders. If the action is initiated by the entity, the devisee of the original securities receives these additional securities as well. UPC § 2-605(a)(1) does not require that the additional securities be the same as the original securities.

b. Securities of Another Entity

UPC § 2-605(a)(2) covers securities of another organization acquired as a result of a merger, consolidation, reorganization, or other distribution by the organization or any successor, related, or acquiring organization.

Example 18-19. Ted executed his will when he owned 100 shares of ABC Corporation stock. He devised his 100 shares of ABC Corporation stock to his friend Freda. He devised the residue of his estate to his friend Frank. A year before Ted died, LLL Corporation acquired ABC Corporation. Each ABC shareholder received 5 shares of LLL Corporation stock for every share of ABC he owned. Ted died owning 500 shares of LLL Corporation stock. ABC Corporation no longer existed. Freda will receive the 500 shares of LLL stock. If LLL later splits or declares a stock dividend, Freda will also receive those shares.

c. *Securities Acquired Through a Plan of Reinvestment*

UPC § 2-605(a)(3) covers securities acquired through a plan of reinvestment. This provision applies to mutual funds if the shareholder has chosen to have the fund reinvest the cash dividends she would have otherwise received. It can also apply to dividend reinvestment plans (DRPs or DRIPS) sponsored by the issuing corporation. If a corporation sponsors such a plan, shareholders can elect to receive additional shares of stock—including fractional shares—instead of some or all of the cash dividends they would otherwise receive. Because they include the ability to acquire fractional shares, both mutual funds and individual plans offer less-affluent investors a relatively low-cost method for increasing their investment in a fund or a single company.

Note that, unlike true stock dividends, shareholders who participate in mutual fund reinvestment plans and DRPs must report the value of the shares received as gross income. The exclusion for true stock dividends does not apply because shareholders could choose between additional shares and money or other property. Even those who choose shares are taxed. I.R.C. § 305(b)(1).

d. *Cash Dividends*

UPC § 2-605(b) applies to cash dividends paid with respect to securities. It provides that cash distributions with respect to a security covered by that section are not part of the devise if they are paid before the testator's death. Receipts after the testator's death will likely be governed by the state's principal and income act or by provisions in its probate code.

e. *Other Situations*

UPC § 2-605 does not address every situation involving after-acquired securities. One omission relates to a testator who sells securities after executing his will but later repurchases securities in that company. Another relates to a testator who did not actually own the securities when he executed his will, as could be the case with a general devise, but acquired them before he died. The comments to UPC § 2-605 indicate that it does not cover the treatment of any additional securities acquired with respect to those securities. The comments indicate that UPC § 2-605(a) does not prevent a court from determining that the devisee would receive not only the devised securities but also any securities that would otherwise be covered by UPC § 2-605(a).

3. State Statutes

State statutes might diverge from UPC § 2-605 by limiting themselves to specific devises of securities. They might also diverge by limiting the categories to which their accessions statutes apply.

F. Nonademption of Specific Devises

Ademption by extinction is the term used when a devise fails because the testator does not own the property when she dies. It applies only to specific devises. In that situation, there are two possibilities: the devisee receives nothing or the devisee receives a substitute devise. To determine the appropriate outcome, we consider the language used in the devise and the relevant ademption statutes.

1. Language Used in Devise

The testator might indicate what is to occur if he does not own the property when he dies. To make it absolutely clear that the devisee is to receive the property devised and no other property, he might use the following language: "I devise my painting by Picasso to Dahlia if I own it at my death; I make no substitute devise if I do not own this painting when I die." The testator can also provide for a substitute devise. For example, the devise might read: "I devise my painting by Picasso to Dahlia; if I do not own it at my death, Dahlia is to receive $100,000." Instead of a devise of money, the testator could have devised Dahlia another item of property.

If the specific devise reads only "I devise my painting by Picasso to Dahlia," the testator has not indicated what should happen if he does not own the painting when he dies. Before turning to the relevant statute, you should look elsewhere in the will for guidance. There might be a group of provisions that apply to all specific devises, indicating whether the testator wants the devisee to receive a substitute gift.

2. UPC Provisions

The UPC separates ademption events into two categories. The first category provides an umbrella rule. The second involves dispositions that occur when a testator's property was sold or mortgaged when he was incapacitated and represented by a conservator or by an agent acting under a durable power of attorney. The section also applies to receipt of a condemnation award, insurance proceeds, or a recovery for injury to property. A devisee's rights under the second category are reduced by any rights he obtains under the first category.

The distinction between testator action and fiduciary action is important. If the testator is under a conservatorship, he might lack testamentary capacity and thus have no ability to provide an alternate gift for the devisee. If the testator is in control of his property and has testamentary capacity, he can make a substitute gift by amending his will or by providing for the devisee in another fashion.

a. UPC § 2-606(a)

The first three subdivisions of UPC § 2-606(a) cover money owed the testator on account of specifically devised property. The testator might have sold the property, it might have been taken by condemnation, or it might have been damaged or destroyed. If he specifically devised that property, and the will does not provide otherwise, the devisee is entitled to the unpaid sales proceeds and any security interest, the unpaid condemnation award, or the unpaid insurance recovery or other damages. If only part of the property was disposed of, the devisee is also entitled to the property the testator still owned at death. This section does not give the devisee a right to any proceeds the testator received before death.

> **Example 18-20.** Tyrone devised Whiteacre to Dale; his will did not indicate what should happen if he did not own Whiteacre when he died. Tyrone sold Whiteacre to Bob, in exchange for Bob's promise to pay \$150,000 in \$15,000 installments over the next ten years. Bob also gave Tyrone a security interest in shares of GGG Corporation stock worth \$150,000 as security for the payment owed. Tyrone died after receiving three installments. Dale is entitled to receive the remaining seven installments from Bob and the security interest for unpaid installments.

The fourth subdivision gives the specific devisee the right to any property the testator received if he foreclosed on the security interest he received when he disposed of specifically devised property. It also applies to property he received in lieu of foreclosure.

> **Example 18-21.** After making the second payment, Bob defaulted. Tyrone was still alive and exercised his right to the GGG shares instead of retaking Whiteacre. He owned those shares at his death. Dale is entitled to the GGG shares.

The fifth and sixth subdivisions involve judgment calls. UPC § 2-606(a)(5) gives the specific devisee any real property or tangible personal property that the testator acquired as a replacement for the specifically devised real property or tangible personal property. This provision does not trace funds used to acquire the new property, but the term "replacement" limits the type of property to which it applies.

> **Example 18-22.** Tricia devised "the car that I own when I die to Delores." When Tricia died, she owned a different car than when she executed her will. Because Tricia did not specify a particular car, Delores receives the car. This devise does not involve ademption.
>
> **Example 18-23.** Tricia instead devised "my Chevrolet sedan" to Delores. Two years later, Tricia traded in her Chevrolet and purchased a Buick. If the jurisdiction has adopted the principles of UPC § 2-606(a)(5), Delores receives the Buick.

UPC § 2-606(a)(6), which applies only if none of the other five subdivisions applies, gives the specific devisee a pecuniary devise equal to the value of the specifically devised property on the date of its disposition during the testator's lifetime. This rule requires establishing that ademption would be inconsistent with the testator's manifested plan of distribution or that the testator did not intend ademption at the relevant date.

> **Example 18-24.** After Tricia failed the vision test and could not renew her driver's license, she sold her Chevrolet for $2,000. If the jurisdiction has adopted the principles of UPC § 2-606(a)(6), the specific devise to Delores is likely to be converted into a $2,000 general pecuniary devise.

Because UPC § 2-606(a)(6) focuses on value, it can apply even if the testator received nothing in exchange for the property. That might be the case if the testator uses his own funds to replace uninsured property that was lost or stolen. The comments indicate that ademption is likely to apply, and the devisee will receive nothing, if the testator voluntarily gave the property away before death.

The fifth and sixth subdivisions rely on the "intent" theory and do not reflect the traditional view of ademption. That view, the "identity" theory, favors ademption when the testator does not own the specifically devised property when he dies. Some jurisdictions employ a modified version of the intent theory and allow the devisee to receive the proceeds from selling the property. The devisee might have to establish that the funds can be traced to the sale and that the testator did not intend to disinherit her.

b. UPC § 2-606(b)

UPC § 2-606(b) provides additional rights if a disposition occurs or property is mortgaged during a conservatorship or pursuant to a durable power of attorney when the principal is incapacitated. These rights are reduced to the extent UPC § 2-606(a) applies. UPC § 2-606(c).

When a conservator or agent sells specifically devised property, the devisee is to receive a general pecuniary devise equal to the net sales price. The same rule applies if the property is taken by a government and the conservator or agent receives condemnation proceeds, or a casualty occurs and the conservator or agent receives insurance proceeds or damages. In each case, the devisee receives a substitute devise, but it is transformed from a specific devise to a general devise. Its amount is fixed by the net proceeds received; it does not increase or decrease to reflect changes in the property's value between the date of disposition and the date of the testator's death.

> **Example 18-25.** Tom devised "Blackacre to Dora." His will did not include any language concerning what would occur if he did not own Blackacre when he died. While Tom was under a conservatorship, his conservator sold Blackacre to Ralph for its $100,000 value; the conservator incurred selling expenses of $6,000. Tom died two years later, while still under the conservatorship. Blackacre was then worth $150,000. Because Tom's will did not preclude a substitute devise, his specific devise of Blackacre to Dora is treated as a general devise to her of $94,000.

If the conservator or agent mortgages the property instead of selling it, the specific devisee will receive the property because the testator owned it at death. The property will be subject to the mortgage (unless the will provided for exoneration). If the will does not provide for exoneration, the devisee should also receive a general pecuniary devise equal to the amount of the mortgage. Because the property was mortgaged by the conservator or agent, and not by the testator, the rules of construction covering nonexoneration do not apply.

A conservatorship could end before the testator's death because he regains competency. At that point, we must determine whether the devisee should receive the substitute general pecuniary devise or should receive nothing. The testator could revise his will to address the situation, but he might die before doing so. UPC § 2-606(d) covers this situation. If the testator dies less than one year after it is adjudicated that his incapacity has ceased, the devisee receives the substitute general devise. If the testator dies one year or more after the conservatorship ends, the devisee does not receive the substitute general devise. In other words, if the testator had sufficient time to revise the will in favor of the devisee and did not do so, the UPC treats his non-action as ratifying the sale and ademption by extinction of the specific devise. UPC § 2-606(d) does not contain a comparable rule governing actions taken by an agent acting under a durable power of attorney.

UPC § 2-606(b) also applies to dispositions and mortgages by an agent for an incapacitated person acting under a durable power of attorney. It applies even if the principal has not been adjudicated incapacitated. If the agent is acting under a durable power of attorney, the principal is presumed to be incapacitated. UPC § 2-606(e). The devisee is entitled to the pecuniary devise even if the principal later terminates the agency.

Some state statutes substitute the term guardian for conservator. They might also limit their version of UPC § 2-606(b) by not including dispositions by an agent acting under a durable power of attorney.

G. Nonexoneration

If a specifically devised item of property is encumbered by a mortgage or other security interest, the devisee would prefer to have the property but not have to pay the underlying obligation. Because the will likely read "I devise my car to Devisee," not "I devise my car, subject to any loan encumbering it, to Devisee," the devisee would argue that the car loan should be satisfied from funds that would otherwise go to residuary devisees. Exoneration is the term used when a loan encumbering specifically devised property is paid from the residue.

At common law, the specific devisee was entitled to exoneration. He received the devised property free of any debt encumbering it. The interest of the residuary devisee was reduced by the amount of the unpaid debt. UPC § 2-607 applies the opposite rule. The specific devisee takes the property subject to the mortgage unless the will provides otherwise.

The testator's will might provide "My personal representative shall satisfy claims against the estate, debts, and administrative expenses." That provision is not a sufficient indication that she wants the specific devisee to take the property free and clear. State probate statutes already require that the personal representative pay debts and expenses. The statement reinforces the personal representative's duty, or perhaps the testator included it to remind the devisees that creditors generally are paid first. UPC § 2-607 provides that a general direction to pay debts is not sufficient to give the specific devisee a right to exoneration.

If the devise above had read "I devise my car to Devisee free and clear of any loan encumbering it," the specific devisee would be entitled to exoneration. The same result would occur if the devise of the car was silent but another section of the will provided for payment of any secured debt before distributing those assets to devisees. Note that although UPC § 2-607 uses the term "mortgage," a state's nonexoneration statute might use the term "encumbrance."

The comments to UPC § 2-607 refer to UPC § 2-403, which covers the surviving spouse's rights to exempt property. If exempt property is encumbered, any dollar limit on her rights is increased by the amount of the encumbrance. In other words, exempt property rights are based on the net value of the property. If they were based on the value before the encumbrance, the spouse's rights could be considerably weakened. States that do not impose dollar limits on the amount of exempt property a spouse receives might not provide for an increase to offset the encumbrance.

H. Exercise of Power of Appointment

Chapter 21 focuses on powers of appointment. It describes the types of power, when they can be exercised, and limitations on the power. It also mentions tax consequences and creditor access when property subject to a power is held in trust. The discussion in this chapter covers whether the holder of a testamentary power is treated as exercising a power she did not specifically mention in her will.

A powerholder has a testamentary power if she can exercise it only in her will. A will provision that reads: "I exercise my power of appointment over the ABC Trust created on March 1, 2010, in favor of [one or more objects of the power]" is an exercise of a power. But a will provision might instead read "I exercise any power of appointment that I have in favor of my residuary devisees," "I devise the residue of my estate, including any property over which I have a power of appointment, to [residuary devisees]," or simply "I devise the residue of my estate to [residuary devisees]." If the residuary devisees are objects of the power, we must determine if any of those devises is a sufficient exercise of the power.

UPC 2-§ 608 treats a nonspecific reference as an exercise in two situations. These rules apply only if the instrument creating the power did not require that the power be exercised by a reference to the power. First, a residuary devise is deemed to show that the testator intended to exercise the power if the power is exercisable in favor of the powerholder's estate and the instrument creating the power did not create an effective gift in the absence of exercise. This rule is based on the drafters' belief that the donor of the power would rather have property pass to the powerholder's residuary takers than have his own estate reopened. Because this provision applies only if the powerholder can exercise the power in favor of his estate, a general power that does not include the estate as an object will not suffice.

> **Example 18-26.** Thirty years ago, Tom devised property to a testamentary trust. His niece Nell was to receive the income for life. Nell could withdraw the principal at any time until age 40. If she failed to withdraw the principal, the trust would continue until her death. Because he assumed Nell would withdraw the principal, Tom did not provide for a taker after Nell's death. Nell died at age 50; in her will she devised her estate to various family members. Although Nell had a general power of appointment, it had lapsed before her death. She did not have a general power to appoint property to her estate. The property in the trust reverts back to Tom's estate.

UPC 2-§ 608 also treats a residuary devise as an exercise if the powerholder's will manifests an intention to exercise the power. The comments indicate that a residuary devise that includes language such as "including any property over which I have a power of appointment" is a manifestation of intent. Even then, the exercise is effective only if a residuary devisee is an object of the power.

A state statute might reflect either or both of these provisions. It might also reject the UPC rule.

I. Ademption by Satisfaction

A devisee who received money or other property from the testator before the testator's death might be subject to ademption by satisfaction. The earlier transfer is treated as in partial or total satisfaction of the devise. Unlike ademption by extinction, which is limited to specific devises, ademption by satisfaction can apply to any type of devise.

1. Requirements

Ademption by satisfaction applies only if there is a writing that satisfies the statutory mandate. UPC § 2-609 provides for three types of writing. A testator can use all of them but only one is required. First, the testator can provide in a writing that is contemporaneous with the transfer that it is in satisfaction of a devise in the will. Second, the devisee can provide in writing that he is receiving the transfer in satisfaction of a devise in the will. Third, the testator can provide for ademption by satisfaction in the will itself. Neither of the first two writings requires any formalities; a statement in the will is subject to the state's requirements for a valid will. Only the first writing must be contemporaneous with the transfer.

2. Application

If the testator used a contemporaneous writing, he might use the following language: "I am making this transfer in complete satisfaction of any devise to you in my will." In that situation, the devisee receives nothing when the testator dies. Alternatively, the testator might say: "This transfer reduces any devise to you in my will." In that situation, the devisee might receive a devise, but it will be reduced because of the earlier gift. The result would be the same if the devisee used a written acknowledgement that the gift is in full or partial satisfaction of any devise in the will.

UPC § 2-609 applies the doctrine to cover gifts to third parties if the writing indicates that intent. Gifts to third parties are likely when the donor wants to take advantage of multiple gift tax exclusions. Not every state uses the UPC language covering gifts to third parties.

> **Example 18-27.** Greta wants to reduce her potential estate tax by making lifetime gifts to her grandchildren, but she wants to treat her two sons equally. Because one son has four children and the other has only one child, she might use a contemporaneous writing or a will provision that reduces the share of her estate to be received by the son with four children because his family received greater inter vivos gifts from her.

If the jurisdiction's antilapse rules apply to a devise, a deceased devisee's descendants receive his devise. UPC § 2-609(c) applies ademption by satisfaction to the substitute takers unless the donor's contemporaneous writing provides otherwise. In this situation, the gift to the intended devisee could reduce what his descendants take by representation.

3. Computing Partial Satisfaction

If the transfer is in partial satisfaction of the devise, its effect depends on what was transferred and any language in the will. The easiest transfer to deal with is an outright transfer of money. Unless the relevant writing provides for a different offset, the devise is reduced by the amount of money received. If the writing provides a formula, that formula applies.

> **Example 18-28.** Talia transferred $10,000 to Dennis and $30,000 to Dustin in 2014. Her will provides that "Any devise to Dennis is to be reduced by the transfer I made to him in 2014. Any devise I made to Dustin is to be reduced by 10% of the transfer I made to him in 2014."

If the testator transferred property other than money and did not provide a formula for reducing the devise, we use the statutory formula. It uses the value of the property on the earlier of two dates: (1) the date the testator died or (2) the date the devisee came into possession or enjoyment of the property. UPC § 2-609(b). These two dates can differ if, for example, the testator made the transfer in trust instead of outright.

> **Example 18-29.** Terrie made two transfers in 2010. She transferred a silver bracelet worth $10,000 to Denise. She transferred a parking lot worth $15,000 to a trust. Jeff will receive the rental income until he dies; the trustee will then distribute the parking lot to Dorothy. When Terrie

died this year, the bracelet and the parking lot were each worth $18,000. Terrie's will provides that gifts made to Denise and Dorothy in 2010 will reduce any devises to them. Dorothy's devise is reduced by its value when Terrie died. Denise's devise is reduced by only $10,000. Note that although we value Dorothy's interest at Terrie's death, it will not become possessory until Jeff dies. The $18,000 value will be reduced by the value of Jeff's life estate.

Because the inter vivos transfer was a gift, not a loan, UPC § 2-609 makes no provision for returning an excess gift to the estate. If the inter vivos gift exceeded the value of the donee's devise, he simply receives none of the property covered by that devise.

4. Comparing Ademption by Satisfaction and Ademption by Extinction

Ademption by satisfaction reduces or eliminates a devise because it was satisfied, or partially satisfied, by an inter vivos gift. The concept applies to each type of devise. Ademption by extinction eliminates a devise because the testator did not own the property at death, and the will (or a rule of construction) did not provide for a substitute gift. The concept applies only to specific devises.

If the testator specifically devises property and later transfers that property to the devisee by inter vivos gift, the distribution of his estate is affected by which concept applies. If there is a writing indicating that the gift is in satisfaction of the devise, ademption by satisfaction applies. In the absence of a writing, ademption by extinction applies unless the will is interpreted to include a substitute devise.

Example 18-30. Tinsley devised "Blackacre to my son Serge, but if I do not own Blackacre at my death, Serge is to receive $100,000." He devised the residue of his estate to charity. Two years later, Tinsley transferred Blackacre to Serge. Tinsley included a letter with the deed of gift, indicating that the transfer is in satisfaction of any devise to Serge. Serge will receive nothing when Tinsley dies. If Tinsley had not written the letter, Serge might receive $100,000 when Tinsley died even though he had already received Blackacre.

5. Comparing Ademption by Satisfaction and Advancement

Ademption by satisfaction (testate estates) and advancement (intestate succession) reduce or eliminate a beneficiary's share of the donor's estate. Each requires a writing as evidence that the reduction is to occur. Neither requires a donee who receives more than his share of the estate to return the excess property.

These concepts differ in one important respect, at least in jurisdictions that use the UPC's antilapse rules. When ademption by satisfaction is coupled with the antilapse statute, the donee's descendants receive only what the deceased devisee would have received unless the donor's contemporaneous writing provides otherwise. When advancement is coupled with taking by representation under the intestacy statutes, the advancement is ignored in computing the share of the deceased heir's descendants unless the donor's contemporaneous writing provides for a different result.

Example 18-31. Tillie gave her daughter Debra $100,000 five years ago. Debra died two years later. When Tillie made the gift to Debra, she sent her a letter indicating that the money was to count against any property Debra would receive when Tillie died. Tillie died today, survived by her sons Sam and Sid and by Debra's daughter Denise. If Tillie died intestate, we ignore any gift to Debra. She predeceased Tillie and the contemporaneous writing says nothing about Debra's descendants. The estate is divided evenly between Sam, Sid, and Denise.

Example 18-32. Same as Example 18-31 except that Tillie executed a will four years ago. Her will devised her estate evenly between her three children. Denise will receive less than Sam and Sid. Because Tillie's contemporaneous writing says nothing about Debra's descendants, ademption by satisfaction applies to reduce Denise's share. She receives only what her deceased mother would have received.

CHECKPOINTS

- The UPC and state statutes include several rules of construction that apply to wills.
- These rules do not apply if there is sufficient evidence of the testator's contrary intent.
- The testator's will disposes of property she owns at death and property she acquired after death unless a state statute or her will indicates otherwise.
- If a devisee to whom antilapse applies fails to meet a survival condition, but is survived by descendants, those descendants take the property devised to him. The devise is not voided even if the devisee predeceases the testator.
- Antilapse applies only if the devisee is the testator's grandparent or a descendant of that grandparent. It can apply to other devisees only if the will provides that it applies.
- Antilapse applies to devises to individuals and devises to a class.
- If a pre-residuary devise fails, the residuary devisees share the failed devise.
- If a residuary devisee fails to survive, and antilapse does not apply, the other residuary devisees share the failed devise even if the devise is not made to them as a class.
- If there is no surviving residuary devisee and antilapse does not apply, the failed residuary devise is distributed through intestate succession.
- The devisee of a certain amount of securities is entitled to that amount if the testator owned the securities at death.
- The devisee is also entitled to additional securities of that issuer, or securities of another issuer, if the testator acquired them through entity action. Entity action includes the payment of stock dividends, stock splits, and reorganizations.
- The devisee is also entitled to additional securities in the issuer that the testator acquired through a plan of reinvestment.

- Some jurisdictions give the devisee the right to additional securities only if the securities are specifically devised. The UPC applies to both general and specific devises of securities owned when the will was executed.
- The UPC includes several provisions designed to prevent the ademption by extinction of specific devises. It substitutes a pecuniary devise equal to the unpaid proceeds if the testator sold the property, it was taken by condemnation, or it was damaged or destroyed.
- The UPC also provides a substitute devise if the testator disposed of real property or tangible personal property and acquired replacement property. The devisee receives the replacement property.
- The UPC provides for a substitute pecuniary devise if the property was disposed of in any other situation and the testator did not intend to have ademption by extinction apply.
- Although the UPC follows the intent theory in trying to limit ademption by extinction, many states follow the identity theory. They are less likely to allow the replacement devise or the substitute pecuniary devise.
- The UPC provides for pecuniary devises equal to the net proceeds when a conservator or agent sells specifically devised property or receives a condemnation award or damages.
- A devisee of encumbered property is not entitled to have the debt paid from the residue unless the will indicates that intent. A statement that the personal representative should pay the testator's debts is not a sufficient indicator of intent.
- The donor of a power of appointment can prescribe the conditions for the power's exercise.
- If the donor did not require a specific reference to the power, the power is treated as exercised by a residuary clause in the powerholder's will if she could have exercised it in favor of her estate and the donor did not provide for an eligible taker in default.
- A nonspecific reference also exercises the power of appointment if the will indicates that intent, usually by a residuary clause devising any property over which the testator has a power of appointment.

- Ademption by satisfaction applies when an inter vivos gift is made in full or partial satisfaction of a devise.
- Inter vivos transfers reduce or eliminate devises to the devisee only if there is a writing indicating the gift is in full or partial satisfaction of the devise. The writing can be made contemporaneously by the testator or made in his will; it can be an acknowledgement by the devisee.
- A devisee who receives an inter vivos gift that exceeds the value of any devise to him does not have to return the excess gift.
- When antilapse applies, the descendants of a deceased devisee have their devises reduced for ademption by satisfaction unless there is a writing that provides otherwise.

CHAPTER 19

Rules of Construction for Governing Instruments

ROADMAP

- Survival requirements
- Choice of law
- Power of appointment specific reference requirement
- Construing class gifts
- Deceased beneficiary
- Survivorship with respect to future interests in trust
- Class gifts to descendants and similar categories
- Representation
- Worthier-title doctrine abolished
- Future interests in heirs
- State statutes

A. Chapter Overview

The previous chapter discussed UPC rules of construction that apply only to wills. This chapter covers UPC rules of construction that apply to wills, trusts, and other instruments. If a rule applies only to some instruments, the statute indicates its limitations. Because these rules are not mandatory, a property owner can provide for other outcomes, usually by doing so in the relevant document.

The discussion in this chapter focuses on UPC rather than UTC provisions. It does so because UTC § 112 provides for following the jurisdiction's rules of construction used in interpreting wills as appropriate to the interpretation of trust provisions and the disposition of the trust property. Individual jurisdictions might depart from the UTC by including rules of construction in their trust codes. These rules might be identical to those in the state's probate code or might differ from them in one or more aspects. The jurisdiction might also have its own rules for transfers pursuant to a non-trust beneficiary provision.

B. Survival Requirements

Survivorship requirements might appear in wills or trust instruments, be imposed by statute, or be part of contracts between a property owner and a bank, insurer, or other entity. The requirement might be for actual survival, survival for a specific period, or survival until a stated event. Those requirements involve actual survival. Statutes often extend beyond requiring actual survival and treat a surviving beneficiary as predeceased based on his killing the decedent, disclaiming a devise, or taking other disqualifying actions. This section focuses on actual failure to survive in the context of wills, trusts, and other dispositive instruments.

1. Language of the Instrument

Survival terms commonly appear in wills, trusts, and other instruments. A will might devise "$100,000 to my son but only if he survives me." A trust might provide for distributing the trust principal "to my surviving descendants." If the instrument imposes a survival requirement, the beneficiary must survive to take. To determine whether the named beneficiary (or class member) takes, we must determine if the instrument actually imposes a survival requirement and what it means by "survival."

The instrument might be specific regarding survival, often to prevent successive rounds of probate when the beneficiary dies soon after the original decedent. Thus, a will might devise "$100,000 to my daughter if she survives me by at least 30 days" or "150,000 to my wife if she and I do not die as a result of a common event." A trust might provide for distributing "$10,000 to each of my grandchildren who survives to age 21." Survivorship conditions based on a time period or event rarely postpone transfers indefinitely. For transfers to a surviving spouse, there might be estate tax issues relating to delay beyond the six-month or common disaster safe harbor in I.R.C. § 2056(b)(3). For transfers to unborn beneficiaries in trust, conditions must avoid rule against perpetuities problems.

Survival conditions and definitions might appear in the language describing the potential transfer, as in the paragraphs above. They might also appear elsewhere in the instrument, particularly in a will or trust. Before using the statutory default provisions, always look for blanket survival definitions or conditions in administrative or other parts of the governing instrument.

2. UPC Default Provisions

The instrument might not use survival terms, or it might use "surviving" without defining that word. In the first situation, we must determine whether the transferor intended an absolute gift, with no survivorship requirement imposed on the beneficiary. In the second situation, we must determine whether he meant only actual survival or preferred a longer survival period. Although the UPC imposes survival conditions and defines survival, it is subject to an overriding rule based on transferor intent. UPC § 2-701.

a. 120-Hour Survival Requirement

The UPC imposes a 120-hour survival requirement. Merely surviving a decedent, or even surviving for 119 hours, is not sufficient. UPC §§ 2-104(b) (intestate succession, homestead, and exempt property), 2-702 (wills and other governing instruments). The UPC provisions require establishing survival for the requisite period by clear and convincing evidence.

The UPC survival requirements apply to surviving an event. The testator's death is one such provision, but UPC § 2-702 covers other events, such as the termination of a preceding trust interest or attaining a specific age.

The comments to UPC § 2-702 indicate that it requires survival by 120 hours in situations covered by the Uniform Simultaneous Death Act. Under that act, for example, survivorship tenancy property passes as if each tenant survived as to his or her share of the property. UPC § 2-702(c) applies that rule when there is not clear and convincing evidence of survivorship by at least 120 hours.

Example 19-1. Sam created a testamentary trust to pay income for life to his wife Irma, followed by a remainder to Sam's surviving children. When Sam died two years ago, he was survived by Irma and his three children, Cindy, Clara, and Curt. Irma died last week, and Curt died 15 hours later. Although Curt survived Sam by more than 120 hours, he did not survive Irma by more than 120 hours. Cindy and Clara will share the trust property after Irma's death. If Curt had died more than 120 hours after Irma's death, he would have received his share of the trust principal.

Example 19-2. Jerry and Jane purchased Blackacre as joint tenants with right of survivorship. Jerry died 48 hours ago; Jane died 12 hours later. Although Jane survived Jerry, she did not do so by 120 hours. As a result, one-half of Blackacre passes through Jerry's estate and one-half passes through Jane's estate.

Example 19-3. Tina, Terry, and Ted purchased Whiteacre as joint tenants with right of survivorship. Tina died six days ago. Terry and Ted survived Tina by at least 120 hours. Terry and Ted continue to own Whiteacre as joint tenants with right of survivorship. The 120-hour survivorship rule will apply again when either of them dies.

b. Exceptions to the 120-Hour Survival Requirement

The exceptions covered below are UPC provisions. Individual states might impose shorter survival requirements. In addition, certain federal statutes, primarily the Employee Retirement Income Security Act of 1974 (ERISA), may preempt conflicting state laws (whether or not based on the UPC).

UPC § 2-702(d) contains four exceptions to the 120-hour survival requirement. The first two apply if language in the governing instrument effectively preempts the UPC default. The other two are based on avoiding failure of an interest or power or other unintended consequences. Because these are exceptions to the 120-hour rule, they are designed for situations involving shorter actual survival periods. They are not, however, invalidated if they result in longer survival requirements. Each requires clear and convincing evidence of meeting the survival condition.

The first exception covers two commonly used survivorship provisions: simultaneous death and death in a common disaster. The exception applies if the governing instrument applies to one or both of those occurrences. Its language must explicitly apply to the facts involved.

Example 19-4. Imogene devised "$10,000 to Dora if she survives me by at least 120 hours *and* she and I do not die as a result of a common disaster." If Dora survives 300 hours after Imogene, but dies as a result of a common disaster, the devise fails.

Example 19-5. Imogene instead devised "$10,000 to Dora if she actually survives me *or* if we die under circumstances in which our order of death cannot be determined by clear and convincing evidence." If Dora and Imogene are found dead, and the order of death cannot be established by clear and convincing evidence, Dora's estate will receive the $10,000 even though she probably failed to survive Imogene by 120 hours.

The second exception applies to two different provisions. Survival by 120 hours is not required if the instrument expressly indicates that the beneficiary does not have to survive by any specified time period. Survival by 120 hours is also unnecessary if the instrument expressly includes its own survival period.

Example 19-6. Sybil created an inter vivos trust, retaining the right to income for her life. The trust instrument provides for trust principal to be distributed "to those of my children who survive my death by at least 10 hours." The trust principal will be shared by those children who survive Sybil by at least 10 hours. Survival by 120 hours is not required.

The third exception is designed to prevent a nonvested interest or power from being invalidated under the common-law or the 90-year wait-and-see version of the rule against perpetuities included in UPC § 2-901.

The final exception applies to prevent unintended consequences if applying the 120-hour requirement to more than one governing instrument causes an unintended failure or duplication. The comments refer to spousal mutual wills that make a charity the substitute taker. Application of the 120-hour rule might result in the charity receiving devises from both spouses when only one such devise was intended. It is less likely that this exception would apply if the substitute devisees were instead the couple's children or other descendants that they had in common.

3. Provisions in the Governing Instrument

The governing instrument might impose survival requirements or definitions that differ from the relevant statutory rules. For example, a testator might consider 120 hours too short an enjoyment period to justify passing property through two successive rounds of probate. In that case, he might impose a longer period.

A transferor has other options. Instead of a particular number of days or hours, he might require that he and the trust beneficiary not die as a result of a common disaster or that the beneficiary be located within a certain time period. He might even reverse the presumption in the simultaneous death statute and treat the beneficiary as the survivor; this is often done for estate tax reasons.

A testator who inserts his own survival provisions can apply them to all transfers under a particular instrument, but he does not have to do so.

> **Example 19-7.** Ted made the following devises: "I devise Redacre to Rita if she survives me by at least three months. I devise Blueacre to Ben unless he and I die as a result of a common disaster. I devise Purpleacre to Pam." Because Ted's will did not include a survival provision for Purpleacre, Pam is not subject to the survival conditions imposed on either Rita or Ben. If the will is silent, the statutory default rules might apply to Pam's devise. Alternatively, the court might determine that Ted's failure to mention survival meant that he imposed no condition on Pam.

4. Deemed Failure to Survive

A beneficiary who satisfies a survival condition might still be treated as predeceased. Actions that result in this treatment might occur before or after she would normally have become entitled to the property or power. Some of these situations involve any beneficiary; others apply only to the surviving spouse. Situations such as murder, disclaimer, or waiver by a beneficiary are covered in more detail elsewhere in this book.

Simultaneous death statutes can result in a potential taker being treated as predeceased. These statutes may be unnecessary in states that have adopted the UPC provisions discussed above. But those statutes serve a valuable purpose in states that require survival only for an instant rather than for 120 hours. Statutes that mirror the Uniform Simultaneous Death Act provide rules that apply when we cannot establish that death was not simultaneous. These rules generally treat the beneficiary as predeceasing the property owner and divide jointly owned property between the deceased joint owners.

> **Example 19-8.** Tom devised $100,000 to Donna. If Donna dies a day before Tom, she fails to meet the survival requirement. If she dies 26 hours after Tom, she meets the survival requirement if the state requires only actual survival. She fails it if survival by 120 hours (or any number of hours greater than 26) is required. If Tom and Donna are found dead at the scene of an accident, medical evidence might establish their respective times of death. If there is not sufficient evidence to do so, Donna does not meet the survival requirement.

5. Alternative Taker

A governing instrument that includes a survival requirement might provide for an alternative taker. A statute that treats a beneficiary as predeceased effectively provides for an alternative taker even if it does not specifically do so. Depending on the relevant language, the alternative taker might be someone named in the governing instrument, a residuary beneficiary of a will or trust, an intestate heir, or the descendants of a beneficiary who failed the survival requirement. Several of the rules of construction in this chapter are relevant in determining who ultimately takes the property interest.

C. Choice of Law

In a mobile society, it is likely that an individual might execute a will in one jurisdiction but later move to and die in another. Likewise, a settlor might reside in one state when he creates a trust, while his trustee is located in another jurisdiction. Or an individual might simply prefer rules of law in effect in a state other than the state of his residence or the state in which he holds property. UPC § 2-703 provides a general choice of law rule and three exceptions. As a general rule, the instrument will be governed by the law of the state selected in the governing instrument. That state's law will apply even to property that has a different situs.

The general rule will not apply, and the law of the decedent's residence or the property's situs will instead apply, in three situations. The first relates to the spouse's elective share, the second to exempt property, and the third to any other public policy of the state of residence or situs.

Note that this provision lets the transferor select the governing law. It does not give the transferee that power.

D. Power of Appointment Specific Reference Requirement

The donor of a power of appointment might require the powerholder to exercise the power at a specific time and in a specific manner. The instrument creating the power might require the powerholder to exercise it by a writing that is separate from her will, require witnesses to the exercise, or limit exercise to a will. The donor might specify that the instrument must refer to the power in a particular way.

UPC § 2-704 provides that the powerholder's substantial compliance with those requirements is sufficient if two conditions are met. First, the powerholder must know she has the power, and she must intend to exercise it. This requirement prevents inadvertent exercise that rises to the level of substantial compliance. Second, her manner of exercising the power must not impair a material purpose of the power's donor.

The comments indicate that this provision should reduce litigation over whether a powerholder's reference to the particular power is sufficiently detailed to satisfy the donor's "make reference to the power" requirements. Because the instrument creating the power is the governing instrument regarding exercise requirements, that instrument should be consulted to determine if the donor had a material purpose for requiring strict compliance with any exercise requirements.

If the power must be exercised in a will, UPC § 2-608, discussed in the previous chapter, is relevant in determining if the powerholder's residuary clause exercises a power.

E. Construing Class Gifts

UPC § 2-705 provides rules for determining when individuals in specified categories are included in class gifts. If the governing instrument doesn't define qualifications for class inclusion or exclusion, these provisions apply.

1. Terms of Relationship

If a class gift includes a term of relationship, it is to be construed using the rules for intestate succession. UPC § 2-705(b). Those rules are described in Chapter 5. Exceptions apply to situations involving relatives by marriage and transferors who are not a potential beneficiary's parent.

> **Example 19-9.** Geraldine created a trust to pay income to herself for life, then pay income to her children for their lives, and then distribute principal to her children's descendants. The trust included no definitional terms. Geraldine's daughter Dahlia adopted an infant, Danielle, after Geraldine died. Danielle is included as a beneficiary of trust principal.

a. *Relatives by Marriage*

Some terms of relationship indicate that the individual is related to the transferor by blood or by marriage. For example, a daughter is related by blood, while a son-in-law is related by marriage. Other relationships do not involve separate terms. The transferor's aunt or cousin could be related to him by blood or by marriage. UPC § 2-705(c) applies to those situations.

If the instrument indicates whether relationships by marriage are included or excluded, the instrument governs. If the instrument is silent, the class excludes relationships by marriage unless one of two exceptions applies. It includes relationships by marriage if the class was otherwise empty when the instrument was executed and would foreseeably continue to be empty. This exception makes sense, as we would not expect a transferor to make a meaningless class gift. This exception is more objective than the second exception. That exception includes relationships by marriage in the class if the language or circumstances of the transfer indicate that they should be included.

> **Example 19-10.** Sam had two brothers, each of whom had one child, a son, who was Sam's nephew. Each of those sons married and then died without issue. After both of his brothers and both of his nephews died, Sam created a trust that would pay him the income for life and then distribute trust principal to "my nieces." Although the nieces are related to

Sam only by virtue of their marriage to his nephews, they will receive the trust principal when he dies. The class of nieces related to him by blood was empty when he executed the trust and would foreseeably continue to be empty.

Example 19-11. Same as Example 19-10 except that Sam also had a sister. She died giving birth to a daughter before Sam created the trust. That daughter died after Sam created the trust. Sam's nieces by marriage would not be included in the class based on its being empty when Sam created the trust. They might be included based on his use of the word "nieces" instead of "niece," as he had only one niece by blood and—because all his siblings were dead when he created the trust—could not expect to have another.

UPC § 2-705(a)(5) defines "in-laws" to include step relatives and former step relatives.

Example 19-12. Same as Example 19-10 except that Sam was also survived by his late wife's niece. His wife and all her other relatives died before Sam created the trust. Although some nieces are related to Sam only by virtue of their marriage to his nephews, and one is a step-niece, they will receive the trust principal when he dies. The class of nieces related to him by blood was empty when he executed the trust and would foreseeably continue to be empty.

b. *Transferor Is Not the Parent*

UPC § 2-705(d) applies to construing class gifts in a governing instrument when the transferor is not the parent of an individual who might be included in a class. For example, a grandmother might establish a trust for her children, with remainder to her grandchildren. She is obviously not the parent of those grandchildren. She might not even know that some of them exist.

The individual will be treated as his parent's child if the parent performed customary parental functions before the child reached age 18. These functions can also be performed by the parent's spouse or close relative or by a surviving spouse of either. The individual will also be treated as his parent's child if the parent intended to perform those functions but was prevented by death or some other reason. The intent must be proved by clear and convincing evidence. The comments to UPC § 2-705 provide an extensive list of parental functions.

UPC § 2-705(d) is most likely to affect adult adoptees.

2. Class-Closing Rules

Because class membership can increase or decrease over time, we must consider what to do about hypothetical, unborn class members when the time for distribution arrives. The comments to UPC § 2-705(e) begin with the general class-closing rule found in the Restatement (Third) of Property: Wills and Other Donative Transfers § 15.1. The transferor's intent governs. In the absence of an expression of intent, we close the class to future members if there is a class member eligible take on the distribution date.

UPC § 2-705(e) indicates the treatment of four sets of potential class members. First, a child who is in gestation when the distribution date arrives is not precluded from taking if she survives at least 120 hours after birth. Second, a posthumously conceived child is not precluded from taking even though her parent's death was the distribution date. To be part of the class, she had to be *in utero* no later than 36 months after her parent's death or be born no later than 45 months after her parent's death. In either situation, she must live at least 120 hours after birth. In addition, the person with distribution power must have known or received notice of the intent to use genetic material in assisted reproduction; notice or knowledge must have occurred no more six months after the parent's death. Third, a child who is in the process of being adopted when the class closes is part of the class if the adoption actually occurs. Fourth, a child is included in the class if he is in the process of being adjudicated a de facto child and the de facto parentage is subsequently established.

Note that only the second rule in UPC § 2-705(e) requires the death of the child's parent to be the class-closing date.

F. Deceased Beneficiary

UPC § 2-706 is designed to follow (as is UPC § 2-707 for trusts) the antilapse provisions described in UPC § 2-603 for wills. It applies when a beneficiary who would have taken under a life insurance policy, a retirement plan, a pay on death account, or a transfer on death account is ineligible to receive the benefit because he did not survive the decedent. It applies if the deceased beneficiary is the only beneficiary or if he is a member of a class. It does not apply to survivorship tenancies, such as a joint tenancy with right of survivorship, or to joint and survivorship bank accounts. Money or other property covered by those ownership forms passes by survivorship rather than by virtue of a beneficiary designation.

UPC § 2-706 does not apply if the instrument creating the benefit provides for a different distribution in an alternative beneficiary designation. UPC § 2-706(a)(1). If its application is preempted by a federal statute, it provides that the actual recipient is to return the property to the beneficiary who would have received it in the absence of preemption. UPC § 2-706(e)(2). State law might include this provision, but that will not always be the case and there is no guarantee such a provision would escape a preemption challenge.

UPC § 2-706(b) applies antilapse rules if the beneficiary who failed to survive the decedent falls into one of three categories: the decedent's grandparent; a descendant of the decedent's grandparent; or the decedent's stepchild. It does not apply these rules if the beneficiary is the decedent's spouse or a descendant of the decedent's stepchild. When this provision applies, it creates a substitute gift.

If the beneficiary designation is not expressed as a class gift, the descendants of the deceased beneficiary take in his place, by representation. If the beneficiary designation is expressed in class gift form, the surviving beneficiaries and the descendants of the deceased beneficiary share the benefit, again using representation rules. The provision for class gifts does not apply if the class is expressed using the terms "issue," "descendants," "heirs of the body," "heirs," "family," or similar language.

> **Example 19-13.** Inez insured her life for $600,000; the beneficiary designation on her life insurance policy read "my children." Inez died, survived by her son Stuart and his daughter Dora, her son Steven, and her grandson Gordon, the son of her deceased son Simeon. Because "children" constitutes a class and the deceased member (Simeon) was a descendant of Inez's grandparents, the proceeds are divided into thirds. Gordon takes the share that Simeon would have received. Dora takes nothing because Stuart survived Inez and takes his one-third share.
>
> **Example 19-14.** If Inez had instead been survived only by Dora and Gordon, the proceeds would have been divided equally between Dora and Gordon. Because the beneficiary designation was to a class, the surviving class members share the entire proceeds. Steven is removed from the class because he was not survived by descendants.

The UPC continues its construction, discussed in the previous chapter regarding will provisions, that the terms "my surviving" or "if he survives me" do not automatically preclude antilapse. The UPC requires additional evidence of the decedent's intent to require survivorship by the named beneficiary. UPC § 2-706(b)(3).

If the instrument contains an alternative beneficiary designation, it supersedes the substitute beneficiary provisions. UPC § 2-706(b)(4). But if no one named in the alternative designation is eligible to take, the substitute beneficiaries receive the property. It does not revert to the decedent's estate. The alternative beneficiary designation can be to a class or to an individual. If the expressly named individual does not survive, the alternative beneficiary designation does not supersede the substitute gift even if the alternative beneficiary is herself survived by descendants.

> **Example 19-15.** Bob opened a bank account in the name of "Bob, POD my children, alternative beneficiary my sister." When Bob died, he was survived by his two sons, a child of his deceased daughter, and by his sister. Although Bob's daughter predeceased him, two of his children survived. Because eligible takers in the class survived Bob, the class—including the substitute beneficiary (his grandchild)—receives the bank account. Bob's grandchild would not have received a share of the account if the form that Bob signed when he opened the account contained terms indicating that survivorship was required.
>
> **Example 19-16.** If Bob was instead survived only by several grandchildren and by his sister, his sister would take the bank account. The alternative designation supersedes the substitute gift.

UPC § 2-706(c) deals with situations in which the decedent established alternative designations, neither designated beneficiary survived, but each was survived by descendants. As a general rule, it favors the descendants of first-listed beneficiary, referred to as the primary beneficiary.

> **Example 19-17.** If Bob was instead survived only by several grandchildren and by the son of his deceased sister, his grandchildren would take the bank account by the relevant rules of representation. The expressly designated alternative beneficiary (his sister) failed to survive. Antilapse reinstates the gift to the substitute beneficiaries of the primary beneficiaries rather than to the descendants of the alternative beneficiary.

UPC § 2-706(c) includes an exception when the alternative designation is to a descendant of the primary beneficiary. In that case, we favor the younger-generation substitute beneficiary. Example 19-18 illustrates this concept for trust interests.

G. Survivorship with Respect to Future Interests in Trust

UPC § 2-707 applies to trusts that provide for alternative takers of a future interest. For example, the trust might provide income to one beneficiary for life, with trust principal paid to a second beneficiary if living but otherwise to a third beneficiary. One or both of those alternative beneficiaries might fail to survive but be survived by descendants. If either designation was to a class rather than to an individual, some or all of the class members might fail to survive.

This provision is analogous to UPC § 2-603 for wills and to UPC § 2-706 for various will substitutes. It is designed to preserve the future interest in descendants of a deceased beneficiary unless there is evidence that the settlor had a contrary intent. Antilapse applies in some states only if the primary beneficiary has the required relationship to the settlor; UPC § 2-707 does not include this requirement. It applies only if the settlor did not expressly require survivorship or provide an alternative beneficiary if the primary beneficiary failed to survive. The UPC continues its construction, discussed in the previous chapter regarding will provisions, that the terms "my surviving" or "if he survives me" do not automatically preclude antilapse. It requires additional evidence of the decedent's intent to require survivorship by the named beneficiary. UPC § 2-707(b)(3).

The starting point is determining the required survival date. UPC § 2-707(b) makes the distribution date, not the trust creation date, the relevant date for this purpose. In other words, a future interest does not vest in the named beneficiary when the trust is created. This is a change from the original common law rule that vested the interest when it was created. A beneficiary who had a vested interest could dispose of it by will to someone other than his descendants. A beneficiary whose interest was contingent on satisfying a condition, and who failed to do so, had nothing to dispose of by will. The comments indicate that the taker must survive the distribution date by at least 120 hours.

If the instrument contains an alternative future interest, it supersedes the substitute beneficiary provisions. UPC § 2-707(b)(4). But if no one named in the alternative designation is eligible to take, the substitute beneficiaries receive the property. It does not revert to the decedent's estate. The alternative beneficiary designation can be to a class or to an individual. If the expressly named alternative beneficiary does not survive, the alternative beneficiary designation does not supersede the substitute gift even if the alternative beneficiary is herself survived by descendants.

Because a trust is often created by will, and a will usually includes a residuary devise, we need to determine if the will creates an alternative future interest in the residuary devisee. UPC § 2-707(a)(1) provides that a residuary clause does not create such an interest with respect to a future interest that is not created in the residuary clause. This rule applies even if the residuary devise specifically mentions lapsed or failed devises. If the future interest would fail for lack of primary or alternative takers (including substitute takers), the interest passes under the residuary clause of the transferor's will. This rule applies if the interest was created in a nonresiduary clause of his will or in a codicil to the will. UPC § 2-707(d). If there is no eligible residuary taker, it passes to his intestate heirs. The rules of UPC § 2-711, described in Section K, apply in determining those heirs.

Because a trust's settlor might have created a power of appointment, it is possible that the powerholder might exercise it to create a future interest in trust property. When that occurs, UPC § 2-707(e) applies to provide a taker if there is no surviving beneficiary, alternative beneficiary, or substitute beneficiary. If the person who created the power provided for a taker in default, that person receives the property. If no recipient is eligible to take, a fallback provision looks to the residuary clause of the transferor's will or his intestate heirs. When the fallback provision applies, the term transferor depends on what type of power was created. The donor of the power is the transferor if the power was nongeneral; the powerholder is the transferor if the power was general.

UPC § 2-707(c) deals with situations in which the decedent established alternative designations, neither designated beneficiary survived, and each was survived by descendants. As a general rule, it favors the descendants of the primary beneficiary. But if the alternative beneficiary was a descendant of the primary beneficiary, descendants of the alternative beneficiary receive the property. The settlor is treated as preferring a particular descendant of the primary beneficiary rather than all eligible descendants.

Example 19-18. Sally created a trust with income to her brother Brad for life, remainder to her sister Dora, but if Dora did not survive, remainder to Dora's son Seth. Dora and Seth both died before Brad. Dora was survived by her sons Seymour and Serge and by Seth's daughter Denise. Seymour, Serge, and Denise all survived Brad. Although Dora had the primary future interest, the holder of the alternative future interest

(Seth) was Dora's descendant. Because Sally is treated as preferring Seth to his siblings, Denise is the substitute beneficiary who takes.

H. Class Gifts to Descendants and Similar Categories

A gift to a single-generation class is divided equally among class members unless the will or other instrument provides otherwise. All class members are of the same rank. That is not the case for transfers to a multigenerational class, which might have members in two or more ranks when the transfer becomes effective. The instrument might provide a method for distributing property among members of a multigenerational class. The UPC provides a rule that applies if the governing instrument does not address that issue.

UPC § 2-708 provides that transfers to descendants, issue, or heirs of the body are distributed among class members based on how the property would be distributed to them if the designated ancestor had died intestate owning the relevant property. The designated ancestor might be the transferor but that is not required. The comments indicate that, by providing for using the applicable intestacy statute, the UPC is rejecting the use of per stirpes provided by the Restatement (Second) of Property: Donative Transfers § 28.2.

Example 19-19. Trey created an inter vivos trust and retained income for life. The principal would then be distributed to his descendants. Trey was survived by his son Phil, his daughter Lisa, and four grandchildren. One grandchild was Phil's son; the other three were children of Trey's predeceased son Bob. No matter what method of representation the state follows, Phil would receive one-third, Lisa would receive one-third, and Bob's three children would each receive one-ninth. Phil's son would receive nothing.

Example 19-20. If Trey was instead survived only by Phil's son and by Bob's three children, the shares each grandchild would take depend on the representation method used in that jurisdiction. In a per stirpes system, Phil's son would receive one-half; Bob's three children would each receive one-sixth. In a per capita with representation system or a per capita at each generation system, each of the four grandchildren would receive one-fourth; we would ignore the intervening generation (Trey's children) because it had no surviving members.

Example 19-21. Trey amended the terms of his trust. After his death, the trustee was to pay income to his children for life. When his last surviving child died, the trustee was to accumulate income for 10 years and then distribute the principal and accumulated income to his children's surviving descendants. Each child was the designated ancestor for his share of the trust. One of Bob's three children died before the 10-year accumulation period ended, survived by his spouse but no descendants. Because Bob's daughter-in-law would not have been his intestate heir if he had died intestate at the end of the tenth year, she does not receive a distribution from this trust.

I. Representation

The fiduciary distributing property based on provisions in a will, trust, or other instrument distributes it among those persons who survive to the distribution date unless they are treated as not surviving based on some act such as disclaiming their interest or killing a transferor. If the instrument either provides for distribution to a group such as descendants, or antilapse applies to the share of a deceased taker, the fiduciary distributes the deceased beneficiary's property by representation.

UPC § 2-709 provides definitions for two common methods of representation that might be required by statute or a governing instrument. The two methods are per stirpes and per capita at each generation. Although it does not provide a definition for per capita with representation, a transferor can choose to mandate that system in the governing instrument. All three systems are described in Chapter 5 in the context of intestate succession.

Although UPC § 2-709 does not mandate the use of per capita at each generation, the language in UPC § 2-709(b) establishes that method as preferred. Distribution is to be made by this method if the statute or governing instrument does not specify a method and merely calls for distribution by representation.

J. Worthier-Title Doctrine Abolished

The common-law doctrine of worthier title provided for a reversion in the transferor if the transfer was made to his heirs. The same result occurred if the transfer was to heirs at law, next of kin, distributees, relatives, family, or similar language. UPC § 2-710 provides that the doctrine is abolished as a rule of law and as a rule of construction. A state might have retained the doctrine in some form. Wash. Rev. Code § 11.12.185.

K. Future Interests in Heirs

UPC § 2-711 applies when a statute or a governing instrument provides for distributions to an undifferentiated category of a designated individual's relatives. The statute lists heirs, heirs at law, next of kin, relatives, and family as examples. Those terms, and others like them, should be contrasted with such terms as children, descendants, and ancestors, to which this section does not apply. The intestacy statutes are deemed to apply to distributions covered by one of these designations. If no qualifying heir survives to the distribution date, the state takes the property by escheat. The transferor can, of course, prevent escheat by providing for an alternative taker in the governing instrument.

Because UPC § 2-711 applies to both present and future distributions, those statutes could give different results depending on the date of the distribution. Each distribution is made based on treating the designated individual as dying on the date the distribution is to take effect.

UPC § 2-711 treats the designated individual's surviving spouse differently from his other heirs. A spouse who survives the designated individual but remarries before the distribution date is not treated as his surviving spouse.

L. State Statutes

States might adopt some or all of the UPC rules of construction for wills, trusts, and other instruments. If a state varies from a UPC provision, the differences are likely to relate to survival conditions, relationships, and affected governing instruments. The discussion below covers some potential areas of difference. Careful reading of the relevant state statute is essential.

1. Survival

A state might have enacted a pre-1993 version of the Uniform Simultaneous Death Act or similar statute. In that case, survival rather than survival by 120 hours suffices. If the relevant statute requires only that the beneficiary survive a person or an event, and no separate rule of construction applies, you should assume that mere survival is the only requirement.

The state might provide separate survival provisions in its probate code, in its trust code, and in various statutes governing property in survivorship tenancies and beneficiary designations. Do not assume that a rule included in one set of statutes applies to all relevant transfers.

States might also differ from the UPC in their treatment of the terms "surviving" and "if he survives." The UPC does not treat those terms, standing alone, as indicating a survival condition. A state statute might explicitly provide that those terms do require survival. Fla. Stat. §§ 732.603(3)(a), 736.1106(3)(a). Alternatively, a statute might not address the issue, leaving the interpretation to the courts. *Gibney v. Hossack*, 230 N.E.3d 1009 (Mass. 2024).

2. Relationships

As was true for intestacy statutes, states might not provide benefits to every relationship category included in the UPC. They might omit stepchildren and might have different—or no—provisions covering children conceived by an assisted reproduction method, posthumously conceived children, or adult adoptees. They might treat half-blood relationships differently from whole-blood relationships, or they might apply their half-blood statutes to some types of transfers but not to others. They might not have adopted the Uniform Parentage Act's de facto parentage concept.

3. Other Differences

States might not follow the UPC in allowing substantial compliance for exercising a power of appointment. They might use per stirpes instead of per capita at each generation in determining the shares of substitute beneficiaries. They might not provide that the descendants of an alternative beneficiary take instead of the descendants of a primary beneficiary when the deceased alternative beneficiary is a descendant of the primary beneficiary. They might limit their general rules of construction to wills and trusts. They might use preponderance of the evidence instead of clear and convincing evidence.

CHECKPOINTS

- Unless limited to a particular instrument, the rules of construction listed below apply to wills, trusts, and other governing instruments.
- Survival requirements might appear in a governing instrument or in a statute.
- Survival requirements might be based on surviving a particular person or surviving until an event occurs.
- Survival requirements prevent successive rounds of probate within a relatively short time period.
- Survival requirements usually treat the potential beneficiary as predeceasing the property owner. As a result, property might pass to someone other than the deceased beneficiary's heirs or devisees.
- The UPC requires surviving the individual or the event by 120 hours. It includes a clear and convincing evidence standard for establishing survival.
- The UPC survival requirement does not apply if the governing instrument uses simultaneous death or death in a common disaster language.
- The UPC survival requirement does not apply if the instrument expressly indicates that the beneficiary does not have to survive by any specified time period or if it expressly includes its own survival period.
- The UPC survival requirement does not apply if that would result in invalidating a nonvested interest or power under the common-law or the 90-year wait-and-see version of the rule against perpetuities.
- The UPC survival requirement does not apply if applying it to more than one governing instrument causes an unintended failure or duplication, as might be the case with mutual wills.
- A transferor can select the state whose law will apply to the governing instrument. That law will apply even to property with a different situs. Exceptions apply to protect the spouse's elective share, exempt property, and any other public policy of the state with situs.
- If the holder of a power of appointment does not strictly comply with the exercise requirements, substantial compliance might be sufficient.

The powerholder must know she has the power and intend to exercise it, and her manner of exercising it must not impair a material purpose of the power's creator.

- Class gifts are generally construed according to the rules for intestate succession. Children of assisted reproduction, posthumous children, and adult adoptees often are subject to different rules in determining from whom they inherit.
- In the absence of a contrary expression of intent, we close a class to future members if there is a class member eligible take on the distribution date.
- Antilapse provisions can apply to a life insurance policy, a retirement plan, a pay on death account, transfer on death account, or similar contracts if the instrument doesn't expressly require survival. The deceased beneficiary's descendants take as substitute beneficiaries.
- If the instrument provides an alternative beneficiary designation, that designation applies instead of antilapse.
- Antilapse provisions can apply to a future interest in a trust if the named beneficiary fails to survive to the distribution date. A substitute future interest is created in the deceased beneficiary's descendants.
- A residuary clause in a will, even one that includes lapsed or failed devises, is not sufficient to constitute an alternative future interest if the future interest was created in a nonresiduary devise.
- If a class gift to descendants, issue, or heirs of the body does not specify the distribution method, the fiduciary distributes the property based on the method used for intestate succession. It treats the designated ancestor as dying intestate on the distribution date.
- Distribution by representation applies to devises, trust interests, and other donative transfers unless the instrument provides otherwise. The UPC provides definitions for per stirpes and per capita at each generation distributions and indicates that per capita at each generation is used unless the instrument provides for using per stirpes.
- The UPC and many state statutes have abolished the doctrine of worthier title, which provided a reversion if the transferor made a gift to his heirs.

- Distribution of a future interest to a designated individual's heirs is based on treating the designated individual as dying intestate on the distribution date.
- State statutes might differ from the UPC in their treatment of survival conditions, relationships, taking by representation, and other rules of construction. They might limit their coverage to wills and trusts, particularly with respect to antilapse and length of survival.

CHAPTER 20

Disqualifying Acts

ROADMAP

- Marital dissolution
- Killers and abusers
- Disclaimers
- Undue influence
- Duress
- Fraud or mistake
- Relationship to lack of capacity
- Spoliation or alteration
- Remedies

A. Chapter Overview

In a perfect scenario, all beneficiaries meet any survival requirements imposed on them and are eligible to receive property designated for them. But while survival may be a necessary condition for receiving property, it is not always sufficient. In addition to simultaneous death acts, other statutes might treat a beneficiary as predeceased or as disclaiming an interest or power. This chapter addresses three groups of potential beneficiaries: former spouses; killers and abusers; and disclaimants.

In addition to acts affecting a beneficiary's relationship with the decedent, problems may arise based on actions affecting an instrument. Previous chapters described the capacity and formalities necessary to execute a valid will or create a valid trust as well as requirements for amending or revoking an instrument. A disappointed family member might challenge the execution or revocation of a will or trust based on lack of capacity or failure to follow the required formalities. But those are not the only available challenges. This chapter discusses the requirements for challenges based on undue influence, fraud, mistake, and duress. The chapter concludes with a discussion of spoliation and alteration and remedies available to redress disqualifying acts.

B. Marital Dissolution

1. Effect on Treatment as Surviving Spouse

UPC §2-802 determines whether an individual qualifies as a surviving spouse. It applies to marital dissolutions, both divorces and annulments. It does not apply to informal separations, separation decrees, desertion, or abandonment unless the decedent's marriage was dissolved. A state law might apply to one or more of those situations.

An individual whose marriage to the decedent was dissolved is not a surviving spouse. If, however, the individual and the decedent are married when the decedent died, we ignore their prior divorce or annulment. UPC §2-802(a).

UPC §2-802(b) includes circumstances that preclude an individual from qualifying as a surviving spouse even if the dissolution was invalid. The first of these is based on estoppel. It applies if the individual obtained the dissolution or consented to it even though the decree was not recognized as valid in the relevant jurisdiction. But if she and the decedent then remarry or live together as spouses, she retains her status as a surviving spouse. The second of these is based on actions she took that appear to ratify the dissolution. Even if she neither obtained the dissolution nor consented to it, she is not a surviving spouse if she participates in a marriage ceremony with a different person. She is also precluded from claiming surviving spouse status if she was a party to a valid proceeding which ended with an order purporting to terminate all her marital property rights.

If an individual is not a surviving spouse, even though she survived the decedent, she forfeits her rights to an intestate share, elective share, homestead allowance, exempt property, and family allowance.

2. Effect on Devises and Other Transfers to Former Spouse or Former Spouse's Family

The provisions discussed in this section apply unless expressly provided otherwise in one of three documents: the governing document covering the benefit involved; a court order; or a contract between the spouses related to the division of the marital estate. The contract applies whether it is entered into before or after the marriage, divorce, or annulment. UPC § 2-804(b).

If a benefit is revoked under this section, the UPC treats the former spouse or relative as disclaiming the benefit. A former spouse or relative who is prevented from serving as a fiduciary is treated as having died immediately before the divorce or annulment. UPC § 2-804(d). State law might treat the former spouse or relative as having died in both situations rather than having disclaimed with respect to benefits and died with respect to serving as a fiduciary.

This UPC section includes rules protecting third parties who dealt with the former spouse or her relatives without notice of the revocation. It also imposes an obligation on the former spouse or her relatives to return benefits received because federal preemption prevented cancellation of the designation. UPC § 2-804(h)(2). The comments regarding this provision indicate the drafters hope that it provides a viable way around ERISA preemption. The plan benefits can be paid to the former spouse (assuming the other spouse never changed the beneficiary designation), but the UPC effectively imposes a constructive trust on her by requiring their return. The comments note that the U.S. Supreme Court applied preemption to a Virginia statute that was similar to the UPC provision. *Hillman v. Maretta,* 569 U.S. 483 (2013).

a. *Revocable Instrument*

For purposes of UPC § 2-804, an instrument is considered revocable if the individual had the power at the time of the dissolution to cancel any beneficiary or other designation made to his former spouse or her relatives. The source of his power—statute or the governing instrument—does not matter. In addition, the instrument is deemed revocable for this purpose even if he could not substitute his own name in place of his former spouse's name (or that of her relatives). It is deemed revocable even though he lacked the capacity to revoke.

> **Example 20-1.** Horace's father created a trust under which Horace receives income for life. Horace has the power at any time to appoint the trust principal to anyone other than himself, his estate, his creditors, or

the creditors of his estate. The trust instrument gives him the power to change the appointee until he dies. Horace exercised the power in favor of his wife Wilhelmina several years ago. If Horace and Wilhelmina divorce today, she will not receive the trust principal when Horace dies. Horace's appointment of the property to Wilhelmina is considered revocable.

b. Former Spouse

UPC § 2-804(b)(1) revokes benefits the spouse would have received under a will or other revocable governing instrument the individual executed before the dissolution. Revocable governing instruments might include inter vivos trusts (unless the settlor did not have a right of revocation), life insurance policies, and pay on death and transfer on death accounts. This section also revokes any appointments made in favor of the former spouse in a governing instrument and any powers conferred on the former spouse. It also revokes any nomination the former spouse received to serve as a fiduciary. The former spouse cannot serve as personal representative, trustee, conservator, agent, or guardian.

Example 20-2. Winnie married Hank five years ago. She executed a will two years ago devising one-half of her property to Hank and the other one-half to her sister Sondra. Winnie and Hank were divorced last month, and she died yesterday without having revoked or revised her will. The devise to Hank is revoked even if Winnie's will does not refer to him as her spouse.

Example 20-3. Winnie revised her will after the divorce. Her new will devised $50,000 to Hank and the rest to Sondra. Because Winnie made the devise after she and Hank divorced, Hank can receive the $50,000.

Example 20-4. Susan created an irrevocable inter vivos trust 10 years ago. She receives income for life. At her death, the trustee is to split the principal equally between her husband Homer and her brother Bret. UPC § 2-804(b) does not apply to Homer's interest in this trust. Susan did not retain the right to revoke the trust.

UPC § 2-804(b)(2) severs the spouses' interests in property they jointly owned with right of survivorship, converting their ownership into a tenancy in common. It applies this treatment even if the instrument does not refer to the individuals as spouses.

c. *Family of Former Spouse*

UPC § 2-804(b)(1) also applies to benefits that would be received under a revocable instrument by the former spouse's relatives. The affected relatives are those individuals who are related to the former spouse by the rules governing parent-child relationships or affinity and who are not so related to the divorced spouse after the divorce occurs. UPC § 2-804(b)(2), which severs the spouses' interests in property they jointly owned with right of survivorship, does not mention relatives of the former spouse.

State statutes do not necessarily follow the UPC in their treatment of the former spouse's relatives. They might apply only to interests and powers designated for the former spouse. Even if a jurisdiction does follow the UPC, it might use the terms "blood or adoption" rather than referring to the rules governing parent-child relationships. The usage will vary depending on whether the jurisdiction has adopted the 2017 version of the Uniform Parentage Act discussed in Chapter 5.

d. *Effect of Remarriage*

If the spouses remarry, UPC § 2-804(e) revives any designation that was revoked by this section. It also revives these designations if the dissolution was invalidated. This is another area where the UPC might diverge from state law. State law might require that the individual affirmatively reinstate a devise, beneficiary designation, or other canceled benefit. State law might even make the remarried spouse eligible for omitted spouse rights.

C. Killers and Abusers

1. UPC

UPC § 2-803, sometimes referred to as the slayer statute or killer statute, applies to benefits the killer might receive through intestacy, as statutory allowances, as a devisee, or as a beneficiary of a revocable trust or other revocable disposition. It also applies to revocable powers of appointment exercised in his favor or to powers granted him by the decedent. Finally, it severs any survivorship tenancy between the decedent and his killer, so that the property passes as if it was owned by them as tenants in common. UPC § 2-803(f) provides that its principles apply to any wrongful acquisition by the killer not specifically covered by the list of revoked benefits.

UPC §2-803 applies to anyone who feloniously and intentionally kills the decedent, including a co-conspirator or accomplice. When this statute applies, the killer is treating as having disclaimed the property or power he would have otherwise received. The killer's descendants might receive the forfeited benefit if the antilapse statute applies to a killer who is treated as predeceasing the decedent.

> **Example 20-5.** Calvin had a brother (Bob) and two sisters (Jill and Susan) but no surviving parents, spouse, or descendants. Calvin and Bob owned Blackacre as joint tenants with right of survivorship. Bob was the beneficiary of a bank account titled Calvin POD Bob, alternative beneficiary Jill. Calvin devised $10,000 to Bob and the residue of his estate to Susan. Bob feloniously and intentionally killed Calvin. The joint tenancy in Blackacre will become a tenancy in common. Bob will retain his one-half. Susan will receive the other one-half as Calvin's residuary devisee. Jill will receive the funds in the POD account as the alternative beneficiary. Bob's descendants, if any, will receive the $10,000 devise; if there are none, Susan will receive those funds as residuary devisee.

In categorizing the acts that apply, the UPC looks to the law of the relevant jurisdiction. It revokes benefits to anyone who was convicted under a statute that establishes criminal accountability for the intentional and felonious killing. This rule applies after all appeals have been exhausted. The slayer statute also might apply if the wrongdoer was not convicted because he died before being tried or he pled guilty to a lesser offense. In those situations, the court uses a preponderance of the evidence standard in determining whether the statute applies. It is unlikely to apply the statute if the devisee establishes self-defense, necessity, or even insanity.

2. State Law

State law might adopt the UPC rules in whole or in part. In applying the law of a particular state, focus on which criminal convictions trigger the statute, the standard of evidence used to bar someone who was not convicted of that type of behavior, and what happens if someone other than the devisee killed the testator or if the devisee killed someone other than the testator. A state might also allow the probate court to apply the statute before the alleged killer exhausts all his appeals.

State statutes or judicial interpretations might also apply when a devisee was not involved in the killing but would benefit from it. For example, a devisee's spouse might kill the devisee's father, thus causing the devisee to inherit. Different rules might also apply if an alternative devisee killed a primary devisee and thus would receive the devise when the testator later died.

Although the UPC does not address abuse, a state statute might treat the wrongdoer similarly to its treatment of killers. Florida, for example, has a statute applicable to those who commit manslaughter or elder abuse. It treats a conviction as establishing a rebuttable presumption that the section applies. Fla. Stat. § 732.8031. Its killer statute treats a conviction as conclusive. Fla. Stat. § 732.802.

D. Disclaimers

A disclaimer is a refusal to accept outright ownership of property, an interest less than outright ownership, or a power over property. The discussion of disclaimers in other chapters indicated that they might affect the ultimate ownership of property. This chapter focuses on disclaimer terminology, interests or powers that can be disclaimed, formalities necessary to make a valid disclaimer, limitations on the right to disclaim, and who takes property following a disclaimer.

Tax reasons often motivate disclaimers, and state disclaimer statutes often refer to these rules. This chapter briefly explains the federal gift and estate tax rules for making a valid disclaimer.

1. Terminology

A person who refuses to accept an interest or power has disclaimed that interest or power. Although the term renunciation may be used for that refusal, the more common term is disclaimer.

The relevant UPC provisions do not use specific terminology to refer to the person who creates, or attempts to create, the interest or power. In this chapter, we refer to him using terminology appropriate to the interest or power he is creating. A person who makes an outright transfer of an interest is a donor. A person who creates an interest by establishing a trust is a settlor. A person who creates a power is a donor of the power. If he grants the power in a trust he is creating, he is both the trust's settlor and the donor of a power over trust property.

The person who would have received the interest or power in the absence of the disclaimer is the disclaimant. She is referred to as the disclaimant even if the disclaimer is actually made by a fiduciary acting on her behalf. The interest or power that she rejects is the disclaimed interest or power.

2. Interests and Powers That Can Be Disclaimed

The Uniform Disclaimer of Property Interests Act (UDPIA) lists the interests and powers that can be disclaimed. Because the UDPIA is part of the UPC, this discussion uses UPC section numbers.

UPC § 2-1103 provides that the disclaimer provisions apply to disclaimers of any interest in or power over property. It does not matter when the interest or power was created. UPC § 2-1104(a) indicates that principles of law and equity supplement the UPC disclaimer provisions unless those provisions displace those principles. UPC § 2-1104(b) indicates that the UPC disclaimer provisions do not limit a person's right to "waive, release, disclaim, or renounce" interests or powers under a different law. For example, spouses might waive rights in each other's property as part of a marital settlement valid under state matrimonial law.

State statutes based on the UDPIA often begin with this language: "This [part of the statutes] may be referred to as the [name of State] Uniform Disclaimer of Property Interests Act." That statute might vary from the UDPIA if the legislature prefers a different outcome in certain circumstances. Conversely, statutes of a state that has not formally adopted the UDPIA might nevertheless closely resemble it.

UPC § 2-1105 provides a broad right of disclaimer. It allows a person to disclaim any interest in or power over property. The disclaimer can be of the entire interest or power or it can be a partial disclaimer. The UPC allows a disclaimer even if the instrument creating the interest or power includes a spendthrift provision, other provisions restricting alienation, or restrictions on the right to disclaim itself. It gives a fiduciary the same broad ability to disclaim unless that ability is limited by another statute or by the instrument creating the fiduciary relationship.

a. *Fee Simple Ownership*

A completed gift requires both offer and acceptance. A potential donee can refuse to accept the property offered, thus making a disclaimer. If the proposed transfer is by inter vivos gift, there might be no record of the offer or the disclaimer. The donee might simply refuse to accept the gift, and no transfer occurs.

The disclaimer statute is more likely to apply to a transfer made when the original property owner dies. In that case, the potential recipient would take as a devisee under the decedent's will or as an heir of the intestate decedent. Taking as the beneficiary of a trust or as the appointee under a power of appointment is addressed later in this section.

b. *Interests in a Survivorship Tenancy*

Joint tenancies with right of survivorship and tenancies by the entirety are both survivorship tenancies. The ability to disclaim an interest in one of these tenancies is likely to depend on the type of property involved. This section focuses on three types of property that could involve survivorship rights: bank accounts; securities accounts; and real estate.

Opportunities to disclaim an interest in a survivorship tenancy arise at several points. First, if one tenant provides all the consideration for the property involved, one or more of the other potential tenants can refuse to take an ownership interest. In that case, the outcome is much like the refusal to accept an outright gift. The noncontributing individual refuses to sign the bank account or securities account application, or she refuses to accept the transfer. She never takes an interest in the property.

If the noncontributing owner accepts the transfer, or all owners contribute funds, our attention shifts to an owner's death. If there are only two tenants, as must be the case with tenancies by the entirety and might be the case for joint tenancies with right of survivorship, the surviving tenant is entitled to the property in fee simple absolute. If there are more than two tenants, the surviving tenants receive an increased interest in the tenancy property but the tenancy does not terminate.

> **Example 20-6.** Joe purchased real property and had it titled in a joint tenancy with right of survivorship with Jane. When Joe dies, Jane becomes the sole owner unless she effectively disclaims her survivorship interest.
>
> **Example 20-7.** Jessica purchased real property and titled it in a joint tenancy with right of survivorship with Jeff and Jerry. Each has a one-third interest in the real property. When Jessica dies, Jeff and Jerry continue

as joint tenants with right of survivorship. Each of them will have a one-half interest. Unless one of them effectively disclaims his interest, the survivor of Jeff and Jerry will eventually become the sole owner.

The examples above assume that none of the joint tenants has the property partitioned, converting the joint tenancy into a tenancy in common. If that had occurred, each tenant could then transfer his or her interest by inter vivos gift, by will or intestacy, or in trust. The recipient would be subject to the disclaimer rules for transfers by gift, by will or intestacy, or in trust.

c. *Beneficial Interest in an Express Trust*

Trust interests take many forms. A beneficiary might have only a vested interest or only a contingent interest. He might instead have a vested interest in part of the trust and a contingent interest in another part. He might have an interest in income, in principal, or in both. He might have an absolute right to distributions. Alternatively, his ability to receive distributions might be subject to a standard, to a trustee's discretion, or to the discretion of someone who holds a power of appointment. The nature of his interests determines what he can disclaim and when he must make that disclaimer.

d. *Status as a Beneficiary*

Status as a beneficiary arises when the owner of a pay on death, transfer on death, or in trust for account dies or when the person insured under a life insurance policy dies. It also arises if an annuitant or retirement account owner dies, leaving a beneficiary to continue receiving benefits. There is generally no requirement that the beneficiary know of his status before the relevant death occurs. Until that death occurs, his interest is really only an expectancy unless the creator of the interest has surrendered both the right to cancel the policy, account, or contract and the right to change the beneficiary.

e. *Parties to a Power of Appointment*

Several persons might be able to make a disclaimer involving a power of appointment: the donee of the power (powerholder); one or more of the objects of the power (permissible appointees) before it is exercised; and the person who takes if the power is not validly exercised (the taker in default). If the powerholder appoints the property subject to the power, we also consider any actual appointee's power to disclaim.

f. Power as a Fiduciary

Individuals or corporations acting as fiduciaries owe duties to the person over whose property they have control or to that person's beneficiaries. Depending on the circumstances, the fiduciary might be the personal representative or the curator of a decedent's estate, the trustee of a trust, a trust director, the holder of a power of attorney, or a powerholder whose power of appointment is held in a fiduciary capacity.

A person who is nominated to be a fiduciary need not agree to serve. Even after agreeing to serve, the fiduciary might later resign. Declining an appointment or resigning is likely to be addressed by statutes governing fiduciaries instead of by the disclaimer statutes.

3. Requirements for Disclaiming

An effective disclaimer must satisfy any state law requirements with respect to eligibility. It must comply with any required formalities, and it must be made within the time period provided by law. State law provisions focus on the transmission of property. Substantive federal tax law provisions relate to whether the disclaimer will be effective for those purposes. The two sets of provisions might be identical, but that is not necessarily the case. Likewise, a disclaimer that meets the requirements of state law might fail if a federal tax lien is involved. *Drye v. United States,* 528 U.S. 49 (1999).

a. Eligibility

As noted above, UPC § 2-1105 does not place any limits on the right to disclaim interests in, or powers over, property. UPC § 2-1113(a) prevents disclaimers by persons who have given a written waiver of their right to disclaim. It applies to disclaimers of both interests and powers. UPC § 2-1113(e) also applies to interests and powers. It prevents or limits a valid disclaimer if a law other than the UPC disclaimer provisions bars or limits the right to disclaim.

The UPC distinguishes between interests and powers. UPC § 2-1113(b) prevents disclaimers of interests in property. It applies to persons who accepted the interest being disclaimed before the disclaimer became effective or who voluntarily took certain actions with respect to the interest before the disclaimer became effective. These actions include assigning, encumbering, or transferring the interest—or entering into a contract to do so. It is also too late to make a valid disclaimer if a judicial sale of the interest occurs before the disclaimer is effective.

UPC §§2-1113(c) and (d) apply to powers. The holder of a power held in a fiduciary capacity can disclaim a future exercise of the power even if he has previously exercised the power. The same rule applies if the power is not held in a fiduciary capacity, but with one exception. If the power is exercisable in favor of the disclaimant, a previous exercise prevents a valid disclaimer of any future exercise.

State laws might include additional limits on the right to disclaim. The comments to UPC §2-1113 list several such limitations. Some states bar disclaimer if the disclaimant is insolvent; some prevent disclaimers made to qualify for certain types of public assistance, including Medicaid.

b. Formalities

UPC §2-1105(c) requires a disclaimer to be in a writing that indicates that a disclaimer is being made and that describes the interest or power being disclaimed. The writing must be signed by the disclaimant and it must be delivered or filed. UPC §2-1105(c) does not require that the document be witnessed. This provision also allows the disclaimant to use an "other record" instead of a writing. It defines that term as "information that is inscribed on a tangible medium or that is stored in an electronic or other medium and is retrievable in perceivable form." The signature requirement can be met by an electronic sound, symbol, or process that is associated with the record.

A disclaimer can be delivered in person, by first-class mail, or by any other means that is likely to result in its being received. UPC §2-1112(b). It must be delivered to the person designated in the relevant disclaimer subsection. UPC §2-1112(c)–(l). For example, if an inheritance from an intestate decedent is being disclaimed, delivery must be made to the personal representative. If one has not yet been appointed, the disclaimant must deliver the disclaimer to the court that has jurisdiction to appoint a personal representative. These rules are designed to provide notice of the disclaimer and limit the possibility that the property will be transferred incorrectly.

c. Time Period for Disclaiming

The actions barred by UPC §2-1113 create outside limits for disclaiming. For example, a disclaimer is ineffective if the disclaimant has accepted the benefits of the interest. The UPC does not include a specific time limit on the right to disclaim. The comments note that limits might apply under other statutes.

d. Disclaimer Valid for Federal Tax Purposes

UPC § 2-1114 provides a safe harbor for making a valid disclaimer. If the disclaimer is valid under the Internal Revenue Code, it is effective for purposes of the UPC's disclaimer provisions.

The Internal Revenue Code covers disclaimers in its gift tax provisions and refers to that coverage in its estate tax provisions. I.R.C. §§ 2046 (estate tax), 2518 (gift tax). The discussion below covers issues related to each tax. The estate and gift tax rules are important for two reasons. First, failure to follow their requirements can result in adverse transfer tax consequences for the disclaimant. Second, state statutes are likely to treat following the federal tax disclaimer provisions as sufficient for state law disclaimer purposes.

Although the discussion below refers to interests in property, I.R.C. § 2518 also applies to powers. The regulations interpreting it include examples of its application to outright ownership, a joint tenancy with right of survivorship, and a tenancy by the entirety.

I.R.C. § 2518 determines whether the disclaimant has made a taxable gift to the person who will receive the disclaimed interest. I.R.C. § 2046 determines whether the value of the interest disclaimed is included in the disclaimant's gross estate; it relates back to the rules in I.R.C. § 2518. A disclaimer that fails to comply with the I.R.C. § 2518 requirements can thus affect the computation of both taxes.

> **Example 20-8.** Tom devised $100,000 to his friend Doug and the residue of his estate to his friend Rita. Doug made a disclaimer that was valid under state law but did not satisfy the requirements of I.R.C. § 2518. Doug is treated as making a taxable gift to Rita for gift tax purposes. Because the estate tax is computed based on Doug's gross estate, increased by his adjusted taxable gifts, the transfer to Rita will eventually be included in the computation of Doug's estate tax.

I.R.C. § 2518(b) lists the requirements for making a valid disclaimer of an interest in property. The disclaimer must be irrevocable and unqualified. It must be in writing. It must be received no later than nine months after the later of two dates: (1) the day on which the transfer creating the interest in the disclaimant becomes effective; or (2) the day on which the disclaimant attains age 21. The disclaimant must not have accepted the interest or any of its benefits. An individual is not barred from disclaiming because of actions taken before attaining age 21. Treas. Reg. § 25.2518-2(d)(3).

The final requirement in I.R.C. § 2518(b) relates to the ultimate recipient of the property. The disclaimant cannot direct to whom the property passes. In addition, the property must pass either to the decedent's spouse or to someone other than the disclaimant. In other words, a surviving spouse can disclaim and still benefit from the interest disclaimed; another beneficiary cannot.

Example 20-9. Twyla devised one-half of her estate to her husband Hugh and one-half to her daughter Donna. Twyla's will provided that any property disclaimed by Hugh would be transferred to a trust in which Hugh received a life estate, with the remainder to Twyla's brother. Any property disclaimed by Donna would be transferred to a trust in which Donna received a life estate, with the remainder to Twyla's sister. Hugh can disclaim his devise and receive benefits from his trust without having adverse gift or estate tax consequences. If Donna disclaims her devise but does not disclaim her income interest in the trust, she has made an inter vivos gift of the remainder interest to Twyla's sister. Donna will be treated as the settlor of the trust because her disclaimer caused the property to go into the trust. When she dies, the value of the trust property is included in her gross estate as property over which she retained an income interest for life.

4. Effective Date of Disclaimer

The date the disclaimer becomes effective depends on the type of interest or power involved. State law might provide different dates for one or more of these interests and powers.

The general effective date rule appears in UPC § 2-1106(b). It makes the disclaimer effective when the instrument creating the interest becomes irrevocable. If the interest is created by the death of an intestate, the disclaimer is effective as of the date of the intestate's death, not the later date on which a distribution would occur. The same is true for an interest created by a testate decedent's will.

The disclaimer of a survivorship interest in property held as a joint tenant with right of survivorship or tenancy by the entirety is effective as of the date of a tenant's death. UPC § 2-1107(b). If there are more than two joint tenants, there are potentially multiple dates on which a survivor can disclaim an interest.

The effective date of the disclaimer of a power of appointment or other power not held in a fiduciary capacity depends on whether the power had previously been exercised. UPC § 2-1109. If the disclaimant has not previously exercised the power, it is effective as of the date the instrument creating the power became irrevocable. If he has previously exercised the power, and the power is *not* a presently exercisable general power of appointment, the disclaimer is effective as of the last date on which he exercised the power.

> **Example 20-10.** A month before she died, Samantha created a revocable inter vivos trust. Income is paid to Isabelle for life; the principal will be distributed to Samantha's descendants when Isabelle dies. The trust instrument gives Samantha's brother Brad the power to invade principal for Samantha's descendants before Isabelle dies. Five years later, without ever exercising the power, Brad disclaimed it. The disclaimer is effective as of the date Samantha died, which is the date the trust became irrevocable.
>
> **Example 20-11.** If Brad exercised the power to distribute part of the principal to Samantha's daughter Debby, his disclaimer of any further exercise would be effective as of the date he exercised the power in favor of Debby.
>
> **Example 20-12.** If Brad's power had included the power to distribute principal to himself, he would have received a presently exercisable general power of appointment. If he never exercised the power, he could disclaim it; the disclaimer would be effective as of the date Samantha died. If he had exercised the power, UPC § 2-1113(d) precludes him from later disclaiming it.

5. Taker of Disclaimed Property

A disclaimer might cover less than all of the disclaimant's interest or power. In that situation, some of the property might remain with the disclaimant. The disclaimant can disclaim a fraction, percentage, or monetary amount. He can also disclaim a term of years, part of a power over the property, or any other interest or estate in the property. UPC § 2-1105(d). The comments indicate that he can even disclaim a contingent interest.

a. General Rules

To determine who receives the property after an interest or power has been disclaimed, we look to the instrument creating the interest or power. UPC § 2-1106(b)(2). It can provide for disclaimers of a particular devise or other interest, or it can cover all transfers covered by the instrument. The following are examples of provisions that might appear in a will:

- I devise $100,000 to Son. Any portion of this devise that he disclaims shall be distributed to my other children.
- I devise $100,000 to Daughter. Any portion of this devise that she disclaims shall pass as part of the residue of my estate.
- I devise $100,000 to Sister. Any portion of this devise that she disclaims shall pass to those individuals who would receive my estate if I died intestate.
- I have made several devises of real property in this will. Any devise, or portion thereof, that is disclaimed shall pass to my descendants.

If the instrument does not provide for an alternative taker, we follow the statutory rules. UPC § 2-1106(b)(3) provides most of those rules. It first divides disclaimants into two categories: those that are not individuals and those that are. If the disclaimant is not an individual, the property passes as if the disclaimant did not exist. If the disclaimant is an individual, it passes as if he had died immediately before the time for the property to be distributed.

The time of distribution is defined in UPC § 2-1106(a)(2) as the time when the interest being disclaimed would have taken effect in possession or enjoyment. The comments indicate that this occurs with respect to property that is devised (or that would pass by intestate succession) when the decedent dies. It occurs with respect to property in trust when the beneficiary would have possession or enjoyment. If the beneficiary has a present interest, the distribution date occurs when the settlor can no longer retake the property. If the beneficiary has a future interest, it occurs when her interest becomes a present interest.

Two additional rules apply if disclaimants are individuals. The first applies if the instrument or relevant statute makes the disclaimant's descendants the alternative takers by representation if the disclaimant dies before the time for distribution. Only those descendants who survive the distribution date take the property. UPC § 2-1106(b)(3)(C). The second applies if the property would pass to the disclaimant's estate if he dies before the time for distribution. In that case, the disclaimed interest passes by representation to the descendants of the disclaimant who survive to the time of distribution. If no descendants survive, the property passes to those individuals (other than the disclaimant) who would take the transferor's estate by intestacy if the transferor died on the date of distribution. The transferor is treated as unmarried for this purpose if his surviving spouse has remarried by the date of distribution. UPC §2-1106(b)(3)(D). This provision includes the possibility that the property will escheat to the state.

b. *Acceleration of Future Interests*

If the disclaimant has a partial interest, such as a life estate or a term for years, the person who would take after that interest ceases has her interest accelerated because of the disclaimer. No acceleration occurs, however, if the disclaimant holds the future interest. UPC §2-1106(b)(4).

> **Example 20-13.** Father created a testamentary trust, giving Son income for 10 years, followed by the principal to Daughter. Son disclaimed his interest. Daughter receives the principal immediately unless the trust provides otherwise. If Son had been named the remainder beneficiary, he would still have to wait 10 years to receive trust principal even if he disclaimed his income interest.

c. *Survivorship Tenancies*

The disclaimer rules for jointly held property allow a surviving joint tenant to disclaim the larger of two amounts. The first is simply a fraction of the property based on the number of tenants before the death occurred. The second is the entire property reduced by the value attributable to her contributions. The disclaimant can disclaim less than the maximum allowable. The property passes as if the disclaimant predeceased the actual deceased joint owner. UPC §2-1107.

> **Example 20-14.** Jacqueline, Jessica, Jill, and Julie purchased Blackacre as joint tenants with right of survivorship. Each paid 25% of the cost. When Jacqueline died, Jessica, Jill, or Julie could each disclaim up to 75% of the value of Blackacre.
>
> **Example 20-15.** Jessica actually provided 60% of the consideration for Blackacre; Jacqueline and Jill each provided 20%. Julie provided none of the consideration. When Jacqueline died, Jessica could disclaim 40% of the value of Blackacre. This is greater than her 25% ownership share. Jill could disclaim 80% of the value of Blackacre. Julie could disclaim the entire value of Blackacre. It is possible, depending on how much the surviving tenants disclaim, that Blackacre will be distributed as an asset of Jacqueline's estate.

E. Undue Influence

The UPC does not directly provide for voiding a will based on undue influence. It does so indirectly in its coverage of will contests. UPC § 3-407 places the burden of establishing undue influence on the party contesting the will. A state statute might shift that burden to the proponent if the challenger establishes a presumption of undue influence. Fla. Stat. § 733.107(2). UTC § 406 specifically provides that a trust is void to the extent its creation was the product of undue influence. The Restatements, state statutes, and judicial decisions also invalidate instruments (or portions thereof) based on undue influence.

Undue influence goes beyond mere suggestions. It requires a finding that the testator or settlor was influenced in such a way that the document—or a portion of it—reflected the goals of the influencer rather than those of the testator or settlor. Because a will or revocable trust is generally not subject to challenge until the testator or settlor dies, the facts surrounding undue influence are generally proven by facts that support a presumption of undue influence. The burden then shifts to the proponent of the challenged instrument. Each jurisdiction decides whether the proponent must meet the burden or overcome it and whether the relevant standard is preponderance of the evidence or clear and convincing evidence.

A disappointed relative is likely to allege undue influence in one of two situations. Either one relative received significantly more than others who were similarly situated, or a nonrelative received a significant portion of the property covered by the instrument. The term "unnatural disposition" is often used in these situations, particularly when a nonrelative is the beneficiary.

The facts that raise a presumption of undue influence tend to involve three factors. First, the disposition was substantial. This generally means substantial in relation to what the individual might have received in intestacy or substantial in relation to what similarly situated individuals received. A devise of a year's salary to a long-time, trusted employee might be substantial or it might not; a devise of all of the testator's property, on the other hand, is likely to be treated as substantial. The same is true when a will or trust benefits one of the testator's children significantly more than his other children.

But a substantial benefit alone does not result in a finding of undue influence. The testator or settlor might have had valid reasons of his own for the gift. Those reasons can be offered in testimony by the proponent of the will or trust or by others testifying on his behalf.

The second factor involves whether the beneficiary had a confidential relationship with the testator or settlor. A confidential relationship is one of trust or reliance. Individuals with whom the testator or settlor had such a relationship include family members (particularly a spouse or a child), religious advisers, attorneys, health professionals, social services workers, and other professionals. When a confidential relationship is involved, particularly if the testator or settlor is in declining physical or mental health, a court might infer that he was particularly susceptible to undue influence.

The relationship between an individual and his spouse might be viewed differently from other confidential relationships. This is particularly true if neither spouse has descendants from another relationship. In that situation, it is not unusual for spouses to consult an attorney together and draft wills or trusts that are largely, if not entirely, mirror images of each other. As a result, courts might refuse to apply the presumption of undue influence to a spouse in the absence of other evidence. If a jurisdiction has enacted a statute addressing marriages induced by fraud, duress, or undue influence, relatives—particularly when a second marriage is involved—might seek to apply that statute to eliminate any exemption from undue influence the spouse might otherwise enjoy.

The third factor relates to the beneficiary's involvement in the execution of the will or the creation of the trust. The beneficiary might have accompanied the testator or settlor to an attorney's office and might even have been present when the attorney interviewed the testator or settlor. The beneficiary might have selected the attorney. The beneficiary might have kept the original instrument or a copy of it. It may be impossible to sustain a claim of undue influence against a beneficiary who had no involvement in any aspect of the instrument's creation.

F. Duress

Duress is also grounds for voiding a will or trust or a portion thereof. A finding of duress requires establishing that the testator or settlor was forced to make the challenged disposition. The beneficiary might have physically abused the testator or threatened to expose information that the testator would prefer to have kept private. Duress is similar to undue influence in that the testator or settlor's free will is overcome by the wrongdoer. But when duress is involved, the testator or settlor knows he is making a disposition that he would prefer not to make. The victim of undue influence might not realize the extent of the beneficiary's influence.

G. Fraud or Mistake

Fraud involves intentional deception by a third party. Mistake can be the product of a third party's unintentional error or a misconception by the testator or settlor. The fraud or mistake can relate to the document itself or to its terms.

Inducement and execution are terms used regarding why a document included or excluded particular terms or why a property owner signed the document. As a general rule, a document is void if its execution was a product of fraud or mistake. Thus, a document is void if it was executed by an individual who believed he was signing a different type of document. On the other hand, if he knew what he was signing, there is no fraud or mistake in the execution. If the document included terms that were the product of a mistaken belief or fraudulent conduct by another person, the document involved fraud or mistake in the inducement. It is not necessarily void. But the erroneous terms can be changed if the jurisdiction allows reformation.

H. Relationship to Lack of Capacity

Disappointed relatives might challenge a document or its revocation based on lack of capacity in addition to any challenge based on undue influence, duress, fraud, or mistake. Their decision regarding challenges involves the evidence available to them, the existence of an earlier document, and the outcome they hope to achieve.

For example, a testator's old will might have favored family members, but his new will devised his property to a nonrelative. In that case, the family members might claim both lack of capacity and undue influence, fraud, or duress. If the later will was declared void on either ground, the earlier will could be probated. If, on the other hand, they wished to challenge only a particular portion of the later will, they might challenge only that portion based on undue influence, fraud, or duress. If reinstating the earlier will would not suit their purposes, they would avoid challenging based on lack of capacity.

Example 20-16. Tammy executed her first will five years ago. It devised $100,000 to charity and the residue to her sisters, her only surviving relatives. She executed her second will a month before she died. It revoked her first will and devised her entire estate to an individual who had been her caretaker for three months. Tammy's sisters and the charity will challenge the second will based on both lack of capacity and undue influence.

Example 20-17. If Tammy's second will devised $100,000 to the caretaker and the residue to her sisters, her sisters might consider challenging it based only on undue influence. Voiding the entire second will and reinstating the first will does not increase their share of Tammy's estate. Because voiding the devise to the caretaker might increase their share, they may decide not to raise the specifics of Tammy's declining mental capacity in a judicial proceeding. The charity, on the other hand, might challenge the second will based on both lack of capacity and undue influence.

I. Spoliation or Alteration

Spoliation and alteration are terms for changes to an instrument after it has been executed and—if necessary—witnessed. Spoliation refers to changes made by a third party, while alteration refers to changes made by the testator or settlor. Spoliation and alteration can be difficult to detect if the document was not stapled, which makes inserting new pages more difficult, or initialed by the maker and witnesses on all relevant pages, which makes forgery more difficult. If a challenger can establish that spoliation or an impermissible alteration occurred, and can establish the document's original terms, it can be administered according to those terms.

Not every alteration is impermissible. A testator can informally amend an attested will by a signed separate writing if the will provides for separate writings. UPC § 2-513. In addition, if the jurisdiction allows holographic wills, the testator might be able to amend the will by adding additional terms in his own handwriting. Finally, UPC § 2-507(a)(2) allows partial revocation by act; some jurisdictions limit revocation by act to total revocation.

J. Remedies

Individuals who challenge a will or trust based on a wrongful act hope to have the will probated or the trust administered as it would have appeared if the wrongful act had not occurred. Those who challenge the revocation of a will or trust based on a wrongful act hope to have the instrument reinstated and administered according to its terms. Those outcomes might be possible in some situations, but they are not universally available.

If a will is voided based on undue influence, duress, fraud, or mistake in the execution, the court is unlikely to rewrite the will to suit the disappointed beneficiary. The more likely outcome is probating an earlier will or allowing the property to pass by intestacy. If only part of the will is attributable to undue influence, striking that part might result in the residuary beneficiary receiving a larger share of the estate; if the portion that is voided is the residuary, that part of the estate will likely pass by intestacy. If a trust is voided based on one of those acts, the property is likely to revert to the settlor or his estate and pass under the terms of his will or by intestacy. In appropriate cases, the court might impose a constructive trust on the person who receives the property because of the wrongdoing. In some states, the challengers may be able to sue the wrongdoer for damages caused by interference with their expectancy. *In re Estate of Osguthorpe*, 491 P.3d 894 (Utah 2021). That challenge may barred if the challengers could have received adequate relief in a probate proceeding.

If the revocation of a will, codicil, or trust was attributable to one of those acts, the court might allow the original document to be administered if the proponent can establish its terms. The same is true for wills affected by spoliation or alteration. States that follow the principles of UPC § 2-515 allow a testator to deposit the will, under seal, with a court. In those situations, the will as written is available. Even if a state does allow it, testators are not required to take advantage of this opportunity.

UPC § 3-402(a) requires the proponent of a will that is lost or destroyed to state its contents. But it does not mandate the requirements for doing so. State statutes might establish procedures, such as testimony by a specified number of non-beneficiaries who were familiar with the will's contents. The number required may vary depending on whether a copy of the will can be produced. For example, Florida requires only one disinterested witness if a correct copy of the will exists; otherwise, it requires the testimony of two disinterested witnesses to the will's contents. Fla. Stat. § 733.207. If the lost document cannot be established, the proponents might seek a constructive trust or damages.

Unlike a killer, an individual who obtains a devise by undue influence or similar wrongdoing might still be eligible to share in a devise or gift in trust.

> **Example 20-18.** Terence had never executed a will. After his wife died, he executed a will that was a product of his son Seth's undue influence and devised his entire estate to Seth. Unless the jurisdiction disinherits a wrongdoer in this situation, Seth will receive the same inheritance as his brothers and sisters.

If wrongdoing does not involve a will or trust, disappointed beneficiaries could have a particularly difficult time recovering property from a wrongdoer. For example, they might be unable to prove that a family member's potential estate was depleted by outright gifts. Even if they prove that the wrongdoing occurred, they can recover only if the wrongdoer has assets they can recover.

CHECKPOINTS

- An individual who is divorced from a decedent or whose marriage to the decedent has been annulled is not a surviving spouse.
- Status as a surviving spouse can be regained if the former spouses remarry.
- The UPC revokes benefits the spouse (or her family) would have received under a will or other revocable governing instrument the individual executed before the divorce or annulment. It reinstates those benefits if the spouses remarry.
- State laws might differ from the UPC by not revoking benefits to the former spouse's family or by not automatically reinstating benefits if the former spouses remarry.
- An individual who intentionally and feloniously kills or participates in the killing of another person cannot benefit from his wrongdoing.
- A killer loses his status as the decedent's devisee, intestate heir, revocable trust beneficiary, or beneficiary under another revocable transfer. His descendants might take in his place if the state's killer statute does not preclude taking by representation. A state law might also eliminate benefits that would be received by an abuser or a person who commits aggravated manslaughter.

- A beneficiary who has not accepted the benefits of a transfer can disclaim an interest in the property or in a portion of it.
- A powerholder might be able to disclaim if he has not exercised the power in favor of himself.
- As a general rule, disclaimed property interests pass as if the disclaimant had died immediately before the distribution date.
- The disclaimant's descendants might be eligible to take in his place.
- A valid disclaimer requires complying with statutory formalities. These include Internal Revenue Code rules if the disclaimant wants to avoid making a taxable gift of the disclaimed interest or having it included in his gross estate.
- Wills and trusts, or portions thereof, can be challenged based on undue influence, duress, fraud, or mistake. Revocation caused by undue influence, duress, fraud, or mistake can also be challenged.
- A wrongdoer might attempt to alter a document by adding language, inserting pages, or substituting pages. If spoliation is proven, a court can strike the language added by the wrongdoer.
- Challenges to a will or trust can include the above types of wrongdoing in addition to, or instead of, challenges based on lack of capacity.
- There might be no way to establish how a will or trust would have been written in the absence of undue influence or other wrongdoing.
- If a challenger is unable to establish the will or trust as originally written, he may ask the court to impose a constructive trust on the person who received the property because of the wrongdoing. He might also be able to bring a suit for damages caused by tortious interference with his expectancy.

CHAPTER 21

Powers of Appointment

ROADMAP

- Relevant uniform acts
- Terminology
- Exercising the power
- Elective share
- Creditor access
- Miscellaneous powers of appointment issues

A. Chapter Overview

Powers of appointment are not ownership interests. They are powers to determine who will ultimately own property or an interest in property. They are commonly used to select the recipient of a partial or full distribution of trust principal. The powerholder might have the ability to benefit himself, but that is not always the case.

Although this chapter focuses on powers of appointment, it includes information about how these powers interact with other aspects of trusts and estates. These include the spouse's elective share, creditor access to trust property, the rule against perpetuities, and federal transfer taxes.

B. Relevant Uniform Acts

Although the UPC and UTC both refer to powers of appointment, neither contains a comprehensive set of rules governing those powers. The Uniform Powers of Appointment Act (UPAA), which the Uniform Law Commission approved in 2013, has been adopted by 13 states. It is based on principles contained in the Restatement (Third) of Property: Wills and Other Donative Transfers.

UPAA § 203 provides three default characteristics for a power of appointment. If the instrument does not provide otherwise, a power of appointment is presently exercisable, exclusionary, and general. These terms are explained in the next section.

C. Terminology

The UPAA defines most of the relevant terms in UPAA § 102. Some terms are based on language in the Internal Revenue Code or the Treasury regulations interpreting it.

1. Parties

The terminology used for powers of appointment can be confusing. The person who creates the power is the donor of the power. The person to whom the power is given is the powerholder. UPC sections and comments variously use the term power holder, powerholder, and power-holder. The UPAA uses the term powerholder. Although the comments to UPAA § 102 indicate that the traditional term for the powerholder—donee—is "potentially confusing," state statutes or judicial decisions might refer to a donee of the power rather than to a powerholder. Treasury regulations use the term donee.

The UPC refers to persons for whose benefit the power can be exercised as the objects of the power; the UPAA refers to them as the permissible appointees. The donor of the power can preclude the powerholder from exercising in favor of certain potential recipients by making them impermissible appointees. The beneficiaries of an exercised power are the appointees. The persons who will receive the property if the powerholder does not validly exercise the power are the takers in default.

Do not confuse a power of appointment with a power of attorney. A power of attorney is a power to act on behalf of another person, often—but not necessarily—a person who is incapacitated. The agent who has the power of attorney is a fiduciary (and is not necessarily an attorney). The holder of a power of appointment might hold the power in a fiduciary capacity, but that is not required. If the power is general, thus allowing the powerholder to benefit at least one of himself, his creditors, his estate, or his estate's creditors, he is unlikely to hold it in a fiduciary capacity.

2. General and Nongeneral Powers

If the powerholder can exercise the power in favor of himself, his estate, his creditors, or the creditors of his estate, he has a general power of appointment. The power is general even if only one of these options is a permissible appointee. The power is general even if there are additional permissible appointees. If the power is not a general power, it is referred to as a nongeneral power, a limited power, or a special power of appointment. The UPAA uses the term nongeneral power of appointment.

Example 21-1. Sam created a trust that will terminate when his youngest child reaches age 50. He gave his oldest child, Cora, the power to direct how the trustee distributes trust principal among Sam's descendants. Cora has a general power of appointment, even though she is not specifically named, because she is one of Sam's descendants. If she can instead appoint only to Sam's grandchildren, her power is nongeneral.

3. Powers of Invasion and Ascertainable Standards

The powerholder might be limited to appointing the trust principal when the trust terminates (or to terminating the trust by appointing the trust principal). He might also be able to invade principal without terminating the trust. If his power to invade principal is unlimited, and he can invade in favor of himself, his estate, his creditors, or the creditors of his estate, his power of invasion is a general power of appointment.

If his power to invade is subject to an ascertainable standard, it is not a general power even if he can benefit himself, his estate, his creditors, or the creditors of his estate. The term ascertainable standard does not require that the power be limited to a fixed amount or to a formula. Instead, a power is subject to an ascertainable standard if it is based on a purpose that a court could determine is being met. The Internal Revenue Code lists four purposes that are acceptable for tax purposes: health, education, support, or maintenance. I.R.C. §§ 2041(b)(1)(A), 2514(c)(1). Practitioners often refer to these as "HEMS" powers. UTC § 103(2) refers to the relevant Internal Revenue Code provisions and uses the same terminology. UPAA § 102 does not include "ascertainable standard" in its list of definitions.

Powers that are not subject to ascertainable standards include those that the holder can exercise for his "comfort, welfare, or happiness." Treas. Reg. §§ 20.2041-1(c)(2), 25.2514-1(c)(2). The regulations cover situations in which ascertainable standard and general power terms are mixed. For example, the power to exercise to support the powerholder in reasonable comfort is treated as subject to an ascertainable standard.

4. Powers of Invasion and Powers of Withdrawal

The terms power of invasion and power of withdrawal both refer to a power to remove property from the trust. They can be differentiated by the status of the person removing the trust property. An invasion power usually covers property that would otherwise remain in the trust until a future date. Although it could be held by a beneficiary, the power is usually held by a trustee, who can invade on behalf of a beneficiary. The power to invade gives the trustee the flexibility to invade principal when trust income is not sufficient to carry out the settlor's purpose.

A settlor might give a withdrawal power to a trust beneficiary; the power is usually limited in duration and amount and often applies only to that year's contribution to the trust. A settlor often gives the beneficiary this power so that the transfer in trust will qualify for the gift tax exclusion discussed in Chapter 26. This power of withdrawal is a general power of appointment.

> **Example 21-2.** Seth created a trust several years ago. Each year he adds $40,000 to the trust principal and gives each of his four children the power to withdraw up to $10,000 of that year's contribution. The withdrawal power lapses after three months. If a child does not withdraw the $10,000, it becomes part of the trust principal administered by the

trustee. Each child has a presently exercisable general power of appointment over $10,000—but only for three months.

5. Power to Revoke and Powers of Appointment

The settlor of an inter vivos trust generally retains the right to revoke that trust until he dies or relinquishes the power. The comments to UPAA § 102 treat this right as a power of appointment; they cite to comments to Restatement (Third) of Trusts § 56. That usage is unnecessary for federal estate tax purposes, as a provision other than that governing powers of appointment applies to transfers with a retained right of revocation. I.R.C. § 2038. Uniform acts other than the UPAA cover the right of revocation separately or as a general power. For example, UTC § 505(a)(1) makes property of a revocable trust available to the settlor's creditors during the settlor's lifetime. UTC § 505(b)(1) treats the holder of a power of withdrawal as if he were the settlor of a revocable trust. UPC § 2-201(6) treats a power of revocation as a presently exercisable general power of appointment for purposes of computing the spouse's elective share.

6. Exclusionary and Nonexclusionary Powers

A power that can benefit more than one person is exclusionary if the powerholder can omit one or more of the permissible appointees. If he must exercise the power in favor of all permissible appointees, the power is nonexclusionary.

Example 21-3. Paul holds a nongeneral power of appointment over assets in the TUV Trust. Paul's wife established the trust before she died. Her four grandchildren are the permissible appointees. If the power is exclusionary, Paul can exercise it in favor of one, two, three, or all four grandchildren. If the power is nonexclusionary, he must exercise it in favor of all of them or not exercise it all. He does not have to give each grandchild an equal amount.

If the instrument creating the power does not specify whether it is exclusionary or nonexclusionary, UPAA § 203(2) provides that it is exclusionary. This treatment avoids any disputes over how small an amount the powerholder can give a permissible appointee of a nonexclusionary power without violating the terms of the power.

7. Presently Exercisable and Testamentary Powers

If the powerholder can exercise the power only in his will, he holds a testamentary power. Only his will is relevant. The power is testamentary even if the donor of the power is alive when the powerholder dies.

If the powerholder can exercise the power at any time, he holds a presently exercisable power. If he can exercise it before his death, but only after a condition is met, the power is not presently exercisable because of failure to meet a condition. When the condition is met, the power becomes presently exercisable.

> **Example 21-4.** Pam holds a power of appointment over the assets in a trust her sister established. Pam can exercise the power any time after attaining age 35. Because Pam is currently age 30, the power is not presently exercisable. If Pam dies before attaining age 35, the power will never become exercisable.

D. Exercising the Power

1. Purpose

The instrument granting the power might limit the purpose for which the powerholder can exercise the power. For example, it might allow her to exercise the power to invade only for a permissible appointee's education. In that case, she cannot exercise it to pay his medical bills.

2. Manner of Appointee's Enjoyment

The instrument might also limit the powerholder's ability to delay an appointee's enjoyment. For example, it might require that the appointee receive property outright. Alternatively, the powerholder might be allowed to exercise the power to create a trust benefiting the appointee. UPAA § 305(c)(1) allows an appointment in trust if the instrument does not provide otherwise.

3. Method of Exercise

A power of appointment is personal to the named powerholder. She cannot transfer it to a third party. UPAA § 202. The comments to that section indicate that other uniform acts or state laws govern whether an agent or guardian can exercise a power on behalf of a principal or ward. In a jurisdiction that has enacted the UPAA, the powerholder must exercise the power in a manner that satisfies the requirements set by the donor and do so in a manner that indicates an intent to exercise. UPAA § 301. The substantial compliance provisions in UPAA § 304 reflect those in UPC § 2-704.

4. Exercise in Favor of a Deceased Appointee

UPAA § 306(a) makes an exercise in favor of a deceased appointee ineffective unless the relevant antilapse statute provides otherwise. But, unless the instrument creating the power provides otherwise, the powerholder can appoint the property to the permissible appointee's descendants even if they are not themselves permissible appointees. UPAA § 306(b).

5. Disclaimer of Power or Property Subject to Power

A disclaimer is a refusal to accept a power over or interest in property. Given that a powerholder does not have to exercise a power, we might think she has no reason to decline the power when it is granted or at a later date. That might be true for a nongeneral power of appointment, but the donee of a general power of appointment might decide to disclaim the power because of the effect it has on her gross estate for federal estate tax purposes. A permissible appointee, an actual appointee, or even a taker in default might want to avoid receiving property that is covered by the power, particularly if rejecting the property avoids or limits probate, transfer taxes, or creditor access.

E. Elective Share

Powers of appointment are relevant to two aspects of the elective estate. First, the value of property over which the deceased powerholder had a general power of appointment might be included in determining the value of the spouse's elective share interest. Second, if a decedent uses a trust to satisfy a spouse's elective share, a power of invasion is a factor that affects how much of the trust's value is treated as satisfying the spouse's rights.

1. Computing the Powerholder's Elective Estate

If a decedent held a presently exercisable general power of appointment over property when he died, the value of the property he could have received is likely to be included in computing the value of his elective estate. The fact that he did not exercise the power is irrelevant. UPC § 2-205(1)(A). State law might include both presently exercisable and testamentary general powers, or it might omit both powers from the computation.

> **Example 21-5.** Paul held a general power of appointment over the principal of a trust established by his father. If he did not exercise the power, the trust principal would be paid to Paul's sister when the trust terminated. If Paul could exercise the power before he died, the property subject to the power would be included in his elective estate even though he did not transfer the property into trust or create the power. If the power was testamentary, it would not be included.

2. Valuing the Spouse's Elective Share

Powers of appointment are also relevant in determining to what extent the surviving spouse's elective share is satisfied when she receives something less than an outright interest in property. An income interest in a trust is worth less than outright ownership of the underlying property. But an income interest coupled with a power of invasion or a general power of appointment comes closer to approximating the value of outright ownership.

State law determines how to value the surviving spouse's interest for purposes of satisfying the elective share. The state might use either actuarial values or a fixed percentage of trust assets. The percentage used might vary based on the rights the spouse receives in the trust.

F. Creditor Access

The extent to which a creditor can access a beneficiary's interest in a trust is affected by the type of trust. For example, if the beneficiary is entitled to a mandatory distribution of income, the creditor can access that income. If the trustee can distribute income only for the beneficiary's support, the creditor cannot force the trustee to pay the income to it.

1. Settlor's Interest

Creditors can access a settlor's trust interest unless the trust is in a jurisdiction with asset protection statutes that protect a settlor. A state is likely to allow creditor access to the entire trust if the settlor has a power of revocation. It would allow access only to the settlor's interest in the trust if he does not have a power of revocation.

2. Trust Beneficiary as Settlor

A trust beneficiary who receives a power of withdrawal has a general power of appointment. Although the power could lapse after a short time, creditors can access the amount subject to the power before it lapses. Even after the power lapses, creditors might retain rights. If the beneficiary who allowed the withdrawal power to lapse has an income interest in the trust, he is treated as transferring the lapsed amount into the trust. This nonexercise of his general power of appointment makes him a settlor of the transferred amount. Although he has no power to revoke, he does have a retained interest that creditors might be able to access.

Statutes protect the beneficiary from creditor access if the power of invasion was limited in amount, usually by a so-called "5 and 5 power." The statutory protection applies to lapses that do not exceed the greater of $5,000 or 5% of the trust assets. UTC § 505(b)(2). The UTC refers to the amount that avoids being treated as the lapse of a general power of appointment for federal transfer tax purposes. I.R.C. §§ 2041(b)(2), 2514(e).

Example 21-6. Sally created a trust last year. In January of both last year and this year she transferred $100,000 to the trustees. They were to distribute income for her son Seth's support, in the amounts they deemed necessary. The trust will terminate when Seth dies and Sally's surviving grandchildren will receive the trust principal. She gave Seth a power to withdraw up to $3,000 of each year's contributions to the trust; his power would lapse 90 days after she made the contribution. For 90 days after last year's contribution, Seth's creditors could access up to $3,000 of trust assets; for 90 days after this year's contribution, his creditors could access up to $3,000 of trust assets. After Seth's power lapsed, his creditors could no longer treat him as the holder of a general power of appointment.

Example 21-7. If Seth had instead received the power to withdraw $9,000 each year, the result would be different. After the 90-day withdrawal period expired last year, assuming the trust assets were worth $100,000, he would be treated as the settlor of $4,000 of trust assets. After the 90-day withdrawal period ended this year, he would be treated as the settlor of additional trust assets unless the value of the trust property at that time was more than $180,000. If the trust property was worth more than $180,000, Seth's power to withdraw $9,000 did not exceed 5% of the trust assets. The fact that it exceeded $5,000 would not matter.

3. Trustee as Settlor

A trustee might have the power to invade trust principal for his own benefit. If the power is limited by an ascertainable standard, it is a nongeneral power. If it is not so limited, the trustee has a general power of appointment and his interest could be subject to the rights of creditors.

G. Miscellaneous Powers of Appointment Issues

1. Rule Against Perpetuities

Unless the power can be exercised only to create a fee simple interest, a powerholder might use a power to create a new trust and further delay vesting. Unless that power was covered by the rule against perpetuities, its limitation on delayed vesting would be meaningless. Perpetuities statutes cover both interests in and powers over property.

2. Federal Estate and Gift Taxes

The value of property an individual owns at death is included in his gross estate. If he owns less than an outright interest, adjustments could be made to reflect the value of his interest, but the property is not necessarily excluded from the estate tax base.

a. General and Nongeneral Powers

The gross estate includes property interests and powers that end at death. One such inclusion relates to powers of appointment. The value of property subject to a general power of appointment is included in the powerholder's gross estate if he could have exercised it in favor of himself, his estate, his creditors, or the creditors of his estate. I.R.C. § 2041. If he relinquishes the power before death, he makes a taxable gift to the individuals who take in default of exercise of the power. I.R.C. § 2514. If he merely allows the power to lapse, he makes a taxable gift to the extent the property subject to the power exceeds the greater of $5,000 or 5% of the value of the property that could have been used to satisfy his power. I.R.C. § 2514(e).

If the individual held only a nongeneral power, the property subject to the power is not included in his gross estate when he dies. It does not matter whether he exercises the power or allows it to lapse. He does not make a taxable gift by exercising the power before he dies, relinquishing it before he dies, or allowing it to lapse before he dies.

b. Powers of Invasion

An unlimited power of invasion is treated as a general power of appointment and is subject to the rules for general powers. A power of invasion that is subject to an ascertainable standard is treated as a nongeneral power. A power is not subject to an ascertainable standard merely because the instrument creating the power includes a purpose for which invasion is permissible. To avoid treating the power of invasion as a general power, the purpose should reflect the language of I.R.C. § 2041: "health, education, support, or maintenance." For estate tax purposes, a power to invade for the powerholder's comfort, welfare, or happiness is a general power of appointment. Treas. Reg. § 20.2041-1(c)(2).

c. Powers of Withdrawal

Creditor access is not the only issue to consider when a trust includes a power of withdrawal. Potential gift or estate tax liability is another aspect of this power.

To qualify a transfer in trust as a present interest gift, and thus exclude some or all of its value from the computation of gift and estate tax, a settlor might give a beneficiary a power, exercisable for a limited time, to withdraw the property transferred. Until it expires, that withdrawal power is a general power of appointment. The property subject to the power is included in the powerholder's gross estate if he dies before the power lapses.

If the powerholder survives the lapse period, he no longer has a power of appointment, but he might still be subject to transfer tax. First, he might be treated as making a gift to the trust beneficiaries who will ultimately receive that property. Second, if he is an income beneficiary of the trust, his gross estate might include the value of that portion of the trust on the grounds that he transferred property to the trust and retained a life estate (or other income interest that did not terminate before his death) in that property.

If the property subject to the withdrawal right does not exceed a statutory de minimis amount, the lapse does not cause gift or estate tax consequences. The statutory de minimis amount is the greater of $5,000 or 5% of the property subject to the withdrawal right. I.R.C. §§ 2041(b)(2), 2514(e).

d. Marital Deduction

An individual can reduce her taxable estate by the value of property she devises to her spouse, that he receives through intestate succession, or that he receives as a surviving tenant or beneficiary. I.R.C. § 2056(a). Presumably those transfers will increase his wealth and, ultimately, increase his estate tax when he dies. The marital deduction is thus seen as a postponement of the estate tax.

She might not want to transfer property outright for a variety of reasons. Her spouse might be in poor health and expected to die relatively soon. In that case, the property goes through a second round of probate, which has costs. In addition, the spouses might have different potential beneficiaries. He might not be adept at managing money, or his hypothetical, potential new wife might acquire spousal rights in the property. To avoid these potential problems, she might prefer placing property in trust for her spouse rather than devising it to him outright.

If the surviving spouse receives a life estate in the trust income, and someone other than his estate will receive the principal when he dies (or at a later date), he has received a terminable interest. The first spouse's estate can take a marital deduction only if the terminable interest is a *qualified* terminable interest. If the surviving spouse has a general power of appointment in addition to his income interest, he has a qualified terminable interest. I.R.C. § 2056(b)(5). Because he has a general power of appointment, the value of the trust property will be included in his gross estate when he dies. For purposes of the marital deduction, the power must be exercisable in favor of the spouse or his estate. A power that can be exercised only in favor of creditors will not suffice.

If he does not receive a general power of appointment, the deceased spouse's estate receives a marital deduction only if her estate's personal representative makes a qualified terminable interest property (QTIP) election. That election includes the trust property in the surviving spouse's gross estate even though he has no power to select the ultimate taker. His only rights are to receive the income for life, at least annually. Although the trustee might have a power to invade, it can do so only for the surviving spouse's benefit while he is alive. I.R.C. § 2056(b)(7)(B)(ii)(II).

CHECKPOINTS

- The donor (creator) of a power of appointment gives the donee of the power (powerholder) the ability to designate the ultimate taker of property covered by the power.
- The powerholder might have a general power, which he can exercise in favor of himself, his estate, his creditors, or the creditors of his estate, or he might have a nongeneral power.
- Even if the powerholder can benefit himself, the power is nongeneral if its exercise is subject to an ascertainable standard, generally for health, education, support, or maintenance.
- The power might be presently exercisable, or it might be subject to a condition before it can be exercised.
- The persons in whose favor the power can be exercised are the permissible appointees, also referred to as the objects of the power.

- If the power is exclusionary, the powerholder can exclude some of the permissible appointees when he exercises the power. He cannot do this if the power is nonexclusionary.
- The instrument creating the power usually provides for a taker in default, who receives the property if the powerholder does not effectively exercise the power.
- The instrument creating the power usually provides any conditions regarding the method of exercise. A statute might include conditions under which substantial compliance is permissible.
- An individual who is offered a general power of appointment will consider transfer tax, creditor access, and elective share consequences in deciding whether to accept the power.

CHAPTER 22

Rule Against Perpetuities

ROADMAP

- Historical context
- Potential benefits and downsides of avoiding vesting
- Relevant Uniform Probate Code provisions
- State laws

A. Chapter Overview

A property owner might not want to give his beneficiaries fee simple ownership of property. This chapter addresses the benefits he seeks and his methods for delaying vesting. The primary focus is the common-law rule against perpetuities and the wait-and-see rule allowed by the UPC. It concludes with a brief discussion of state statutes that extend vesting limitations well beyond the UPC limit or completely eliminate them.

B. Historical Context

The common-law rule against perpetuities reflected a bias in favor of vesting. Subjecting property to unvested rights spanning many generations limited its marketability and often prevented its being put to its best and highest use. Courts devised the rule against perpetuities, which initially required vesting during a period based on a life in being, and which was later extended to a life or lives in being plus 21 years and possibly a period of gestation. The interest was judged at its inception. Unless it was certain to vest or to fail during the permissible period, it was void.

Although the common-law rule against perpetuities still exists and is often codified, it generally coexists alongside wait-and-see provisions. Rather than requiring certainty when an interest is created, a wait-and-see statute judges that interest at the end of the relevant wait-and-see period. These statutes also cover how to distribute the property if no interest vests within the statutory time period.

C. Potential Benefits and Downsides of Avoiding Vesting

Property owners have various reasons for using a trust instead of transferring fee simple ownership to their beneficiaries. If the beneficiary does not own property outright, her creditors will have more difficulty in accessing it. The new spouse of a widowed beneficiary will not be able to claim omitted spouse or elective share rights based on its value. And, if the settlor's children or more remote descendants have marital difficulties, the trust might avoid being included as divisible marital property. Property that remains in a trust avoids probate when each successive beneficiary dies. Before the generation-skipping transfer tax was enacted, skipping generations also meant skipping estate tax as the beneficial interest passed from one generation to another.

Some of these benefits—such as those related to federal transfer taxes—have been curtailed or eliminated, but others—such as protecting property from a new spouse—remain viable. Some jurisdictions promote delayed vesting by allowing trusts to continue indefinitely. Others retain a perpetuities rule but extended the permissible vesting period by statute. As a result, a settlor might be able to take advantage of the benefits of delayed vesting for a period that extends well beyond the traditional lives in being plus 21 years.

The longer a trust continues without distributing its principal, the more likely it is that trust provisions will not serve the beneficiaries' interests. States that allow vesting periods longer than 90 years may give more weight to the beneficiaries' interests than to the settlor's purpose when deciding whether to modify or terminate a trust.

D. Relevant Uniform Probate Code Provisions

1. Statutory Rule Against Perpetuities

UPC § 2-901 provides two methods for satisfying the rule against perpetuities. If an interest or power satisfies the common-law rule when it is created, no further inquiry is necessary. Failure to satisfy the common-law rule at creation does not void the interest or power. Instead, we wait a prescribed period to see if an interest vests or terminates or if a power is exercised or terminates. If vesting, exercise, or termination occurs within that time period, the interest or power is valid.

The UPC drafters chose a 90-year wait-and-see period as their alternative to the common law rule. The comments indicate that most interests or powers will vest, be exercised, or terminate within that period and that it likely gives approximately the same results as the common-law rule would using life expectancies and a minor as the youngest life in being.

Because the UPC provisions operate differently for interests in property and powers over property, the discussion below separates interests from powers. In either case, you must focus on when the interest or power is created and on when it vests, is exercised, or terminates.

a. Application to Interests in Property

UPC § 2-901(a) applies to nonvested property interests. An interest is valid if is certain to vest or terminate no later than 21 years after the death of an individual alive when it is created. UPC § 2-901(a)(1). This determination is made when the interest is created and reflects the common-law rule. As was true under the common law, it does not guarantee that a particular beneficiary will ultimately receive the property.

> **Example 22-1.** Samantha devised property to a testamentary trust. The trustee is to pay income to Samantha's children for life. When her youngest child dies, the trustee is to distribute the trust principal to Samantha's then-living descendants using the relevant rules of representation. If no descendant survives, the trustee is to distribute the assets among several charities named in the trust. The remainder interest in the trust principal satisfies the rule against perpetuities. Because all of Samantha's children had been born or adopted when she died, the remainder interest will vest in either her descendants or the charities within 21 years after

the deaths of the lives in being when the trust was created. It does not matter that the trustee cannot determine the actual recipients until all of Samantha's children die.

The remainder interest in Samantha's property was created when Samantha died. It does not matter that she executed her will several years earlier or that she executed her will before all of her children were born or adopted. The trust term was based on the lives of the children alive when she died.

If Samantha had instead created an inter vivos trust, there are three possibilities. She either retained a right of revocation that did not end until her death; retained a right of revocation but relinquished it before her death; or retained no right of revocation. In the first situation, the remainder interest was created when she died. In the second situation, it was created when she relinquished her right to revoke. In the third situation, in which she created an irrevocable trust, the remainder interest was created when she created the trust. Only the first situation guarantees the trust satisfies the common-law rule. In the other two situations, it is possible she would have another child after the irrevocable trust was created or after she relinquished her right to revoke a revocable trust. A child born or adopted after a trust becomes irrevocable cannot be a measuring life. That child would not have been alive when the interest was created. Because such a child could die more than 21 years after the death of all his siblings, the remainder interest would not necessarily vest or terminate within the common-law perpetuities period.

UPC § 2-901(a)(2) allows an interest to be tested based on actual vesting or termination. It validates any interest that vests or terminates within 90 years after its creation. Thus, if all of Samantha's children die within 90 years after she creates the trust, the remainder interest is valid. It will not matter that she had one or more children after she is treated as creating the remainder interest.

b. *Application to Powers of Appointment*

When considering powers of appointment that are not subject to a condition precedent, focus on whether they must be irrevocably exercised or terminate within the common-law period or are actually irrevocably exercised or terminate within the wait-and-see period. When a condition precedent is involved, consider whether the condition must be (common-law) or is (wait-and-see) satisfied within the relevant period.

For purposes of the rule against perpetuities, there are three categories of powers of appointment: (1) a general power of appointment that is presently exercisable; (2) a general power of appointment that is not presently exercisable because it is subject to a condition precedent; and (3) a testamentary power of appointment or a limited (nongeneral) power of appointment. The third category actually covers two types of power. Powers in categories (2) and (3) are subject to the rule against perpetuities; powers in category (1) are not.

> **Example 22-2.** Sylvia created an irrevocable inter vivos trust. The trustee is to pay income to Sylvia's children until the youngest child living when the trust is created dies. At that time, the trustee is to distribute the trust principal to Sylvia's descendants. Sylvia gave her brother Bob the power to appoint the trust principal to himself at any time before the trust terminated. Bob has a general power of appointment because he can appoint the trust principal to himself. His power is presently exercisable; there is no condition precedent that must occur before he can exercise it. Bob's power must be exercised or must terminate by the time he dies (or the earlier date on which the trust terminates); it easily satisfies the common-law rule against perpetuities. This type of power is not covered by UPC §2-901.

1. Nontestamentary General Powers Subject to a Condition Precedent

A power is both general and nontestamentary if it meets the criteria of both those terms. A power is general if the powerholder can exercise it in favor of himself, his estate, his creditors, or the creditors of his estate. It is general even if he can exercise it in favor of only one of those categories. His power can include additional permissible appointees, such as his children, and still be a general power.

A power is nontestamentary if the powerholder can exercise it before his death. A nontestamentary power can be immediately exercisable, as in Example 22-2, or it can be subject to one or more conditions precedent. Those conditions can be based on an event or on the passage of time. UPC §2-901(b) validates nontestamentary general powers that are *not* presently exercisable if they satisfy the common-law rule. It also validates them if the condition precedent is satisfied or becomes impossible to satisfy within 90 years of its creation.

As was true for interests in property, the date of creation varies based on the type of transfer. A power created by an irrevocable inter vivos trust carries the most risk because of the possibility that a powerholder will be able to exercise it more than 21 years after the death of everyone who was alive when the power was created or of its not being exercised or terminating within 90 years of its creation.

Example 22-3. Sylvia instead gave Bob a power to appoint the trust principal to himself after he completes his Ph.D. program if he completes the program before the trust would otherwise terminate. Although Bob's general power of appointment is not presently exercisable, it does not violate the rule against perpetuities. Bob will either finish his Ph.D. program before the trust terminates or he will be unable to satisfy the condition before the trust terminates. The power is valid under the common-law rule because the condition must be satisfied or terminate within Bob's lifetime even if the trust terminates after Bob's death.

Example 22-4. Sylvia instead gave Bob's youngest grandchild a power to appoint the trust principal to himself or herself upon attaining age 30. The trustee is not to distribute trust principal to Sylvia's descendants until Bob's youngest grandchild attains age 30 or dies before attaining age 30. Because it is possible Bob could have a child after the trust is created, and that child could have a child of his own, Bob might have a grandchild who attains age 30 more than 21 years after the death of any individual alive when Sylvia created the power. This power will fail the rule against perpetuities unless the condition is satisfied or becomes impossible to satisfy within 90 years after Sylvia created it.

2. Nontestamentary Limited Powers and Testamentary Powers

UPC § 2-901(c) governs the validity of nontestamentary limited powers and all testamentary powers. The powerholder has a nontestamentary limited power if he can exercise the power before his death but cannot exercise it in favor of himself, his estate, his creditors, or the creditors of his estate. If the powerholder can exercise the power only at death, it is testamentary. In that case, it does not matter if the power is general or limited.

A power subject to UPC § 2-901(c) is valid if it satisfies either the common-law rule or the 90-year wait-and-see period. It must be certain that the power will be irrevocably exercised or terminate within 21 years after the death of an individual who was alive when the power was created. Alternatively, it must actually be irrevocably exercised or must terminate within 90 years after it is created.

Example 22-5. Sylvia instead gave her brother Seth the power to appoint one-half the trust principal 10 years after the trust was created and to appoint half of the remaining one-half 30 years after the trust was created. Seth could exercise the power in favor of his children and Bob's children. Each power would lapse after six months. Seth received two non-testamentary limited powers. The first power satisfied the common-law rule; it will be exercised or lapse within 21 years after its creation. The second power will satisfy the 90-year rule, as it will be exercised or lapse only 30 years after its creation.

2. Posthumous Child Exception

UPC §2-901(d) provides an exception in applying the common-law rule to property interests, to general powers of appointment subject to a condition precedent, and to limited powers and testamentary powers of appointment. In determining whether the interest or power satisfies the common-law rule, we ignore the possibility that a child will be born to an individual after that individual has died. The comments to that subsection indicate that this rule applies only in determining compliance with the common-law rule. It does not overturn the rule, discussed in Chapter 5, that a child in gestation who is later born alive is treated as alive for purposes such as intestate succession.

3. Nondonative Transfer Exception

UPC §2-904(1) exempts nondonative transfers from the rule against perpetuities. The term "nondonative" does not mean that every involuntary transfer is exempt. Nor does it necessarily exempt every situation in which the transferor received some consideration. The exception for nondonative transfers does not apply to nonvested interests or powers of appointment created as a result of a prenuptial or postnuptial agreement, a separation or divorce settlement, or a spousal election. Likewise, it does not apply to contracts to make or revoke a will or to exercise or not exercise a power of appointment, to transfers to satisfy a support obligation, or to reciprocal transfers.

Example 22-6. Brad and his brother Bill entered into a contract to establish trusts for each other's families. The trustee of the trust Brad established is to pay Bill's children income for life, then pay Bill's grandchildren income for life, then pay Bill's great-grandchildren income for life. The trustee of the trust Bill established is to pay Brad's children income for life, then pay Brad's grandchildren income for life, then pay Brad's great-grandchildren income for life. Each trust terminates at the death of the last eligible recipient. When the trust Brad created terminates, the trustee is to pay principal to Bill's descendants by representation. When the trust Bill created terminates, the trustee is to pay principal to Brad's descendants by representation. Each trust provided for a charitable taker in the event no descendant survived the termination date. Each of these reciprocal trusts fails the common-law rule against perpetuities and is likely to fail the 90-year wait-and-see period.

4. Charity to Charity Exception

As a general rule, governments encourage charitable transfers, outright or in trust. Federal and state income and transfer taxes allow deductions for gifts to charity. Charitable trusts are exempt from the UTC's definite beneficiary requirement. Not surprisingly, charitable trusts can be structured in a manner that exempts them from the rule against perpetuities. UPC § 2-904(5).

The UPC exemption applies to nonvested property interests held by charities, governments, and governmental agencies and subdivisions if the preceding interest is held by a charity, government, or governmental agency or subdivision.

Example 22-7. Samantha created a trust to pay income to her two children for life. When her last surviving child dies, the trustee is to pay the trust principal to the local food bank. Although the interest preceding the charity's interest is not held by another charity, the charity's interest satisfies the common-law rule against perpetuities.

Example 22-8. Sara created a trust to pay income to the local food bank for 250 years and then pay the principal to the university from which she graduated if it was still in existence; if not, to a nonprofit entity that aids disaster victims. Although the university's interest in principal will not vest within 90 years of its creation (and might never vest if it ceases existence), it is exempt from the rule against perpetuities. The preceding interest is held by a charity. The same analysis applies to the contingent interest that takes effect if the university's interest fails.

5. Other UPC Exceptions

UPC § 2-904 exempts certain powers related to fiduciaries. These include fiduciary powers to administer or manage assets and to determine income and principal, powers to appoint a fiduciary, and a trustee's discretionary power to distribute principal to a beneficiary before the trust terminates. UPC

§ 2-904(2)–(4). The last power is exempted from the rule only if the beneficiary has an indefeasibly vested interest in both income and principal.

UPC § 2-904(6) exempts various interests in and powers over employee benefit plans. UPC § 2-904(7) exempts interests and powers that would not have been subject to the common-law rule. It also exempts interests and powers exempted by any other state statute.

6. Determining When Interest or Power Is Created

UPC § 2-902(a) provides a general rule for determining when an interest or power is created. The creation is determined using the jurisdiction's general principles of property law. That rule is subject to two exceptions.

The first exception applies if the governing instrument gives an individual the unqualified power to make himself the beneficial owner of a nonvested property interest or a nonvested interest that is subject to a power of appointment. In that situation, the nonvested interest or the power is treated as created when that individual's power terminates. UPC § 2-902(b). The second exception applies to property (or a power over property) added to an existing trust. The perpetuities period begins when the nonvested property interest (or power) in the original contribution was created, not at the later date of the transfer. UPC § 2-902(c).

Example 22-9. Seth created a revocable inter vivos trust. The trustee is to pay income to Seth's children for life, then to his grandchildren. When the last grandchild dies, the trustee is to distribute the trust principal to Seth's descendants. Because the trust is revocable, all nonvested interests are created when Seth dies.

Example 22-10. Sigmund created an irrevocable inter vivos trust. The trustee is to pay income to Sigmund's children for life, then to his grandchildren. When the last grandchild dies, the trustee is to distribute the trust principal to Sigmund's descendants. The trust instrument gives Sigmund's daughter Diane the unlimited power to invade trust principal for five years after he created the trust. Because Diane had a power to make herself the beneficial owner of trust property, all nonvested interests are created when Diane's power ends, not when Sigmund created the irrevocable trust.

Example 22-11. Stuart created an irrevocable inter vivos trust. The trustee is to pay income to Stuart's children for life, then to his grandchildren, and then to his great-grandchildren. The trustee is to distribute property to Stuart's descendants after the death of all his great-grandchildren. Six years later, Stuart added more property to the trust. Both the original nonvested interest and the nonvested interest in the later contribution are created when Stuart created the trust.

7. Distribution of Trust Property

If the interest or power fails, the nonvested property interest must be distributed. The recipient might be determined by language in the trust instrument or by statutory default rules. A state might provide for distribution among current trust beneficiaries, adopt the UPC's language regarding reformation, or provide for a totally different distribution scheme.

UPC § 2-903 allows an interested person to petition the court to reform the disposition in the manner that most closely approximates the transferor's manifested plan of distribution and occurs within the 90-year wait-and-see period. Reformation is required if a nonvested interest or a power becomes invalid, a class gift might become invalid but at least one class member is eligible to have possession or enjoyment of a share of the property, or a nonvested interest can vest but not within the 90-year period. In the first situation, reformation takes place at the end of the 90-year period. In the other two situations, reformation can occur earlier to avoid postponing distribution of a vested class interest or because it is certain that vesting will not occur until after 90 years.

Example 22-12. Sally created a testamentary trust to pay income to her children for life, then to her grandchildren for life. The trustee is then to distribute a proportionate share of principal to each of Sally's great-grandchildren when they attain age 25. If a great-grandchild dies before attaining age 25, that share is to be distributed to charity. Ninety years after the trust's creation, two of Sally's great-grandchildren had attained age 25 and received their share of trust principal. Three other great-grandchildren had not attained age 25. The trustee can petition the court to reform the trust. It is likely that distributing principal to the remaining great-grandchildren most closely follows Sally's plan. Because Sally did provide an alternative gift to charity, the court must take that into account in determining her plan of distribution.

Example 22-13. Sally's trust instrument also included this provision: "If any trust principal has not been distributed within 90 years following my death, the trustee is to distribute that undistributed principal to a charity benefiting the local community. The trustee is to do so even if I have great-grandchildren who have not yet attained age 25." In that situation, the great-grandchildren who had not yet attained age 25 will not receive trust principal.

Example 22-14. Serena created a testamentary trust to pay income to her children for life, then to her grandchildren for life. The trustee is to distribute a proportionate share of principal to each of Serena's great-grandchildren who have attained age 25 and are alive when the last great-grandchild attains age 25. Eighty years after the trust's creation, two great-grandchildren had attained age 25, but the third great-grandchild was only 10 years old. The trustee can petition the court to reform the trust so that the trustee can distribute their share to the older beneficiaries immediately and distribute the remaining share to the other beneficiary when the 90-year period expires. That distribution most closely follows Serena's plan.

E. State Laws

State laws vary in their treatment of delayed vesting. Some states have enacted the common-law rule; others have enacted the uniform act. Some states have abolished the rule against perpetuities. N.J. Stat. § 46:2F-9. Others have abolished it if the instrument exempts the trust from the rule and gives the trustee the power to alienate trust property. N.H. Rev. Stat. §§ 564:24, 564-B:4-402A. Some states have extended the wait-and-see period. Florida, for example, has 90-year, 360-year, and 1,000-year wait-and-see periods. Fla. Stat. § 689.225. Colorado uses a 1,000-year period. Colo. Rev. Stat. § 15-11-1102.5. Other states have different rules for real property and personal property. Del. Code tit. 25, § 503. Read RAP statutes carefully to determine the extent of any variation from the common-law rule or 90-year wait-and-see rule.

Not surprisingly, standards a court uses in deciding whether to modify a trust may be more heavily weighted in favor of the beneficiaries when a settlor selects a long vesting period. The longer that vesting is deferred, the more likely it is that the settlor has not anticipated how changing conditions affect the beneficiaries' interests. Modification, which is discussed in Chapter 16, can occur long before the time the state requires for vesting.

CHECKPOINTS

- The rule against perpetuities began as a common-law rule to prevent remote vesting.
- The common-law rule against perpetuities required that a nonvested interest had to be certain to vest or terminate no later than a period that ended 21 years after the death of a life in being. Powers had to be certain to be irrevocably exercised or terminate during the same period.
- Interests and powers subject to the common-law rule were judged at their creation.
- Statutes providing a fixed wait-and-see period can save an interest or power that would fail the common-law rule. These interests and powers are judged at the end of the wait-and-see period rather than at their creation. They are judged on what actually occurs.
- An interest in (or power over) property created by will, including in a testamentary trust, is created when the testator dies.
- An interest in (or power over) property created by an inter vivos trust is created when the trust becomes irrevocable.
- The UPC includes a 90-year wait-and-see period.
- The UPC provides exceptions from the rule, including those for non-donative transfers and for transfers in which a charitable or governmental interest follows another charitable or governmental interest.
- The UPC provides for reforming an interest or power that fails to vest within the necessary time period. The trust instrument can also provide rules for distributing the trust principal.
- Many states have lengthened the perpetuities period (or even abolished the rule) in addition to easing rules regarding reformation and modification when a trust uses a longer vesting period.

CHAPTER 23

Claims, Expenses, and Distributions to Beneficiaries

ROADMAP

- Expenses and claims
- Abatement of devises
- Tax apportionment
- Beneficiary requests and private agreements

A. Chapter Overview

The personal representative of a decedent's estate and trustee of a trust exercise powers and perform duties pursuant to the governing instrument and the relevant statutes. Subject to the rights of creditors and other claimants, they administer the entity's assets for the benefit of its beneficiaries. Their powers and duties extend to selecting investments, allocating income and expenses between categories of beneficiaries, and distributing assets to eligible beneficiaries. This chapter and the two that follow it address those matters.

B. Expenses and Claims

Each jurisdiction has statutes covering the personal representative's duty to notify creditors directly or provide notices that creditors are likely to read. After any relevant period for filing claims has ended, the personal representative satisfies valid claims and pays expenses before distributing assets to the devisees or intestate heirs. A trustee or other fiduciary has similar responsibilities. The trustee will interact with creditors throughout the trust's existence.

C. Abatement of Devises

Before the personal representative distributes probate assets to devisees, he must satisfy claims based on debts, funeral expenses, and expenses of administration. With limited exceptions, those claims "outrank" the rights of heirs and devisees. Surviving spouses and omitted children might also have rights that supersede those of other beneficiaries. To satisfy these claimants, the personal representative uses money or other property that would otherwise be distributed to devisees and heirs. This process is called abatement.

1. Will Clauses

The testator can specify the order of abatement in her will. UPC § 3-902(b). She can provide for abatement by category of devise, or she can prefer some devises within a category to others. The testator can also change the order of abatement for certain claims but not for others. The following are examples of potential will provisions:

- The order of abatement shall be residuary devises, specific devises, and general devises.
- Devises to my siblings shall abate before any other devise. All other devises shall abate in the statutory order.
- Devises shall abate in the statutory order, but only to the extent the residuary devise is not reduced below 10% of my probate estate.
- General devises shall abate before residuary devises to provide for any spousal rights. Abatement to pay other claims and expenses shall be in the statutory order.

The examples above use the term "abate." There is no requirement that the testator use that term. The testator could instead say "My personal representative shall reduce the share of my siblings before reducing any other devise."

UPC § 3-902(b) includes language that might not appear in state statutes concerning abatement. It allows abatement according to the testator's intention, even if there is no will provision, if the statutory defaults would defeat the testamentary plan or would defeat the express or implied purpose of the devise.

> **Example 23-1.** Tom's will did not mention abatement. He devised 25% of his estate to his daughter and 75% to his granddaughter. His will contained the following language: "I am devising more to my granddaughter than to my daughter in recognition of her ongoing medical expenses." A court might determine that charging 75% of the estate's claims and expenses against the granddaughter's share would defeat the purpose of this devise.

2. Statutory Defaults

UPC § 3-902(a) provides for the following order of abatement: property passing by intestate succession; residuary devises; general devises; and specific devises. Because demonstrative devises are eventually categorized as specific, general, or partly each, they are subsumed into those categories by the UPC language. This section also provides the rules for abatement within a category of devises. Abatement is pro rata by the amount of the devise, not by the number of devisees.

> **Example 23-2.** Terry devised $100,000 to be shared by her children, $300,000 to her sister, and the residue to her brother. Expenses exceeded the value of property that Terry's brother would have received. Unless Terry's will provides otherwise, excess claims will be paid 25% from the devise to her children and 75% from the devise to her sister. It does not matter how many children Terry had.

The reference to property that passes by intestate succession applies in several situations. Obviously if there is no valid will, all non-exempt property passes by intestate succession. Even if there is a will, property might pass by intestate succession because there is no residuary clause. It might also pass by intestate succession if there is no eligible residuary devisee, even after applying the antilapse statute.

In addition to its exception for any abatement order provided by the testator, UPC § 3-902(a) is also subject to an exception for the surviving spouse's elective share. UPC § 3-902(a) does not mention omitted spouse or child rights, homestead allowance, exempt property, or family allowance, but the UPC provisions covering those rights could be relevant in determining abatement. UPC § 2-402 exempts the homestead allowance from all claims against the estate and makes it superior to those claims. UPC § 2-403 makes the right to exempt property superior to all claims except those for homestead allowance and family allowance. UPC § 2-404 exempts the family allowance from all claims against the estate and makes it superior to all claims except homestead allowance. These rights are discussed in greater detail in Chapter 9.

The rights of an omitted spouse are satisfied using the UPC § 3-902 abatement rules, but with one exception. A devise to the testator's child does not abate for this purpose if the child was born before the testator married the surviving spouse and is not the surviving spouse's child. Antilapse might save that devise from abatement even if the child predeceased the testator. UPC § 2-301. Abatement to satisfy the rights of an omitted child follows the UPC § 3-902 order if the testator had no living child when he executed the will, and either did not devise substantially all his estate to the other parent of the omitted child or did but the parent was ineligible to take the devise. UPC § 2-302(d). If the testator did have one or more living children when he executed his will, they share their devises with the omitted child. UPC § 2-302(a)(2). The devise to the reconstituted group of children is subject to the normal abatement rules.

State statutes follow the UPC in providing for testator intent to govern. They might diverge from the UPC in their treatment of family rights. They might, for example, change the order of priority for those rights or make some rights subject to claims of creditors. They might put different limits on different types of exempt property instead of putting furniture, automobiles, furnishings, appliances, and personal effects into a single group, with an overall dollar value limit. They might provide for different family members to benefit from homestead, exempt property, or family allowance. They might compute omitted spouse or child rights differently.

3. Claims Against the Estate

UPC § 3-805 lists categories of claims against the estate and ranks them. Ranking is important if the estate does not have sufficient assets to cover all claims. The order of priority is: (1) costs and expenses of administration;

(2) reasonable funeral expenses; (3) debts and taxes with preference under federal law; (4) reasonable and necessary medical and hospital expenses of the last illness of the decedent, including compensation of persons attending him; (5) debts and taxes with preference under other laws of the state; and (6) all other claims. Tax apportionment provisions are provided by a separate UPC section. A secured creditor will generally take the property subject to his security interest.

State statutes might vary from the UPC by ranking claims in a different order. They might add items that would otherwise fall into the UPC's fifth or sixth categories. They might place dollar limits on a ranked item; amounts above the dollar limit would be covered under the "all other claims" category.

If the probate estate is not sufficient, the personal representative might have other sources from which to obtain funds for paying claims. If, for example, the decedent had a revocable trust, the trustee might be required to transfer trust assets to the personal representative. UTC § 505(a)(3).

D. Tax Apportionment

1. Overview

Transfers during life and at death are subject to the federal estate tax if they exceed a cumulative amount. That amount increases from year to year because of an inflation adjustment. The relevant amount for 2024 is $13,610,000 ($13,990,000 for 2025). The statute governing the amount will expire at the end of 2025. Congress could extend the current exemption or could allow it to revert to its pre-2017 Act level (but with an inflation adjustment).

The federal estate and gift taxes cover many nonprobate transfers, including inter vivos gifts, transfers to a revocable trust and other revocable transfers, and transfers with a retained life estate. They also cover some or all of a decedent's interest in property held in a survivorship tenancy, proceeds of a policy insuring the decedent's life if she had incidents of ownership in the policy, and the value of annuity payments received by a surviving beneficiary.

Computing the federal transfer tax is not important for this discussion. Instead, you should focus on the fact that the decedent's nonprobate transfers might result in her estate owing federal gift or estate tax or owing more tax than would otherwise be due. If the tax is paid solely from probate assets, nonprobate takers benefit at the expense of devisees or intestate heirs.

Example 23-3. When Teresa died in 2024, she devised all her property to her son Sam. Her probate estate was $150,000. A trust over which she held a general power of appointment was worth $20 million. If she had only a nongeneral power, her estate would owe no estate tax. Because she had a general power, her estate is subject to an estate tax liability that exceeds the value of her probate assets. If the normal rules of abatement applied, Sam would receive no assets from her probate estate; the $150,000 would be needed to pay the estate tax and other claims.

If Sam is the trust's beneficiary, he might not care that the probate estate is eliminated. If someone else is the beneficiary, Sam might object to being disinherited in favor of the nonprobate beneficiary.

Not surprisingly, the normal rules of abatement might not apply in this situation. Instead, the relevant tax apportionment and collection provisions apply. These provisions could appear in several places: the decedent's will if she died testate; any nonprobate instruments she executed; the jurisdiction's tax apportionment statute; and any applicable tax statutes (federal and possibly state). Written agreements between the decedent and transferees of her nonprobate assets might also apply.

2. Tax Apportionment Provisions

The Uniform Estate Tax Apportionment Act is included as UPC Article III, Part 9A. This discussion, which focuses on the primary apportionment rules, uses UPC section numbers. It covers apportioning the tax among persons who receive an interest in the apportionable estate. Whenever possible, these rules apportion tax to persons who receive interests that are included in the gross estate but that are not eligible for deductions in computing the taxable estate.

UPC § 3-9A-103(a) provides three rules, one each for language in wills, in revocable trusts, and in other instruments. First, the estate tax is to be apportioned as provided in the decedent's will if that document expressly and unambiguously provides for apportionment. Express, unambiguous will provisions govern even if other instruments also have express, unambiguous provisions.

Second, any portion of the tax not apportioned pursuant to a direction in the will is to be apportioned as provided in a revocable trust of which the decedent is the settlor if that instrument expressly and unambiguously provides for apportionment. The provisions concerning revocable trusts indicate that the most recent trust provisions govern if there are two or more conflicting sets of provisions. A trust is considered revocable for purposes of tax apportionment if it was revocable when created. It is irrelevant that the settlor later relinquished the power to revoke.

With respect to interests in property passing by virtue of another instrument, the tax is to be (or not to be) apportioned if the other dispositive instrument expressly and unambiguously directs that such interest is to be (or is not to be) subject to apportionment.

UPC § 3-9A-103(b) provides several default rules that apply if the decedent did not expressly and unambiguously provide otherwise. One of these rules covers reapportioning tax that would otherwise apply to interests the decedent has exonerated from payment of estate tax. Another of the rules is designed to limit the effect of tax apportionment on interests eligible for an estate tax marital or charitable deduction.

State statutes might diverge from the UPC by exempting certain interests allocable to family members even if those interests do not qualify for a federal estate tax deduction. A state might also limit the primacy of express will provisions over express trust provisions if the trust was created after the will was executed.

3. Applicable Federal Statutes

Several federal tax statutes allow for recovery of estate tax from a person who received nonprobate property. For example, I.R.C. § 2206 provides for contribution by a recipient of life insurance proceeds that were included in the gross estate. It is expressly made subject to a contrary provision in the decedent's will. I.R.C. § 2207 provides for contribution by a person who receives property because of the decedent's exercise, nonexercise, or release of a general power of appointment. It is also expressly made subject to a contrary provision in the decedent's will and applies only to amounts included in the gross estate.

> **Example 23-4.** When Tom died, the value of his probate estate exceeded the relevant estate tax exemption. Tom held a nongeneral power of appointment over property in a trust established by his grandfather; he exercised it in favor of his daughter Debra. His son Steve was the beneficiary of a policy insuring Tom's life. Tom owned the policy at his death. Tom's will did not mention estate tax apportionment. Steve must contribute to paying any estate tax due; his contribution will be based on the ratio of the insurance proceeds to Tom's total taxable estate. Debra does not have to contribute. Because Tom had only a nongeneral power of

appointment, the trust property Debra received is excluded from Tom's gross estate.

Chapter 14 includes a brief discussion of QTIP trusts. These trusts allow the first spouse to die a marital deduction even though the surviving spouse does not receive a general power of appointment over the trust assets. When the surviving spouse dies, the trust assets are included in her gross estate and might result in an estate tax or increase an estate tax that would otherwise be due. I.R.C. § 2207A(a) provides for recovery of the increased estate tax from the recipients of the trust property. The surviving spouse can waive contribution by a provision in her will or in a revocable trust she has established. I.R.C. § 2207A(b) provides comparable rules for the recovery of any gift tax paid by the surviving spouse.

I.R.C. § 2207B deals with estate tax payable because the decedent retained a life estate in property he previously transferred. The trust assets will be included in the decedent's gross estate under I.R.C. § 2036. The estate is entitled to recover estate tax from the person who receives the property. The decedent can waive recovery in his will or in a revocable trust he has established.

The provisions outlined above apply only if the property is included in the decedent's gross estate. They differ in two respects. First, I.R.C. §§ 2207A(a) and 2207B expressly provide that the decedent can waive recovery in a will or in a revocable trust; I.R.C. §§ 2206 and 2207 only mention waiver in a will. Second, I.R.C. § 2207A(a) provides for recovering the amount that the estate tax was increased by including the relevant property in the decedent's gross estate. The other three provisions use a ratio to determine the tax increase. The ratio is the value of the included property to the total taxable estate.

Example 23-5. Ilene died in 2024. If she had owned only probate assets, her gross estate would have been $15,610,000. After taking into account potential deductions, her taxable estate would have been exactly $13,610,000. No estate tax would be due. Ilene had powers over or interests in nonprobate property, which increased both her gross and taxable estates by $3,000,000 and resulted in an estate tax of $1,200,000, which is 40% of the additional $3,000,000. The additional property represented 18.06% of her $16,610,000 taxable estate. If the property included in her gross estate was covered by I.R.C. § 2207A(a), the QTIP trust beneficiaries would be liable for the $1,200,000 tax. If the property included in her gross estate was covered by I.R.C. § 2206, the beneficiaries of her life insurance policy would be liable for $216,720, which is 18.06% of $1,200,000.

E. Beneficiary Requests and Private Agreements

1. Beneficiary Requests

The UPC establishes distribution in kind as the preferred method for transferring estate assets to beneficiaries. UPC § 3-906. Specific devisees have the right to the property devised; the rights of other devisees are more limited. Because distribution in kind is preferred, the personal representative can distribute property other than money to satisfy a general pecuniary devise. Residuary devisees receive any property that remains after satisfying specific and general devises. The personal representative is to distribute the residue in an equitable manner. UPC § 3-906(a)(4). This is particularly important if there are multiple residuary devisees.

Family rights are not subject to those general rules. A surviving spouse or child who is entitled to exempt property can select qualifying items of property in taking a distribution in kind. UPC § 3-906(a)(1). A surviving spouse or child who is entitled to homestead allowance or family allowance can request distribution of money rather than distribution in kind. If distribution in kind is made to satisfy these rights, the personal representative cannot distribute items that a residuary devisee requested remain in the residue. UPC § 3-906(a)(2).

2. Private Agreements

Private agreements between beneficiaries are most likely to involve the administration of a decedent's probate estate. Perhaps an ambiguity exists, and the personal representative is unsure which of two or more potential devisees was to benefit. Perhaps the dispute is over an item of property. Perhaps a beneficiary's actions suggest undue influence but other beneficiaries are not sure they would succeed if they litigated. Or perhaps one or more devisees would prefer receiving property devised to one or more other devisees.

Rather than incur litigation costs—and risk losing altogether—beneficiaries might enter into agreements regarding the estate's distribution. They could, of course, simply reallocate the property after the personal representative distributes it. But receiving the desired property directly from the estate eliminates the need for a second round of transfers, some of which might require new deeds or other title documents.

UPC § 3-912 allows the successors to the estate to rearrange their interests by a binding written contract. The contract cannot adversely affect the rights of any beneficiary who does not sign it. Nor can it limit the rights of creditors and taxing authorities.

The UTC provides for distributing trust principal according to terms agreed on by the beneficiaries if the trust is terminated pursuant to UTC § 411. That provision is discussed in Chapter 16.

CHECKPOINTS

- The personal representative must satisfy claims against the estate and pay expenses of administration before distributing the remaining assets to devisees or heirs. The trustee of a trust must pay expenses and claims before distributing income or principal to beneficiaries.
- The testator can specify an order in which devises abate for the payment of claims and expenses.
- If the testator does not specify an abatement order, claims and expenses are satisfied in this order: (1) property that would pass by intestacy; (2) property otherwise in the residuary devise; (3) general devises; and (4) specific devises.
- Abatement provisions might apply differently for satisfaction of certain rights based on family status. These include homestead allowance, exempt property, family allowance, elective share, and omitted spouse or child rights.
- The trustee of a revocable trust might be required to transfer trust property to the personal representative to pay expenses and claims.
- Transfer taxes owed by the decedent's estate might be apportioned among recipients of interests in the probate estate and in other property included in the decedent's gross estate. Apportionment provisions appear in governing instruments, state statutes, and the Internal Revenue Code.

- Beneficiaries might rearrange their shares of the estate by private agreements. These agreements cannot affect the rights of creditors or of beneficiaries who are not parties to the agreement.
- Trust beneficiaries might agree on the distribution of trust principal when a trust terminates.

CHAPTER 24

Trustees and Other Fiduciaries

ROADMAP

- Fiduciaries other than trustees
- Trustees and trust directors

A. Chapter Overview

In covering probate estates and trusts, this book has discussed various aspects of the relationship between a transferor (intestate, testator, or settlor), a fiduciary (personal representative or trustee), and various beneficiaries. Although this chapter briefly describes other fiduciaries and the sources of their powers, it focuses on trustees. Because the trustee's relationship to trust beneficiaries can begin during the settlor's lifetime and continue long after her death, the trustee's powers and duties are a model to which you can compare the treatment of other fiduciaries. Keep in mind that state law can differ from the uniform acts discussed in this chapter.

B. Fiduciaries Other Than Trustees

1. Agent Under a Power of Attorney

An individual might appoint an agent to act on his behalf for a variety of reasons. The individual being represented is the principal; the person acting on his behalf is variously referred to as an agent under a power of attorney or as an attorney in fact. Despite the language used, there is no requirement that the agent be an attorney.

The principal might need someone to manage his affairs because he will be away for a long period. Although he could place his property in trust, the trust has two potential drawbacks. First, if he anticipates returning and terminating the arrangement, he might not want to incur the cost of creating a trust, transferring property to that trust, and then retransferring it back to himself. Second, he might want to give his fiduciary powers that extend beyond managing his property.

For many individuals, appointing an agent under a power of attorney serves an even more important function. If the power is durable, it is not extinguished when the principal becomes incapacitated. The principal can avoid the court's appointing a conservator to manage his property. Even if a conservator is appointed, the power of attorney remains operative; the conservator does not have the authority to revoke a durable power. If the principal is placed under a conservatorship, the agent makes reports to the conservator as well as to the principal. UPC § 5B-108.

The Uniform Power of Attorney Act is also part of the UPC, and this discussion uses UPC section numbers. The discussion below assumes the agent received a durable power because that is the uniform act's default rule. UPC § 5B-104. The principal can create a nondurable power, in which case the power ceases when the principal becomes incapacitated, but must expressly indicate that the power is terminated by the principal's incapacity. State law might reverse the language requirement. For example, Fla. Stat. § 709.2104 requires an affirmative statement that incapacity does not terminate the power.

a. Creation and Termination of Power of Attorney

The principal creates the power by a signed writing; the UPC does not require witnesses. UPC § 5B-105. A state might require witnesses, notarization, or both.

The principal selects the time when the power becomes effective. Unless the instrument provides for a standby power ("springing power") that becomes effective upon the happening of an event or the passage of time, the power is effective immediately. UPC § 5B-109. A state might allow for a delayed power or might require that the power become effective immediately.

The agent's ability to act pursuant to the power ends when he no longer has authority to act. The UPC differentiates events that terminate the particular agent's authority and events that terminate the power itself. In either case the particular agent's authority ends. UPC § 5B-110. The agent's authority terminates if the principal revokes it, if the agent is no longer able to act because of his own death or incapacity, if the agent resigns, or if the power terminates. If the agent and principal are married to each other, an action to dissolve the marriage also terminates the power unless the instrument creating it provides otherwise.

The power terminates when the principal dies or revokes the power, a termination event specified in the instrument occurs, or the purpose of the power is accomplished. If the power is not durable, it terminates when the principal becomes incapacitated. The power itself also terminates if the particular agent's authority terminates and the instrument did not provide for a substitute agent.

b. *Agent's Authority*

An agent can act only within the specific authority granted in the power of attorney or a general grant of authority covered by the relevant statute. UPC § 5B-201(c) provides that language in the instrument allowing the agent to perform all acts a principal could perform is a general grant of authority. That language authorizes the agent to perform acts listed in UPC §§ 5B-204 through 5B-216. UPC § 5B-202 indicates language the instrument can use to incorporate those provisions into the instrument. UPC § 5B-201(a) lists acts for which the agent needs a specific grant of authority. These include creating, revoking, or amending an inter vivos trust, making gifts, and creating or changing survivorship or beneficiary designations.

UPC § 5B-301 is a form that a principal can use to indicate the agent's general authority, specific authority, limitations on authority, and special instructions to the agent. The form is not mandatory.

c. *Agent's Duties and Liability*

UPC § 5B-114 lists three duties that cannot be waived in the instrument creating the power: acting in accord with the agent's knowledge of the principal's expectations and otherwise acting in the principal's best interest; acting in good faith; and acting only within his scope of authority. Other duties can be waived in the instrument. Those duties are acting loyally; avoiding conflicts of interest that might prevent the agent from acting impartially on the principal's behalf; acting with care, competence, and diligence; keeping records of transactions made on behalf of the principal; cooperating with anyone with authority to make health care decisions for the principal; and attempting to preserve the principal's estate plan, including tax minimization aspects of that plan. If the agent acts in good faith, the act exempts him from liability to beneficiaries for failure to preserve the estate plan. If he acts with care, competence, and diligence for the principal's best interest, he is not liable even if he benefits from an action or he has a conflict of interest.

UPC § 5B-115 validates any exoneration provisions in the instrument. The agent is not liable to the principal or the principal's successors in interest for breach of duty covered by the exoneration provision. The exoneration provision is inapplicable if the agent abused his confidential or fiduciary relationship with the principal to have it inserted. It is also inapplicable to exonerate actions by the agent that involved dishonesty, an improper motive, or reckless indifference.

UPC § 5B-116 provides a lengthy list of persons that can petition the court to construe the power, review the agent's actions, and grant any appropriate relief. An agent that violates the act is required to restore the principal's property value and reimburse the principal for attorney's fees and costs paid on the agent's behalf. UPC § 5B-117.

2. Conservator or Guardian

A court appoints a conservator to manage the affairs of a person who is incapacitated. The court determines the scope of the conservator's authority. In some jurisdictions, the conservator is referred to as a guardian or as a guardian of the property. An incapacitated person might have a conservator (or guardian of the property) to manage his property and a separate fiduciary (guardian or guardian of the person) to manage other aspects of his life.

The UPC includes two sets of provisions that are denominated uniform acts, the Uniform Guardianship and Protective Proceedings Act and the Uniform Adult Guardianship and Protective Proceedings Jurisdiction Act. The first act has general provisions as well as separate provisions covering minors, incapacitated persons, and the property of an incapacitated person. The second act deals with various procedural issues, particularly those involving multiple jurisdictions.

Unlike agencies under a power of attorney, in which courts function only when someone invokes their jurisdiction, guardianships and conservatorships are regularly overseen by courts. A conservator of a protected person's property is appointed by the court. UPC § 5-102(1). A guardian of an incapacitated person is appointed by the court or—in some cases—by a parent or spouse. UPC § 5-102(3). An individual for whom a conservator has been appointed is referred to as a protected person. UPC § 5-102(8). An individual for whom a guardian has been appointed is referred to as a ward. UPC § 5-102(10). An individual can be a protected person, a ward, or both a protected person and a ward. A court issues letters of guardianship and letters of conservatorship to the persons appointed to serve in those capacities. The letters include any limitations on the fiduciary's powers. UPC § 5-110.

The UPC recognizes the parent's ability to appoint a guardian for his child by will or by some other writing. UPC § 5-202. The court can confirm the appointment or appoint another person if another appointment is in the child's best interest.

The separate provisions covering minors and incapacitated persons list the fiduciary's powers and duties in great detail, provide for the termination of the guardianship when appropriate, and indicate when accountings are due and any other information the guardian is to provide about the ward. UPC § 5-310 provides an extensive order of priority a court can follow in appointing a guardian for an incapacitated person; UPC § 5-413 provides the order of priority for appointing a conservator. UPC § 5-411 lists actions a conservator can take after receiving express court approval in dealing with the property. The listed powers go beyond mere purchase and sale of property. In a jurisdiction that adopts this or a comparable provision, a court can authorize the conservator to make gifts, exercise or release a power of appointment, or make, amend, or revoke a will. UPC § 5-418 holds the conservator to the standards of care that are applicable to a trustee.

Guardianships and conservatorships might be temporary in duration or might essentially be permanent. If the ward or protected person regains capacity, the relationship can be terminated. In addition, the court might limit the fiduciary's powers over a ward or protected person who has at least limited capacity to participate in managing his affairs.

The UPC does not currently include the Uniform Guardianship, Conservatorship, and Other Protective Arrangements Act. It was adopted in 2017 and has been enacted in two states. This act's drafters rejected the earlier act's use of "ward" and "incapacitated person." It uses "adult (or minor) subject to guardianship" and "adult subject to conservatorship." It focuses on providing the least restrictive means for protecting the individual and provides information and forms for less restrictive alternatives to traditional guardianships and conservatorships.

3. Custodian for UTMA Account

A donor who wants to benefit a minor but does not want to create a trust can transfer property to a custodianship account. The donor can name herself or nominate another person to act as custodian. UTMA § 3. The Uniform Transfers to Minors Act calls the fiduciary a custodian. UTMA § 1(7). It refers to a minor as an individual who has not yet attained age 21. UTMA § 1(11). The age of majority does not matter. The Uniform Law Commission retained age 21 in part because that age is allowed by the federal gift tax exclusion for certain transfers of future interests. I.R.C. § 2503(c).

The UTMA is not part of the Uniform Probate Code, but several UPC provisions authorize payments to the custodian of a UTMA account. Unlike the UPC, the UTMA has been enacted in every state. UTMA § 9 provides language a transferor can use in making a transfer to a custodianship account.

A custodianship account can have only one custodian and be for the benefit of only one minor. UTMA § 10. In that regard, it is more limiting than a trust with respect to the fiduciary's discretion regarding distributions. The custodian must use the standard of care that a prudent person would use in dealing with another person's property. It must maintain records and allow inspection by the minor's parent or legal representative. A minor who is at least age 14 also has the right to inspect these records. UTMA § 12.

The custodian has the same powers over the minor's property as an unmarried adult would have over her own property. The custodian must exercise those powers only in a custodial capacity. UTMA § 13. The UTMA includes provisions for use of custodial property, actions against the custodian, and termination of the custodianship when the minor attains a specified age or dies.

The UTMA was adopted more than 40 years ago. Not surprisingly, it does not address developments such as the use of prepaid tuition savings plans (authorized by I.R.C. § 529) or ABLE accounts (authorized by I.R.C. § 529A). The Uniform Law Commission's Transfers to Minors Committee plans to address these matters, raising the termination age, and allowing joint custodianships.

A related statute, the Uniform Custodial Trust Act, operates in similar fashion but allows for adult beneficiaries. It was adopted in 1987, and has been enacted in 18 states.

4. Health Care Fiduciary

An individual who worries about being unable to communicate with health care professionals because of declining physical or mental capacity might authorize another person to act on his behalf or might issue other advance directives concerning his care. The Uniform Health-Care Decisions Act provides for designating an agent to make health-care decisions on his behalf. Only a handful of states enacted the 1993 version, and only one has enacted the 2023 version; only three states have enacted the Uniform Recognition of Substitute Decision-Making Documents Act. Most states do have statutes dealing with advance decisionmaking and health care surrogates These statutes might be grouped with provisions dealing with health care rather than with a state's probate or estates and trusts provisions.

5. Personal Representative

The discussion of the personal representative's powers and duties focuses on an estate that is subject to a traditional probate administration process. It ignores UPC and comparable state provisions governing international wills, informal probate, succession without administration, and matters related to jurisdiction and venue. Discussion in this chapter does not repeat material, such as the preference for distributing the estate in kind, covered earlier in the book. Discussion here is relatively brief to limit duplication of the topics covered below for trustees.

A testator can nominate a personal representative, but she does not have to. Even if she does nominate a personal representative, her nominee might not ultimately serve. The nominee might fail to satisfy any relevant state qualifications, be unwilling or unable to serve, or die before the testator. The court overseeing the probate process will either appoint the person selected by the testator or appoint another person. If the decedent was intestate, the court will appoint the representative. State statutes provide an order of priority.

a. Powers

UPC § 3-711 describes the personal representative's powers in general terms. He has the same power over the title to property of the estate that an absolute owner would have, but he holds his power in trust for the benefit of creditors and other interested persons. Twenty-seven specific powers are listed in UPC § 3-715. These powers can be limited by the will or by the court. These powers include retaining assets, receiving assets, performing or compromising contracts entered into by the decedent, satisfying charitable pledges (including pledges that are not binding), prudently investing funds not yet needed, acquiring or disposing of assets, leasing or mortgaging property, and satisfying claims.

b. *Duties*

UPC § 3-703 begins by stating that the personal representative is a fiduciary and is held to the standards of care imposed on a trustee. It establishes a general duty: settle and distribute the decedent's estate in accordance with the terms of any will and do so expeditiously and efficiently in the best interests of the estate. The personal representative must notify heirs and devisees of his appointment. UPC § 3-705. They are entitled to information and are most likely to be involved in any will contests or other disputes involving the estate. He must compile an inventory of the estate, have it valued, and take possession of estate property. UPC §§ 3-706 through 3-709.

The personal representative must notify creditors by publication, mail, or other means required or allowed by statute. UPC § 3-801. He must satisfy claims in the order provided in UPC § 3-805 if estate assets are insufficient to pay all claims. The personal representative can complete his duties by distributing estate assets according to the rules in UPC §§ 3-902 through 3-915. Those provisions cover topics discussed earlier (abatement, exoneration, and distribution in kind) and other matters, such as offsets for debt owed by a beneficiary and partition of undivided property interests.

c. *Liability*

UPC § 3-712 makes the personal representative liable to interested persons for damages or loss caused by his breach of his fiduciary duty. He is liable to the same extent as he would be if he was the trustee of an express trust. In addition, if he has dealt with the estate in a manner that involves a substantial conflict of interest, an interested person can have the transaction voided. UPC § 3-713. The transaction will not be voided if the decedent expressly authorized it or the court approved it.

The personal representative can also be liable on contracts he enters into on behalf of the estate if he fails to indicate to the other party that he is acting in a representative capacity. He is liable for torts only if he is personally at fault. UPC § 3-808.

C. Trustees and Trust Directors

A trustee might begin serving while the settlor of an inter vivos trust is alive; if a testamentary trust is created, her service will not begin until the testator dies. In each instance, the term trustee can refer to the original trustee, a successor trustee, or a cotrustee. Because the settlor can serve as trustee, the original trustee is not necessarily the person who will ultimately administer the trust after the settlor's death. Although the discussion below refers to the trustee as she, a trust with significant assets that is intended to benefit several generations is likely to have a corporate trustee.

The discussion in this section focuses on a sole trustee who is not the settlor. It considers the trustee's powers, duties, and potential for liability. The trustee's powers and duties come primarily from three sources: the trust instrument; the relevant statutes; and court orders. Because the relevant statutes often indicate that common-law rules also apply if not superseded by statute, those rules can also be relevant. The discussion in this chapter focuses on two uniform acts, the Uniform Trust Code (UTC) and the Uniform Directed Trust Act (UDTA).

To some extent, the trustee's powers and duties depend on whether the trust is revocable. Until the settlor of an inter vivos trust releases his power to revoke or dies, the trustee owes her duties to him rather than to the other beneficiaries. UTC § 603(b). This provision contains optional language that terminates the settlor's power if he lacks capacity to revoke the trust. Her duty to the settlor affects how she administers the trust. UTC § 603(a) allows her to follow the settlor's directions, even if they contradict the terms of the trust, while the trust is revocable.

Even if the trust is irrevocable, the instrument might have given another person (the trust director) the power to direct the trustee's actions. In that case, she is to follow those directions unless she would be engaging in willful misconduct by complying. UDTA § 9(b). The trust director has the same fiduciary duty and liability as a trustee. UDTA § 8(a).

1. Powers

UTC § 815 lists the trustee's general powers. The first of the general powers is simple; it allows the trustee to exercise powers granted by the terms of the trust. Unless the jurisdiction allows oral trusts, those terms will appear in the trust instrument. The settlor need not grant any powers in the trust instrument and might not do so if he is satisfied with the statutory defaults. He can use the trust instrument if he wants to limit or expand powers covered by statutory defaults. He might also use the trust instrument to instruct the trustee regarding his preferences for the exercise of discretionary powers.

The other three general powers apply unless and to the extent that the trust instrument provides otherwise. First, the trustee can exercise the powers that an unmarried, competent individual could exercise over his own property. Unlike the power an individual can exercise over his own property, however, the trustee's power is subject to her fiduciary duty to the beneficiaries. Second, the trustee can also exercise any powers that are appropriate to achieving her three main duties as a trustee: properly investing, managing, and distributing trust property. Third, the trustee can exercise any powers conferred by the trust code.

UTC § 816 lists 26 specific powers or groups of powers. This section complements UTC § 815. A trustee may exercise a power not listed in UTC § 816 if it is appropriate under the other section's general grant of powers. The 26 powers relate to trust property, to trust administration, and to distribution of trust assets and termination of the trust.

Powers related to trust property include collecting the trust property and accepting (or rejecting) additions to that property; acquiring or selling property; partitioning property; depositing funds at a financial institution; borrowing money and using trust property as security; continuing to operate a business placed in trust; exercising the rights that an owner would over stocks and other securities owned by the trust; improving or repairing real property; entering into leases as lessor or lessee; granting or acquiring options to purchase or sell property; insuring property; abandoning property whose value makes it not worth the costs of administering it; and investigating and dealing with environmental issues related to property.

Powers with respect to administration include paying trust administration expenses; making tax elections; selecting payment methods for any benefits to which the trust is entitled under an insurance policy, pension plan, or other benefit plan; loaning trust funds, including to beneficiaries; pledging trust assets to third parties who have made loans to beneficiaries; and appointing a trustee to act with regard to trust property in another jurisdiction. Other powers related to administration include resolving disputes over trust interpretation and administration; prosecuting or defending claims to protect trust property; and executing contracts that facilitate the exercise of the trustee's powers.

Powers with respect to distributions include options for distributing funds to or on behalf of a beneficiary who is under a legal disability or appears to be incapacitated; making distributions of divided or undivided interests; and exercising any powers necessary to wind up the trust and distribute its assets.

UTC § 814 imposes a fiduciary limit on the trustee's exercise of discretionary powers. Even if the trust instrument uses language that purports to give her power to act in her sole discretion, she is to act in good faith and in the beneficiaries' interests. UTC § 814 imposes two other limits, which can be waived if the settlor expressly waives them in the trust instrument. First, if as trustee she has the power to make discretionary distributions to herself as beneficiary, she can do so only in accordance with an ascertainable standard. Even if she can distribute property to other beneficiaries for their "happiness" or other indefinite purpose, she cannot do so for herself. Second, she cannot make discretionary distributions to satisfy her legal obligation of support. Neither of these limits applies to the settlor's spouse if she is the trustee of a trust for which the settlor received a marital deduction based on the spouse having a life estate and a general power of appointment. These limits are also inapplicable while the trust is revocable. Finally, these limits do not apply if the trust qualifies for the gift tax annual exclusion based on the power of withdrawal qualifying as a present interest. Marital deduction trusts and powers of withdrawal are discussed in other chapters.

The trust instrument might give a power of direction to a trust director. UDTA § 6. The comments to that section list numerous powers the trust instrument might grant. These include acquiring property, modifying the trust, determining whether the trustee (or even the settlor) has capacity, and adopting a valuation method for trust property. As noted above, a directed trustee follows these directions unless that would result in her engaging in willful misconduct.

2. Duties

Trustee duties are listed in a group of provisions, beginning with UTC § 801. Keep in mind that any duty listed in UTC § 105(b) cannot be waived by a provision in the trust instrument. The first nonwaivable duty is to act in good faith and in accordance with the terms and purposes of the trust and in the best interests of the beneficiaries. UTC § 105(b)(2). That duty appears in UTC § 801.

UTC § 802 imposes a duty of loyalty. The trustee must act solely for the beneficiaries. This provision makes self-dealing by the trustee and transactions that involve a conflict of interest voidable by a beneficiary. The trustee does not breach this duty if the trust instrument authorized the transaction, a court approved it, the beneficiary did not challenge it soon enough, the beneficiary consented to the conduct, ratified it, or released the trustee from liability, or the transaction involved a contract or claim that the trustee entered into before she became the trustee or contemplated becoming the trustee.

Example 24-1. Tonya is the trustee of the ABC Trust. The trust instrument allows her to purchase trust property after receiving three competent appraisals. If Tonya purchased land from ABC without obtaining an appraisal, she has breached her duty of loyalty.

UTC § 802 applies both to direct and indirect benefit. It can apply if the other party to the transaction is related to the trustee instead of actually being the trustee. In addition, this section allows a beneficiary to void a transaction he entered into with the trustee and from which the trustee derived an advantage. The beneficiary can void the transaction even though no trust property is involved unless the trustee establishes that the transaction was fair to the beneficiary.

UTC § 803 applies to trusts with more than one beneficiary. The trust might have multiple beneficiaries with respect to the same interest, such as two beneficiaries receiving current trust income. It might have sequential beneficiaries, such as one or more income beneficiaries who will be succeeded by successor income beneficiaries or by recipients of trust principal. Some, but not necessarily all, current beneficiaries might want the trustee to maximize trust income; principal beneficiaries will prefer an investment strategy that increases the value of the underlying trust principal. UTC § 803 requires the trustee to act impartially in investing, managing, and distributing trust property and to give due regard to the beneficiaries' respective interests. The trust instrument can authorize or mandate the trustee to prefer one group to another, and it often will do so. The investment and distribution powers discussed in the next chapter are relevant to the trustee's performance of this duty.

UTC § 804 requires the trustee to act prudently and to exercise reasonable care, skill, and caution. The trustee is to consider the trust's purposes, terms, distributional requirements, and other circumstances.

UTC § 805 imposes a duty of incurring only reasonable costs in administering the trust. This requirement takes into account the trust property and purposes as well as the trustee's skills. A trustee who is not a professional fiduciary, for example, might reasonably incur additional costs in seeking investment or other advice. This section can be read in conjunction with UTC § 807, which allows a trustee to delegate powers and duties that a prudent person would delegate under the circumstances. The trustee must use reasonable care, skill, and caution in selecting the agent, defining the scope of the agent's authority, and reviewing the agent's actions.

UTC § 806 requires a trustee with special skills or expertise to use them in administering the trust. It also applies to a trustee who was selected because she represented that she had such skills or expertise.

UTC § 809 requires the trustee to take reasonable steps to take control of and protect the trust property. UTC § 810 requires the trustee to maintain adequate records of the trust's administration and not to commingle her property with that of the trust. If trust property is registered or titled, she is to take steps to see that the property is identified as that of the trust on the other party's records. UTC § 812 requires her to take reasonable steps to claim trust property from a predecessor trustee and to seek redress of breaches by that trustee.

UTC § 811 requires the trustee to take reasonable steps to enforce the trust's claims against others. It also requires her to take reasonable steps to defend claims brought against the trust.

The reporting duties imposed by UTC § 813 are owed to different groups. Qualified beneficiaries are entitled to be reasonably informed about the trust administration and about material facts necessary for them to protect their interests. She must notify them within 60 days after she accepts the trusteeship of her name, address, and telephone number. She must also notify them of the trust's existence, the settlor's identity, their right to request a copy of the instrument, and their right to a trustee's report. These duties arise within 60 days after she learns of the creation of an irrevocable trust or of a revocable trust's becoming irrevocable. Finally, she must notify them in advance of a change in her rate of compensation or method of computing her compensation.

She must also make available an annual report of the trust property, liabilities, receipts, and disbursements, including information about her compensation, and information about trust assets and, if feasible, their respective market values. She must send this report to distributees and permissible distributees. She does not have to send it to other beneficiaries unless they request it.

Example 24-2. Tammy is the trustee of the DEF Trust. The trust instrument requires her to distribute one-half of the trust income each year to Ben. She has the discretion to distribute the other half to Beth in whatever amount she considers appropriate and to add undistributed income to principal. After the death of the survivor of Ben and Beth, the trust will continue for another 50 years, paying income to their children. The trust will then terminate and a local charity will receive the principal. Ben is a distributee; he is entitled to distributions. Beth is a permissible distributee. They both are qualified beneficiaries because they are distributees or permissible distributees. If they already have children, those children would be qualified beneficiaries now, but they would not be distributees or permissible distributees until Ben and Beth have both died.

Beneficiaries can waive their rights to notice; they do not have to make an irrevocable waiver. The UTC places limits on the settlor's ability to waive these rights. UTC § 105(b)(8)–(9).

3. Liability

Because a trustee is a fiduciary, she might be liable to beneficiaries when she violates a fiduciary duty. In some instances, she could be liable despite the beneficiaries' not suffering a loss. In limited situations, she could be personally liable to third parties.

a. Liability to Trust Beneficiaries

The trustee's liability to trust beneficiaries depends on the nature of the breach and on the effect of exculpatory language or the beneficiaries' own actions. The starting point in determining trustee liability is with UTC § 1001, which provides that any violation of a trustee's duties to beneficiaries is a breach of trust. That section lists actions a court can take in response to the breach of trust. Some of these responses involve the administration of the trust. The court can compel the trustee to perform her duties, enjoin her from committing a breach, order her to account, appoint a special fiduciary, suspend her, remove her, void her actions, or order any other appropriate relief. Other actions are financial. The court can compel her to pay money or restore property; it can also reduce or deny her compensation. The court can also impose a constructive trust on trust property or trace and recover property wrongfully disposed of by the trustee. These remedies are derived from the Restatement (Second) of Trusts § 199.

UTC § 1002 provides a formula for determining damages for which the trustee is liable. The first alternative is based on making the beneficiaries whole. The trustee must restore the trust property and distributions to what they would have been if there had not been a breach. Because this option might result in no damages, where a breach occurred but did not cause financial loss, we look to the second alternative. The trustee must disgorge any profit she made because of the breach. The trustee must pay whichever of those two amounts is greater.

Example 24-3. While serving as trustee of the GHI Trust, Teri sold trust property to herself for $5,000 less than its appraised value. Three weeks later, she sold the property for a profit of $8,000. Teri must pay damages of $8,000. If she had made only a $2,000 profit, she would be liable for damages of $5,000.

UTC § 1003(a) goes further and makes a trustee liable for any profit she makes from administering the trust even if she does not breach a duty. If, for example, a trustee accepted a gratuity for using a particular professional to work on trust business, this section would apply. The mere fact that the trust loses value or fails to make a profit on a transaction does not result in trustee liability if the trustee did not commit a breach. UTC § 1003(b).

A trustee might commit an "innocent" breach by reasonably relying on the terms of the trust instrument. She is not liable for damages for a breach caused by that reliance. UTC § 1006. The trustee is also not liable for failing to act in response to a change in circumstance of which she was unaware so long as she used reasonable care to determine if the event had occurred. UTC § 1007. This section is a change from the common law's imposition of strict liability.

1. Exculpatory Language in Instrument

If the trust instrument includes exculpatory language, its effectiveness depends on the type of behavior being covered. The UTC does not specifically preclude relieving the trustee of liability for profit derived from the breach. It makes an exculpation provision unenforceable if it relieves the trustee of liability for a breach of trust committed in bad faith or with reckless indifference to the trust's purposes or the beneficiaries' interests. UTC § 1008(a)(1). It is also unenforceable if it was inserted into the trust instrument as a result of the trustee's abuse of a fiduciary or confidential relationship to the settlor. UTC § 1008(a)(2). An exculpatory term drafted by the trustee is treated as an abuse unless she establishes that the term was fair under the circumstances *and* that the term and its contents were adequately explained to the settlor. UTC § 1008(b). The comments indicate that this provision is satisfied if the settlor was represented by independent counsel. UTC § 105(b)(10) provides that the trust instrument cannot prevail over the language of UTC § 1008.

2. Consent, Release, or Ratification

Under general principles of equitable estoppel, a beneficiary under no disability who requested or consented to an action by the trustee cannot, in equity, complain of that action. The same is true if the beneficiary discharges by release or contract the trustee's liability for breach of trust or if the beneficiary ratifies, after the fact, the breach of trust. Restatement (Second) of Trusts §§ 216–218. UTC § 1009 does not allow the trustee to avoid liability based on consent, release, or ratification if her improper conduct induced the beneficiary to take that action. She is also prevented from avoiding liability if the beneficiary was unaware of his rights or of the material facts related to the breach.

b. Liability to Third Parties

UTC § 1010(a) limits the trustee's liability for contracts made in the proper course of administration of the trust. The trustee is not personally liable on such contracts if she discloses the fiduciary capacity in the contract. UTC § 1010(b) limits her personal liability for torts committed in the administration of a trust. She is liable for acts or omissions only if she was personally at fault. The trust instrument cannot waive this liability to third parties. UTC § 105(b)(11).

c. Liability to Settlor

While a trust is revocable, the trustee owes her duties to the settlor. But the trustee might act in good faith before she receives notice that the settlor has amended or revoked the trust's terms. For example, she might distribute trust property to a beneficiary before she receives notice that the settlor has revoked or amended the trust. The UTC provides that she is not liable to the settlor or the settlor's successors in interest for actions taken based on her assumption that the trust had not been revoked or amended. UTC § 602(g).

4. Multiple Fiduciaries

A trust might have a single trustee or multiple trustees. UTC § 703 anticipates that cotrustees will act unanimously but allows them to act by majority decision if they cannot all agree. Each trustee must exercise reasonable care to prevent a cotrustee from committing a breach of trust. When there is a breach of trust by more than one trustee, a trustee who pays damages is entitled to contribution from any other breaching trustee. The trustee is not entitled to contribution if she was substantially more at fault, acted in bad faith, or acted with reckless indifference to the interests of the trust and its beneficiaries. UTC § 1002(b).

A trust might have a trust director in addition to one or more trustees. Unless the trust instrument requires monitoring, a trust director is not required to monitor a trustee, and a trustee is not required to monitor a trust director. Likewise, neither is required to inform the settlor, a beneficiary, or another fiduciary that she might have acted differently than the other fiduciary did. UDTA § 11.

CHECKPOINTS

- An individual can appoint an agent to act on her behalf under a power of attorney. Court intervention is limited. If the power is durable, it remains in effect even if the principal becomes incapacitated.
- A minor or an incapacitated person might have a guardian appointed for his person and a conservator for his property. These fiduciaries are subject to court supervision.
- A donor can make transfers for a minor to a custodian who will act on the minor's behalf. The custodian must provide reports to the minor's parents or other designated recipient.
- An individual can appoint a surrogate to make health care decisions on her behalf.
- The personal representative of an estate is responsible for taking control of the decedent's property, satisfying claims, and distributing any remaining property to beneficiaries.
- The personal representative's powers and duties are comparable to those of a trustee.
- A trustee owes duties only to the trust's settlor until the trust becomes irrevocable.

- The trust instrument might list the trustee's powers and duties. The applicable statute applies to the extent powers and duties are not covered in the instrument or the statute overrides the instrument.
- The UTC lists powers and duties related to trust property, to trust administration, to distribution of trust assets and termination of the trust, and to notice to beneficiaries.
- A trustee is liable to beneficiaries for damages caused by a breach of her duty or, if greater, for any profit she made on account of the breach.
- Trustee duties include acting in good faith, loyalty, impartiality, and exercising reasonable care and skill.
- A trustee can be held liable to third persons with respect to contracts if she failed to indicate she was acting as a representative. She is liable for torts only if she is personally at fault.
- The trust instrument might provide for a trust director, who can direct a trustee's actions as provided for in the trust instrument. The trust director is a fiduciary but is not acting as a trustee.

CHAPTER 25

Income, Expense, and Investment

ROADMAP

- Relevant documents
- Overview of accounting principles
- Principal and income: probate estate
- Principal and income: property held in trust
- Investing trust assets

A. Chapter Overview

Because other topics are likely to exhaust the available time, the allocation of receipts and outlays between principal and income beneficiaries might receive little discussion in a trusts and estates course. Not surprisingly, in practice these concepts are important to the fiduciary, who must treat all beneficiaries impartially, and to the beneficiaries themselves. This chapter introduces the concepts of principal and income and the general rules for allocating them among beneficiaries. It focuses on the Uniform Fiduciary Income and Principal Act (UFIPA). Keep in mind that, although you might often hear the terms used interchangeably, income does not have the same meaning as receipts, and expenses are not necessarily the same as outlays.

The fiduciary, again primarily the trustee because of the longer time period involved, must do more than allocate current income and expense between principal and income. She must invest the assets in a manner that benefits income beneficiaries, successor income beneficiaries, and the ultimate recipients of the underlying assets. The discussion of investments in this chapter focuses on obligations imposed by the Uniform Prudent Investor Act (UPIA).

B. Relevant Documents

As is true for the general administration of wills and trusts, the intent of the testator or the settlor governs unless a statute or judicial decision provides otherwise. State law is likely to diverge from that expressed intent only to effectuate an important public policy.

The Uniform Fiduciary Income and Principal Act, approved in 2018, replaced the Revised Uniform Principal and Income Act. By mid-September 2024, it had been enacted in eight states. As is true for other uniform acts, a state that has enacted UFIPA might have enacted provisions that differ from it in various respects; the relevant statute in a state that has not enacted UFIPA might nevertheless resemble it.

The UFIPA requires the fiduciary to follow the allocation rules provided in the instrument even if those differ from UFIPA provisions. UFIPA § 201(a)(3). If the fiduciary exercises a discretionary power of allocation authorized by the instrument, that exercise does not create an inference of abuse of discretion even if the outcome differs from that in the act. UFIPA § 201(b). If the instrument neither contains a different rule nor gives the fiduciary a discretionary power, the act's allocation provisions apply. UFIPA § 201(a)(4). If a receipt or outlay is not addressed in the instrument or in the act, the fiduciary is to allocate it to principal. UFIPA § 201(c)(1).

The act echoes provisions in the UTC about impartiality. Unless the governing instrument favors a particular beneficiary or group of beneficiaries, the fiduciary is to administer the entity in a manner that is fair and reasonable to all beneficiaries. If she follows the UFIPA provisions, she is presumed to have acted in a fair and reasonable manner. UFIPA § 201(b).

Federal tax statutes relating to an entity's taxable income are also relevant. These statutes cover the computation of the entity's taxable income and allocating it between the entity and its beneficiaries.

C. Overview of Accounting Principles

Trusts and estates compute their income for several purposes: allocating receipts and outlays between income and principal; making periodic reports to beneficiaries; computing the entity's income taxes; and reporting entity-related tax consequences to beneficiaries. The fiduciary must select an accounting period and an accounting method. The discussion below only introduces the issues. It is not a comprehensive discussion of trust accounting.

1. Accounting Period

Entities report their net income on an annual basis, although they might issue more frequent reports to their beneficiaries. An entity that reports on a calendar-year basis ends its year on December 31. If it reports on a fiscal-year basis, it ends its year on the last day of a month other than December. If the fiduciary does not select a fiscal year, the entity reports using a calendar year. UFIPA § 102(1).

An entity begins its first accounting period when it comes into existence. It ends its final accounting period when it ends its existence, which can include a reasonable period for winding up its affairs. As a result, those two periods are likely to be shorter than a year. Accounting periods used to report to beneficiaries might also be shorter than a year when a beneficiary's income interest begins or ends at a time other than the normal year end. UFIPA § 102(1).

For federal income tax purposes, a trust must use a calendar year. I.R.C. § 644(a). This rule does not apply to estates.

2. Accounting Method

The testator or settlor can select the accounting methods unless the relevant state statute requires a particular method. Federal tax statutes might mandate particular accounting methods for tax reporting even if the entity uses different methods for other reporting purposes.

The two most common accounting methods are the cash receipts and disbursements method (cash method) and the accrual method. Entities using the cash method report income when it is actually or constructively received; they report expenses when they are paid. Entities using the accrual method report income and expenses when they are due. The "due date" varies depending on whether the income or expense is based on an event or accrues over time.

The accrual method uses the term "incurred" to report expenses that do not accrue over time and the term "accrued" to report expenses that accrue over time. A bill for legal fees to the estate would be an incurred expense. Interest owed on a debt would be an accrued expense.

> **Example 25-1.** In January, the trustee of the ABC Trust deposited \$30,000 in a certificate of deposit (CD) at the XYZ Bank. Interest accrues at the rate of 4% a year. Interest is payable quarterly (at the rate of 1%) and is added to the balance in the account. During the period ended March 31, XYZ deposited \$300 in ABC's account. If the trustee reported income to the beneficiaries on February 28, it would include nothing on the cash method but would include \$200 on the accrual method. Interest received or paid accrues over time even though payable only at fixed dates. The same is true for rents received or paid.

The distinction between cash and accrual is relevant in determining in which accounting period to report the item. But that distinction is not the only one the fiduciary must make. The entity might own an asset that is subject to wear and tear, exhaustion, or obsolescence. The fiduciary must account for depreciation of assets that become less useful over time or depletion if it owns a mineral deposit. Although the entity does not expend funds, failure to account for the diminutions in value results in reports that overstate entity assets.

> **Example 25-2.** In his will, Seth devised a rental house worth \$100,000 to the trustee of the STU Testamentary Trust. The trustee is to pay the trust's net income to his daughter Denise for life. After Denise dies, the trustee is to distribute the trust principal to Seth's descendants. This year the trustee received \$10,000 in rents and paid \$2,000 in property taxes and minor repairs. The trustee might also compute a reasonable deduction for depreciation, based on the useful life of the building, because buildings are subject to wear and tear. (Because land does not depreciate, the trustees must first allocate the initial \$100,000 between the building and the land on which it sits.) The trustee will distribute less than \$8,000 to Denise if it transfers cash receipts from income to principal to reflect reasonable depreciation. This adjustment offsets the potential reduction in the value ultimately received by the remainder beneficiaries. UFIPA § 503.

Not every outlay is an expense. As a general rule, outlays to acquire or improve assets are treated as part of the cost of those assets; they are not current expenses. In effect, trust cash is being replaced by other assets.

A final item that can cause difficulty relates to gains and losses. Entity assets might increase or decrease in value after the fiduciary acquires them. Until the fiduciary disposes of the property, the gain or loss is unrealized. When the fiduciary disposes of the property, the entity realizes the gain or loss. Realized gains and losses might reflect changes that took place over many years. The fiduciary must determine how to take those into account in computing entity income and allocating it among current and future beneficiaries.

D. Principal and Income: Probate Estate

1. Overview

Investment property in the probate estate could produce income before the personal representative completes the probate process and distributes the estate's assets to devisees or intestate heirs. Expenses paid or incurred during probate might relate to the estate as a whole or to particular items of property.

During probate administration, the personal representative might receive payments from two sources. First, if the decedent owned income-producing property, the personal representative might receive interest, dividends, rents, or royalties with respect to that property. Second, she might receive amounts owed the decedent for services he performed before his death; these include unpaid salary or fees. Estate assets might also include rights to income that the personal representative does not receive before probate ends.

The personal representative must also make outlays, including her own fee and other expenses of administration, expenses of the decedent's funeral, expenses to maintain probate property, and claims against the decedent that were unpaid at his death. To pay these obligations, she might sell probate property, which could result in a gain or a loss.

If the decedent died intestate, his intestate heirs simply receive whatever is left after accounting for these items and for any superior rights of the surviving spouse and children. The results are similar if the decedent used only a residuary devise in his will. The residuary devisees share the remaining property in the proportions specified in the will. If the will fails to specify proportions, they will share equally unless some of them are taking by representation. In that case, they share according to the jurisdiction's representation rules. The only exceptions relate to property to which the spouse or other family members have superior rights, for example, the right to exempt property or an elective share.

> **Example 25-3.** Tom devised "my estate to my children." All five of Tom's children survived. After collecting the estate assets and paying claims and expenses, the personal representative will distribute one-fifth of the remaining assets to each child.

If the testator's will included specific or general devises, we must determine if those devisees are entitled to any income earned, and are subject to any expenses incurred, during probate. Residuary devisees receive any remaining property after expenses, claims, and devises with priority are satisfied.

2. Uniform Act Provisions

In administering property devised by will, the personal representative must first determine whether devises are specific, general, or residuary. It then allocates receipts and disbursements among the devisees.

A specific devisee is entitled to the net income and the net principal receipts attributable to specifically devised property. UFIPA § 601(b).

> **Example 25-4.** Ted devised his rental land to his brother Ben. Ben receives the land and any rent the personal representative receives during administration, offset by any appropriately allocated outlays. If the will provided that all net income received during administration was to be paid to the residuary devisee, Ben would receive only the land. The language of the instrument governs.

After accounting for specifically devised property, the personal representative then computes the estate's remaining net income. UFIPA § 601(c) includes rules for this computation. The recipient of an outright pecuniary devise will receive both the amount devised and interest allocable to that devise if the will provides for interest. If the estate's income is not sufficient, the personal representative is to pay the allocable income from other estate assets. UFIPA § 601(d). The devisee's share of estate income is determined by the terms of the will or by applicable law if the will is silent. For example, the UPC provides that the recipient of a general pecuniary devise is entitled to the statutory rate of interest, but that interest does not begin to accrue until one year after the personal representative is appointed. This rule is subject to contrary language in the will. UPC § 3-904. State laws might differ from the UPC by accruing interest from a time based on the testator's death, which the comments note is the common-law rule, or by not providing for interest on pecuniary devises.

E. Principal and Income: Property Held in Trust

1. Overview

Principal and income provisions are generally more important for a trustee than for an estate's personal representative because of the longer time period involved. A decedent does not have a probate estate until she dies. Unless that estate is particularly complicated, it will probably be closed and the property distributed within a year and often sooner. If she wants to create a trust, she can do so while she is alive or in her will.

Both inter vivos and testamentary trusts can last for as long as allowed by the jurisdiction's rule against perpetuities. The trustee's allocation between principal and income thus affects the current income beneficiaries, any successor income beneficiaries, and—ultimately—any beneficiaries who receive trust principal. Not surprisingly, the UFIPA trust provisions are more extensive than UFIPA estate provisions.

2. General Uniform Act Provisions

A trust is likely to have several beneficiary groups. It might have one or more current income beneficiaries and be required to terminate when their interest ends. Alternatively, it might have successive income interests, which might continue as long as the rule against perpetuities allows. The trustee might be required to distribute all the trust income to its income beneficiaries, or it might have the discretion to retain income. The trustee might have to treat all income beneficiaries equally, or it might have discretion to distribute unequal amounts. The trustee might even have the discretion to invade principal for an income beneficiary who would not otherwise receive a distribution of principal when the trust terminates.

The trust instrument might indicate how the trustee is to allocate income among groups of beneficiaries and whether to favor any particular group or beneficiary within a group. In the absence of such directions, we consider UFIPA provisions covering when an income interest begins and ends and how receipts and outlays are to be allocated between income and principal.

3. Beginning and Ending an Income Interest

UFIPA § 701(a) and (c) provide general rules about when an income beneficiary's right to income begins. Unless the trust instrument provides otherwise, the right begins on the day an asset becomes subject to the trust. A successive income beneficiary's interest begins on the day after the preceding income interest ends.

UFIPA § 701(d) provides rules for ending the beneficiary's right to income. An income interest that ends because of the beneficiary's death ends on the day before that death occurs. An income interest that ends because of a different terminating event ends on the day before that event occurs. An income interest also ends on the last day of a period during which there is no beneficiary to receive distributions even if the trust continues.

The time when an asset becomes subject to the trust depends on how the trust is created and funded. If the settlor creates an inter vivos trust, the asset becomes subject to the trust as soon as it is transferred to the trust. If the trust is established in the testator's will, the asset becomes subject to the trust when she dies. It does not matter that the asset will not be distributed to the trust until the estate administration concludes. Finally, property might be transferred to a trust because of an individual's death, but the transfer could be made by someone other than the personal representative. For example, the trust might be the beneficiary of a policy insuring the decedent's life. The insurance company will transfer the proceeds to the trustee after it receives evidence of the insured's death. The property is treated as subject to the trust on the date of that death. UFIPA § 701(b).

Example 25-5. Sarah created an inter vivos trust by transferring property to a trustee. Her 5-year-old grandson George will receive the income for 15 years. Income will then be paid to George's children until the youngest child attains age 25. The trust will terminate at that point, and the trustee will distribute the trust principal to Sarah's descendants. George's income interest begins on the day the trust is funded; it ends the day before the 15-year term ends. At that point, George could not possibly have a child who has attained age 25; he might not yet have had any children. If George has at least one child, the successive income interest begins when the 15-year period expires. If George does not yet have a child when his income interest ends, there is no beneficiary to receive the income until a child is born.

4. Allocation When Interest Begins and Ends

The cash versus accrual distinction has relevance in determining whether distributions to a trustee are allocated to income or principal. UFIPA § 702(a) applies when a trustee that receives property from an estate has income receipts or disbursements with a due date that precedes the decedent's death. The section treats the item as principal. That treatment makes sense; if the decedent had received the income or made the disbursement while alive, the amount transferred to the trust would have reflected the income received by or the outlays made by the decedent. The same rule applies to receipts or disbursements before an income interest begins.

If an income receipt or disbursement has a periodic due date *and* is due on or after the decedent's death, the trustee is to allocate it to income. UFIPA § 702(b). If the item does not have a periodic due date, or has no due date, the trustee is to treat it as accruing from day to day. The portion accruing before the decedent dies is allocated to principal; the rest is allocated to income. The same rule applies to receipts or disbursements before an income interest begins. UFIPA § 702(c).

UFIPA § 702(d) and (e) define the meaning of the terms used in the preceding paragraphs. A due date is the date on which the payor is to make the payment. The payment does not have a due date if none is specified. Due dates are periodic if payment is due, or customarily made, at regular intervals. The UFIPA treats corporate dividends as due on the date the entity fixes for determining who is entitled to receive them; that is often referred to as the record date. If the entity does not use a fixed date, the payment is due on the date the entity declares it. UFIPA § 702(f).

UFIPA § 703(b) applies to the time when an interest ends. Unless the terms of the trust provide otherwise, the beneficiary of mandatory income distributions is to receive her share of any undistributed income. If she has died, and her death caused the interest to end, the trustee distributes her share of undistributed income to her estate. UFIPA § 703(a) indicates that undistributed income is defined with respect to income actually received.

> **Example 25-6.** Barbara is the sole income beneficiary of the ABC Trust, which her grandfather created several years ago. The trustee distributes all trust income to her on the last day of each calendar quarter. After her death, the trustee will distribute the trust principal to her descendants. Barbara has no power over trust principal. If she dies on March 1, her estate is entitled to income the trustee received in January and February. It is not entitled to receive income due but not yet received by the end of February.

Additional rules apply if the beneficiary had the power to withdraw more than 5% of the trust principal before his income interest ended or was entitled to a fixed annuity amount or fixed fraction of the trust's value. UFIPA § 703(c) and (d).

5. Trustee's Power to Adjust

The remainder of this section focuses on rules that trustees may or must follow in the absence of a governing trust provision. One of the most important rules appears in UFIPA § 203(a), which authorizes the trustee to adjust between income and principal if it believes exercising the power will assist it in administering the trust impartially.

UFIPA § 201(e) lists factors the trustee is to consider in deciding whether to make an adjustment. This list, which is not exclusive, covers the trust's terms, the beneficiaries' circumstances, needs—which can often conflict—for liquidity, regular income, and capital appreciation, anticipated economic conditions, trust terms relating to the trustee's power to invade principal or accumulate income—including prohibitions on invading or accumulating—and actual use of those powers in the past, and any anticipated tax consequences from an adjustment.

UFIPA § 203(e) lists several situations in which a trustee cannot make an adjustment, including making an adjustment that reduces an income interest in a trust that qualified for a special tax benefit, that changes the amount a beneficiary of a fixed annuity or unitrust interest would receive, or that involves a charitable interest unless both income and principal interests are set aside for charity. Not surprisingly, the trustee cannot make an adjustment if he is not an independent person.

6. Conversion to a Unitrust

It should not surprise you that current income beneficiaries might prefer that the trustee invest to maximize current income while remainder beneficiaries would prefer that the trustee invest to grow the trust principal. If the trust instrument provides which group should be favored, the trustee can act accordingly. If the trust instrument is silent, the trustee must follow an investment policy that meets its duty of impartiality.

One option is a unitrust, often referred to as a total return unitrust. Instead of distributing actual trust income to the current income beneficiary, the trustee will distribute a fixed percentage of the trust's value. If the trust value increases, both the income interest and the remainder interest share in that increase.

UFIPA Article 3 provides rules for using a unitrust model. Its comments note that 36 states had enacted unitrust provisions by the end of 2016. N.C. Gen. Stat. § 37A-1-104.4 (between 3% and 5%); N.Y. Est. Powers & Trusts Law § 11-2.4 (4%).

State unitrust provisions often mirror federal tax regulations for unitrusts. Those regulations specify a unitrust rate of between 3% and 5%. Treas. Reg. § 1.643(b)-1. The comments note that the UFIPA provisions for unitrusts are more flexible than those statutes mirroring the regulation. For example, UFIPA § 306 provides for fixed or varying unitrust rates and does not specify a minimum or maximum unitrust rate, and UFIPA § 308 provides more options for determining the valuation period.

7. Allocation of Receipts and Disbursements Between Income and Principal

The UFIPA has both general and specific provisions for allocating receipts and disbursements during the administration of a trust. Provisions governing receipts appear in UFIPA Article 4; provisions governing disbursements appear in UFIPA Article 5. The allocation provisions cover items that are normally apportioned between income and principal and those that are not.

It provides rules for trusts conducting a business, for assets such as copyright and minerals, and for taxes.

F. Investing Trust Assets

The discussion of allocating receipts and outlays between income and principal is based on an obvious premise, that the trust will have net receipts even after making any necessary outlays. In other words, the trust will have income to distribute or to add to principal.

Unless a trust produces income, the trustee cannot make distributions to income beneficiaries or must deplete principal to cover those distributions. The first option disadvantages the income beneficiaries; the second disadvantages beneficiaries who will receive trust principal. Even if the trust assets produce income, the trustee must determine if—given the settlor's goals for both income and principal beneficiaries—she is properly investing trust assets. The trustee must decide whether to retain the assets received from the settlor and, if she replaces those assets, what investments are appropriate.

The trust instrument might provide guidance by indicating whether the trustee should prefer the current income beneficiaries to the ultimate takers or vice versa. It might indicate any particular asset that the trustee should retain even if she disposes of other assets. It might indicate whether the settlor prefers that the income beneficiaries receive a predictable amount of income, even if the trustee must invest conservatively to guarantee that flow. It might provide instructions that vary based on the beneficiaries' age, health, or other circumstances.

If the trust instrument does not provide adequate guidance, the trustee can refer to statutes that list permissible investments or that describe factors she should consider in investing trust principal. The Uniform Prudent Investor Act (UPIA), approved by the Uniform Law Commission in 1994, is an example of a guiding statute. It has been adopted by every state except Delaware, Florida, Kentucky, Louisiana, New York, and Pennsylvania (with a substantially smaller version in Georgia).

To some extent the UPIA's terms overlap with the UTC trustee duty provisions discussed in the previous chapter. The use of the term prudent investor instead of the term prudent person focuses the trustee's attention on this particular aspect of her relationship to the trust's present and future beneficiaries. A reasonably prudent person might generally act with care in her dealings with others but might never be called on to invest assets on behalf of a third party.

The act imposes a duty on the trustee to comply with the prudent investor rule as a default rule. The trust provisions can expand, restrict, alter, or even eliminate the trustee's duty. UPIA § 1. The trustee's duties begin when she accepts her position or receives the assets. At that time, she is to review the assets and make decisions about which to retain and which to dispose of so that the portfolio complies with the statute, as modified by the trust instrument. UPIA § 4.

The Act covers both the investment and management of trust assets. In carrying out her duties, the trustee must take into account the trust purposes, the trust terms, any distribution requirements, and any other relevant trust circumstances. She must act with reasonable care, skill, and caution. This section requires that the overall risk and return objectives be reasonably suited to the trust. The trustee is judged in the aggregate, not on any single trust asset. If she has special skills or expertise, or her representation of herself as having those traits led to her appointment as trustee, she must use those skills or expertise. UPIA § 2.

Unlike the permissible investment lists that once were a common feature of state trust law, UPIA § 2(c) does not limit the trustee to acquiring any particular type of asset or preclude her from acquiring any particular type of asset. She is expected to consider relevant circumstances, including the economy as a whole, the possibility of inflation or deflation, which could affect the value of trust assets as well as beneficiary income requirements, potential tax consequences, how each investment fits as part of an overall portfolio, the total return expected from trust assets, the beneficiaries' other sources of income or capital, the trust's requirements for liquidity, regular income, and capital preservation or appreciation, and—with respect to individual assets—any special relationship or value those assets have to the trust or to a beneficiary.

Not surprisingly, the act imposes a duty to diversify. Appreciation or declines in value in one asset type may be less painful if the trust includes other assets that are influenced by different economic indicators. At the same time, the trustee can fail to diversify if she reasonably determines that, because of special circumstances, she can better serve the trust's purposes without diversifying. UPIA § 3. The comments note that a family business might constitute a significant trust asset; retaining the business might suit the settlor's purpose while making diversification almost impossible. The trustee might also decide to retain appreciated assets because of potential income tax concerns.

The trustee must invest solely for the beneficiaries' interests, and she must treat those beneficiaries impartially. She can consider the beneficiaries' different interests and still act impartially. UPIA §§ 5, 6. She should avoid incurring unreasonable or unnecessary costs. UPIA § 7. If she delegates investment or management functions to an agent, she must use care, skill, and caution in selecting the agent, setting the terms of delegation, and reviewing the agent's actions on a periodic basis. UPIA § 9.

CHECKPOINTS

- A fiduciary must determine which receipts and disbursements are allocable to principal and which to income.
- The fiduciary's decision affects beneficiaries of both estates and trusts.
- Because trusts generally last for long periods of time, the fiduciary's allocation can have cumulative effects on each category of beneficiaries.
- The Uniform Fiduciary Income and Principal Act provides rules covering when an interest begins and when it ends, receipts that are usually allocated and those that are not, and allocation of disbursements. In addition to general rules, it provides specific allocation rules for such assets as copyrights, minerals, and businesses operated by the trustee.
- The Uniform Fiduciary Income and Principal Act gives the trustee power to adjust the share of net income that is allocable to the income and principal beneficiaries if necessary to fairly allocate trust income.
- A trustee might have the power to convert a trust to a unitrust. In that case, the income beneficiary receives a percentage of the trust's value instead of the trust's actual income for the year. The trustee invests trust assets to produce an overall rate of return that benefits both income and principal beneficiaries.
- If the trust instrument does not provide otherwise, a trustee in most states is subject to the Uniform Prudent Investor Act in deciding how to invest trust assets.

- The act uses a reasonably prudent investor standard rather than a reasonably prudent person standard.
- The act judges a portfolio as a whole rather than judging a single asset.
- The trustee is to invest based on a variety of factors related to the economy and beneficiary circumstances.

CHAPTER 26

Federal Transfer Taxes

ROADMAP

- Gift tax
- Estate tax
- Generation-skipping transfer tax
- Miscellaneous tax consequences

A. Chapter Overview

Many of the transfers described in this book are structured to avoid probate or to limit creditor access. Others are designed to reduce the federal transfer taxes imposed on the property owner or his beneficiaries. Some of these devices originated in an era of relatively high transfer tax rates and low tax exemptions. Others are of more recent vintage. This chapter summarizes the interaction between the probate estate, other transfers, and the relevant federal transfer taxes; it covers only transfers between U.S. citizens. Transfer taxes are addressed in detail in courses on estate and gift tax and estate planning.

This chapter is general in nature for several reasons. First, the credits allocated to many trusts and estates courses do not justify spending significant class time on them. Second, the transfer tax exemptions in effect in 2024 are currently due to expire at the end of 2025. Congress will then have several choices: (1) extend the expiring exemptions; (2) do nothing, in which case the much lower exemptions in effect through 2017 will take effect; (3) enact exemptions that are less generous than those about to expire but more generous than those in effect before 2018; (4) eliminate exemptions; or (5) eliminate transfer taxes altogether. Options (4) and (5) are probably unlikely.

B. Gift Tax

The federal gift tax is currently imposed only if an individual's lifetime taxable gifts exceed an inflation-adjusted amount. That amount, which was $13,610,000 in 2024, is variously referred to as an exemption, a unified credit, an applicable credit, or an applicable exclusion. This book uses the term exemption to reflect the fact that the relevant amount is exempt from tax. It is computed and applied as a credit against the tax otherwise due. I.R.C. §§ 2010, 2505.

Individuals compute their taxable gifts annually. They pay no gift tax until their cumulative taxable gifts exceed the exemption in effect that year. A tax rate of 40% currently applies. I.R.C. §§ 2001(c), 2502.

The gift tax applies to *taxable* gifts, not to the gross amount of gifts. First, we must determine that the transferor made a gift subject to the gift tax. Second, we determine whether any exclusions or deductions reduce the gross amount to the amount that is potentially taxable.

1. Completed Gift

A transfer is subject to federal gift tax if it is a *completed gift*. Both italicized words are critical. For example, a transfer to a revocable trust does not constitute a completed gift; the settlor can retake the property at any time. The same is true if the settlor retains the right to change the beneficiaries, even if he has no right to revoke the trust, unless he has only a fiduciary power that is subject to a fixed or ascertainable standard. Treas. Reg. § 25.2511-2(c). On the other hand, if the settlor retains the right to income for life but has no right to retake the trust principal, he makes a completed gift of the principal. The value of that gift is less than the full value of the property because the donee cannot enjoy the property until the settlor's life estate terminates.

Not every completed transfer is a gift. A gift, for gift tax purposes, is a transfer in which the consideration received in money or money's worth, if any, is less than the value of the property being transferred. In other words, there can be a gift for gift tax purposes even in situations involving consideration that would be sufficient for an enforceable contract. Mere detriment to the recipient, for example, is not sufficient consideration to prevent the gift tax from applying. Treas. Reg. § 25.2512-8.

2. Gift Tax Exclusions

a. Gifts of a Present Interest

I.R.C. § 2503(b) provides a per-donee, per-year exclusion. In 2024, the exclusion was $18,000. Although the amount is adjusted for inflation, the adjustment formula does not result in an increase every year. The exclusion is large enough to let individuals of average means avoid keeping detailed records of annual birthday and holiday gifts.

The exclusion is available only for transfers that qualify as gifts of a present interest. As a general rule, the donor would have to make an outright gift. A vested remainder would not qualify because it is not presently enjoyed. A life estate, valued at its present value, could qualify because it is a presently enjoyed interest.

The present-interest requirement has several exceptions. One relates to trusts for minors. Not surprisingly, a donor might not want to transfer large sums of money to a relatively young donee. I.R.C. § 2503(c) lets the donor use the exclusion for transfers to individuals who have not attained age 21 if the transfer meets its requirements. The property and the income it produces must be paid to the donee or accumulated for his benefit. The property and any accumulated income must be transferred to him when he attains age 21. If he dies before attaining age 21, the property must be payable to his estate or must pass pursuant to a general power of appointment he exercises. This provision is an exception to the normal present interest requirements; it is not an exception to the annual exclusion limit.

A judicially sanctioned method of satisfying the present interest requirement relates to so-called *Crummey* powers. *Crummey v. Commissioner*, 397 F.2d 82 (9th Cir. 1968). The donor of trust property gives a beneficiary the right to withdraw some or all of that year's contribution. The power to withdraw is sufficient to make the amount subject to the power a gift of a present interest.

> **Example 26-1.** Mother transferred $50,000 in trust in 2024 and plans to do so every year for the foreseeable future. The trustee is to pay all trust income to Son for life; when Son dies, the trustee is to pay principal to Daughter. The value of Son's income interest is a present interest gift. If Mother also gives Daughter the power to withdraw $10,000 from the trust, she has made a $10,000 present interest gift to Daughter even

if Daughter does not exercise her power. Although Mother transferred $50,000 to the trust, the amount of her taxable gifts is less than $50,000. She can exclude the value of Son's income interest (up to $18,000 in 2024) and the $10,000 that Daughter could have withdrawn.

Donors have successfully used the *Crummey* power very aggressively. For example, the Tax Court has allowed exclusions for withdrawal powers given to both vested and contingent beneficiaries. *Estate of Cristofani v. Commissioner*, 97 T.C. 74 (1991).

b. *Transfers to Educational Institutions and Medical Care Providers*

A second gift exclusion is available for transfers for tuition and medical care. I.R.C. § 2503(e). Unlike the exclusion for present-interest gifts, there is no dollar limit on this exclusion. A donor can use it in addition to the per-donee, per-year exclusion.

Example 26-2. In 2024, Mother wrote a $30,000 check to State University to cover Son's tuition. She also gave Son $18,000. Neither transfer is treated as a taxable gift. The result would be the same if Mother also paid $6,000 to Son's dentist to replace teeth he lost in a car accident.

This exclusion is available only if the donor pays the educational institution or the health care provider directly. It does not apply to amounts given to the donee to use for these purposes. Nor does it apply to amounts paid to a prepaid college savings plan. Those plans allow tax-advantaged savings for college, but they are not payments *to* an educational institution. Contributions to these plans are treated as present-interest gifts, subject to the annual exclusion amount. I.R.C. § 529(c)(2)(A). They do have one gift tax advantage: a donor who transfers funds to these plans can elect to spread the amount over five years. That reduces or eliminates any additional present-interest exclusion for gifts to that donee during the five-year period. I.R.C. § 529(c)(2)(B).

c. *Gift-Splitting*

A married couple can agree to treat gifts made by one of them to a third person as gifts made by both of them. This allows a double present-interest exclusion even if only one of them is transferring property to a donee. I.R.C. § 2513.

Example 26-3. Harry and Wilma were married in 2024. Each has children by a prior marriage. Harry transferred $22,000 to his daughter Darleen shortly after the wedding. If Wilma agreed to a split-gift election, each of them is treated as giving Darleen $11,000; neither Harry nor Wilma made a taxable gift. In the absence of such an agreement, Harry made a taxable gift of $4,000.

d. *Effect of Exclusions on Trusts and Estates Concepts*

In computing the surviving spouse's elective share, the UPC includes both the decedent's probate estate and the value of certain other property interests transferred before the decedent died. Among those interests are transfers to third parties made during the marriage and within two years of his death. However, any transfer in excess of a specific annual amount (currently $12,000) or the applicable federal gift tax exclusion (if a state adopts that UPC alternative) is not included in this computation. UPC § 2-205(3)(C). Transfers in which the spouse has joined (or to which she consented) are also excluded. The comments to UPC § 2-208 indicate that a spouse's consent to gift-splitting does not constitute joinder or consent.

Some state elective share statutes vary from the UPC by using a different pre-death time period for including gifts. Some also exclude transfers to educational institutions and medical care providers from the computation.

A donee who has a *Crummey* power might subject trust assets to the claims of her creditors before the power expires. UTC § 505(b)(1). After the power expires, if the donee has an income interest in the trust, she can be treated as a settlor with respect to the amount she could have withdrawn. If she is treated as a settlor, creditors might have continued access to her interest to the extent her withdrawal power wasn't subject to a "5 and 5" power limitation. UTC § 505(b)(2). A "5 and 5" power is a power to withdraw property that is limited to the greater of $5,000 or 5% of the value of the property subject to the power. The lapse of the power also avoids gift and estate tax consequences even though the powerholder could be indirectly making a transfer to other beneficiaries. I.R.C. §§ 2041(b)(2), 2514(e).

3. Gift Tax Deductions

a. *Transfers to a Spouse*

Transfers to a spouse can be deducted in computing taxable gifts if made in a form described in I.R.C. § 2523. They are not limited by the annual exclusion amount, and they do not have to be made directly to an educational institution or a medical care provider.

Outright gifts to the donor's spouse qualify for the gift tax deduction. Gifts in trust also qualify if they are made in one of three formats. The donor can give her spouse an income interest for life, coupled with a general power of appointment over the trust property. She can give her spouse an income interest for life, no power of appointment, and make a qualified terminable interest property election. Or she can simply have any trust property not previously distributed to the spouse paid to his estate when he dies. These trusts have estate tax counterparts for transfers made at death.

b. Transfers to a Charity

Outright gifts to a charity qualify for a gift tax deduction. Gifts in trust also qualify if they are made in an appropriate format. These formats are designed to ensure that the charity actually receives the benefit for which a deduction was allowed for gift or estate tax purposes. I.R.C. § 2522. In addition to being allowed a gift tax deduction, the donor might also receive a deduction in computing his federal income tax. I.R.C. § 170.

C. Estate Tax

Congress enacted a federal estate tax several years before it enacted a gift tax. The estate tax was initially imposed on the value of the probate estate and certain other interests or powers. Because no gift tax existed at that time, individuals who wished to avoid the federal estate tax could do so by making inter vivos gifts to their beneficiaries. At one time the estate and gift taxes operated separately, with different exemptions and rate structures. Under current law, taxable gifts affect the amount subject to the estate tax, and an individual pays both taxes at the same rate. The exemption ($13,610,000 in 2024) applies to the sum of cumulative taxable gifts and the taxable estate. The transferor does not have separate gift tax and estate tax exemptions.

An individual does not pay estate tax unless his cumulative taxable gifts and taxable estate exceed any remaining exemption to which he is entitled. A tax rate of 40% currently applies. I.R.C. § 2001(c).

The discussion below ignores the effect of various credits to which the estate might be entitled. It also ignores the alternate valuation rules in effect for certain interests in farms and other real property and other special valuation rules. These topics are addressed in estate and gift tax and estate planning courses.

1. Gross Estate

The taxable estate is computed as the difference between the decedent's gross estate and any deductions available. Unlike the gift tax, the estate tax does not have exclusions for transfers to pay for medical care or tuition or for present-interest devises.

The gross estate is based on ownership, enjoyment, or control; it might even include events that occurred within three years of the decedent's death. The components of the gross estate are covered in detail in I.R.C. §§ 2033, 2034, 2035, 2036, 2037, 2038, 2039, 2040, 2041, 2042, 2043, and 2044. Disclaimers are given effect if they meet the requirements in I.R.C. § 2518. I.R.C. § 2046.

The listing below is only a summary of the relevant interests and powers. The elective share provisions discussed earlier in this book are similar in their coverage of these items. To the extent the decedent received full and adequate consideration in money or money's worth for the transfer involved, these provisions do not apply. His estate will have been enhanced by the consideration he received.

Property owned at death. The gross estate includes the value of the decedent's probate estate. It also includes other property in which the decedent had an interest even if that property is not state law probate property. The regulations specifically include state law homestead and other exempt property. Treas. Reg. § 20.2033-1(b).

Retained interests and powers. The gross estate includes the value of property over which he retained the right to income or possession until he died. It includes the value of certain reversions that might take effect if a transferee must survive him to obtain possession or enjoyment, but only if the reversion is worth more than 5% of the value of the property involved. It includes the value of property he previously transferred if he retained the right to alter, amend, revoke, or terminate the transfer. It includes the value of an annuity or retirement account received by someone who survived him if he had retained the right to payments from the account until he died.

Example 26-4. Dan transferred property into an irrevocable trust 10 years ago. He retained the right to income for life, after which his children would receive the trust principal. The value of the trust principal is included in Dan's estate when he died. He retained the right to income even though he no longer had title to the property. I.R.C. § 2036.

Survivorship tenancies. If the decedent owned property in a survivorship tenancy with his spouse and no other joint tenant, his gross estate includes 50% of the property value. If he owned property in a survivorship tenancy with another person, the amount included in his gross estate is based on the percentage of consideration he supplied. I.R.C. § 2040. The rules for survivorship tenancies can give surprising results when the tenants are married to each other.

Example 26-5. Harry and his brother Bob purchased Blackacre and placed it in a joint tenancy with right of survivorship. Harry paid 60% of the cost; Bob paid the other 40%. When Harry dies, Bob will own Blackacre as the surviving tenant. Harry's gross estate will include 60% of Blackacre's value.

Example 26-6. Harry instead purchased Blackacre with his girlfriend Wendy. All other terms were the same. If Harry dies before they marry, his gross estate will include 60% of Blackacre's value. If he dies while married to Wendy, his gross estate includes 50% of its value.

Example 26-7. If Wendy provided 60% of the consideration and Harry provided 40%, Harry's gross estate will include 50% of Blackacre's value if he and Wendy are married when he dies. It will include only 40% of Blackacre's value if he dies before they marry.

General power of appointment. The gross estate includes the value of property over which the decedent had a general power of appointment. A power is general if the decedent could appoint the property to himself, his estate, or to the creditors of either. It does not matter whether the decedent ever owned the property.

Life insurance policies. The gross estate includes the proceeds of a life insurance policy if the death benefit was payable to the insured's estate. It also includes the proceeds if the insured had incidents of ownership in the policy at death. Incidents of ownership include the right to name the beneficiary and the right to borrow against the policy's cash surrender value. The regulations focus on the right to obtain economic benefits. Treas. Reg. § 20.2042-1(c)(2).

QTIP property. As discussed below, a decedent can deduct certain transfers to his spouse in computing his taxable estate. If the spouse received outright ownership or a general power of appointment over a trust interest, the value of the property would be taxed when she died. Thus, the marital deduction was designed to postpone rather than eliminate estate tax. A QTIP (qualified terminable interest property) trust does not give the surviving spouse a general power of appointment. Nevertheless, the decedent's estate receives a marital deduction if his personal representative elects the deduction with respect to a QTIP trust. The property in that trust is included in the surviving spouse's gross estate even though she was not able to select its ultimate taker.

Actions within three years of death. Many of the powers and interests discussed above cause property to be included in the gross estate because the decedent retained them until death. If the decedent relinquishes the interests and powers before death, he has made a completed gift but the item might still be included in his gross estate when he dies. I.R.C. § 2035 includes in the gross estate any gift tax the decedent paid with respect to gifts made within three years of his death. It also includes the value of any property that would have been in his estate had he not released interests or powers within three years of his death. The latter inclusion relates to retained income or possession, retained reversions, retained powers to alter, amend, revoke, or terminate, and incidents of ownership over life insurance. I.R.C. § 2041 provides similar rules for exercises or releases of a general power of appointment.

2. Estate Tax Deductions

a. *Expenses, Debts, and Taxes; Losses*

In computing the taxable estate, the personal representative can deduct funeral expenses, administration expenses, claims against the estate, and mortgages and other encumbrances on property if the value included in the gross estate was not reduced by those debts. Even expenses for administering nonprobate property can be deducted. I.R.C. § 2053.

The estate can also deduct losses sustained during administration arising from fire, storm, shipwreck, other casualty, or theft. The personal representative must first reduce the loss by any insurance or other compensation received. I.R.C. § 2054.

Some of the items allowed would also be deductible in computing the estate's taxable income. The personal representative cannot deduct them in computing taxable income if he deducts them in computing the taxable estate. I.R.C. § 642(g).

b. Transfers to a Spouse

A marital deduction is allowed for transfers to a surviving spouse. Outright gifts to the surviving spouse qualify for the estate tax deduction. As was true for inter vivos gifts to the spouse, gifts in trust qualify if they are made in one of three formats. The decedent can give her spouse an income interest for life, coupled with a general power of appointment over the trust property. She can give her spouse an income interest for life, no power of appointment, and have the personal representative make a qualified terminable interest property (QTIP) election. Or she can simply have any trust property not previously distributed to the spouse paid to his estate when he dies. I.R.C. § 2056.

c. *Transfers to a Charity*

Outright gifts to a charity qualify for the estate tax charitable deduction. Gifts in trust also qualify if they are made in an appropriate format. These formats are designed to ensure that the charity actually receives the benefit for which a deduction was allowed. I.R.C. § 2055.

3. Tax Base, Tentative Tax, and Exemption

After computing the taxable estate, the decedent's personal representative adds any adjusted taxable gifts the decedent made. An inter vivos transfer could be subject to both gift and estate tax if the decedent retained an interest or power until death or relinquished it within three years of death. The adjusted taxable gifts are reduced on account of such transfers before we compute the estate tax due.

The personal representative computes a tentative tax on the combined amount and then offsets that tax by an amount that is the equivalent of the decedent's lifetime exemption. I.R.C. §§ 2001, 2010.

A decedent is entitled to a larger exemption if he was a surviving spouse and his spouse did not fully use her exemption. The decedent can offset his tax by his own exemption and by what is called the deceased spousal unused exclusion amount. I.R.C. § 2010(c)(4).

D. Generation-Skipping Transfer Tax

As states relaxed the common-law rule against perpetuities, trusts that spanned multiple generations became possible. These trusts had two advantages. First, each generation could enjoy trust income without having the assets producing that income included in their probate estates when they died. Second, those income beneficiaries could also avoid having trust principal included in their gross estates. Each time the income interest passed from one generation to another in trust, rather than outright, probate costs and transfer taxes were avoided.

Example 26-8. Father died with a taxable estate of $50 million. He devised all his assets to Daughter. Daughter received the assets left after paying estate tax. When Daughter died, she devised all her assets to Grandson. He received the assets left after paying estate tax. When Grandson died, he devised all his assets to his child. That child received the assets left after paying estate tax. So long as the family's wealth exceeded the estate tax exemption in effect when one of them died, part of the estate would be subject to tax. If Father had instead placed the property in trust, giving income to Daughter for life, then to Grandson for life, then to Grandson's child for life, and so on, the estate tax would be paid only when Father died.

To prevent the use of trusts and other devices to avoid the gift and estate taxes, Congress enacted the generation-skipping tax. It is currently imposed at the highest estate tax rate, 40%. I.R.C. § 2641. It applies in a variety of situations involving transfers that skip one or more generations. Because the generation-skipping tax applies the exclusions used in computing the gift tax, it does not apply to every inter vivos transfer that skips a generation. A lifetime exemption, equal to that used for the estate and gift tax, is also available. A property owner can allocate the exemption to a trust, which can then provide the tax and probate-avoidance devices available before the generation-skipping tax was enacted.

The tax is imposed when a skip person benefits. A skip person is an individual who is two or more generations below the transferor. When a transfer is made in trust, the identity of its beneficiaries as skip persons or non-skip persons is relevant. I.R.C. § 2613. If the transferor and the beneficiary or the transferor's spouse and the beneficiary are related lineally, we count actual generations. If they are not, we use the difference in their ages as a surrogate for generations. The transferor and beneficiary are in the same generation if the beneficiary was born not more than 12.5 years after the transferor. Each successive generation spans 25 years. I.R.C. § 2651. This section includes additional, detailed rules for assigning generations; they include beneficiaries related to the transferor by marriage and beneficiaries whose parents are deceased.

The examples below illustrate three situations to which this tax applies: taxable distributions; taxable terminations; and direct skips. Each of these transfers is subject to tax to the extent it exceeds any available exclusion (inter vivos transfers) or exemption. A detailed explanation of the generation-skipping transfer tax is beyond the scope of this book.

Example 26-9. Serena created the Serena Family Trust. The trustee has the discretion to distribute trust income or principal to her son Sam and his descendants for the next 30 years. At that time, the trust will continue but Sam's interest will terminate. Serena did not allocate any of her generation-skipping tax exemption to this trust. This year, the trustee distributed $40,000 to Serena's grandson Gary. The distribution is a taxable distribution because Gary is a skip person. I.R.C. § 2612(b).

Example 26-10. When Sam's interest in the trust terminated at the end of 30 years, Gary became its only beneficiary. The termination of Sam's interest is a taxable termination. After the non-skip person's interest terminated, no non-skip person held an interest in the trust. I.R.C. § 2612(a).

Example 26-11. George gave $20 million to his granddaughter Glenda. George's son Sid (Glenda's father) was alive when George made this gift. This transfer is a direct skip; Glenda is a skip person. I.R.C. § 2612(c). If Sid had died before George made the transfer to Glenda, it would not be treated as a generation-skipping transfer. I.R.C. § 2651(e) provides a limited exception in that case.

E. Miscellaneous Tax Consequences

1. Tax-Inclusive and Tax-Exclusive Transfers

Because the gift tax is imposed on the value of the property at the time of the gift, it does not include the tax itself. Because the estate tax is imposed on the value of the property owned or treated as owned at death, it is imposed on property that will be used to pay the tax. The gift tax is tax-exclusive; the estate tax is tax-inclusive. This distinction does not matter if the individual will not be subject to transfer tax. It can be an important distinction in larger estates.

The difference between the gift and estate taxes is illustrated by the examples below. The examples ignore any gift tax exclusions and assume there is no surviving spouse.

Example 26-12. Tom expects to own property worth $8 million in excess of his estate tax exemption. The estate tax imposed on $8 million at the current 40% rate is $3,200,000. Of that $8 million, Tom's devisees will receive $4,800,000 plus the amount sheltered by his exemption; the government will receive $3,200,000.

Example 26-13. If Tom made taxable gifts totaling $5 million greater than this exemption, his gift tax would be $2 million. When he dies, assuming no changes in the value of his property or increase in the exemption, he will own property worth $1 million. The government will receive $400,000 and his devisees will receive the remaining $600,000. His combined gift and estate taxes will total only $2,400,000. His inter vivos donees will receive $5 million plus the gifts sheltered by his exemption; his devisees will receive $600,000. By transferring property before he dies, Tom reduces his transfer taxes by $800,000. He would have reduced them further if any of his inter vivos gifts had qualified for an exclusion.

Tom saved $800,000 because the gift tax is tax-exclusive. No tax was due on the $2 million he paid in gift tax. But, as indicated earlier in this chapter, he must live at least three years after making a taxed inter vivos gift. Otherwise, the gift tax is included in his gross estate.

2. Income Tax Basis Rules

Given that making inter vivos gifts and paying gift tax can reduce the overall transfer tax burden, why might a person continue to hold property until death? He might fear that he will need the property if his economic circumstances change, worry that the donees will treat their early wealth as a disincentive to work, or feel "locked in" by the disparate basis rules that will affect his beneficiaries.

As a general rule, the donee of an inter vivos gift takes an income tax basis equal to the donor's basis for the property, and the donee of a testamentary gift takes an income tax basis that reflects the property's estate tax value (even if the estate is not subject to tax). I.R.C. §§ 1014, 1015. An individual who owns appreciated property might hold the property until death to limit his beneficiaries' income tax on selling the property. This concern does not apply to money or to property that has declined in value.

> **Example 26-14.** Tammy purchased Blackacre several years ago for $100,000. It is currently worth $1 million. If Tammy gives Blackacre to her daughter Dora as an inter vivos gift, Dora's basis will be $100,000. If Dora sells Blackacre for $1 million, she will be taxed on a gain of $900,000. If Tammy holds Blackacre until she dies, and devises it to Dora, Dora's basis (assuming no change in value) will be $1 million. Dora will have no taxable gain if she sells Blackacre for $1 million.

3. Trust Income Tax Rates and Creditor Access to Trust Assets

If a beneficiary has an absolute right to trust income, the beneficiary will be subject to income tax on that income. The rates in effect in 2024 ranged from 10% to 37%. An unmarried individual reached the 37% rate bracket when her taxable income exceeded $609,350. If the trustee has the power to accumulate trust income rather than distributing it, the trust will be taxed on undistributed taxable income. In 2024, a trust reached the 37% rate bracket when its taxable income exceeded $15,200.

Although the disparate income tax rates would seem to favor distributing income, creditor access is also relevant. As discussed in Chapter 15, creditor rights can be affected by making trust distributions mandatory or discretionary or by including a spendthrift provision. The settlor must consider both income tax and creditor access issues when providing for trust income.

CHECKPOINTS

- Individuals whose wealth exceeds $13,610,000 (2024 amount) consider federal transfer taxes in addition to other aspects of their estate plans.
- The exemption and the exclusion for present-interest gifts are subject to inflation adjustments.
- The federal gift tax is imposed on the value of the property transferred. The federal estate tax is imposed on the value of the taxable estate.

- Inter vivos present-interest gifts below a certain amount and transfers to a medical care provider or educational institution are excluded from the gift tax computation. The donor can deduct transfers to a spouse or to a charity that meet statutory requirements.
- The federal estate tax is imposed on property owned at death and on property in which the decedent retained interests or over which he retained powers. He might also be taxed on the value of property subject to a general power of appointment even if the power is over property he never owned.
- The estate can take deductions for qualifying transfers to a surviving spouse or charity, for certain costs of administration and debts, and for casualty and theft losses during administration.
- An inter vivos transfer may be subject to both gift and estate tax if the decedent relinquished an interest or power within three years of death. The adjusted taxable gifts are reduced on account of such transfers before we compute the estate tax due.
- A decedent can use both his exemption and any exemption his deceased spouse did not use.
- The income tax basis rules might cause an individual to hold appreciated property until death. The income tax basis rules for property acquired from a decedent eliminate any pre-death appreciation in the property. Beneficiaries of an inter vivos gift do not receive this advantage.
- The generation-skipping tax is imposed on transfers, distributions, and terminations of an interest that skip a generation.
- The generation-skipping tax is imposed at the highest transfer tax rate, currently 40%.
- Transfers eligible for the gift tax exclusion are eligible for the exclusion from the generation-skipping transfer tax. Each individual also has an exemption from tax equal to the gift and estate tax exemption amount.
- The current exclusion and exemption amounts were enacted in a statute that expires at the end of 2025. Changed amounts or tax rates could become law in 2026.

Mastering Trusts and Estates Checklist

CHAPTER 1 • INTRODUCTION TO TRUSTS AND ESTATES

- ☐ Property owners can transfer property to their beneficiaries before they die or at death.
- ☐ They may choose to make outright transfers or transfers in trust.
- ☐ Transfers at death can be made by a will; otherwise, the relevant intestacy statutes will apply.
- ☐ The choice of transfer method reflects the transferor's concerns about privacy, transfer costs, taxes, and a donee's ability to manage funds.

CHAPTER 2 • SOURCES OF LAW

- ☐ The rules regarding trusts and estates can be found in federal and state statutes and judicial decisions.
- ☐ State laws often reflect uniform acts and Restatements, but they are not required to do so.
- ☐ Most disputes concerning transfers from an owner to a beneficiary are based on state law rather than on federal law and are litigated in state courts.
- ☐ Residents of community-property states have different wealth transmission rules for marital property than do residents of other states.

CHAPTER 3 • TERMINOLOGY AND ABBREVIATIONS

- ☐ Terminology used for one type of transfer may differ from that used for other types, and some terms have multiple meanings.
- ☐ Relevant statutes or groups of statutes might include definitions.
- ☐ Several types of property transmission are commonly referred to by initials.

CHAPTER 4 • PROBATE AND OPTIONS FOR AVOIDING IT

- ☐ Probate involves administering property the decedent owned at death.
- ☐ A property owner can avoid probate by making outright inter vivos transfers and transfers that take effect at death. These include survivorship tenancies and beneficiary designations.
- ☐ Probate-avoiding transfers are not necessarily treated as testamentary but do not necessarily avoid the transferor's creditors, the elective share rights of a spouse, or federal taxes.

CHAPTER 5 • INTESTATE SUCCESSION

- ☐ Probate property that is not disposed of by a will passes by intestate succession to the intestate decedent's heirs.
- ☐ Heirs are usually related to the decedent by blood or marriage.
- ☐ Heirs other than the decedent's surviving spouse are either lineal or collateral. Lineal heirs are ancestors or descendants. Collateral heirs are other blood relatives, including siblings, aunts, uncles, nieces, nephews, and cousins.
- ☐ The UPC and many state statutes limit the rights of remote ancestors to inherit.
- ☐ Intestacy statutes rank heirs in terms of priority and establish the share that each heir takes.
- ☐ The surviving spouse is the highest-ranked heir. The spouse's share is usually smaller if she and the decedent did not have all their descendants in common.
- ☐ The remaining ordering generally covers the decedent's descendants, parents, siblings, grandparents, and descendants of grandparents.

- ☐ Some jurisdictions may include stepchildren or great-grandparents.
- ☐ Some jurisdictions treat half-blood collateral heirs less generously than whole-blood heirs who share both sets of ancestors with the decedent.
- ☐ If the intestate decedent has no heirs, the state takes the property by escheat.
- ☐ When a deceased heir's descendants take in her place, they take by representation.
- ☐ The UPC uses the per capita at each generation method for determining representation. That method begins dividing the estate at the first generation with at least one surviving member. It pools the shares of deceased heirs in the same generation and redistributes those shares among their combined next-generation descendants.
- ☐ Some states use the per stirpes method for determining representation. That method begins dividing the estate at the highest generation, even if all members of that generation are deceased. Descendants of deceased heirs take only the share their ancestor would have taken.
- ☐ UPC provisions regarding adoptions, nonmarital births, de facto parentage, assisted reproduction, and posthumous conception reflect language in the Uniform Parentage Act.
- ☐ An advancement to an heir reduces her share of the intestate estate only if that intention is declared in a contemporaneous writing by the donor or an acknowledgement by the donee.
- ☐ Because the advancement was a gift, a donee who receives more than her intestate share does not have to transfer the excess back to the estate.
- ☐ If the intestate loans money to an heir, the unpaid loan reduces the heir's share of the estate.

CHAPTER 6 • REQUIREMENTS FOR A VALID WILL

- ☐ A will is not valid unless the testator has testamentary capacity.
- ☐ Litigation over capacity generally focuses on whether the testator understands the nature of her property, the identities of the objects of her bounty, and the effect of her estate plan.

- ☐ States generally require that the testator execute the will and that there be at least two attesting witnesses.
- ☐ Witnesses need not see the contents of the will or know they are witnessing a will.
- ☐ The UPC has looser witnessing requirements than many states.
- ☐ The UPC uses a conscious presence test for acts that must occur in the presence of the testator or a witness. This test is often easier to meet than the line of sight test.
- ☐ The UPC validates a will (or its revocation) if there is harmless error regarding formalities for execution or revocation.
- ☐ A minority of states allow oral wills in limited circumstances, such as a testator who will be fighting in the military.
- ☐ States that allow holographic wills may require that they be entirely in the testator's handwriting or that the material portions be handwritten.
- ☐ A notarized self-proving affidavit indicates the steps taken in signing and witnessing the will.
- ☐ Self-proving affidavits allow offering the will for probate without presenting the testimony of any witnesses to its execution.

CHAPTER 7 • CATEGORIZING DEVISES

- ☐ Precatory language does not create an enforceable devise.
- ☐ A specific devise is a devise of a particular asset. The devise is conditional; it may fail if the testator does not own the devised asset at death.
- ☐ A general devise is usually a devise of a particular amount of money, but it could be a devise of other property. The devise does not fail if the testator does not own the property at death.
- ☐ A demonstrative devise has characteristics of both specific and general devises and is ultimately treated as one or the other or partially as one and partially as the other.
- ☐ A residuary devise covers property that was not specifically, demonstratively, or generally devised.

CHAPTER 8 • AMENDING, REVOKING, AND REVIVING A WILL

- ☐ A new will or a codicil requires the same formalities as the original will.
- ☐ A testator can also amend a will by transferring property to a trust, by incorporating another document into the will, or by devising property in a separate writing.
- ☐ A separate writing is valid only if the will indicates that one is possible. It can be used only for limited types of property.
- ☐ A will that makes a full disposition of the testator's property is treated as revoking the original will even if words of revocation are not used.
- ☐ A will that does not make a full disposition of the testator's property generally revokes only the inconsistent portions of the earlier will.
- ☐ A testator can revoke a will—or a part of a will—by performing a revocatory act. The UPC lists several revocatory acts: burning; tearing; canceling; obliterating; or destroying. Some states do not allow partial revocation by act.
- ☐ A testator can reinstate a revoked document by reviving it. If the original document was only partially revoked by the later document, he can reinstate the earlier document by revoking the later document.
- ☐ Dependent relative revocation revives an earlier will if the later will was invalid and the court determines the valid revocation of the earlier will was conditioned on the validity of the later will.
- ☐ A change in marital status does not revoke a will but may affect the validity of some of its provisions.
- ☐ Individuals can make written succession agreements that cover rights to make a will or a devise, not to revoke a will or devise, or to die intestate.
- ☐ Joint or mutual wills are not sufficient evidence to establish the existence of a contract.

CHAPTER 9 • FAMILY PROTECTION STATUTES

- ☐ A surviving spouse may receive rights to a homestead allowance, exempt property, and a family allowance.

- ☐ If the decedent does not have a spouse, or if the spouse has waived his rights, his children may take those rights.
- ☐ A spouse or child who is not mentioned in the decedent's will may be entitled to a share of the decedent's estate. Neither has omitted spouse or child rights (pretermission) if the omission was intentional or if the decedent provided for the spouse or child by other transfers.
- ☐ A surviving spouse has elective share rights, which entitle him to a percentage of the value of the deceased spouse's probate estate.
- ☐ The UPC and many states also extend the surviving spouse's rights to a percentage of the value of the decedent's nonprobate property, including property transferred outright within a certain period before death.
- ☐ The elective share computation may also include the spouse's property. This inclusion prevents the spouse from taking an elective share even though he owns significant property, received nonprobate transfers from the decedent, or gave away property before the decedent died.
- ☐ The UPC bases the elective share percentage on the length of the marriage. Some states simply apply a flat percentage to the value of the property comprising their version of the elective estate.
- ☐ Other recipients (or potential recipients) of a decedent's property have their probate or nonprobate receipts reduced to satisfy homestead allowance rights, exempt property rights, family allowance, pretermission rights, and elective share.
- ☐ Community-property states treat each spouse as owning one-half of the community property. Only the decedent's one-half is probated.
- ☐ Spouses can waive their rights before or during the marriage. An enforceable waiver must be in writing and may require disclosure of the other party's property and financial obligations.

CHAPTER 10 • INTRODUCTION TO TRUSTS

- ☐ More than two-thirds of the states have enacted the Uniform Trust Code.
- ☐ Trusts separate legal and beneficial ownership of property.

- ☐ The trustee has legal title and acts on behalf of the trust beneficiaries. The settlor of the trust might be a trustee, a beneficiary, both, or neither.
- ☐ Qualified beneficiaries generally have more rights than other beneficiaries.
- ☐ Trusts are created by transfer to a trustee, by self-declaration, or by exercise of a power of appointment.
- ☐ Private express trusts generally have one or more definite beneficiaries. Charitable express trusts are designed to further a public good.
- ☐ A resulting trust is imposed based on the transferor's inferred intent. A constructive trust is imposed as a remedy to prevent unjust enrichment. They are not actual trusts.

CHAPTER 11 • CREATING AN EXPRESS TRUST

- ☐ A settlor who creates a testamentary trust or a revocable inter vivos trust must have testamentary capacity.
- ☐ Creating an irrevocable inter vivos trust requires the capacity to make an outright gift.
- ☐ The settlor must have the intent to create a trust.
- ☐ Private express trusts usually must have at least one definite beneficiary.
- ☐ A trust must have a trustee with duties. A court can appoint a trustee if the trust instrument fails to do so.
- ☐ If a trust's only beneficiary and only trustee are the same person, the legal and equitable interests merge and the trust fails.

CHAPTER 12 • TRUST PURPOSE, FORMALITIES, AND FUNDING

- ☐ A trust must have a purpose that is not unlawful, contrary to public policy, or impossible to achieve.
- ☐ The formalities necessary to create a trust may be identical to those required for a valid will, but trusts may require fewer formalities.

- ☐ If a will purports to create a trust, but omits required trust terms, it is a semisecret trust. Its terms will not be enforced because that would violate the requirement that a will's terms be in writing.
- ☐ If the will does not include trust language, but the testator intended a trust, it is a secret trust. Its terms might be enforced as a constructive trust if the testator acted in reliance on the purported trustee's promise to carry out the trust.
- ☐ If the settlor creates a trust by transfer, he must observe any formalities—deed, delivery, etc.—necessary to validate the transfer and take the property out of his probate estate.

CHAPTER 13 • TRUST DISTRIBUTION PROVISIONS

- ☐ A trust may include mandatory provisions governing the distribution of trust income or principal, or the trustee may have discretion regarding distributions.
- ☐ A beneficiary or third party may have a power to withdraw contributions or invade principal.
- ☐ Powers to withdraw, invade, or revoke have consequences involving creditor access to trust assets, computing a surviving spouse's elective share, and computing the powerholder's estate or gift taxes.

CHAPTER 14 • SPECIFIC USES FOR TRUSTS

- ☐ Express trusts offer privacy and professional management, and they avoid delays caused by probate.
- ☐ A settlor may use a trust to avoid ancillary administration or the potential claims of a surviving spouse's new spouse or children.
- ☐ Trusts for spouses are often structured to satisfy elective share rights or reduce estate taxes.
- ☐ The UTC includes provisions validating trusts for animals and for noncharitable purposes.
- ☐ Irrevocable life insurance trusts can be used to fund estate expenses—through loans—without increasing the settlor's estate taxes.
- ☐ Charitable trusts do not have to have definite beneficiaries or a specific purpose; they are subject to the other requirements for creating a valid express trust.

CHAPTER 15 • CREDITOR ACCESS TO TRUST ASSETS

- ☐ The settlor's creditors can generally access trust assets while the trust is revocable.
- ☐ The settlor's creditors are generally limited to accessing his retained interest, if any, in an irrevocable trust.
- ☐ Some jurisdictions let settlors avoid creditor access by establishing asset protection trusts.
- ☐ A settlor may limit access by a beneficiary's creditors by including a spendthrift provision in the trust or by making distributions subject to the trustee's discretion.
- ☐ To be effective, a spendthrift provision must bar voluntary *and* involuntary transfer or alienation of the beneficiary's interest in the trust.
- ☐ Spouses, ex spouses, and children with court orders for support may be able to gain access despite a spendthrift provision.
- ☐ A beneficiary with a power of withdrawal may be treated as a settlor unless the power is limited by an ascertainable standard.

CHAPTER 16 • MODIFICATION, REFORMATION, TERMINATION, AND REVOCATION

- ☐ An irrevocable noncharitable trust can be modified or terminated without court approval if the settlor and all beneficiaries agree. It can be modified or terminated with court approval without the settlor's agreement if all beneficiaries consent.
- ☐ A court can modify administrative or dispositive terms, or even terminate the trust, if that will further the trust's purposes.
- ☐ A court can modify or terminate a charitable trust if its purpose has become unlawful, impracticable, impossible to achieve, or wasteful. When the court applies the doctrine of cy pres, it attempts to follow the settlor's purpose as closely as possible.
- ☐ A trust can be terminated or modified if its value is not sufficient to justify the cost of administration.
- ☐ A court can reform a will or trust if there is clear and convincing evidence that the challenged terms were based on a mistake of fact or law. The document can be reformed even if it is unambiguous.

- ☐ A court can authorize modification of a trust if its terms do not comport with the settlor's tax objectives (or probable objectives if the transferor is dead).
- ☐ A trustee can combine separate trusts into a single trust or split a single trust into separate trusts after giving notice to the qualified beneficiaries. The trustee cannot impair the rights of any beneficiary or adversely affect achieving the trust purpose.
- ☐ An authorized fiduciary may have the power to decant trust assets from one trust to another or to amend the initial trust to make it into a new trust. The fiduciary must have discretionary powers over trust principal.
- ☐ The fiduciary cannot exercise its power to decant in a manner that eliminates or reduces vested interests even if it has expanded distributive discretion.
- ☐ A fiduciary with limited distributive discretion must provide beneficiaries of the first trust as a group with substantially similar rights in the second trust.
- ☐ The settlor of an inter vivos trust generally has the power to revoke or amend the trust or withdraw trust principal. The settlor must have the capacity to do so and must comply with required formalities.

CHAPTER 17 • INTERPRETING INSTRUMENTS AND RULES OF CONSTRUCTION

- ☐ A document may contain an ambiguity or an incorrect description.
- ☐ Ambiguities are latent if they are not apparent until it is time to act on the document.
- ☐ Ambiguities are patent if they are apparent from the text of the document.
- ☐ Jurisdictions may allow taking extrinsic evidence to determine what the ambiguous term meant.
- ☐ Beneficiaries can be identified by name, in which case the transferor has made a transfer to one or more individuals.
- ☐ Beneficiaries can also be identified by a group characteristic, in which case the transfer is to a class.

- ☐ If an instrument identifies the recipients by both name and group characteristic, a gift to individuals is presumed in the absence of evidence of contrary intent.
- ☐ A class can expand or contract between the time the transfer document is executed and the time for distribution. A class that can only contract is possible.
- ☐ When the time for distribution arrives, surviving class members share the property equally.
- ☐ Courts may rely on canons of construction, such as giving terms their everyday meaning. Courts also rely on rules of construction, which apply if they cannot determine the drafter's intent from the document or by other means.

CHAPTER 18 • RULES OF CONSTRUCTION FOR WILLS

- ☐ Rules of construction do not apply if there is sufficient evidence of the testator's contrary intent.
- ☐ The testator's will disposes of property she owns at death and property she acquired after death unless a state statute or her will indicates otherwise.
- ☐ If a devisee to whom an antilapse statute applies fails to meet a survival condition, but is survived by descendants, those descendants take the property devised to him.
- ☐ Antilapse applies only if the devisee is the testator's grandparent or a descendant of that grandparent. It can apply to other devisees only if the will provides that it applies.
- ☐ If a pre-residuary devise fails, the residuary devisees share the failed devise.
- ☐ If a residuary devisee fails to survive, and antilapse does not apply, the other residuary devisees share the failed devise even if the devise is not a class gift.
- ☐ If there is no surviving residuary devisee and antilapse does not apply, the property is distributed through intestate succession.
- ☐ The devisee of a certain amount of securities is entitled to that amount if the testator owned the securities at death.

- ☐ The devisee is also entitled to additional securities of that issuer, or securities of another issuer, if the testator acquired them through entity action or a plan of reinvestment.
- ☐ Some states give the devisee the right to additional securities only if the securities are specifically devised. The UPC applies to both general and specific devises.
- ☐ Although the UPC follows the intent theory in trying to limit ademption by extinction, many states follow the identity theory. They are less likely to allow a replacement devise or a substitute pecuniary devise.
- ☐ The UPC provides substitute pecuniary devises when a conservator or agent sells specifically devised property or receives a condemnation award or damages.
- ☐ A devisee of mortgaged property is not entitled to have the mortgage paid from the residue unless the will indicates that intent. A statement that the personal representative should pay the testator's debts is not a sufficient indicator of intent.
- ☐ The donor of a power of appointment may prescribe the conditions for the power's exercise.
- ☐ If the donor did not require a specific reference to the power, the UPC treats the power as exercised by a residuary clause in the powerholder's will if she could have exercised it in favor of her estate and the donor did not provide for an eligible taker in default.
- ☐ Ademption by satisfaction applies when an inter vivos gift is made in full or partial satisfaction of a devise.
- ☐ Inter vivos transfers reduce or eliminate devises to the devisee only if there is a writing indicating the gift is in full or partial satisfaction of the devise. The writing can be made contemporaneously by the testator or in his will; it can be an acknowledgement by the devisee.
- ☐ A devisee who receives an inter vivos gift that exceeds the value of any devise to him does not have to return the excess gift.

CHAPTER 19 • RULES OF CONSTRUCTION FOR GOVERNING INSTRUMENTS

- ☐ Survival requirements may be based on surviving a particular person or surviving until an event occurs.

- ☐ Survival requirements usually treat the potential beneficiary as predeceasing the property owner. As a result, property may pass to someone other than the deceased beneficiary's heirs or devisees.
- ☐ The UPC requires surviving the individual or the event by 120 hours. It includes a clear and convincing evidence standard for establishing survival.
- ☐ The UPC survival requirement does not apply if the governing instrument uses simultaneous death or death in a common disaster language or if the instrument expressly indicates that the beneficiary does not have to survive by any specified time period or includes its own survival period.
- ☐ A transferor can usually select the law of the state that will apply to the governing instrument.
- ☐ If the holder of a power of appointment does not strictly comply with the exercise requirements, substantial compliance may be sufficient in a state that has adopted the UPC.
- ☐ Class gifts are generally construed according to the rules for intestate succession. There may be exceptions for children of assisted reproduction, posthumous children, and adult adoptees.
- ☐ In the absence of a contrary expression of intent, we close a class to future members if there is a class member eligible take on the distribution date.
- ☐ Antilapse provisions can apply to a life insurance policy, a retirement plan, a pay on death account, a transfer on death account, or similar contracts if the instrument doesn't expressly require survival.
- ☐ If an instrument provides an alternative beneficiary designation, it applies instead of antilapse.
- ☐ Antilapse provisions can apply to a future interest in a trust if the named beneficiary fails to survive to the distribution date.
- ☐ A residuary clause in a will, even one that includes lapsed or failed devises, is not sufficient to constitute an alternative future interest if the future interest was created in a nonresiduary devise.
- ☐ Distribution by representation applies to devises, trust interests, and other donative transfers unless the instrument provides otherwise.

The UPC uses per capita at each generation unless the instrument provides for using per stirpes.

- ☐ The UPC and many state statutes have abolished the doctrine of worthier title, which provided a reversion if the transferor made a gift to his heirs.
- ☐ Distribution of a future interest to a designated individual's heirs is based on treating the designated individual as dying intestate on the distribution date.
- ☐ State statutes may differ from the UPC in their treatment of survival conditions, relationships, taking by representation, and other rules of construction.

CHAPTER 20 • DISQUALIFYING ACTS

- ☐ The UPC revokes benefits the former spouse (or her family) would have received under a revocable governing instrument the individual executed before the divorce or annulment. It reinstates those benefits if the spouses remarry.
- ☐ States may differ from the UPC by not revoking benefits to the former spouse's family or by not automatically reinstating benefits if the parties remarry.
- ☐ An individual who intentionally and feloniously kills or procures the killing of another person cannot benefit from his wrongdoing.
- ☐ The killer's descendants might take in his place if the state's killer statute does not preclude taking by representation.
- ☐ A state might also eliminate benefits that would otherwise be received by abusers.
- ☐ A beneficiary who has not accepted the benefits of a transfer may disclaim an interest in the property or in a portion of it.
- ☐ As a general rule, disclaimed property interests pass as if the disclaimant had died immediately before the distribution date. The disclaimant's descendants may be eligible to take in his place.
- ☐ Wills and trusts, or portions thereof, are void if procured by undue influence, duress, fraud, or mistake. Revocation caused by undue influence, duress, fraud, or mistake is also void.

- ☐ A wrongdoer may attempt to alter a document by adding language, inserting pages, or substituting pages. If spoliation is proven, a court can strike the language added by the wrongdoer.
- ☐ Challenges to a will or trust can include the above types of wrongdoing in addition to, or instead of, challenges based on lack of capacity.
- ☐ A challenger who is unable to establish the will or trust as originally written may ask the court to impose a constructive trust on the person who wrongfully received the property. He may also be able to bring a suit for damages caused by tortious interference with his expectancy.

CHAPTER 21 • POWERS OF APPOINTMENT

- ☐ The donee of the power (powerholder) can designate the ultimate taker of property covered by the power.
- ☐ The powerholder may have a general power, which he can exercise in favor of himself, his estate, his creditors, or the creditors of his estate, or he may have a nongeneral power.
- ☐ Even if the powerholder can benefit himself, the power is nongeneral if its exercise is subject to an ascertainable standard, generally for health, education, support, or maintenance.
- ☐ The power may be presently exercisable, or it may be subject to a condition before it can be exercised.
- ☐ The persons in whose favor the power can be exercised are the permissible appointees, also referred to as the objects of the power.
- ☐ If the power is exclusionary, the powerholder can exclude some of the permissible appointees when he exercises the power. He cannot do this if the power is nonexclusionary.
- ☐ The instrument creating the power usually provides for a taker in default, who receives the property if the powerholder does not effectively exercise his power.
- ☐ The instrument also usually provides any conditions regarding the method of exercise.
- ☐ An individual who is offered a general power of appointment may have to consider transfer tax, creditor access, and elective share consequences in deciding whether to accept the power.

CHAPTER 22 • RULE AGAINST PERPETUITIES

- ☐ The rule against perpetuities began as a common-law rule to prevent remote vesting.
- ☐ The common-law rule required that a nonvested interest had to be certain to vest or terminate no later than a period that ended 21 years after the death of a life in being. Powers had to be certain to be irrevocably exercised or terminate during the same period.
- ☐ Statutes providing a fixed wait-and-see period can save an interest or power that would fail the common-law rule. These interests and powers are judged at the end of the wait-and-see period rather than at their creation.
- ☐ An interest in (or power over) property created by will, including in a testamentary trust, is created when the testator dies.
- ☐ An interest in (or power over) property created by an inter vivos trust is created when the trust becomes irrevocable.
- ☐ The UPC includes a 90-year wait-and-see period. Some states include longer periods; a few have abolished the rule altogether.
- ☐ The UPC provides exceptions from the rule, including those for non-donative transfers and for transfers in which a charitable or governmental interest follows another charitable or governmental interest.
- ☐ It may be possible to reform an interest or power that fails to vest, be exercised, or terminate within the necessary time period.

CHAPTER 23 • CLAIMS, EXPENSES, AND DISTRIBUTIONS TO BENEFICIARIES

- ☐ The fiduciary must satisfy claims and pay expenses of administration before making distributions to devisees, heirs, or trust beneficiaries.
- ☐ If the testator does not specify an abatement order, expenses and claims against his estate are satisfied in this order: (1) property that would pass by intestacy; (2) property otherwise in the residuary devise; (3) general devises; and (4) specific devises.
- ☐ Abatement provisions may apply differently for satisfaction of certain rights based on family status.

- ☐ The trustee of a revocable trust may be required to transfer trust property to the personal representative to pay expenses and claims.
- ☐ Transfer taxes owed by the decedent's estate may be apportioned among recipients of interests in the probate estate and in other property included in the decedent's gross estate.
- ☐ Beneficiaries may rearrange their shares of the estate by private agreements. These agreements cannot affect the rights of creditors or of beneficiaries who are not parties to the agreement.
- ☐ Trust beneficiaries may agree on the distribution of trust principal when a trust terminates by unanimous agreement.

CHAPTER 24 • TRUSTEES AND OTHER FIDUCIARIES

- ☐ In addition to personal representatives and trustees, fiduciaries include agents acting under a power of attorney, conservators, guardians, custodians under a Uniform Transfers to Minors Act account, and health care surrogates.
- ☐ The personal representative of an estate is responsible for taking control of the decedent's property, satisfying claims, and distributing any remaining property to beneficiaries.
- ☐ A trustee owes duties only to the trust's settlor until the trust becomes irrevocable.
- ☐ The trust instrument may list the trustee's powers and duties. The applicable statute applies to the extent powers and duties are not covered in the instrument or the statute overrides the instrument.
- ☐ The UTC lists powers and duties related to trust property, trust administration, distribution of trust assets and termination of the trust, and notice to beneficiaries.
- ☐ A trustee is liable to beneficiaries for damages caused by a breach of her duty or, if greater, by any profit she made on account of the breach.
- ☐ Trustee duties include acting in good faith, loyalty, impartiality, and exercising reasonable care and skill.
- ☐ A trustee can be held liable to third persons with respect to contracts if she failed to indicate she was representing a trust. She is liable for torts only if she is personally at fault.

- ☐ The trust instrument might provide for a trust director, who can direct a trustee's action on matters specified in the trust instrument.

CHAPTER 25 • INCOME, EXPENSE, AND INVESTMENT

- ☐ Fiduciaries allocate receipts and disbursements to principal or income.
- ☐ The Uniform Fiduciary Income and Principal Act (UFIPA) applies when the will or trust does not provide different allocation rules.
- ☐ The UFIPA gives the trustee power to adjust the share of net income that is allocable to the income and principal beneficiaries if necessary to fairly allocate trust income.
- ☐ A fiduciary may have the power to convert a trust to a unitrust and invest for total return.
- ☐ A beneficiary may be taxed on income he has not yet received because of differences in trust and tax accounting rules.
- ☐ If the trust instrument does not provide otherwise, a trustee in most states follows the Uniform Prudent Investor Act in deciding how to invest trust assets.
- ☐ That act judges a portfolio as a whole rather than judging a single asset.

CHAPTER 26 • FEDERAL TRANSFER TAXES

- ☐ Individuals whose wealth exceeds $13,610,000 (2024 amount) consider federal transfer taxes in addition to other aspects of their estate plans.
- ☐ The federal gift tax is imposed on the value of the property transferred. The federal estate tax is imposed on the value of the taxable estate.
- ☐ Gift tax exclusions are available for present-interest gifts below a certain amount and transfers to a medical care provider or educational institution.
- ☐ Gift and estate tax deductions are available for transfers to a spouse or to a charity.

- ☐ The federal estate tax is imposed on the value of property owned at death and the value of property in which the decedent retained interests or over which he retained powers.
- ☐ A decedent can use both his own exemption and his deceased spouse's unused exemption.
- ☐ The income tax basis rules may cause an individual to hold appreciated property until death.
- ☐ The generation-skipping tax is imposed on transfers, distributions, and terminations of an interest that skip a generation.
- ☐ The generation-skipping tax is imposed at the highest transfer tax rate, currently 40%.
- ☐ The current transfer tax rates and exemptions were enacted in a statute that expires at the end of 2025. Changed amounts could become law in 2026.

TABLE OF CASES

Crummey v. Commissioner, 389–391
Drye v. United States, 301
Estate of Cristofani v. Commissioner, 390
FTC v. Affordable Media, LLC, 203
Gibney v. Hossack, 287
Hillman v. Maretta, 293
In re Estate of Hodtum, 87
In re Estate of Osguthorpe, 312
In re Robertson's Estate, 87
In re Totten, 34
In re Wells, 168
Lewis G. Allen Family Tr. v. Gov't of the United States, 163
Marshall v. Marshall, 15
Morris v. Trust Co. of Virginia, 87
Obergefell v. Hodges, 50, 51, 59
Olliffe v. Wells, 175
Pickelner v. Adler, 175
Ponzelino v. Ponzelino, 163
Romaniello v. Romaniello, 232
Wehrheim v. Golden Pond Assisted Living Facility, 121

TABLE OF STATUTES

Federal Statutes

I.R.C. § 102(a), 43
I.R.C. § 170, 392
I.R.C. § 305(a), 252
I.R.C. § 305(b)(1), 253
I.R.C. § 305(b)(4), 252
I.R.C. § 401(k), 41
I.R.C. § 403(b), 41
I.R.C. § 529, 358
I.R.C. § 529(c)(2)(A), 390
I.R.C. § 529(c)(2)(B), 390
I.R.C. § 529A, 358
I.R.C. § 642(g), 395
I.R.C. § 644(a), 373
I.R.C. § 652(a), 180
I.R.C. § 674, 224
I.R.C. § 674(b)(5)(A), 224
I.R.C. § 1014, 43, 399
I.R.C. § 1015, 43, 399
I.R.C. § 2001, 396
I.R.C. § 2001(c), 388, 392
I.R.C. § 2010, 388, 396
I.R.C. § 2010(c)(4), 396
I.R.C. § 2033, 393
I.R.C. § 2034, 393
I.R.C. § 2035, 141, 393, 395
I.R.C. § 2035(a), 195
I.R.C. § 2036, 348, 393
I.R.C. § 2037, 393
I.R.C. § 2038, 225, 319, 393
I.R.C. § 2039, 393
I.R.C. § 2040, 393, 394
I.R.C. § 2041, 325, 393, 395
I.R.C. § 2041(b)(1)(A), 209, 210, 318
I.R.C. § 2041(b)(2), 323, 326, 391
I.R.C. § 2042, 39, 393
I.R.C. § 2042(1), 195
I.R.C. § 2042(2), 195
I.R.C. § 2043, 393
I.R.C. § 2044, 194, 393
I.R.C. § 2046, 303, 393
I.R.C. § 2053, 395
I.R.C. § 2054, 395
I.R.C. § 2055, 396
I.R.C. § 2056, 396
I.R.C. § 2056(a), 326
I.R.C. § 2056(b)(1), 193
I.R.C. § 2056(b)(3), 271
I.R.C. § 2056(b)(5), 193, 327
I.R.C. § 2056(b)(7), 194
I.R.C. § 2056(b)(7)(B)(ii)(II), 327
I.R.C. § 2056(b)(8), 193
I.R.C. § 2206, 347, 348
I.R.C. § 2207, 347, 348

I.R.C. § 2207A(a), 348
I.R.C. § 2207A(b), 348
I.R.C. § 2207B, 348
I.R.C. § 2502, 388
I.R.C. § 2503(b), 4, 389
I.R.C. § 2503(c), 358
I.R.C. § 2503(e), 390
I.R.C. § 2505, 388
I.R.C. § 2513, 390
I.R.C. § 2514, 325
I.R.C. § 2514(c)(1), 318
I.R.C. § 2514(e), 323, 325, 326, 391
I.R.C. § 2518, 303, 393
I.R.C. § 2518(b), 303–304
I.R.C. § 2522, 392
I.R.C. § 2523, 391
I.R.C. § 2523(b), 193
I.R.C. § 2523(e), 193
I.R.C. § 2523(f), 194
I.R.C. § 2523(g), 193
I.R.C. § 2612(a), 398
I.R.C. § 2612(b), 398
I.R.C. § 2612(c), 398
I.R.C. § 2613, 397
I.R.C. § 2641, 397
I.R.C. § 2651, 397
I.R.C. § 2651(e), 398
29 U.S.C. § 1055, 42
42 U.S.C. § 402, 42

State Statutes

Cal. Prob. Code § 6402, 65
Cal. Prob. Code § 6402.5, 65
Cal. Prob. Code § 6454, 76
Colo. Rev. Stat. § 15-11-901(2), 190
Colo. Rev. Stat. § 15-11-1102.5, 339
Colo. Rev. Stat. § 15-15-404, 37
Del. Code tit. 25, § 503, 339
Fla. Stat. § 689.225, 339
Fla. Stat. § 709.2104, 354
Fla. Stat. § 731.1065, 112
Fla. Stat. § 732.103(4), 58
Fla. Stat. § 732.103(5), 65
Fla. Stat. § 732.105, 56
Fla. Stat. § 732.2095(2)(d), 194
Fla. Stat. § 732.2095(2)(f), 194
Fla. Stat. § 732.4015, 33, 130
Fla. Stat. § 732.502, 90
Fla. Stat. § 732.502(1)(a), 92
Fla. Stat. § 732.502(2), 89
Fla. Stat. § 732.506, 117
Fla. Stat. § 732.515, 112
Fla. Stat. § 732.517, 88
Fla. Stat. § 732.603(3)(a), 287
Fla. Stat. § 732.802, 297
Fla. Stat. § 732.8031, 297
Fla. Stat. § 732.806, 96
Fla. Stat. § 733.107(2), 308
Fla. Stat. § 733.207, 312
Fla. Stat. § 736.0503(3), 206
Fla. Stat. § 736.0902, 196
Fla. Stat. § 736.1106(3)(a), 287
Fla. Stat. § 743.08(4)(b), 86
Ga. Code Ann. § 53-3-1, 139
755 Ill. Comp. Stat. Act 5 § 4-7, 117
Ind. Code § 29-1-21-4(b), 91
La. Civ. Code art. 1493, 147
La. Civ. Code art. 1494, 147
La. Civ. Code art. 1495, 147
Neb. Rev. Stat. § 12-512, 192
N.H. Rev. Stat. § 564:24, 339
N.H. Rev. Stat. § 564-B:4-402A, 339
N.J. Stat. § 46:2F-9, 339
N.Y. Est. Powers & Trusts Law § 3-2.1(a)(1)(A)–(B), 92

N.Y. Est. Powers & Trusts Law §3-2.1(a)(3), 91
N.Y. Est. Powers & Trusts Law §3-2.1(a)(4), 91
N.Y. Est. Powers & Trusts Law §3-2.2, 89, 90, 173
N.Y. Est. Powers & Trusts Law §3-3.2, 93
N.Y. Est. Powers & Trusts Law §3-3.5(b), 88
N.Y. Est. Powers & Trusts Law §11-2.4, 381
N.C. Gen. Stat. §31D-3-311(2), 164
N.C. Gen. Stat. §36C-5-503, 206
N.C. Gen. Stat. §37A-1-104.4, 381
Ohio Rev. Code §5302.22, 37
Okla. Stat. tit. 84, §222, 57
Tex. Est. Code §113.052, 36
Tex. Est. Code §251.001, 86
Va. Code §64.2-200(A)(5)(c), 55
Wash. Rev. Code §11.12.160, 93
Wash. Rev. Code §11.12.185, 286
Wis. Stat. §853.55, 89
Wis. Stat. §854.20(a)–(b), 73

TABLE OF REGULATIONS

Federal Regulations

Treas. Reg. § 1.643(b)-1, 381
Treas. Reg. § 1.674(b)-1(b)(5)(i), 224
Treas. Reg. § 20.2033-1(b), 393
Treas. Reg. § 20.2041-1(c)(2), 182, 318, 325
Treas. Reg. § 20.2042-1(c)(2), 394
Treas. Reg. § 25.2511-2(c), 388
Treas. Reg. § 25.2512-8, 389
Treas. Reg. § 25.2514-1(c)(2), 318
Treas. Reg. § 25.2518-2(d)(3), 303
Treas. Reg. § 25.2702-5, 189

TABLE OF RESTATEMENTS AND UNIFORM ACTS

Restatements

Restatement (Second) of Property: Donative Transfers § 28.2, 284
Restatement (Third) of Property: Wills and Other Donative Transfers § 13.1, 238
Restatement (Third) of Property: Wills and Other Donative Transfers § 13.2, 238
Restatement (Third) of Property: Wills and Other Donative Transfers § 15.1, 279
Restatement (First) of Trusts § 26, 176
Restatement (First) of Trusts § 55, 175
Restatement (Second) of Trusts § 156, 203
Restatement (Second) of Trusts § 199, 366
Restatement (Second) of Trusts §§ 216–218, 368
Restatement (Second) of Trusts § 330 comment o, 202
Restatement (Third) of Trusts § 9, 157
Restatement (Third) of Trusts § 13, comment a, 176
Restatement (Third) of Trusts § 18, 175
Restatement (Third) of Trusts § 24, 158
Restatement (Third) of Trusts § 25 comment e, 202
Restatement (Third) of Trusts § 47, 166
Restatement (Third) of Trusts § 56, 319
Restatement (Third) of Trusts § 58(1), 204
Restatement (Third) of Trusts § 58(2), 202
Restatement (Third) of Trusts § 58(2) comment e, 203
Restatement (Third) of Trusts § 59, 206
Restatement (Third) of Trusts § 60, 207, 209
Restatement (Third) of Trusts § 63, 225

Uniform Acts

Uniform Directed Trust Act

UDTA § 6, 363
UDTA § 8(a), 361

UDTA § 9(b), 361
UDTA § 11, 369

Uniform Electronic Wills Act

UEWA § 5, 91

Uniform Fiduciary Income and Principal Act

UFIPA § 102(1), 373
UFIPA § 201(a)(3), 372
UFIPA § 201(a)(4), 372
UFIPA § 201(b), 372
UFIPA § 201(c)(1), 372
UFIPA § 201(e), 380
UFIPA § 203(a), 380
UFIPA § 203(e), 380
UFIPA § 306, 381
UFIPA § 308, 381
UFIPA § 503, 374
UFIPA § 601(b), 376
UFIPA § 601(c), 376
UFIPA § 601(d), 376
UFIPA § 701(a), 378
UFIPA § 701(b), 378
UFIPA § 701(c), 378
UFIPA § 701(d), 378
UFIPA § 702(a), 379
UFIPA § 702(b), 379
UFIPA § 702(c), 379
UFIPA § 702(d), 379
UFIPA § 702(e), 379
UFIPA § 702(f), 379
UFIPA § 703(a), 380
UFIPA § 703(b), 380
UFIPA § 703(c), 380
UFIPA § 703(d), 380

Uniform Parentage Act

UPA § 609, 74

Uniform Powers of Appointment Act

UPAA § 102, 316, 318, 319
UPAA § 202, 321
UPAA § 203, 316
UPAA § 203(2), 319
UPAA § 301, 321
UPAA § 304, 321
UPAA § 305(c)(1), 320
UPAA § 306(a), 321
UPAA § 306(b), 321

Uniform Probate Code

UPC § 1-109, 128, 130, 132
UPC § 1-201(57), 108
UPC § 2-101, 50
UPC § 2-101(b), 50
UPC § 2-102, 59, 80
UPC § 2-102(1), 60
UPC § 2-102(2), 53
UPC § 2-102(2)–(4), 60
UPC § 2-103, 55, 58, 59
UPC § 2-103(c), 61
UPC § 2-103(d), 53, 61–62
UPC § 2-103(e), 62
UPC § 2-103(f), 62
UPC § 2-103(g), 55, 62–63
UPC § 2-103(h), 62
UPC § 2-103(i), 63
UPC § 2-103(j), 50, 64–65
UPC § 2-104(b), 64, 271
UPC § 2-104(b)(2), 75
UPC § 2-104(b)(3), 75
UPC § 2-104(c), 64
UPC § 2-105, 59
UPC § 2-106, 67, 246
UPC § 2-107, 56–58
UPC § 2-109, 77–80

UPC § 2-109(a), 77
UPC § 2-109(b), 78
UPC § 2-109(c), 79
UPC § 2-110, 81
UPC § 2-111, 71
UPC § 2-113, 73
UPC § 2-114(a), 53
UPC § 2-114(a)(1), 53
UPC § 2-114(a)(2), 53
UPC § 2-114(b), 53
UPC § 2-115(1), 73
UPC § 2-115(2), 75
UPC § 2-115(3), 74
UPC § 2-117, 76
UPC § 2-118(a), 72
UPC § 2-118(b), 74
UPC § 2-119(b), 72
UPC § 2-120, 75
UPC § 2-121, 75
UPC § 2-122, 73
UPC § 2-201(6), 319
UPC § 2-202, 194
UPC § 2-202(a), 138
UPC § 2-202(b), 138, 144
UPC § 2-202(c), 138
UPC § 2-203, 144
UPC § 2-203(b)(Alternative A), 138
UPC § 2-204, 139, 143, 144
UPC § 2-205, 139
UPC § 2-205(1), 139, 141, 143, 146
UPC § 2-205(1)(A), 322
UPC § 2-205(1)(B), 142
UPC § 2-205(1)(D), 142
UPC § 2-205(2), 140–141, 143, 146
UPC § 2-205(2)(B), 141
UPC § 2-205(3), 141
UPC § 2-205(3)(B), 146
UPC § 2-205(3)(C), 142, 391
UPC § 2-206, 142–143, 145, 194
UPC § 2-207, 143
UPC § 2-207(c), 144
UPC § 2-208, 143–144, 391
UPC § 2-208(c), 144
UPC § 2-209, 144, 146
UPC § 2-209(d), 146
UPC § 2-213, 121, 148
UPC § 2-213(a), 148
UPC § 2-213(b), 149
UPC § 2-213(c), 149
UPC § 2-213(c)–(e), 149
UPC § 2-213(f), 149
UPC § 2-213(g), 149
UPC § 2-213(h), 149
UPC § 2-301, 132, 133, 344
UPC § 2-301(a), 134
UPC § 2-301(a)(3), 133
UPC § 2-301(b), 135
UPC § 2-302, 12, 132, 135–136
UPC § 2-302(a), 136
UPC § 2-302(a)(2), 344
UPC § 2-302(b), 136
UPC § 2-302(c), 136
UPC § 2-302(d), 136, 344
UPC § 2-402, 128, 129, 344
UPC § 2-402A, 129
UPC § 2-403, 130–131, 259, 344
UPC § 2-404, 131, 344
UPC § 2-405, 146
UPC § 2-405(a), 128, 131, 132
UPC § 2-502, 91, 92, 97, 98, 173
UPC § 2-502(a)(3), 91
UPC § 2-502(a)(3)(A), 92
UPC § 2-502(b), 90
UPC § 2-502(c), 90
UPC § 2-503, 93
UPC § 2-504, 98

UPC § 2-504(a), 98
UPC § 2-504(b), 98
UPC § 2-504(c), 97
UPC § 2-505, 93
UPC § 2-506, 96
UPC § 2-507, 114, 116
UPC § 2-507(a)(1), 113
UPC § 2-507(a)(2), 116–117, 311
UPC § 2-507(b), 114
UPC § 2-507(c), 114
UPC § 2-507(d), 114
UPC § 2-508, 117
UPC § 2-509, 118–119
UPC § 2-509(a), 118
UPC § 2-509(b), 118
UPC § 2-509(c), 118
UPC § 2-510, 214
UPC § 2-511, 109
UPC § 2-511(a), 176
UPC § 2-512, 109
UPC § 2-513, 110–112, 311
UPC § 2-514, 122
UPC § 2-515, 312
UPC § 2-517, 88
UPC § 2-601, 238, 241
UPC § 2-602, 242
UPC § 2-603, 238, 246, 279, 282
UPC § 2-603(b), 244–245
UPC § 2-603(b)(1), 245
UPC § 2-603(b)(2), 245
UPC § 2-603(b)(3), 247
UPC § 2-603(b)(4), 248
UPC § 2-603(b)(5), 246
UPC § 2-603(c), 248
UPC § 2-604(a), 249
UPC § 2-604(b), 249
UPC § 2-605, 250–254
UPC § 2-605(a), 251–254
UPC § 2-605(a)(1), 251–252
UPC § 2-605(a)(2), 252
UPC § 2-605(a)(3), 253
UPC § 2-605(b), 253, 258
UPC § 2-606(a), 255, 257
UPC § 2-606(a)(5), 256
UPC § 2-606(a)(6), 256
UPC § 2-606(b), 257
UPC § 2-606(c), 257
UPC § 2-606(d), 258
UPC § 2-606(e), 258
UPC § 2-607, 259
UPC § 2-608, 260, 276
UPC § 2-609, 261, 263
UPC § 2-609(b), 262
UPC § 2-609(c), 262
UPC § 2-701, 271
UPC § 2-702, 244, 271–272
UPC § 2-702(c), 272
UPC § 2-702(d), 272
UPC § 2-703, 96, 275
UPC § 2-704, 276, 321
UPC § 2-705, 277–279
UPC § 2-705(a)(5), 278
UPC § 2-705(b), 277
UPC § 2-705(c), 277
UPC § 2-705(d), 278
UPC § 2-705(e), 279
UPC § 2-706, 279–280, 282
UPC § 2-706(a)(1), 280
UPC § 2-706(b), 280
UPC § 2-706(b)(3), 280
UPC § 2-706(b)(4), 281
UPC § 2-706(c), 281
UPC § 2-706(e)(2), 280
UPC § 2-707, 279, 282
UPC § 2-707(a)(1), 283
UPC § 2-707(b), 282

UPC § 2-707(b)(3), 282
UPC § 2-707(b)(4), 282
UPC § 2-707(c), 283
UPC § 2-707(d), 283
UPC § 2-707(e), 283
UPC § 2-708, 284
UPC § 2-709, 285
UPC § 2-709(b), 285
UPC § 2-710, 286
UPC § 2-711, 283, 286
UPC § 2-802, 292
UPC § 2-802(a), 292
UPC § 2-802(b), 292
UPC § 2-803, 79, 295–296
UPC § 2-803(f), 295
UPC § 2-804, 293
UPC § 2-804(b), 293–294
UPC § 2-804(b)(1), 294, 295
UPC § 2-804(b)(2), 294, 295
UPC § 2-804(d), 293,
UPC § 2-804(e), 295
UPC § 2-804(h)(2), 293
UPC § 2-805, 123–124, 219
UPC § 2-806, 124
UPC § 2-901, 214, 273, 331, 333
UPC § 2-901(a), 331
UPC § 2-901(a)(1), 331
UPC § 2-901(a)(2), 332
UPC § 2-901(b), 333
UPC § 2-901(c), 334
UPC § 2-901(d), 335
UPC § 2-902(a), 337
UPC § 2-902(b), 337
UPC § 2-902(c), 337
UPC § 2-903, 338
UPC § 2-904, 336
UPC § 2-904(1), 335
UPC § 2-904(2)–(4), 337
UPC § 2-904(5), 336
UPC § 2-904(6), 337
UPC § 2-904(7), 337
UPC § 2-1103, 298
UPC § 2-1104(a), 298
UPC § 2-1104(b), 298
UPC § 2-1105, 298, 301
UPC § 2-1105(c), 302
UPC § 2-1105(d), 305
UPC § 2-1106(a)(2), 306
UPC § 2-1106(b), 304
UPC § 2-1106(b)(2), 305
UPC § 2-1106(b)(3), 306
UPC § 2-1106(b)(3)(B), 79
UPC § 2-1106(b)(3)(C), 306
UPC § 2-1106(b)(3)(D), 307
UPC § 2-1106(b)(4), 307
UPC § 2-1107, 307
UPC § 2-1107(b), 304
UPC § 2-1109, 305
UPC § 2-1112(b), 302
UPC § 2-1112(c)–(l), 302
UPC § 2-1113, 302
UPC § 2-1113(a), 301
UPC § 2-1113(b), 301
UPC § 2-1113(c), 302
UPC § 2-1113(d), 302, 305
UPC § 2-1113(e), 301
UPC § 2-1114, 303
UPC § 3-402(a), 312
UPC § 3-406(1), 99
UPC § 3-406(2), 99
UPC § 3-406(3), 98, 99
UPC § 3-407, 308
UPC § 3-703, 360
UPC § 3-705, 360
UPC §§ 3-706–3-709, 360
UPC § 3-711, 359

UPC § 3-712, 360
UPC § 3-713, 360
UPC § 3-715, 359
UPC § 3-801, 360
UPC § 3-805, 47, 344, 360
UPC § 3-808, 360
UPC § 3-902, 136, 344
UPC §§ 3-902–3-915, 360
UPC § 3-902(a), 343–344
UPC § 3-902(b), 342–343
UPC § 3-904, 144, 377
UPC § 3-905, 88
UPC § 3-906, 349
UPC § 3-906(a)(1), 349
UPC § 3-906(a)(2), 349
UPC § 3-906(a)(2)(C), 105
UPC § 3-906(a)(4), 349
UPC § 3-912, 350
UPC § 3-9A-103(a), 346
UPC § 3-9A-103(b), 347
UPC § 5-102(1), 356
UPC § 5-102(3), 356
UPC § 5-102(8), 357
UPC § 5-102(10), 357
UPC § 5-110, 357
UPC § 5-202, 357
UPC § 5-310, 357
UPC § 5-411, 357
UPC § 5-413, 357
UPC § 5-418, 357
UPC § 5B-104, 354
UPC § 5B-105, 354
UPC § 5B-108, 354
UPC § 5B-109, 354
UPC § 5B-110, 355
UPC § 5B-114, 355
UPC § 5B-115, 356
UPC § 5B-116, 356
UPC § 5B-117, 356
UPC § 5B-201(a), 355
UPC § 5B-201(c), 355
UPC § 5B-202, 355
UPC §§ 5B-204–5B-216, 355
UPC § 5B-301, 355
UPC § 6-102, 36
UPC § 6-201(1), 34
UPC § 6-201(3), 34
UPC § 6-201(5)–(6), 34
UPC § 6-204, 36
UPC § 6-211, 34
UPC § 6-212(a), 35
UPC § 6-212(b)(2), 36
UPC § 6-212(c), 36
UPC § 6-214, 34
UPC § 6-302, 36
UPC § 6-305, 37
UPC § 6-307, 37
UPC § 6-309, 39
UPC § 6-405, 37
UPC § 6-406, 37
UPC § 6-407, 37
UPC § 6-408, 37
UPC § 6-411, 37

Uniform Prudent Investor Act

UPIA § 1, 383
UPIA § 2, 383
UPIA § 2(c), 383
UPIA § 3, 383
UPIA § 4, 383
UPIA § 5, 384
UPIA § 6, 384
UPIA § 7, 384
UPIA § 9, 384

Uniform Transfers to Minors Act

UTMA § 1(7), 358
UTMA § 1(11), 358

UTMA § 3, 358
UTMA § 9, 358
UTMA § 10, 358
UTMA § 12, 358
UTMA § 13, 358

Uniform Trust Code

UTC § 102, 156
UTC § 103(2), 182, 318
UTC § 103(3), 155
UTC § 103(13), 155
UTC § 105(b), 363
UTC § 105(b)(2), 363
UTC § 105(b)(8)–(9), 366
UTC § 105(b)(10), 368
UTC § 105(b)(11), 368
UTC § 112, 238, 270
UTC § 113, 196
UTC § 401, 154, 172, 175
UTC § 401(1), 175
UTC § 401(2), 176
UTC § 401(3), 176
UTC § 402, 161, 162, 167, 171, 173
UTC § 402(a)(1), 162
UTC § 402(a)(3), 165
UTC § 402(a)(3)(A), 197
UTC § 402(a)(3)(B), 167
UTC § 402(a)(3)(C), 167
UTC § 402(a)(4), 167
UTC § 402(a)(5), 168
UTC § 402(b), 165
UTC § 402(c), 165
UTC § 404, 171–173, 214, 217
UTC § 405(a), 197
UTC § 405(b), 197
UTC § 405(c), 197
UTC § 406, 308
UTC § 407, 173
UTC § 408, 190, 191
UTC § 409, 191–192
UTC § 410, 220
UTC § 410(a), 214
UTC § 410(b), 220
UTC § 411, 215, 220, 350
UTC § 411(a), 215
UTC § 411(b), 215
UTC § 411(c), 215
UTC § 411(d), 215
UTC § 411(e), 215
UTC § 412, 216
UTC § 412(a), 216
UTC § 412(b), 173, 216
UTC § 412(c), 216
UTC § 413, 198, 220
UTC § 413(a), 217
UTC § 413(b), 217
UTC § 414, 218
UTC § 414(a), 217
UTC § 414(b), 218
UTC § 414(c), 218
UTC § 414(d), 218
UTC § 415, 124, 216, 218–219
UTC § 416, 219
UTC § 417, 219, 220
UTC § 502(a), 204
UTC § 502(b), 205
UTC § 502(c), 205
UTC § 503, 205
UTC § 503(a), 206
UTC § 503(b), 206
UTC § 503(b)(1), 205
UTC § 503(b)(2), 206
UTC § 503(b)(3), 206
UTC § 503(c), 206
UTC § 504, 207–209
UTC § 504(b), 208
UTC § 504(c), 208
UTC § 504(d), 208

UTC § 504(e), 209
UTC § 505(a)(1), 202, 319
UTC § 505(a)(2), 202, 203
UTC § 505(a)(3), 47, 202, 345
UTC § 505(b), 211
UTC § 505(b)(1), 319, 391
UTC § 505(b)(2), 210, 323, 391
UTC § 507, 211
UTC § 601, 162, 226
UTC § 602, 202, 227
UTC § 602(a), 187, 225
UTC § 602(b), 227
UTC § 602(c)(1), 226
UTC § 602(c)(2)(A), 226
UTC § 602(c)(2)(B), 226
UTC § 602(d), 225
UTC § 602(e), 226
UTC § 602(f), 226
UTC § 602(g), 368
UTC § 603(a), 361
UTC § 603(b), 187, 361
UTC § 603(c), 248
UTC § 703, 368
UTC § 801, 363
UTC § 802, 364
UTC § 803, 12, 180, 364
UTC § 804, 364
UTC § 805, 365
UTC § 806, 365
UTC § 807, 365
UTC § 809, 365
UTC § 810, 365
UTC § 811, 365
UTC § 812, 365
UTC § 813, 187, 365
UTC § 814, 363
UTC § 815, 361–362
UTC § 816, 362
UTC § 816(21), 180
UTC § 1001, 366
UTC § 1002, 367
UTC § 1002(b), 369
UTC § 1003(a), 367
UTC § 1003(b), 367
UTC § 1006, 367
UTC § 1007, 367
UTC § 1008, 368
UTC § 1008(a)(1), 367
UTC § 1008(a)(2), 367
UTC § 1008(b), 368
UTC § 1009, 368
UTC § 1010(a), 368
UTC § 1010(b), 368

Uniform Trust Decanting Act

UTDA § 2(2), 224
UTDA § 2(3)(A), 221
UTDA § 2(10), 221
UTDA § 2(11), 222
UTDA § 2(21), 224
UTDA § 3, 221
UTDA § 7, 222
UTDA § 8, 222
UTDA § 9, 222
UTDA § 11(b), 223
UTDA § 11(c), 223
UTDA § 11(c)(3), 223
UTDA § 11(d), 223
UTDA § 12, 224
UTDA § 13, 223
UTDA § 14, 223, 224
UTDA § 15, 221
UTDA § 23, 191

INDEX

A

Abatement, 102, 104, 108, 135, 136–138, 146, 151, 342–344, 346, 350, 360, 418
Abusers, 291, 297, 313, 416
Acceleration of future interest, 307
Accessions, 250–254
Acts of independent significance, 109–110
Ademption by extinction, 20, 102, 103, 112, 254–258, 261, 263, 266, 414
Ademption by satisfaction, 20, 42
Administrator, 25, 32
Adoptee, 46, 54, 69, 71–74, 82, 132, 135–138, 150, 237–238, 277, 278, 279, 287, 289, 415
Adoptive parents, 46, 53, 54, 61, 71–74, 82
Adult adoptee, 73, 278, 287, 289, 415
Advancements, 20, 42, 45, 49, 77–81, 83, 264, 405
Afterborn (posthumous) child, 75–76, 82, 279, 287, 289, 335, 405, 415
Agent, 24, 25, 215, 226, 230, 255, 257–258, 266, 294, 317, 321, 353–356, 359, 365, 369, 384, 414, 419
Aggravated manslaughter, 313
Alternative beneficiary designation, 243, 247–249, 275, 280–281, 282–284, 286, 287, 289, 297, 306, 415
Ambiguity, 24, 123, 124, 163, 169, 207–208, 218–219, 229, 232–235, 239, 349, 411, 412
Animal trusts, 156, 165, 167, 190–191, 198, 410
Annuities, 39–41, 42, 108, 186, 300, 345, 380, 381, 393
Annulment, 121, 292, 293, 313, 416
Antenuptial agreements, 61, 64, 148–149, 151, 172, 188, 335
Antilapse, 26, 112, 134–135, 233, 236, 242, 243–249, 262, 264, 265, 267, 279–281, 282–283, 285, 289, 290, 296, 321, 343, 344, 413, 415
Appointee, 246–247, 300, 316, 317, 319–321, 327, 328, 333, 417
Ascertainable beneficiary, 91, 159
Ascertainable standard, 181–182, 209, 210, 212, 222, 223, 229, 317–318, 324, 325, 327, 363, 388, 411, 417

Assisted reproduction, 56, 71, 75, 76, 82, 279, 287, 289, 405, 415
Attestation, 89–91, 92, 93, 97–98, 99, 100, 117, 406
Attorney in fact, 25, 353–354
Augmented estate, 20–21, 40, 42, 138–146, 151, 322–323, 328, 408
Authorized fiduciary, 220–222, 229, 412

B

Beneficiary treated as settlor, 210–211, 212, 323–324, 326, 391, 411

C

Capacity, 6, 22, 26, 37, 86–88, 92, 95, 99, 100, 108, 117, 120, 162, 169, 187, 225–226, 230, 255, 258, 293, 310–311, 314, 357, 361, 363, 405, 409, 412, 417
Charitable trusts, 24, 27, 43, 156, 159, 165, 166, 197–198, 199, 215, 216–217, 218, 220, 221, 228, 336, 340, 409, 410, 411, 418
Choice of law, 96, 275–276
Class-closing rule, 236, 279
Class gifts, 97, 136, 155, 164, 165–166, 180, 188
Codicils, 22, 93, 94, 102, 108, 110–111, 113, 114, 117, 118–119, 121, 124, 196–197, 283, 312, 407
Collateral heirs, 52, 54, 55–56, 69–70, 81, 82, 404, 405
Common law marriage, 51
Community property, 17, 32, 36, 147–148, 151, 227, 408
Conflict of interest, 26, 27, 158, 355–356, 360, 364
Conservator, 25, 180, 215, 226, 230, 255, 257–258, 266, 294, 354, 356–357, 369, 414, 419
Construction of instruments, 16, 24, 103, 163, 231–232, 238, 239, 241–267, 269–290, 412, 416
Constructive trusts, 23, 123, 156, 157–158, 159, 175, 177, 293, 312, 314, 366, 409, 410, 417
Creditors' rights, 6, 15, 44, 47, 129, 156, 182, 183, 201–212, 225, 229, 259, 319, 321, 323–324, 328, 330, 342, 344, 345, 350, 351, 359, 360, 391, 400, 404, 410, 411, 417, 419
Crummey power, 389–390, 391
Custodianship under UTMA, 25, 49, 180, 358, 369, 419
Cy pres, 24, 198, 216–217, 220, 228, 411

D

De facto parentage, 50, 53, 56, 71, 74, 82, 279, 287, 405
Decanting of trust, 182, 191, 220–224, 228, 229, 412
Definite beneficiary, 155, 165–166, 167, 169, 171, 174, 191, 192, 197, 198, 199, 336, 409, 410
Degrees of relationship, 46, 57, 70, 82, 147
Demonstrative devise, 102, 104–105, 106, 242, 249, 343, 406
Dependent relative revocation, 27, 99, 119–121, 125, 407
Descendants, 22, 26, 28, 36, 46, 49, 50, 52–55, 56–57, 59, 60–63, 64–65, 66–69, 70, 79, 81, 82, 83, 134–135, 137, 147, 236, 239, 243–248, 262, 264, 265, 267, 275,

280–281, 282–283, 284–285, 286, 287, 289, 296, 306, 313, 314, 321, 404, 405, 413, 416
Disclaimers, 16, 32–33, 79, 81, 128, 131, 149, 297–307, 314, 321, 393
Distributee, 155, 203, 286, 365–366
Divorce, 38, 50, 121, 148, 149, 172, 234, 292–295, 313, 335, 416
Duress, 24, 27, 93, 109, 149, 203, 292, 309–310, 312, 314, 416

E

Elective estate, 20–21, 40, 42, 138–146, 151, 322–323, 328, 408
Elective share, 27, 33, 39, 41, 42, 43, 44, 48, 96, 102, 123, 128, 131, 132, 138–146, 148, 149, 150, 151, 156, 180, 182, 183, 192, 194, 198, 225, 229, 276, 288, 292, 319, 322–323, 328, 330, 344, 350, 376, 391, 393, 404, 408, 410, 417
Electronic documents, 91, 302
Employee Retirement Income Security Act of 1974 (ERISA), 15, 42, 272, 293
Equitable adoption, 73–74
Escheat, 48, 55, 56, 59, 64–65, 82, 286, 307, 405
Exclusionary power of appointment, 316, 319–320, 328, 417
Execution, 24, 89, 90, 91, 93, 94, 96, 97, 98, 99, 100, 109, 121, 122, 125, 174, 225, 292, 309, 310, 406
Executor, 25, 31
Exempt property, 33, 48, 60, 96, 102, 130–131, 132, 138, 139, 143, 146, 149, 150, 151, 259, 271, 276, 288, 292, 344, 349, 350, 376, 393, 407, 408, 409, 410
Exoneration, 257–259, 347, 356
Expanded distributive discretion, 222–223, 224, 229, 412
Expectancy, 39, 46, 176, 300, 312, 314, 417
Express trusts, 23, 156, 157, 159, 161–169, 174, 197, 198, 199, 221, 300, 347
Expression, 24, 123, 218

F

Family allowance, 48, 60, 105, 131–132, 138, 139, 143, 146, 149, 150, 151, 292, 344, 349, 350, 407, 408
Federal preemption, 272, 280, 293
Five and five ("5 and 5") power, 323–324, 325, 326, 391
Forced heirship, 147
Foster child, 76
Fraud, 24, 89, 91, 93, 99, 158, 172, 201, 309, 310, 312, 314, 416

G

General devises, 104–105, 106, 111, 116, 144, 236, 242, 249, 251, 253, 256, 257–258, 266, 342–343, 349, 350, 376, 377, 406, 414, 418
General power of appointment, 139–140, 193, 209, 210, 223, 224, 260, 305, 317, 318–319, 321, 322, 323–324, 325, 326, 327, 328, 332–334, 335, 346, 347–348, 363, 389, 392, 394–395, 396, 401, 417
Generation-skipping transfer tax, 396–398, 401, 421

Gross estate, 16, 21, 39, 40, 41, 42, 193–194, 195, 209, 210, 303–304, 314, 321, 325–326, 327, 346, 347–348, 350, 393–395, 396–397, 399, 419
Guardian, 25, 27, 180, 215, 226, 230, 258, 294, 321, 356–357, 369, 419

H

Half-blood heirs, 49, 52, 56–58, 69–70, 71, 82, 287, 405
Harmless error, 93, 96, 98, 100, 406
Health care fiduciary, 25, 355, 359, 369, 419
Heirs, 20, 21, 22, 26, 33, 45–83, 90, 113, 115, 120, 135, 147, 175, 177, 188, 242, 243–244, 245, 264, 275, 280, 283, 284–285, 286, 288, 289, 290, 299, 313, 342, 345, 350, 360, 375, 404–405, 415, 416, 418
Holographic wills, 89–90, 95, 100, 311, 406
Homestead, 27, 33, 48, 60, 105, 128–130, 131, 132, 138, 139, 143, 146, 148, 150, 151, 271, 292, 344, 349, 350, 393, 407, 408
Honorary trusts, 156, 166–167, 191
Hotchpot, 78–81

I

In terrorem clauses, 88
In trust for accounts, 23, 28, 33–34, 158, 163, 300
Incapacity, 25, 87, 180, 187, 188, 225–226, 255, 257–258, 317, 354–355, 356–357, 363, 369
Incorporation by reference, 22, 110, 112–113, 187
Inducement, 24, 123, 218, 310
Insane delusion, 87
Integration of will components, 93
Inter vivos trusts, 26, 43, 88, 108–109, 112–113, 124, 156, 162, 169, 173, 187, 190, 197, 198, 202, 225–227, 229, 230, 235, 294, 319, 332, 340, 355, 361, 377, 378, 409, 412, 418
Intestacy, 3, 7, 20, 21, 22, 42, 45–83, 94–95, 115, 119–121, 122, 125, 128, 131, 132, 134–135, 136–137, 138, 139, 145, 146, 147, 149, 150, 158, 174, 175, 177, 186, 242, 243–244, 245, 246, 248, 249, 264, 265, 277, 283, 284–285, 286, 289, 290, 295, 300, 302, 304, 306, 308, 312, 313, 326, 335, 343, 350, 359, 375, 403, 404–405, 407, 413, 415, 416, 418
Irrevocable life insurance trusts, 28, 39, 196, 199, 410

J

Joint tenancy, 28, 36, 37–38, 127, 140, 142, 143, 145, 186, 272, 279, 296, 299–300, 303, 304, 307, 394
Joint wills, 122, 125, 407

K

Killers, 27, 50, 64, 79, 270, 285, 295–297, 313, 416

L

Lapse, 109, 112, 140, 211, 243–249, 265, 289, 323–324, 325, 326, 391, 413, 415
Life insurance, 21, 26, 27, 28, 38–39, 43, 47, 108, 140–142, 143, 146, 176, 186, 194–196, 199, 279, 289, 294, 300, 347–349, 378, 394, 395, 410, 415

Limited distributive discretion, 222, 223–224, 229, 412
Limited power of appointment, 164, 212, 224, 317, 319, 321, 324, 325, 327, 333, 334, 335, 346, 347, 417
Lineal heirs, 52–55, 81, 404
Lost wills, 91, 99, 122, 158, 312

M

Marital deduction, 28, 156, 180, 182, 192–194, 326–327, 348, 363, 394–396
Merger of trust interests, 168
Mistake, 24, 99, 123–124, 125, 136, 216, 218–219, 229, 310, 312, 314, 411, 416
Modification, 24, 123–124, 173, 214, 215–218, 219, 220, 228, 229, 340, 411–412
Mutual wills, 122–123, 125, 273, 288, 407

N

No-contest clause, 88
Noncharitable purpose, 165, 166, 167, 190, 191, 198, 410
Noncupative wills, 89, 90
Nonexclusionary power of appointment, 319–320, 328, 417
Nongeneral power of appointment, 164, 212, 224, 317, 319, 321, 324, 325, 327, 333, 334, 335, 346, 347, 417
Nonmarital children, 49, 70, 76, 82, 405
Nonprobate ownership forms, 32–44, 345–349

O

Object of power of appointment, 244, 246–247, 260, 300, 316, 327, 417
Omitted child, 102, 132, 135–137, 147, 150, 151, 238, 342, 344, 350, 408
Omitted spouse, 102, 123, 132–135, 138, 139, 146, 150, 151, 295, 330, 344, 350, 408
Oral trusts, 173, 361
Oral wills, 89, 100, 173, 406

P

Pay on death accounts, 3, 21, 23, 28, 33–36, 47, 140, 158, 279, 289, 294, 300, 415
Per capita at each generation, 46, 64–65, 67, 68–69, 71, 82, 237, 246, 284, 285, 287, 289, 405, 416
Per capita with representation, 46, 67, 68–69, 82, 284, 285
Per stirpes, 28, 46, 66–69, 82, 237, 246, 284, 285, 287, 289, 405, 416
Permissible appointee, 300, 316, 317, 319–320, 321, 327, 328, 333, 417
Permissible distributee, 155, 365–366
Personal representative, 12, 15, 25, 32, 47, 75–76, 78, 81, 94, 102, 105, 106, 108, 110, 131, 139, 175, 193, 202, 259, 266, 294, 301, 302, 327, 342, 345, 349, 350, 359–360, 369, 375–377, 395, 396, 414, 419
Pet trusts, 156, 165, 167, 190–191, 198, 410
Posthumous conception, 75–76, 82, 279, 287, 405, 415

Posthumous heirs, 75, 82, 279, 287, 289, 335, 405, 415
Postnuptial agreements, 61, 64, 148–149, 172, 188, 335
Power of appointment, 28, 33, 47, 139, 140, 154, 155, 159, 164, 175–176, 182, 187–188, 193, 209, 210, 223, 224, 259–261, 266, 276, 283, 287, 288–289, 295, 300, 301, 304–305, 315–328, 332–335, 337, 347, 348, 389, 392, 394–395, 396, 401, 409, 414, 415, 417
Power of attorney, 24, 25, 28, 215, 226, 255, 257–258, 301, 317, 353–356, 369, 419
Power to invade, 176, 181–182, 183, 193, 194, 229, 317–319, 322, 323, 324, 325, 327, 377–378, 380, 410
Power to withdraw, 176, 182, 183, 210–211, 212, 229, 318, 319, 323–324, 326, 350, 389–390, 391, 410, 411, 412
Precatory language, 102, 106, 163–164, 169, 174, 406
Preemption, 272, 280, 293
Prenuptial agreements, 61, 64, 148–149, 151, 172, 188, 335
Presence requirements, 89, 90–91, 97, 98, 100, 116, 406
Pretermission, 102, 123, 132–137, 138, 139, 146, 147, 150, 151, 238, 295, 330, 342, 344, 350, 408
Principal and income, 253, 375–382, 414, 420
Private express trusts, 156, 159, 169, 174, 198, 221, 409
Probate estate composition, 20–21, 32, 44, 46–47
Probate process, 4, 31, 44, 47, 359–360, 419
Prudent investor, 371–372, 382–384, 385, 420
Prudent person, 358, 365, 382–383, 385
Purging of devises, 93

Q

Qualified beneficiary, 21, 155, 159, 187, 214, 217, 219, 220, 222, 228, 229, 365–366, 409, 412
Qualified personal residence trust, 189
Qualified terminable interest trust, 28, 193–194, 327, 392, 394–395, 396

R

Reformation, 6, 24, 26, 123–124, 125, 136, 214, 216, 218–219, 220, 228, 229, 310, 338–339, 340, 411, 419
Renunciation, 121, 149, 297
Representation, binding others, 26, 222
Representation, taking by, 26, 46, 49, 57, 59, 61, 62, 63, 64, 66–70, 82, 83, 147, 239, 243, 245–246, 262, 264, 280, 285, 289, 290, 306, 313, 376, 405, 415, 416
Reproductive technologies, 56, 71, 75–76, 82, 279, 287, 289, 405, 415
Residuary devise, 47, 50, 97, 105, 106, 114, 174, 187, 242–243, 248–250, 258–259, 260, 265, 266, 283, 289, 342–343, 349, 350, 375–376, 406, 413, 414, 415, 418

Resulting trust, 23, 156–157, 159, 167, 174, 175, 409
Reversion, 23, 32, 157, 162, 166, 217, 286, 289, 393, 395, 416
Revival of will, 94, 99, 118–121, 124, 125, 407
Revocable trusts, 22, 33, 43, 47, 108–109, 156, 162, 169, 187, 202, 211, 215, 225–226, 230, 308, 319, 345, 346–347, 350, 361, 368, 369, 388, 409, 411, 419
Revocation by a writing, 113–116, 118–119, 124, 407
Revocation by act, 116–117, 118–119, 120, 124, 311, 407
Rule against perpetuities, 28, 155, 165, 167, 181, 188, 190, 192, 198, 214, 216, 271, 273, 288, 324–325, 329–340, 377, 418

S

Same-sex marriage, 50, 51, 59
Secret and semi-secret trusts, 174–175, 177, 410
Self-proving affidavit, 97–99, 100, 406
Separate writing, 22, 93, 102, 110–112, 121, 124, 125, 311, 407
Settlor capacity, 162, 169, 187, 225–226, 230, 361, 409, 412
Simultaneous death, 64, 272, 273, 274–275, 287, 288, 415
Slayers, 27, 50, 64, 79, 270, 285, 295–297, 313, 416
Social Security benefits, 15, 42, 143
Specific devises, 102–105, 106, 111, 112, 128, 130–131, 132, 226, 235–236, 249, 251–253, 254–259, 261, 263, 266, 343, 349, 350, 376, 406, 414, 418
Spendthrift trusts, 202–203, 204–206, 207–208, 211, 215, 220, 221, 400, 411
Spoliation, 99, 311, 312, 314, 417
Spousal rights, 128–135, 138–146, 148–149, 150, 151, 326, 407, 408
Statute of Frauds, 157, 158, 173
Statute of Uses, 167
Statute of Wills, 174
Step relatives, 278
Stepchildren, 49, 50, 53, 76, 82, 244, 280, 287, 405
Stepparents, 69, 74
Stepsiblings, 69
Substitute beneficiary, 28, 32, 36, 39, 244, 246–248, 262, 273, 280–281, 282–284, 287, 289
Succession agreements, 121–123, 125, 407
Survivorship, 28, 32, 36, 37–38, 42, 47, 128, 140, 142, 143, 186, 247, 270–275, 279–281, 282–284, 287, 294–296, 299–300, 304, 307, 394, 404

T

Tax apportionment and contribution, 16, 47, 194–195, 345–349, 350, 419
Taxable estate, 392–396, 400, 420
Taxable gift, 196, 210–211, 303, 314, 325, 388–392, 401, 420
Taxation of income, 15, 42, 43, 372, 373, 383, 392, 399–400, 401, 421
Tenancy by the entirety, 28, 36, 37, 38, 186, 299, 303, 304

Tenancy in common, 28, 38, 130, 186, 294, 300
Termination of trusts, 26, 190, 214–216, 217–218, 220, 228, 411
Testamentary capacity, 22, 26, 37, 86–88, 95, 99, 100, 107, 108, 117, 120, 162, 169, 225–226, 255, 310–311, 314, 405, 409, 417
Testamentary formalities, 89–94, 96, 99, 100, 108, 114, 118–119, 124, 406, 407
Testamentary intent, 88, 89, 90, 95, 98
Testamentary trusts, 94, 156, 162, 169, 174–175, 189, 340, 361, 409, 418
Tortious interference, 312, 314, 417
Totten trusts, 34
Transfer on death ownership, 21, 29, 36–37, 140, 186, 189, 279, 289, 294, 300, 415
Trust creation formalities, 173–175, 177, 230, 409
Trust creation intent, 156, 157, 161, 163, 169, 174, 176, 409, 410
Trust decanting, 182, 191, 220–224, 228, 229, 412
Trust director, 361, 363, 369, 370, 420
Trust funding, 175–177
Trust principal and income, 23, 179–182, 183, 372–375, 377–382, 384, 420
Trust purposes, 24, 26, 156, 165, 166–167, 171–173, 177, 180–181, 183, 187, 189, 190, 191–192, 197–198, 199, 204, 216–217, 228–229, 330, 363–365, 367, 383, 409, 410, 411, 412
Trustee liability, 205, 361, 364, 366–368
Trustee powers and duties, 167, 361–370, 380–381, 383–385, 419–420

U

Undue influence, 24, 42, 87, 93, 98, 99, 158, 308–309, 310–311, 312–313, 314, 349, 416
Uniform Parentage Act, 53, 63, 71, 82, 287, 295, 405
Unitrust, 381, 384, 420

V

Vesting, 28, 32, 41, 43, 155, 168, 177, 214, 223, 225, 229, 249, 273, 282, 288, 300, 324–325, 329–340, 389–390, 412, 418

W

Waivers, 42, 61, 64, 121–123, 128, 131, 132, 144, 148–149, 150, 151, 188, 222, 298, 301, 348, 355, 363, 366, 368, 408
Will components, 94–99
Will contracts, 122–123, 125, 335, 407
Witnesses, 22, 25, 88, 89, 90–91, 92–94, 95, 96, 97, 98, 99, 100, 110, 111, 112, 117, 120, 121, 173, 174, 276, 302, 311, 312, 354, 406
Worthier-title doctrine, 286, 289, 416